DOLLAR DEMOCRACY
ON STEROIDS:

With Liberty and Justice for Some;

How to Reclaim the Middle-Class Dream for All

By Peter Mathews

i

Digital textbook published 2020 by Cengage
Available at Amazon.com and other retail bookstores

Cover Design and Illustration by Alan Brett Covey

For more information on this and related subjects, including Peter Mathews'
newspaper op-eds, and radio and television interviews and commentary, go to

www.EPeterMathews.com

or email him at:

go2mathews@msn.com

ISBN-13: 978-1-5136-5142-2
Copyright © 2019 by Peter Mathews

Politics is not about power. Politics is not about money. Politics is not about winning for the sake of winning. Politics is about the improvement of people's lives.

-- United States Senator Paul Wellstone

DEDICATION

To my eight-year-old daughter Page, whom I love deeply, I wrote this book to help save our country and our world for you, your generation and those who follow. This is the least that we adults owe you.

CONTENTS

Tables, Graphs, Charts & Exhibits

ACKNOWLEDGMENTS

I would like to acknowledge my wife Toya Baker-Mathews, whose love, understanding, and support have helped make this book possible. She is truly a partner in life.

I would like to thank my father, Ernest Paul Mathews and my mother, Amara Esther Evangelina Mathews for the early nurturing, love, and support they gave me. They taught me to value the dignity of every human being and to cherish education. They were both educators for many decades.

I would also like to acknowledge my fellow professors and colleagues Gloria Badal, Will Heusser, and good friends Dr. Michael Parenti, Frank Dawoodjee, and Brett Covey, with all of whom I have had excellent discussions of some of my thoughts and ideas on politics and society.

Over many years of my life, I have met good and inspiring people who have helped make it possible for me to achieve what I have. Professor Joe Boyle, Professor Neill Cooney, Dr. Robert Dale Judy, Dr. H.W. Kamp, Dr. Rodger Scott, Dr. Nora Hamilton, Professor William Tinsley.

CHAPTER 1

DOLLAR DEMOCRACY HAS BROUGHT US GLOBAL WARMING, CLIMATE CHANGE, CLIMATE DISRUPTION

Seacoast Drive Goes Underwater

It was a sunny sparkling day in Southern California with mild spring temperatures around 70°F (21°C). I was driving with a friend heading south along the beautiful California coast towards the city of Imperial Beach, just south of San Diego. As I viewed the aquamarine Pacific Ocean to the west, the euphoria I felt while gliding over the freeway in my electric Tesla was tempered by my understanding that the State of California had recently ordered coastal cities to come up with plans to address the dangers of rising sea levels due to global warming! I live in a coastal California city and recently attended a presentation to the community of plans by city agencies, architects and engineers to address the threats and challenges of rising sea level. I recall that standing-room-only meeting several months ago at the Golden Sails Hotel on Pacific Coast Highway in Long Beach, California.

I remember several hundred concerned faces in the packed room, as we were told by the experts that within a couple of decades we would have basically one of two choices to avoid the catastrophic effects of rising sea levels due to increased global warming: managed retreat, which means selling your house and moving inland; or if your house was at sea level or only several feet above it, spending thousands of dollars

2

to retrofit your foundation and raise your house, in order to survive devastating flooding, at least for a while. Stanford University doctoral student Miyuki Hino says, "managed retreat" involves the strategic relocation of assets and people away from areas at risk, enabling restoration of those areas to their natural state." ("Adapting to Climate Change Through 'managed retreat', by Miyuki Hino in carbonbrief.org)

The world's oceans have risen by three inches since 1993. Mayor Serge Dedina of Imperial Beach should know. Because of global warming causing the Polar ice caps to melt and ocean temperatures to increase, the sea level rise around Imperial Beach has resulted in more frequent and intense "king tides" generating huge waves crashing through large rock barriers called riprap, even tossing sand bags and flooding streets and homes. The latest of these extreme weather events hit in January 2019 in this tranquil Southern California town of 27,000. Mayor Dedina said, "There's not much we can do once the ocean reaches a certain level and the surf a certain height. There's not much we can do."

Scientists from San Diego's Scripps Institution recently spent time in Imperial Beach studying the rising sea levels in order to develop a warning and prediction system that could save lives. Meanwhile Mayor Serge Dedina, who has to plan for the city's future, poignantly asked, "What are we going to do with our sewer pump stations? What are we going to do with our roads? What are we going to do with our electrical outlets? We're working with SDG&E (San Diego Gas and Electric) on that. We have a school that's on the bayfront. And then how are we going to deal with actually mitigating rising seas and increased erosion?.... What we are learning is that this is kind of the new normal and with a little bit of tide we're seeing a lot more coastal flooding than we used to," Dedina said (kpbs.org, "Scripps Institution Scientists Study Imperial Beach As Sea Level Rises", January 29, 2019, by Erik Anderson).

Image 1-1 | Peter Mathews walks on Imperial Beach, California by house threatened by seal level rise caused by Global Warming

Now my friend Tony and I were driving to Imperial Beach to interview residents and frequent visitors to the Seacoast Drive neighborhood. Houses and condos on Seacoast Drive had backyards that were right up against the beach sand. I began thinking about how the residents of Imperial Beach would deal with the more frequent and powerful storm surges from the ocean that threatened their city, such as the vicious storm and flooding they had recently survived. My friend and I had stopped once on our way for lunch, arriving in Imperial Beach in the early afternoon, with plenty of time and sunlight left to survey the beach and talk to the neighbors on Seacoast Drive. This was where some of the heavy flooding had occurred. The Seacoast Drive neighborhood was truly beautiful. It was nestled between the open Pacific Ocean and the Tijuana Slough National Wildlife Refuge, full of birds and other wildlife. Just beyond the Refuge I could see the hills of the city of Tijuana in Baja California, Mexico.

One of the first people we met and spoke with was Yadira Figueroa, who was enjoying a walk on the beach with her daughter Maya, at the South end of Seacoast Drive. Yadira told us that the January storms and flooding she had experienced a few months ago were unbelievable. She described how the ocean waves had slammed against the protective rock barriers, broken through them and flooded Seacoast Drive. As her little daughter ran around the sand, Yadira said to us that this was the strongest storm with the largest crashing waves that she had experienced in her 12 years of living there, and she expressed deep concern.

Image 1-2 | Ocean Water from Sea Level Rise Floods Seacoast Drive in March 2016, and as recently as January 2019 | Photo/City of Imperial Beach

Another person we met was Steve Padilla Jr., a college student. Steve, carrying his skateboard, spoke to us while accompanying us for some time, as we met and talked to other people in the neighborhood as well. He told us he had been visiting this beach for a few years while living in South Western California all his life. Steve Padilla Jr. said he is "a devout Christian and geology major at Grossmont Cuyamaca College." He said he "Always had a love for Christ and the Earth", and that "the beach doesn't even look like the beach anymore but just a harbor for the fish and sharks of the sea. Just a few steps to reach the ocean.... Within just a few years there has been the highest of dramatic climate change throughout the U.S. and the entire globe." Steve is right about that: In 2018, according to a United Nations estimate, 62 million people worldwide were affected by extreme weather produced by climate change. ("Extreme weather affected 62 million people last year, UN climate change report says", CBS news, March 28, 2019).

Steve, Tony, and I had walked a block up from the beach to show

Steve the Tesla, since he was interested in seeing such a zero- emission car. As Steve and I were chatting, a young woman and her friend had walked up and were talking to Tony. In a minute Tony introduced them to us. I began explaining to Emily and her friend, both of them college students, why we were visiting Imperial Beach. I asked them if they had experienced the severe January storm and flooding, and if they thought that climate change/global warming may have been a factor. Emily, who had experienced the storm and flooding in the area, and her friend also felt that climate change/global warming is playing a role in the severe weather.

Image 1-3 | Our Tesla On Ocean Sand Covered Parking Lot On Seacoast Drive

Robert Sarnie, whom Tony and I met in the driveway of his house at the beach, acknowledged that during the January storm and flooding of the street, his carport had taken in seawater. He was reluctant to mainly blame global warming/climate change for the severe flooding, which he said many politicians tend to do. Instead he suggested that the heavy flooding from the Ocean could be ameliorated by bringing back underwater vegetation, including kelp, as well as reefs, that could slow down underwater wave action and help reduce flooding.

Shawn Gould, a resident of Imperial Beach, remembers rearranging sandbags that had been tossed around by the surf during the January 2019 flooding. "I just pulled one over to cover my neighbor's front door, so they don't get blasted out," he stated. "We live on the wilderness. This is the edge. The ocean's going to win. And we know unless you're living in a cave and in denial. Global warming exists and the tides are coming up," he said. ("Storm Swell, High Tide Soak Imperial Beach", kpbs.org, January 18, 2019 by Erik Anderson).

When I interviewed the mayor of Imperial Beach, Serge Dedina, he said that the city government was focused on repairing and/or moving the public infrastructure: soft solutions would include adding and building up the sand, as well as the restoration of wetlands. Hard solutions would include repairing and/or moving the public infrastructure such as attending to sewage lines, water pipes and electrical lines. Mayor Dedina has lived in Imperial Beach for decades. He said to me, "since I moved to Imperial Beach in 1971, I've never seen the kind of flooding we are seeing now. Flooding caused by climate change is the most important issue facing coastal cities, including Imperial Beach. It requires a lot of effort to deal with it!" Mayor Dedina, who has a PhD in geography and a Bachelors' degree in Political Science may be well-equipped to navigate the treacherous geographic and political terrain of global warming, climate change, and climate disruption!

Dollar Democracy is Endangering American Lives

"Dollar Democracy" is the influence of big-money corporate-funded campaigns and lobbying dollars on the decisions of elected officials, that affect all of us. Politicians, supported by Dollar Democracy in American politics, have handed us climate change (climate disruption, climate chaos, global warming, rising sea levels, melting polar ice caps, severe drought and fires, more frequent and severe hurricanes, and more); they have handed us huge and widening income and wealth inequality; a yawning gap between wealthy public schools, and middle and low income public schools; college students and graduates drowning in debt from skyrocketing tuition costs; unaffordable and inadequate healthcare; a dangerously polluted environment; pesticide coated and genetically modified food; polluted water from fracking, industrial and agribusiness waste , and the Great Recession without a strong recovery. They have also brought us waste fraud and abuse in the Pentagon and unnecessary military spending; a race to the bottom with the middle class shrinking; the rich getting richer and the poor getting poorer; and the biggest fiasco of all, the selection of Global Warming Denier Donald John Trump by the Electoral College, to be the 45th President of United States, despite receiving almost 3 million fewer popular votes than Hillary Clinton.

In the 2016 Republican Presidential Primary Election, Trump had bragged that he would be independent of wealthy special interests by spending his own money to get himself elected. He promised to "drain the swamp" of lobbyists and special interest groups. In addition to the approximate $1 billion worth of free television news coverage that he received, Trump did spend $66 million of his own money to defeat other well-known Republican Primary candidates such as former Florida Governor Jeb Bush, Florida U.S. Senator Marco Rubio, Ohio Governor John Kasich, and other lesser-known Republican candidates.

Immediately after winning the Primary, Republican presidential nominee Trump made an about-face and started raising money for his general election campaign from wealthy special interests including big donors from Wall Street, fossil fuel companies, and other big business corporate interests (track Trump's and his Democratic opponent Secretary of State Hillary Clinton's funding from wealthy donors at opensecrets.org). Trump and Clinton also benefited from spending on their behalf by wealthy super PACs. In 2017, his first year in office, Trump delivered for his wealthy donors: he successfully got the Republican majority in Congress to deregulate their big businesses, and to pass a gigantic tax-cut plan worth $1.5 trillion, 82% of which went to his super-rich donors, including himself. Trump's deregulation included lowering Obama's 54 miles per gallon CAFE (corporate average fuel economy) standard to a resulting 37 miles per gallon for new cars and light duty trucks by 2025. Trump's roll back on auto fuel efficiency increases oil sales and profits, increases global warming emissions by over 870 million tons of carbon dioxide, and "To our knowledge, there's no single policy on the planet with this much climate impact."(Daniel Sperling, Forbes.com, August 2, 2018). The CAFE standard is the average gas mileage that the vehicles in a fleet must attain.

Trump, who called the Paris Climate Accord (to reduce greenhouse gases that produce global warming) a burden on American business and economy, has announced the U.S. will withdraw from it (November 4, 2020 is the earliest allowed withdrawal date). The accord had been painstakingly negotiated among almost 200 nations of the world and supported by the Obama Administration. Trump called Global Warming a "Chinese Hoax" to damage the U.S. economy.

In this first chapter I will show the reader how Dollar Democracy affected the 2016 Democratic Presidential Primary Election contest between Secretary Hillary Clinton and Senator Bernie Sanders. As I analyze the General Election contest between Clinton and Trump, you will see how Dollar Democracy played a key role in making Hillary Clinton the Democratic Presidential Nominee and in bringing us President Donald Trump, after he defeated her in the Electoral College, but not in the popular vote. Most importantly in Chapter 1 you will see how Trump's triumph through Dollar Democracy has brought us to the brink of climate catastrophe through policies perpetrated by President Trump, his cabinet members and administration. The climate change fiasco did not begin with President Trump. Many decades of climate change/global warming denial by gas, coal, and oil fossil fuel corporations and their enablers, who are among many of our politicians in government, have brought us to the brink of climate and societal disaster.

Today we stand at the precipice facing climate catastrophe, reflected by severe weather patterns, including stronger and more frequent hurricanes, "bomb" cyclones that destroyed grain and livestock in the U.S. Midwest, rising sea levels, polar ice caps melting, severe drought and extreme wildfires, millions of climate refugees, including those from island and low-lying nations, and many more dire circumstances. At the helm of our nation stands President Donald John Trump, a climate change denier, whose 2016 general election campaign was heavily funded by corporate interests, including oil and gas corporate interests that gave $1,027,843. In the 2018 election cycle oil and gas gave Trump $223,428 (opensecrets.org). Fossil fuel energy corporations and their executives donated at least $7 million to President Trump's inauguration committee (thehill.com). This has bought them heavy influence with Trump, who gave us cabinet members such as recent Environmental Protection Agency Administrator Scott Pruitt (Oklahoma's pro-fossil fuel recent Attorney General who sued the EPA on behalf of Oklahoma utilities companies), and Acting EPA Administrator Andrew Wheeler, former lobbyist for coal industry giant Murray Energy. Both of them have acted as foxes guarding the chicken coop: using government to serve the interests of the fossil fuel industry, and not protecting the American people and natural environment from it.

Also, because of Dollar Democracy, the lower 99% of Americans are in danger of either losing the Middle-Class Dream that they worked hard to achieve, have lost the Middle-Class Dream they had once achieved, or will never realize the Middle-Class Dream for themselves or their children. It will never become a reality for them if things continue the way they are going in American Elections, Politics, Economics, and Society. The top 1% of Americans will continue doing fine, and even magnificently better, as time passes. The income gap ratio, which today is 361 to 1, was 40 to 1 in 1980. In other words, the richest Americans, who are generally CEOs and owners of large corporations, are making 361 times the income of the average American worker. If you think this is just a dry economic statistic, think again: the economic power of the 1% gives them a tremendous amount of political and social power.

Page and Gilens Study: Policies Preferred by the Wealthy Elite and Corporate Business Groups are Implemented Far More Often than Policies Supported by the Majority of Americans

For example, the bulk of money given to, and spent on, the campaigns of candidates for Congress and candidates for U.S. President, in a presidential election year, is provided by wealthy Americans in the top 1% of the population (opensecrets.org). In a ground-breaking study Political Scientists Martin Gilens and Benjamin Page found that the policies supported by these wealthy people get implemented far more often than the policies preferred by average Americans.
(https://scholar.princeton.edu/sites/default/files/mgilens/files/gilens_and_page_2014_-testing_theories_of_american_politics.doc.pdf).

For example, nearly 81% of Americans support tuition free college for everyone (PSB Research, February 2018), 70% of Americans support Medicare for All universal healthcare (Reuters.com), and 52 % of Americans support a Federal jobs guarantee (Civics Analytics poll, thenation.com). Has the corporate-bought majority of Congress implemented any of these programs yet? No. Instead corporate-bought members of Congress and corporate-funded president Trump implemented a tax reform bill in 2017 with a tax-cut worth $1.5 trillion (Joint Committee on Taxation), 83% of which goes to the richest Americans, the top 1% (Dylan Matthews in Vox.com, December 18, 2017). In contrast, by 2027, 70% of Americans in the middle class would see their taxes go up (Tax Policy Center). This is a clear example of Dollar Democracy, whereby super-rich individuals and corporations with the big dollars to lobby and give to candidates for President and Congress, are rewarded with huge tax cuts and subsidies. These tax cuts and subsidies are passed by Congress and signed by the President, while programs that benefit the middle class, poor, and America as a whole, are slashed, or not expanded to meet the existing need: public education, affordable college, social and physical infrastructure, science and technology research and development, Head Start, health care, child care, and programs that would seriously address devastating Climate Change.

"Dollar Democracy on Steroids: with Liberty and Justice for Some; How to Reclaim the Middle-Class Dream for All" is the story of how the United States of America has been taken off track by wealthy corporate elites. They have bought our government and produced policies that are destroying the middle class and poor, and destroying the Middle-Class Dream and our natural environment, affecting the world as well.

I've told the story by using historical, political, economic, sociological, and philosophical analyses backed by empirical and scientific evidence. Most importantly I include stories of real Americans and their families, many of whom I personally interviewed, whose lives are teetering on the brink, or are being quickly destroyed by the crisis that America and the world are facing. The Mandarin language character for "crisis" has two parts: danger and opportunity. This book provides critically important information that can help us limit the danger of

Crisis = Danger & Opportunity

steeply increased global warming and help us seize the opportunity to get America back on track once again. This would include creating high-paying green technology jobs that save our economy and the natural environment. This book provides an Action Plan and blueprint of how to get there.

Woven throughout the book and clearly elaborated in the last chapter "With Liberty and Justice for All", are specific suggestions and clear-cut plans of how we can take out the corrupting and corroding influence of big money in American politics, and free our citizens to demand from our leaders that they start serving We the People and not their big donor overlords. For example, I will examine the issue of how Big Money in American Politics has prevented our leaders from seriously addressing the global warming crisis.

The Union of Concerned Scientists (UCSUSA) tells us that global warming is already having significant and costly effects on our communities, our health, and our climate (ucsusa.org). The U.N. Intergovernmental Panel on Climate Change (IPCC) report and the U.S. government's Fourth National Climate Assessment, have issued dire warnings for our immediate future, unless we act immediately. The

UCUSA says that "unless we take immediate action to reduce global warming emissions, these impacts will continue to intensify, grow ever more costly and damaging, and increasingly effect the entire planet including you, your community, and your family. (These impacts include) rising seas and increased coastal flooding, longer and more damaging wildfire seasons, more destructive hurricanes, more frequent and intense heat waves, military bases at risk, national landmarks at risk, costly and growing health impacts, an increase in extreme weather events, heavier precipitation and flooding, destruction of marine ecosystems, more severe droughts in some areas, widespread forest death in the Rocky Mountains, increased pressure on groundwater supplies, growing risks to our electricity supply, changing seasons, melting ice, disruption to food supplies, plant and animal range shifts, and the potential for abrupt climate change."

Intergovernmental Panel on Climate Change 2018 Report on Global Warming/Climate Change

The IPCC special report on global warming released in October 2018 says that we have to limit global warming to a maximum of 1.5°C in order to limit the dire effects of climate change. And we only have until 2030 to do so. Global net human caused emissions of carbon dioxide would have to fall by about 45% from 2010 levels by 2030, reaching net zero around 2050. The IPCC report finds that in order to limit global warming to 1.5° Celsius would require "rapid and far-reaching" transitions in land, energy, industry, buildings, transport, and cities. The activities of human beings have already warmed the planet around 1°C since the preindustrial era, which is defined by the IPCC as the second half of the 19th century. With the current rate of warming, the earth would reach the 1.5°C threshold between 2030 and 2052 (climatecentral.org).

U.S. Government Fourth National Climate Assessment 2018 Report on Global Warming/Climate Change

The U.S. government's fourth National Climate Assessment report, released in November 2018, warns of a damaged environment and shrinking U.S. economy.

SUDDEN AND SEVERE INCREASE IN CARBON-DIOXIDE EMISSIONS

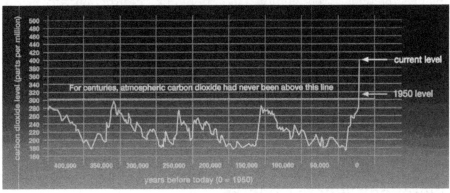

GLOBAL LAND-OCEAN TEMPERATURE INDEX

Data source: NASA's Goddard Institute for Space Studies (GISS). Credit: NASA/GISS

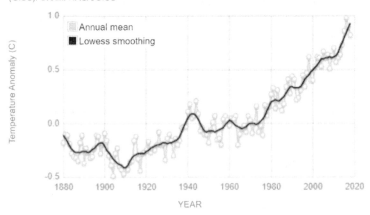

Graphs 1-1 | As carbon dioxide emissions increase, average global temperatures have risen, causing an increase in extreme weather worldwide: hurricanes, droughts, storms, flooding, sea level rising | Graphs/NASA

The 1,656 page assessment "describes the effects of climate change on the economy, health and environment, including record wildfires in California, crop failures in the Midwest and crumbling infrastructure in the South. It says that American exports and supply chains could be disrupted, agricultural yields could fall to 1980s level by midcentury and fire season could spread to the Southeast.... Climate change could slash up to a tenth of gross domestic product by 2100, more than double the losses of the Great Recession a decade ago." (nytimes.com, Nov. 23, 2018, "U.S. Climate Report Warns of Damaged Environment and Shrinking Economy", by Coral Davenport and Kendra Pierre-Louis).

The Green New Deal

The Green New Deal is an ambitious and much-needed program to fight the ravages of climate change. Its roots go back to President Franklin D. Roosevelt's New Deal, created to lift America out of the Great Depression.   FDR's New Deal created federally funded government programs that hired millions of unemployed Americans to go back to work building hydroelectric plants such as the Tennessee Valley Authority and the Hoover Dam, that put Americans to work beautifying and creating national parks, that put artists to work painting murals on the side of buildings to beautify cities, putting actors and directors to work performing plays to American audiences in small towns and rural areas where most had never seen a professional acting troupe before, and building and rebuilding much-needed American physical infrastructure such as roads, bridges, and sidewalks.

Today's Green New Deal is also deeply inspired by the modern-day environmental movement which was launched in the U.S. in the 1970s, including Earth Day. Its environmental component has been galvanized most recently by the scientifically based recognition of climate change, global warming, and climate disruption. The IPCC report, and the U.S. Government's fourth National Climate Assessment report provided extensive scientific evidence for the immediate causes, disruptions, and necessary solutions in order for us to possibly ameliorate the most

15

devastating effects of climate change--- if we act immediately. The deadline set to take concerted and effective action is the year 2030, just 11 years away.

Brand New Congress (BNC), a nationwide activist organization dedicated to electing non-corporate sponsored, grassroots supported progressive candidates to Congress, whose most prominent success was Representative Alexandria Ocasio-Cortez (D-NY), sent out an email to its members dated Wednesday, February 22, 2017 at 6:59 PM. The email outlined the key components of what later came to be called the Green New Deal. Drawing on JFK's visionary pledge to go to the moon within the 1960s decade, BNC outlined another bold vision to "Make America the first 100% clean energy economy in the world within 10 years."(brandnewcongress.org, February 14, 2019). The Brand New Congress' renewable energy plan had several parts in order to create well-paying green jobs and block the increase in global warming:

- Upgrade every home to run on renewable energy and weatherizing it
- Upgrade every building with zero interest loans to invest in new energy upgrades
- build a nationwide, decentralized smart grid designed to improve energy storage and transfer capability
- invest in new solar and wind power projects
- Buy fossil fuel companies
- spin off new profitable companies and take care of displaced workers. Empower energy companies to pursue free market clean energy solutions by purchasing their fossil fuel business segments. As old energy segments strategically wind down, provide support to workers displaced in the transition by funding retraining, relocation, and early retirements
- upgrade transportation by incentivizing car owners to trade in for electric models. Convert or replace all fossil fueled buses and trains, and invest in innovative systems like high-speed rail (brandnewcongress.org, February 14, 2019)

Justice Democrats is a Progressive Political Action Committee that recruits and supports non-corporate Democratic candidates to run for

Congress. They are also strong supporters of the Green New Deal (justicedemocrats.com).

In its current form, the Green New Deal is the "brainchild of the Sunrise Movement, a youth activist group that's been working with (recently elected Representative Alexandria) Ocasio-Cortez (D-New York), since before she got elected. Sunrise was founded about a year and a half ago by six recent college graduates, veterans of organizing climate campaigns from their campuses. ... Sunrise Movement launched in July 2017 with a big idea: the Green New Deal, a series of proposals to move America off fossil fuels fast by creating millions of green jobs."(pri.org, January 14, 2019).

Image 1-5 | Co-Sponsor of the Green New Deal, Representative Alexandria Ocasio-Cortez Launches the GND With Sunrise Movement Co-Founder Varshini Prakash | Photo/Sunrise Movement Website

One of the six co-founders of Sunrise, Varshini Prakash said, "all of us were feeling the sense of unease and frustration that the hurricanes were getting bigger, the fires were getting bigger... But our movements weren't growing with them." (Carolyn Beeler, "The 'Green New Deal' started with six college grads. Now, they're recruiting an army of young people", January 14, 2019). So, Prakash organized a successful fossil fuel divestment campaign at the University of Massachusetts Amherst. In July 2017 the Sunrise Movement launched itself "with a big idea:

the Green New Deal, a series of proposals to move America off fossil fuels fast by creating millions of green jobs.

"We really see it is not just a climate policy, but a socio-economic project to rival some of the greatest projects in American history," Prakash said (pri.org, January 14, 2019). The Green New Deal skyrocketed to fame when the Sunrise Movement staged a sit-in at the office of House Speaker Nancy Pelosi. Upon their invitation for support, Representative Alexandria Ocasio-Cortez showed up in person to join the Sunrise members in Pelosi's office. Immediately, the Green New Deal was put on the world map by the media who showed up. Interest in the group and the Green New Deal immediately skyrocketed.

GREEN NEW DEAL RESOLUTION

Introduced on February 7, 2019, outlined in a House Resolution (H.RES.109), authored by U.S. Congresswoman Alexandria Ocasio-Cortez and co-sponsored by U.S. Senator Edward Markey of Massachusetts, the Green New Deal states:

Exhibit 1-2

RESOLUTION

Recognizing the duty of the Federal Government to create a Green New Deal.

Whereas the October 2018 report entitled "Special Report on Global Warming of 1.5 °C" by the Intergovernmental Panel on Climate Change and the November 2018 Fourth National Climate Assessment report found that—

(1) human activity is the dominant cause of observed climate change over the past century;

(2) a changing climate is causing sea levels to rise and an increase in wildfires, severe storms, droughts, and other

18

extreme weather events that threaten human life, healthy communities, and critical infrastructure;

(3) global warming at or above 2 degrees Celsius beyond pre-industrialized levels will cause—

(A) mass migration from the regions most affected by climate change;

(B) more than $500,000,000,000 in lost annual economic output in the United States by the year 2100;

(C) wildfires that, by 2050, will annually burn at least twice as much forest area in the western United States than was typically burned by wildfires in the years preceding 2019;

(D) a loss of more than 99 percent of all coral reefs on Earth;

(E) more than 350,000,000 more people to be exposed globally to deadly heat stress by 2050; and

(F) a risk of damage to $1,000,000,000,000 of public infrastructure and coastal real estate in the United States; and

(4) global temperatures must be kept below 1.5 degrees Celsius above pre-industrialized levels to avoid the most severe impacts of a changing climate, which will require—

(A) global reductions in greenhouse gas emissions from human sources of 40 to 60 percent from 2010 levels by 2030; and

(B) net-zero global emissions by 2050;

Whereas, because the United States has historically been responsible for a disproportionate amount of greenhouse gas emissions, having emitted 20 percent of global greenhouse gas emissions through 2014, and has a high technological capacity, the United States must take a leading role in reducing emissions through economic transformation;

Whereas the United States is currently experiencing several related crises, with—

(1) life expectancy declining while basic needs, such as clean air, clean water, healthy food, and adequate health care, housing, transportation, and education, are inaccessible to a significant portion of the United States population;

(2) a 4-decade trend of wage stagnation, deindustrialization, and antilabor policies that has led to—

    (A) hourly wages overall stagnating since the 1970s despite increased worker productivity;

    (B) the third-worst level of socioeconomic mobility in the developed world before the Great Recession;

    (C) the erosion of the earning and bargaining power of workers in the United States; and

    (D) inadequate resources for public sector workers to confront the challenges of climate change at local, State, and Federal levels; and

(3) the greatest income inequality since the 1920s, with—

    (A) the top 1 percent of earners accruing 91 percent of

gains in the first few years of economic recovery after the Great Recession;

(B) a large racial wealth divide amounting to a difference of 20 times more wealth between the average white family and the average black family; and

(C) a gender earnings gap that results in women earning approximately 80 percent as much as men, at the median;

Whereas climate change, pollution, and environmental destruction have exacerbated systemic racial, regional, social, environmental, and economic injustices (referred to in this preamble as "systemic injustices") by disproportionately affecting indigenous peoples, communities of color, migrant communities, deindustrialized communities, depopulated rural communities, the poor, low-income workers, women, the elderly, the unhoused, people with disabilities, and youth (referred to in this preamble as "frontline and vulnerable communities");

Whereas, climate change constitutes a direct threat to the national security of the United States—

(1) by impacting the economic, environmental, and social stability of countries and communities around the world; and

(2) by acting as a threat multiplier;

Whereas the Federal Government-led mobilizations during World War II and the New Deal created the greatest middle class that the United States has ever seen, but many members of frontline and vulnerable communities were excluded from many of the economic and societal benefits of those mobilizations; and

Whereas the House of Representatives recognizes that a new national, social, industrial, and economic mobilization on a scale not seen since World War II and the New Deal era is a historic opportunity—

(1) to create millions of good, high-wage jobs in the United States;

(2) to provide unprecedented levels of prosperity and economic security for all people of the United States; and

(3) to counteract systemic injustices: Now, therefore, be it

Resolved, That it is the sense of the House of Representatives that—

(1) it is the duty of the Federal Government to create a Green New Deal—

   (A) to achieve net-zero greenhouse gas emissions through a fair and just transition for all communities and workers;

   (B) to create millions of good, high-wage jobs and ensure prosperity and economic security for all people of the United States;

   (C) to invest in the infrastructure and industry of the United States to sustainably meet the challenges of the 21st century;

   (D) to secure for all people of the United States for generations to come—

(i) clean air and water;

(ii) climate and community resiliency;

(iii) healthy food;

(iv) access to nature; and

(v) a sustainable environment; and

(E) to promote justice and equity by stopping current, preventing future, and repairing historic oppression of indigenous peoples, communities of color, migrant communities, deindustrialized communities, depopulated rural communities, the poor, low-income workers, women, the elderly, the unhoused, people with disabilities, and youth (referred to in this resolution as "frontline and vulnerable communities");

(2) the goals described in subparagraphs (A) through (E) of paragraph (1) (referred to in this resolution as the "Green New Deal goals") should be accomplished through a 10-year national mobilization (referred to in this resolution as the "Green New Deal mobilization") that will require the following goals and projects—

(A) building resiliency against climate change-related disasters, such as extreme weather, including by leveraging funding and providing investments for community-defined projects and strategies;

(B) repairing and upgrading the infrastructure in the United States, including—

(i) by eliminating pollution and greenhouse gas emissions as much as technologically feasible;

23

(ii) by guaranteeing universal access to clean water;

(iii) by reducing the risks posed by climate impacts; and

(iv) by ensuring that any infrastructure bill considered by Congress addresses climate change;

(C) meeting 100 percent of the power demand in the United States through clean, renewable, and zero-emission energy sources, including—

(i) by dramatically expanding and upgrading renewable power sources; and

(ii) by deploying new capacity;

(D) building or upgrading to energy-efficient, distributed, and "smart" power grids, and ensuring affordable access to electricity;

(E) upgrading all existing buildings in the United States and building new buildings to achieve maximum energy efficiency, water efficiency, safety, affordability, comfort, and durability, including through electrification;

(F) spurring massive growth in clean manufacturing in the United States and removing pollution and greenhouse gas emissions from manufacturing and industry as much as is technologically feasible, including by expanding renewable energy manufacturing and investing in existing manufacturing and industry;

(G) working collaboratively with farmers and ranchers in the United States to remove pollution and greenhouse gas emissions from the agricultural sector as much as is technologically feasible, including—

(i) by supporting family farming;

(ii) by investing in sustainable farming and land use practices that increase soil health; and

(iii) by building a more sustainable food system that ensures universal access to healthy food;

(H) overhauling transportation systems in the United States to remove pollution and greenhouse gas emissions from the transportation sector as much as is technologically feasible, including through investment in—

(i) zero-emission vehicle infrastructure and manufacturing;

(ii) clean, affordable, and accessible public transit; and

(iii) high-speed rail;

(I) mitigating and managing the long-term adverse health, economic, and other effects of pollution and climate change, including by providing funding for community-defined projects and strategies;

(J) removing greenhouse gases from the atmosphere and reducing pollution by restoring natural ecosystems through proven low-tech solutions that increase soil carbon storage, such as land preservation and afforestation;

(K) restoring and protecting threatened, endangered, and fragile ecosystems through locally appropriate and science-based projects that enhance biodiversity and support climate resiliency;

(L) cleaning up existing hazardous waste and abandoned sites, ensuring economic development and sustainability on those sites;

(M) identifying other emission and pollution sources and creating solutions to remove them; and

(N) promoting the international exchange of technology, expertise, products, funding, and services, with the aim of making the United States the international leader on climate action, and to help other countries achieve a Green New Deal;

(3) a Green New Deal must be developed through transparent and inclusive consultation, collaboration, and partnership with frontline and vulnerable communities, labor unions, worker cooperatives, civil society groups, academia, and businesses; and

(4) to achieve the Green New Deal goals and mobilization, a Green New Deal will require the following goals and projects—

(A) providing and leveraging, in a way that ensures that the public receives appropriate ownership stakes and returns on investment, adequate capital (including through community grants, public banks, and other public financing), technical expertise, supporting policies, and other forms of assistance to communities, organizations, Federal, State, and local government agencies, and businesses working on the Green New Deal mobilization;

(B) ensuring that the Federal Government takes into account the complete environmental and social costs and impacts of emissions through—

(i) existing laws;

(ii) new policies and programs; and

(iii) ensuring that frontline and vulnerable communities shall not be adversely affected;

(C) providing resources, training, and high-quality education, including higher education, to all people of the United States, with a focus on frontline and vulnerable communities, so that all people of the United States may be full and equal participants in the Green New Deal mobilization;

(D) making public investments in the research and development of new clean and renewable energy technologies and industries;

(E) directing investments to spur economic development, deepen and diversify industry and business in local and regional economies, and build wealth and community ownership, while prioritizing high-quality job creation and economic, social, and environmental benefits in frontline and vulnerable communities, and deindustrialized communities, that may otherwise struggle with the transition away from greenhouse gas intensive industries;

(F) ensuring the use of democratic and participatory processes that are inclusive of and led by frontline and vulnerable communities and workers to plan, implement, and administer the Green New Deal mobilization at the local level;

(G) ensuring that the Green New Deal mobilization creates high-quality union jobs that pay prevailing wages, hires local workers, offers training and advancement opportunities, and guarantees wage and benefit parity for workers affected by the transition;

(H) guaranteeing a job with a family-sustaining wage, adequate family and medical leave, paid vacations, and retirement security to all people of the United States;

(I) strengthening and protecting the right of all workers to organize, unionize, and collectively bargain free of coercion, intimidation, and harassment;

(J) strengthening and enforcing labor, workplace health and safety, antidiscrimination, and wage and hour standards across all employers, industries, and sectors;

(K) enacting and enforcing trade rules, procurement standards, and border adjustments with strong labor and environmental protections—

(i) to stop the transfer of jobs and pollution overseas; and

(ii) to grow domestic manufacturing in the United States;

(L) ensuring that public lands, waters, and oceans are protected and that eminent domain is not abused;

(M) obtaining the free, prior, and informed consent of indigenous peoples for all decisions that affect indigenous peoples and their traditional territories, honoring all treaties and agreements with indigenous peoples, and protecting and enforcing the sovereignty and land rights of indigenous peoples;

(N) ensuring a commercial environment where every businessperson is free from unfair competition and domination by domestic or international monopolies; and

(O) providing all people of the United States with—

(i) high-quality health care;

(ii) affordable, safe, and adequate housing;

(iii) economic security; and

(iv) clean water, clean air, healthy and affordable food, and access to nature.

Widespread Oil and Gas Campaign Contributions Make Congressional Leadership Lukewarm or Hostile to the Green New Deal

After eight long years in the wilderness Democrats recaptured the majority in the House of Representatives in November 2018. The overwhelming majority of them were incumbents who had received corporate oil and gas money for their campaigns over the years. Several progressive Democratic challengers such as Alexandria Ocasio-Cortez, Ilan Omar, Ayanna Pressley, and Rashida Tlaib, had strong grassroots support and refused corporate money. They won impressively and are fighting for progressive policies in Congress. They have been strong leaders in the fight for the Green New Deal. In fact, Congresswoman

Ocasio-Cortez is the lead sponsor of the Green New Deal resolution (H.Res.109) in the House and has been the bold, national leader and public face of the Green New Deal ever since.

With the Democratic sweep of the House and the victory of several high-profile progressives, such as Ocasio-Cortez, Omar, Pressley, and Tlaib, many environmental activists thought that House Democrats would take bold climate action immediately. However since the November, 2018 midterm election the House Democratic leadership has shown a lack of urgency on the climate change issue despite new alarming scientific information showing that the climate crisis is getting much worse at a faster rate than what was thought previously (thinkprogress.org, "New House climate committee even weaker than panel from more than a decade ago," January 4, 2019, by Mark Hand). Congresswoman Ocasio-Cortez and other progressive climate leaders had asked for the establishment of a powerful House Select Committee for a Green New Deal, that would have subpoena power and the power to write legislation. The select committee established by Speaker of the House Nancy Pelosi was given neither power, unlike the previous select committee on climate in 2007, during Pelosi's previous Speakership, which did have subpoena power. This new and much weaker House Select Committee on Climate Crisis will allow its members to accept campaign contributions from fossil fuel companies and will have no language on racial and economic justice, which are important elements of the Green New Deal.

The Senate Republican leadership headed by Senate Majority Leader Mitch McConnell has been even more hostile to and critical of the Green New Deal. McConnell called it "socialism" and a "crippling proposal." In a blatant attempt to shame and divide the Senate Democrats, Majority Leader McConnell scheduled a procedural vote with no time for discussion or debate of this thought-provoking and far reaching resolution. It was voted down by 57 Senators, all Republicans joined by three Democrats and one Independent. 43 Senators, one independent and the rest Democrats voted "present." All 57 Senators who voted "no" on the Green New Deal have received more than $55,000,000 in contributions from fossil fuel companies, according to Oil Change United States. (ecowatch.com).

Here's where the dirty little secret of Dollar Democracy shows its face: in the House of Representatives, the oil and gas industry, in the 2018 election cycle, had donated a total of $14,553,123 to 237 Republicans, an average contribution of $61,405 each; the oil and gas industry had donated a total of $2,357,732 to 161 House Democrats, for an average of $14,644 each. In the Senate the oil and gas industry had donated a total of $3,699,149 to 51 Republicans for an average of $72,532 each; the oil and gas industry had donated a total of $1,331,302 to 47 Democrats for a average of $28,325 each. Two independent senators received a total of $36,598 total for an average of $18,299 each, from the oil and gas industry (OpenSecrets.org). It would surprise many people to know that 92% of the members of the U.S. House of Representatives had taken campaign money from the oil and gas industry; and 100% of the members of the U.S. Senate had received money for their campaigns from the oil and gas industry. This money includes donations from owners, investors, and employees of the corporation.

Those donations were only for one election cycle. Imagine how much more money these elected officials have received for all of their other previous campaigns. Can they truly vote independently on behalf of the public interest and for the American people, not for the oil corporations?

Congressional leaders also receive hundreds of thousands of dollars in campaign donations from the oil and gas industry. For example, Democrat Nancy Pelosi, the Speaker of the House received $126,315 in oil and gas money contributions from 1998 to 2018. Democrat Steny Hoyer, the House Majority Leader received $355,195 during the same period. Republican Kevin McCarthy, the House Minority Leader received $181,374 from 1998 to 2018. Republican Mitch McConnell, the Senate Majority Leader received $6,046,751 from the oil and gas industry from 1998 to 2018. Democrat Chuck Schumer, the Senate Minority Leader received $819,400 from the oil and gas industry during the same period.

Given the millions of dollars donated to the vast majority of Members of Congress is it any wonder that the Green New Deal's momentum has being slowed by corporate-funded Congressional leaders as well as most rank-and-file Members of Congress?

Dollar Democracy in the 2016 U.S. Presidential Election Gave Us Democratic Presidential Nominee Hillary Clinton and Republican President Donald Trump

Secretary of State Hillary Clinton announced her candidacy for the U.S. Presidency in April 2015. She was immediately considered the front runner by the establishment media, the political establishment, and most of the so-called pundits, or political analysts. They based their judgment not only on her long visibility and service in public life, but just as importantly on her ability to raise tremendous amounts of campaign money, which enabled her to establish a nationwide state-by-state presidential campaign organization. After serving as First Lady of Arkansas, she served as First Lady of the U.S. and had a prominent leadership role in the Bill Clinton Administration's healthcare reform. She was then elected U.S. Senator from New York. After losing a high profile Democratic Presidential primary election contest against Senator Barack Obama in 2012, she proceeded to serve as President Obama's U.S. Secretary of State.

In addition to these personal political achievements, Secretary Clinton had at her disposal a juggernaut political fundraising machine built by her and her husband U.S. President Bill Clinton. Through the June 2016 primary elections Hillary's campaign and pro-Hillary super PACs raised $386.1 million and spent $301.4 million. Secretary Clinton's main rival in the Democratic primaries was U.S. Senator Bernie Sanders who raised just over $228 million. Sanders refused, on principle and in practice, to allow super PACs to aid his campaign.

Early Money is Like Yeast, It Makes the Dough Rise!

There is a saying in American politics: "Early Money is like yeast, it makes the dough rise." This was never more true than with Hillary Clinton. Hillary's early money, much of it from wealthy individuals and political action committees, baked her a lot of bread which allowed her to capture the support of more big donors and political action committees from corporate interests, labor, Wall Street, from some small donors, and even from some environmental groups. Just as it takes money to make money in a deregulated capitalist system, it takes early campaign money to attract early support and more campaign money. This is how the Clinton political–financial juggernaut was able to capture the support of the majority of the Democratic Party insiders, organized interest groups, big donors and primary election super-delegates. The Democratic Party super-delegates were elected officials, Democratic members of Congress, Governors and party leaders, and were overwhelmingly supporters of the establishment candidate, Hillary Clinton. The vast majority of super-delegates pledged their support early on to the Hillary for President campaign. Whenever the news media reported primary election or caucus results on the TV screen, the public could see a huge numerical advantage in delegates for Hillary Clinton over Bernie Sanders based on the boost that her super-delegate numbers gave her. Due to reforms championed by the Sanders/Progressive wing of the Democratic Party, the power of super-delegates has somewhat been reduced: super-delegates will not be allowed to vote on the first round at the national convention.

Bernie Sanders and Hillary Clinton were the exact polar opposites of each other as candidates in the 2016 Democratic presidential primary elections. Bernie refused to accept corporate PAC money while Hillary welcomed it and raised a lot of it; Bernie hailed from the small rural state of Vermont and was relatively unknown nationally despite being in the U.S. Senate and House for a couple of decades; Hillary was already a national figure when she was elected U.S. Senator from New York, a large diverse state with the biggest urban financial center of New York City, the home of the huge Wall Street investment banks, whose members and investors provided a great campaign-finance base for her. Hillary was widely criticized for making three private speeches to Wall Street audiences for $250,000 each in personal income. Bernie railed against the big banks and other corporate interests that he felt had bought the American government. His campaign stressed the need to fight for the 99%, not the elite corporate 1%. While refusing their corporate-generated money for his campaign, he relied primarily on campaign money from small individual donors. He had over 2.5 million individual donors in the primary elections; in contrast Hillary had 467,230 individual donors, over half were large donors giving over $200 each, in both the primary and general elections. Sanders relished the chance to remind people that his average donation was $27. Federal Election Commission records show that the majority of his donors were small donors who gave less than $200 each to his campaign (opensecrets.org).

In the 2016 Democratic primaries, Hillary Clinton's early and big-money advantage and fame over Bernie Sanders allowed her to garner early support from Democratic Party and financial donor elites. This enabled her to win a majority of votes cast in the early first-half of the Democratic primaries, which together with her large super-delegate lead, provided her the momentum to win the Democratic presidential nomination. Bernie's remarkable grassroots campaign, despite being outspent by Hillary, galvanized enough support, particularly among young voters, to provide him with a majority of popular votes in the second half of the Democratic presidential primary season. However, this was inadequate to put Bernie over the top in the end. Bernie had other headwinds that he faced: the Democratic Party elite and establishment favored Hillary throughout the primaries. Besides Bernie being a registered Independent voter all his life, until he ran for president in 2016, the Democratic Party and financial elite did not favor his position on the issues such as single-payer Medicare for All healthcare, tuition free college education, and a financial transaction tax on Wall Street to pay for it. The Democratic Party elite also did not like Bernie Sanders' criticism of big money in politics, which they of course accepted and favored. The Democratic Party elite were heavily tied to Wall Street. Just visit opensecrets.org to learn more about campaign contributions from the Finance, Insurance, and Real Estate (FIRE) industries to both the

Democratic and Republican Parties and their candidates for office.

In the 2016 presidential election between Hillary Clinton and Donald Trump, Dollar Democracy was on steroids: Hillary's campaign committee and super PACs that supported her from the outside raised and spent approximately $794,875,608 in the 2016 election cycle. Donald Trump's campaign committee and super PACs that supported them from the outside raised and spent approximately $408,396,207. In addition, Donald Trump was a well-known television personality, a real estate multibillionaire, and a candidate for president. Also, he received approximately $1 billion worth of free airtime from the various television networks, particularly during the Republican primary election season. As pre-election polling data predicted, Hillary Clinton won almost 3 million more popular votes than Donald Trump. Yet she lost the presidential election in the Electoral College. Most of the data from polling after the primary election showed that Hillary Clinton would beat Donald Trump in the November general election by 5 to 7 percentage points. Data from the same polls showed that Bernie Sanders would beat Donald Trump by 8 or 9 percentage points, if he had been the Democratic Nominee. On November 3, 2016, Democrat Hillary Clinton beat Donald Trump in the nationwide popular vote by two percentage points, 48% to 45.9%. She lost the electoral college votes 232 to 306 and lost the presidential election to Donald Trump. (nytimes.com, August 9, 2017).

The American Petroleum Institute, Exxon, and Other Major Multinational Oil and Gas Corporations Knew About Climate Change/Global Warming Over 40 Years Ago, and Concealed It from the Public

The biggest and most prominent lobbying group for the multinational oil and gas corporations is the American Petroleum Institute (API). At the time, its leading members such as Exxon, Mobil, Amoco, Philips, Texaco, Shell, Sunoco, Sohio, as well as Standard Oil of California, and Gulf Oil, Chevron's predecessors, created and used a task force to monitor and share climate research between 1979 and 1983. James J. Nelson, a former career Air Force pilot and director of the first air quality monitoring system in Fairfax County, Virginia served as director of this Climate and Energy Task Force. The task force members included senior scientists and engineers from these oil and gas corporations. This indicates that the oil industry, including Exxon, was aware of the possible impact on the world's climate of its activity of producing fossil fuels, the burning of which, produced global warming greenhouse gases. According to a memo by an Exxon task force representative, a background paper on CO2 informed API members in 1979 that carbon dioxide in the atmosphere was rising steadily and it predicted when the first clearest effects of climate change might be felt. An investigation by the Pulitzer prize-winning nonprofit, nonpartisan news organization, Inside Climate News, found that Exxon "launched its own cutting-edge CO2 sampling program in 1978 in order to understand a phenomenon it suspected could harm its business. About a decade later, Exxon spearheaded campaigns to cast doubt on climate science and stall regulation of greenhouse gases." (insideclimatenews.org, December 22,2015).

Before President George W. Bush handed the fossil fuel industry a major victory by withdrawing the U.S. from the Kyoto Protocol, a worldwide agreement to reduce greenhouse gases, the Environmental Protection Agency's (EPA) authority was growing as early as 1983, and oil companies felt that the EPA was silencing them. It was getting harder for corporations to get scientific papers published or to gain favorable attention from the media. Oil company leaders were worried that this would bring government overregulation. So, the American Petroleum Institute decided that it would not be enough to have scientists meeting in a task force on climate change or other pollution issues. It was going to need lobbyists to influence politicians on environmental issues! (insideclimatenews.org).

By the 1990s the American Petroleum Institute (API) joined Exxon, other fossil fuel companies and major manufacturers in the Global Climate Coalition (GCC). The GCC was a lobbying group with the objective of blocking international efforts to curtail heat trapping emissions. The year after the Kyoto Protocol was adopted by countries to cut back on fossil fuel emissions, in 1998 the API created a campaign to convince American lawmakers and the public that climate science was too uncertain for the U.S. to ratify the treaty. The GCC and the API could declare victory when U.S. President George W. Bush pulled the U.S. out of the Kyoto agreement. A top State Department official is recorded in a June 2001 briefing memorandum, thanking the GCC because Bush "rejected the Kyoto Protocol in part based on input from you."(insideclimatenews.org, December 22,2015).

ExxonMobil: A Case Study in Dollar Democracy and the Politics of Climate Disaster

ExxonMobil's extensive research on the causes and effects of climate change on its business and profitability began even before the research done by the American Petroleum Institute. Exxon's climate change studies were published from 1977 to 2014. Two Harvard researchers, Naomi Oreskes, a professor of the history of science whose work has focused on the energy and tobacco industries, and Geoffrey Supran, a postdoctoral fellow, reviewed nearly 200 documents representing Exxon's research and its public statements. They concluded that the corporation "misled the public about climate change even as its own scientists were recognizing greenhouse gas emissions as a risk to the planet." (New York Times, August 23, 2017, "Exxon Misled the Public on Climate Change, Study Says", by John Schwartz). Oraskes and Supran published their peer-reviewed paper in the journal Environmental Research Letters. They also published their findings in an opinion article in the New York Times. They found that Exxon's climate change studies paralleled the scientific thinking at the time. 80% of the company's research and internal communications concluded that "climate change was real and caused by humans. But 80% of Exxon statements to the broader public, which reached a much larger audience, expressed doubt about climate change."(*New York Times*, August 23, 2017, "Exxon Misled the Public on Climate Change, Study Says", by John Schwartz).

Investigative reporting by the Pulitzer prize-winning Inside Climate

News, the *Los Angeles Times*, and the Columbia Journalism School revealed that top Exxon officials had known everything about climate change that was to be known in the 1980s. Senior company scientist James Black told Exxon's management committee in 1977 "In the first place there is general scientific agreement that the most likely manner in which mankind is influencing the global climate is through carbon dioxide release from the burning of fossil fuels." To verify this, Exxon outfitted an oil tanker with carbon dioxide sensors to measure concentrations of the gas over the ocean, and then funded elaborate computer models to help predict what temperatures would do in the future.(grist.org, February 19, 2016, "It's Not Just What Exxon Did – It's What the Oil Company Is Still Doing", by Bill McKibben).

As Bill McKibben points out, by 1982, in an internal corporate primer, Exxon leaders were told that, despite lingering unknowns, dealing with climate change "would require major reductions in fossil fuel combustion." Unless that happened the primer said, citing independent experts "there are some potentially catastrophic events that must be considered... Once the effects are measurable, they might not be reversible." But that document, "given wide circulation" within Exxon, was also stamped "not to be distributed externally."(grist.org, February 19, 2016). Bill McKibben, environmentalist and author, who has written extensively on the impact of global warming, is the founder of 350.org. McKibben puts it very well:

> "Exxon used its knowledge of climate change to plan its own future. The company, for instance, leased large tracts of the Arctic for oil exploration, territory where, as a company scientist pointed out in 1990, 'potential global warming can only help lower exploration and development costs.' Not only that but, 'from the North Sea to the Canadian Arctic,' Exxon and its affiliates set about 'raising the decks of offshore platforms, protecting pipelines from increasing coastal erosion, and designing helipads, pipelines, and roads in a warming and buckling Arctic.' In other words, the company started climate-

38

proofing its facilities to head off a future its own scientists knew was inevitable."(grist.org, February 19, 2016).

Exxon did not release these actions or information to the public. Instead Exxon started funding think tanks that produced climate denial information and even recruited lobbying talent from big tobacco. Exxon followed the path of the tobacco industry which defended cigarettes by sowing doubts that cigarettes caused cancer. In the same way, Exxon highlighted "uncertainty" regarding the science of global warming. And last but not least, Exxon (ExxonMobil today) donated and still donates heavily to political candidates who often dismiss global warming and weaken policies needed to fight it (opensecrets.org). Policies that would make up the heart of the Green New Deal!

The current track on which to defeat the power of the big corporations in blocking the Green New Deal is to work to elect grassroots, small donor backed, non-corporate, non-oil money candidates to Congress and the Presidency. In this regard the 2020 elections for the Presidency and Congress are extremely crucial. There are Congressional and Presidential candidates in the 2020 elections who are rejecting corporate big money donations, and there are thousands of volunteers organized and organizing to help them win.

The second track on which to defeat the power of the big fossil fuel companies to block the Green New Deal is by holding big oil in particular responsible for concealing information that they had obtained through scientific research in the 1970s and 1980s. As noted earlier that research indicated the devastating effects that the burning of their product, fossil fuels, has had on the lives of Americans, the world's people, and the planet. They must be made to pay for their advent of Global Warming/Climate Change/Climate Disruption. If the U.S. or state governments were to pursue this track, they would only have to learn from the playbook of the government's lawsuits against Big Tobacco.

The attorneys general of 46 states, the District of Columbia, and other jurisdictions sued the tobacco manufacturers to obtain reimbursement for the costs incurred by the state's taxpayers in caring for citizens suffering from smoking-related illnesses. In 1998 the five major tobacco companies reached the "master settlement agreement", an agreement with the states' attorneys general to settle the litigation, estimated to be $206 billion for the first 25 years. The lawyers had uncovered internal tobacco company documents that exposed corporate deception and cover-ups about addiction and nicotine manipulation. Four states-- Florida, Mississippi, Texas, and Minnesota-- settled separately with the tobacco companies. Total settlements for all the states add up to $246 billion. There may be some parallels here with Exxon and/or other oil companies.

In the last few years, two states, New York State and Massachusetts, have started fraud investigations into ExxonMobil over climate change. One state, Rhode Island, is suing ExxonMobil, BP, Royal Dutch Shell, Chevron and other major oil companies for contributing to climate change that is damaging infrastructure and coastal communities in the state. Cities small, medium and large such as Imperial Beach, Richmond, San Francisco, and Oakland in California, and New York City are also suing oil companies for costs related to climate change; so are counties such as San Mateo and Marin in California. If the government is successful in a lawsuit against the big oil companies, perhaps some of that settlement money can be applied to funding Green New Deal policies and help us block the worst effects of Climate Change/Global Warming.

As students of politics and society, what we have learned from the crisis of climate change and its tragic aftermath of human death and suffering is the following: all the money that politicians have taken for their political campaigns from fossil fuel corporations and their lobbyists has enabled them to allow this tragedy to unfold. It has also made them slow, very slow in effectively dealing with it. The power and responsibility rests with We the People to take collective action in order to reverse global warming/climate change through grassroots organizing, political activism, peaceful protests, organized voting and donating small amounts of money to non-corporate funded candidates in our elections in America and the world. As Mahatma Gandhi once said, "When the people lead, the leaders will follow."

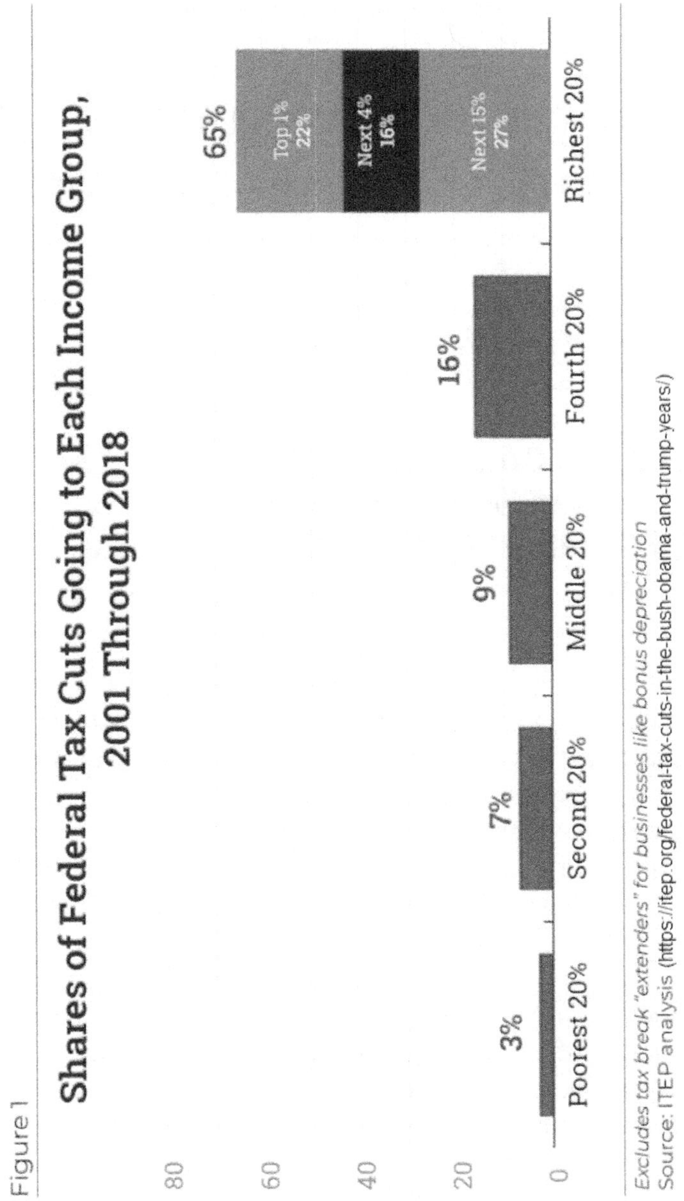
Figure 1
Shares of Federal Tax Cuts Going to Each Income Group, 2001 Through 2018
80
60
40
20
0
3%
7%
9%
16%
65%
Top 1% 22%
Next 4% 16%
Next 15% 27%
Poorest 20%
Second 20%
Middle 20%
Fourth 20%
Richest 20%
Excludes tax break "extenders" for businesses like bonus depreciation
Source: ITEP analysis (https://itep.org/federal-tax-cuts-in-the-bush-obama-and-trump-years/)

Table 1-3

CHAPTER 2

BUYING AMERICAN POLITICS AND
SELLING OUT THE MIDDLE-CLASS DREAM

"...I refused to take part in what former U.S. Congressman Cecil Heftel of Hawaii called 'legalized bribery'."

--Peter Mathews

U.S. Supreme Court: Super Rich Americans Can Now Buy All of Congress and Both Political Parties. McCutcheon v. FEC (2014)

It was another bright and sunny sparkling Southern California morning in June 1994. No worries. Optimism abounded. I had woken up early to shower, shave, and have a hot breakfast of oatmeal and coffee. I had just wrapped up the semester of teaching at the end of May. I drove with relaxed determination to my Congressional campaign headquarters a short four blocks from my house. By 9 o'clock in the morning, the warm sun and blue sky enveloped me with the promise of new beginnings.

As I opened the door with confidence, my campaign manager who was already in the office before me, greeted me with enthusiasm. The campaign headquarters did not have luxuries such as finished floors like most campaign offices; it was a bare room with concrete flooring. However, our enthusiastic volunteer staff had cleaned and organized it beautifully. Nothing like the fruits of victory to galvanize positive attitudes and enthusiasm, even from unpaid volunteers. My campaign manager said "Congratulations Mr. Democratic primary winner. Your reputation precedes you. Are you ready for this important meeting with the ARCO PAC (political action committee)? This is your big day to make an impression. These guys can kick off the raising of hundreds of thousands of dollars that it will take to win in the fall."

I had mixed feelings about this meeting with this oil company's political elite. I had refused to raise money from corporate special interests in my 1992 primary election campaign for the same congressional seat, and still had landed a very strong second-place. As a professor of political science, I knew the strong influence that wealthy corporate donors had over policy votes of candidates who took their money.

Now, as I was facing my campaign manager in that room with desks covered with neatly stacked papers, I looked him in the eye, and seeing his enthusiasm for raising the huge amount of money it would take to defeat a powerful, well-known, well-respected moderate Republican Congressman in November, I said, "Okay let's meet these ARCO guys and see what they have to say." I could see the sense of relief spread over his face. He was probably thinking maybe this guy is not such a crazy, unrealistic, idealist after all. Maybe Mathews has finally come to realize the importance of raising the serious amount of money that it takes to win a general election and become a Congressman. He wasted no time as he drove me to the ARCO PAC offices for our meeting with the political action committee and its chairman.

We had plenty of time to get there, but my manager drove like there was no tomorrow. It felt like he was ready to hit the jackpot. It felt as if we were going to Vegas, not to gamble, but to collect our winnings. After all we only had to show ARCO that I had won more votes in the Democratic primary than my Republican opponent, incumbent Congressman Steve Horn, had won in his Republican primary: 33,000 votes to 26,000 and that this was a strong sign of my likely victory in the fall. Helping us in this argument was the cover story in a magazine in the *Los Angeles Times* with a cover picture of the facial profiles of Steve Horn and me, challenging each other like two prizefighters. The caption accompanying the *LA Times* magazine cover said, "Democrat Peter Mathews poses stiff challenge to incumbent Republican Steve Horn."

We arrived earlier than expected because somewhere on the drive from the campaign office to the ARCO office, my campaign manager had morphed into a Grand Prix racer. The fact that ARCO had taken us seriously enough to invite us to meet and interview with them, and possibly gain their financial support, must have given him an adrenaline boost.

When we arrived and saw the gleaming buildings and offices, I'm sure my campaign manager felt that we had landed a tryout in the major leagues, every baseball player's dream. Of course, major-league baseball players produce a lot of viewing pleasure for the fans and are paid handsomely for playing a superb and professional game. In contrast, major-league politicians such as members of Congress are not about producing a pleasurable game to view but much more importantly, members of Congress gain huge amounts of power to create and shape government policies that benefit or hurt millions of people in major ways. The ARCO political action committee chairman and members were clearly aware of this.

As soon as we walked into the gleaming air-conditioned offices where we were being interviewed, we were treated with professional courtesy and warmth by the receptionist. We did not have to wait very long. The folks in the back room must have been notified of our arrival right away.

A guide was sent to escort us to the room where the interview was to take place with the ARCO PAC members. As my campaign manager and I were ushered in to the immaculately furnished conference room, the committee members rose to greet us and shake our hands very cordially. The atmosphere into which we had walked was very positive and welcoming. I knew that the ARCO PAC members were extremely experienced and aware of their important roles and the power that lay in their hands. After all, these were the men and women who would decide which candidates to support and which to reject in their bids to become members of Congress. These committee women and men knew exactly what kinds of questions to ask of the candidates, both challengers and incumbents running for re-election. The political action committee members knew how to judge the substance and nuances of the answers and presentations provided to them by the hopeful candidates for Congress.

I had been interviewed by political action committees before while seeking the endorsement of public interest groups, so I was not nervous at all while being seated in the hot seat in the conference room facing all those political judges, members of the ARCO PAC. Shaking each person's hand, and making personal contact, including small talk when appropriate, had broken the ice between me and the committee members. I felt at home being interviewed for an endorsement for the U.S. House of Representatives. I told them that government needs to spend its revenues wisely in building the best K-12 and college and university educational systems. Government should ensure that the kindergarten through technical and trade school as well as college and university systems should provide equal opportunity for every single American child and young adult regardless of their parents' economic standing. I added that government should also create policies that would encourage the creation of jobs through small business growth and the rebuilding of America's infrastructure, roads, bridges, water and sewer systems, levies, school buildings etc.

As I looked around the room there seemed to be an expectation for something else. After all we were in the Lions' Den of a corporate big business oil company. I had done my research and knew that in 1994 big business was doing very well in terms of profitability, government subsidies, and corporate tax loopholes given to them by Congress. Big business was getting its way in the area of Free Trade instead of Fair Trade. I knew exactly what the men and women in this room expected to hear from me, if I wanted their political and financial support.

I looked around the room at these women and men playing the role of the political guardians for big oil and once again noticed their expectant expressions. They would have loved it if I had said that what's good for business is good for America. That business, particularly big business, was the engine that drives the train of the American economy. The engine must be constantly fueled by the policies of government, if the boxcars loaded with heavy goods were to be pulled along successfully, and the American economic train was to run smoothly and efficiently.

To Tell You the Truth,
You Can Keep Your Money

What kind of fuel for the big business engine were these ARCO PAC committee members thinking of? I knew that to win their support, endorsement, and full commitment of campaign funding, I had to mention that I supported government policies that would fuel the engine of big business to successfully pull the boxcars of the economic train. All I had to do to gain their support was to say that I supported tax incentives and corporate subsidies so that the big business engine could do its job well in successfully building up and maintaining the American economy. The expectant faces around the room wanted to see that I truly believed in Charles Wilson's claim that what's good for GM is good for America, and vice versa. Charles Wilson, the former CEO of General Motors, served as President Eisenhower's Defense Secretary. I knew that I would disappoint most of those in that room including my campaign manager with what I was about to say, but I was going to say what I believed anyway!

I told them I believed that in order to strengthen and grow the American economy we had to guarantee high-quality, affordable and equal education to everyone; and in order to help create high paying, new technology jobs, the federal government needed to invest in America. As any businessperson knows, productive investment costs money. It would take hundreds of billions of dollars to invest in America's educational systems, small business growth, technological development, and to modernize the aging infrastructure. This investment would be absolutely necessary to create the foundation for a successful 21st Century world-class economy. We will pay now, or we will pay dearly later by falling behind other nations in our productivity. I told them if we don't invest now we will see the rich getting richer, the poor getting poorer, and the middle class disappearing. I looked around the room at the eyes of these eminent, powerful, and influential decision-makers, and said the best way to generate the funds for investment in America is to close the unproductive corporate tax loopholes, and to end the most egregious and unproductive corporate subsidies by government, and use the money generated to educate Americans for the 21st Century jobs just around the corner. I said, "My good friends of ARCO PAC, if we take this path, our economy and our country will be prosperous and successful and corporations like ARCO will be partners and beneficiaries in this venture."

I paused to gauge their reaction. They were smiling nervously at each other, a little shocked at a candidate who would tell them directly what they were not too happy to hear. The chairman proceeded to a couple of more relatively insignificant questions and then the interview was over sooner than expected. The PAC chairman got up to shake my hand and said, "Thank you very much for coming, we appreciate your time. Goodbye." I wasn't sure why I was surprised by this response. I suppose I had thought in the back of my mind that perhaps these people would like to have a serious and vigorous discussion and debate about what it means to close unproductive corporate tax loopholes, and end government subsidies (corporate welfare) of large corporations such as ARCO. No such luck, so I said, "Thank you for your time ladies and gentlemen. Goodbye." I never heard from ARCO PAC again!

"We Have the Best Politicians Money Can Buy"

As we were making our way out of the ARCO offices, my campaign manager reminded me that we had a long way to go to raise the requisite $500,000 minimum that winning candidates for Congress were raising and spending in 1994. In the national elections of 2016, the winning candidates for the U.S. House of Representatives averaged more than $1.7 million raised and spent per district. The losing candidates averaged more than $700,000 raised and spent in each district. That was a total of $1,644,300,000 raised and $1,597,000,000 spent in the 2015-16 election cycle (FEC.gov, March 23, 2017). In the 2018 midterm election, $5.2 billion was raised and spent on House and Senate incumbents and challengers by the candidates, political parties, political action committees (PACs), Super-PACs, and non-profits. (opensecrets.org, Oct. 29, 2018). These were mostly wealthy corporate special interests in the top 1%, who want tax loopholes, subsidies, and other handouts from members of Congress whom they help elect.

They get these favors from Congress, which causes Congress to cut, or not increase, needed spending for programs that provide opportunity and success for the bottom 99% (the middle class and working poor); programs such as public education pre-school through college and university, full universal healthcare (where Obamacare left 20,000,000 Americans uncovered and Trumpcare increased the uninsured by 7 million more), full and secure retirement for all Americans, higher minimum wage and a living wage, investment in small business and entrepreneurial capital and rebuilding and modernizing our infrastructure, scientific research and development, and direct government employment as in Franklin Roosevelt's New Deal, all of which would create millions of new well-paying jobs through increased demand and growth in the American economy. In the two years of the Trump presidency (2017-2018), the rate of uninsured Americans has risen from 10.9 percent to 13.7 percent: 7 million more people, mostly women, young adults, and low-income Americans without health insurance. (news.gallup.com, by Dan Witters, Jan. 23, 2019). Today, in 2019, 44 million Americans have no health insurance, eight out of ten of these are workers or their dependents. Another 38 million have inadequate health insurance coverage!

An FDR type New Deal program has been blocked by Big Money going into Congressional campaigns from the Big Corporations and their wealthy owners and lobbyists. Money and favors go out from Congress to the Wealthy Corporate Special Interests and Super-wealthy Donors. This is "Dollar Democracy", the millions and billions of dollars used by wealthy campaign donors and corporate lobbyists to legally buy influence over our members of Congress, which stops them from representing us, the 99%, and fighting for the American public interest. This reminds me of Will Rogers' quip, *"We have the best politicians money can buy!"*

**CORPORATIONS FUND CONGRESSMEMBER'S CAMPAIGNS AND GET
MILLIONS FROM CONGRESS IN TAX LOOPHOLES AND SUBSIDIES**
60 Profitable Fortune 500 Companies Avoided All Federal Income Tax in 2018

Company	2018 Income	Federal Tax	Tax Rate	Industries
Gannett	$7,000,000	--$11,000,000	--164%	Publishing, printing
Int'l Business Machines	$500,000,000	--$342,000,000	--68%	Computers, Software, Data
Activation Blizzard	$447,000,000	--$228,000,000	--51%	Computers, Software, Data
AECOM Technology	$238,000,000	--$122,000,000	--51%	Engineering & Construction
Pitney Bowes	$125,000,000	--$50,000,000	--40%	Computers, Software, Data
Celanese	$480,000,000	--$142,000,000	--30%	Chemicals
JetBlue Airways	$219,000,000	--$60,000,000	--27%	Transportation
Prudential Financial	$1,440,000,000	--$345,000,000	--24%	Financial
Duke Energy	$3,029,000,000	--$647,000,000	--21%	Utilities, Gas & Electric
Wisconsin Energy	$1,139,000,000	--$128,000,000	--19%	Utilities, Gas & Electric
Aramark	$315,000,000	--$48,000,000	--15%	Misc. Services
Trinity Industries	$138,000,000	--$19,000,000	--14%	Misc. Manufacturing
Deere	$2,152,000,000	--$268,000,000	--12%	Industrial machinery
Whirlpool	$717,000,000	--$70,000,000	--10%	Electronics, Electrical Equip
CMS Energy	$774,000,000	--$67,000,000	--9%	Utilities, Gas & Electric
Eli Lilly	$598,000,000	--$54,000,000	--9%	Pharma & medical products
U.S. Steel	$432,000,000	--$40,000,000	--9%	Metals & metal products
Avis Budget Group	$78,000,000	--$7,000,000	--9%	Motor Vehicles & Parts
SPX	$66,000,000	--$5,000,000	--8%	Industrial machinery
EOG Resources	$4,067,000,000	--$304,000,000	--7%	Oil, Gas & Pipelines
Ryder System	$350,000,000	--$23,000,000	--7%	Transportation
Realogy	$199,000,000	--$10,000,000	--7%	Misc. Services
Arrow Electronics	$167,000,000	--$12,000,000	--7%	Retail & Wholesale Trade
Public Service Entrprise	$1,772,000,000	--$97,000,000	--5%	Utilities, Gas & Electric
MDU Resources	$314,000,000	--$16,000,000	--5%	Oil, Gas & Pipelines
Tech Data	$203,000,000	--$10,000,000	--5%	Retail & Wholesale Trade
Delta Airlines	$5,073,000,000	--$187,000,000	--4%	Transportation
Chevron	$4,547,000,000	--$181,000,000	--4%	Oil, Gas & Pipelines
Penske Automotive Gp	$393,000,000	--$9,000,000	--4%	Motor Vehicles & Parts
Performance Food Gp	$192,000,000	--$9,000,000	--4%	Retail & Wholesale Trade
SpartanNash	$40,000,000	--$2,000,000	--4%	Retail & Wholesale Trade
Principal Financial	$1,641,000,000	--$49,000,000	--3%	Financial
PulteGroup	$1,340,000,000	--$44,000,000	--3%	Misc. Manufacturing
Netflix	$856,000,000	--$22,000,000	--3%	Retail & Wholesale Trade
Goodyear Tire & Rubber	$440,000,000	--$15,000,000	--3%	Motor Vehicles & Parts
General Motors	$4,320,000,000	--$104,000,000	--2%	Motor Vehicles & Parts
Xcel Energy	$1,434,000,000	--$34,000,000	--2%	Utilities, Gas & Electric
American Electric Pwr	$1,943,000,000	--$32,000,000	--2%	Utilities, Gas & Electric
Molson Coors	$1,325,000,000	--$23,000,000	--2%	Food, Beverages, Tobacco
PPL	$1,110,000,000	--$19,000,000	--2%	Utilities, Gas & Electric

Continued on the next page

Continued from the previous page

Company	2018 Income	Federal Tax	Tax Rate	Industries
Halliburton	$1,082,000,000	--$19,000,000	--2%	Oil, Gas & Pipelines
Rockwell Collins	$719,000,000	--$16,000,000	--2%	Aerospace and Defense
MGM Resorts Int'l	$648,000,000	--$12,000,000	--2%	Misc. Services
Atmos Energy	$600,000,000	--$10,000,000	--2%	Utilities, Gas & Electric
Owens Corning	$405,000,000	--$10,000,000	--2%	Misc. Manufacturing
Amazon	$10,835,000,000	--$129,000,000	--1%	Retail & Wholesale Trade
Occidental Petroleum	$3,379,000,000	--$23,000,000	--1%	Oil, Gas & Pipelines
Dominion Resources	$3,021,000,000	--$45,000,000	--1%	Utilities, Gas & Electric
Honeywell International	$2,830,000,000	--$21,000,000	--1%	Industrial machinery
Kinder Morgan	$1,784,000,000	--$22,000,000	--1%	Oil, Gas & Pipelines
First Energy	$1,495,000,000	--$16,000,000	--1%	Utilities, Gas & Electric
Devon Energy	$1,297,000,000	--$14,000,000	--1%	Oil, Gas & Pipelines
DTE Energy	$1,215,000,000	--$17,000,000	--1%	Utilities, Gas & Electric
Ameren	$1,035,000,000	--$10,000,000	--1%	Utilities, Gas & Electric
Alaska Air Group	$576,000,000	--$5,000,000	--1%	Transportation
UGI	$550,000,000	--$3,000,000	--0%	Utilities, Gas & Electric
Cliffs Natural Resources	$565,000,000	--$1,000,000	--0%	Oil, Gas & Pipelines
Arthur Gallagher	$322,000,000	--	--	Financial
Pioneer Nat. Resources	$1,249,000,000	--	--	Oil, Gas & Pipelines
Salesforce.com	$800,000,000	--	--	Computers, Software, Data

Table 2-1

I told my campaign manager that I understood the need to raise $500,000 to be competitive in the November general election against the Republican nominee, Congressman Steve Horn. But I was not going to raise this money from wealthy corporate political action committees who would expect something from their sponsored candidate. Of course, it was illegal for a political action committee to propose providing funds to a specific congressional candidate with a promise that the candidate, once he wins, will propose and work for a specific piece of legislation, or amendments desired by the donor group. This would be called bribery and is definitely illegal.

"A record $5.7 billion was spent on the 2018 elections for Congress"
by Fredreka Schouten, CNN
Updated 11:35AM EST, Thu February 07, 2019

Midterm Election Spending, 1998-2018

CRP projects that more than $5 billion will be spent in the 2018 elections, far surpassing previous midterm totals.

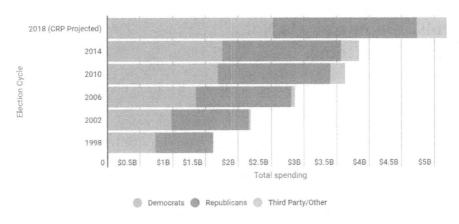

"Third party/Other" represents spending by third party candidates as well as PAC overhead and spending by nonpartisan organizations.

opensecrets.org | graph 1-1

Graph 2-2

However, I refused to take part in what former U.S. Congressman Cecil Heftel of Hawaii called "legalized bribery": an unwritten understanding between wealthy corporate special interests, and candidates receiving their collectively huge donations; the understanding that once this candidate becomes a Congressman, she or he will vote on behalf of positions taken by the wealthy group of donors, on important public issues (taxes, environmental regulations, trade agreements and outsourcing, etc.). Of course, the unwritten understanding cannot be a specific verbal or written agreement. If a specific *quid pro quo* agreement is made, both the member of Congress and the wealthy special interest group representative would probably end up in jail. Many political science studies of voting behavior in Congress have shown patterns of up to 80% support by the members of Congress for the positions taken on key issues by their corporate sponsors. This pattern has also applied to state legislators, and their special interest sponsors, from Big Oil corporations, to Big Tobacco corporations, to Big Pharma, to Big Wall Street Banks, to organized groups of super wealthy individual donors.

Dollar Democracy Is Not a Victimless Crime

As my campaign manager drove us back to our campaign headquarters, this time at a more leisurely pace, we had a very sincere and thought-provoking conversation about campaign finance, and the influence of wealthy special interest groups on American elections and policies made by elected officials. The powerful influence over our government that Corporate America in general has, and in this case Big Oil, is clearly illustrated by the following:

ARCO is one of the top sponsors and funders of politicians elected to the executive and legislative branches of the American Government. It funds their campaigns through its wealthy political action committee (ARCO PAC, whose Southern California branch interviewed me in 1994). In the 1996 election cycle, ARCO PAC gave more than $357,000 to federal candidates. At the same time, it gave $1.25 million in "soft money" (which could only be used for party-building activities such as voter registration and voter turnout) to the Republican and Democratic National Committees. ARCO PAC gave another $500,000 in state elections, where often, as in California, corporations can give directly to candidates' campaigns.

At this time Robert Healy was ARCO's Vice-President for Governmental Affairs. According to *CounterPunch* editor Jeffrey St. Clair, writing in "Dime's Worth of Difference", on October 25, 1995 Healy attended a coffee klatsch with Vice-President Al Gore and Marvin Rosen, finance chair of the Democratic National Committee (DNC). Healy donated the maximum of $1000 to the Clinton-Gore Re- election Campaign. Through July to December 1995, mainly under Healy's direction, ARCO gave $125,000 to the DNC. It so happened that President Clinton's Commerce Secretary Mickey Kantor became the most intense supporter of lifting the export ban on Alaskan oil. Kantor, previously U.S. Trade Representative, promoted this as an important portion of Clinton's Asian Trade Policy.

According to St. Clair, President Clinton hosted a birthday celebration at the White House for ARCO's former CEO, Lodwrick Cook, a personal friend of his. Cook and Clinton's Commerce Secretary Ron Brown traveled together on a trade mission to China in August 1994. On this trip, Cook and Brown negotiated ARCO's investment in the large Zhenhari oil refinery near Shanghai. This got it ready to process crude oil from Alaska. Further evidence of the influence of oil companies, including ARCO, on U.S. government energy policy was seen in 1994 and beyond. Congressman Don Young of Alaska, Chair of the House Resources Committee, received more campaign money from BP, ExxonMobil, ARCO, and Chevron PACs than any other member of Congress.

In 1994, while President Clinton was on his summer vacation in Jackson Hole, Wyoming, oil company executives met with him. According to St. Clair, they "pressed Clinton for concessions: 1) Increased drilling on the outer Continental Shelf, especially in the Gulf of Mexico 2) A break on Royalty Payments 3) Expedited leasing for Coal-bed methane in the Rocky Mountain Front 4) Opening the National Petroleum Reserve—Alaska to drilling 5) Removal on the ban on export of Alaskan Crude oil to overseas refineries." (Jeffrey St. Clair, "Dime's

Worth of Difference", p 201-202).

The National Petroleum Reserve—Alaska is 24 million acres of pristine land and was set aside for entry only in the case of a national emergency. Yet under Clinton's Interior Secretary, Bruce Babbit, the Reserve was opened to the oil corporations for drilling. This was done, despite the fact that it is crossed by a huge migrating Caribou herd, one larger than the herd in ANWR (Arctic National Wildlife Refuge). The National Petroleum Reserve—Alaska is also home to many declining species, including Polar Bears, Arctic Wolves and foxes, and Musk Ox. The largest river on Alaska's North Slope, the Colville River is contained within it. Also, the Colville River Canyon, and nearby marshes and lakes, make up one of the world's most important migratory bird staging areas. But Big Oil's corporations invested enough money in American elections and lobbying to get their way, regardless of Climate Change (Climate Disruption) or the needs of the natural environment.

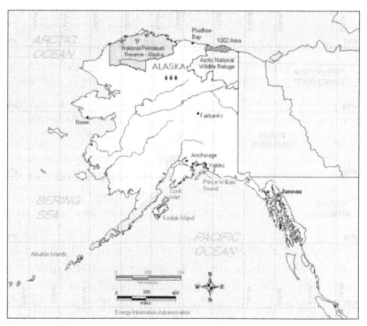

Image 2-1 | ANWR Map of Alaska | Photo/Energy Information Agency

This is the process through which influence is peddled: ARCO and other oil companies contribute heavily to the political campaigns of their favored candidates. Once they are elected to government, ARCO and friends have access to these decision makers, before and while laws and policies are made. It has become a "pay to play" system.

It is not just the majority of Democratic politicians, Bill Clinton, and Al Gore who understand and use this "pay to play" system very well; it is also Republican politicians, including Dick Cheney, and George W. Bush, who know and use this "pay to play" game extremely well. Added to this is the fact that Dick Cheney was the CEO of Halliburton Corporation, the largest oil and gas drilling equipment producer, and George W. Bush was CEO of an oil corporation before he was President.

With influence from the Energy Industry (Big Oil, Big Gas, and Big Coal), President Bush signed the energy bill into law on August 8, 2005. The U.S. House of Representatives had voted 275 to 156 to pass the energy bill on July 28; the U.S. Senate voted on July 29 to approve it. According to *Public Citizen*, since 2001 energy corporations had:

> showered federal politicians with $115 million in campaign contributions—with three-quarters of that amount going to Republicans. This cash helped secure energy companies and their lobbyists exclusive, private access to law makers, starting with Vice-President Dick Cheney's Energy Task Force, whose report provided the foundation of the energy bill passed by Congress and signed by President Bush on August 8.

The energy bill provided billions of dollars in corporate tax loopholes and subsidies to the wealthy oil, gas, and coal corporations. It also repealed the Public Utility Holding Company Act (PUHCA). The PUHCA provided strong consumer protection and effective regulation of the energy sector. Without the PUHCA, insurance companies, oil companies, hedge funds and investment banks are now allowed to own utilities. This gives these corporate owners the right to capture guaranteed revenues from the utilities for leveraging the acquisition of non-utilities. It threw the door wide open to the "price-gouging of ratepayers" (http://www.citizen.org/cmep/article_redirect.cfm?ID=13980).

Under the Cheney-Bush energy bill, the oil and gas industry received

$6 billion in subsidies and corporate tax loopholes. Here are a few of the many sections of the bill that guaranteed the multi-billion-dollar giveaway to the oil and gas men, by a Vice-President and President who were themselves oil and gas men funded by the industry, and Democratic and Republican members of Congress heavily funded by the same oil and gas corporate interests:

Section 1329 speeds up the write-off of "geological and geophysical" costs associated with exploring for oil. This will cost taxpayers over $1.266 billion from 2007-2015. Section 1323 allows the owners of oil refineries to expense 50% of the costs of equipment that is used to increase the capacity of the refinery by at least 5%, which is a governmental giveaway to the oil corporations of $842 million from 2006-2011. Section 1325-6 provides a tax break that allows natural gas corporations to depreciate their property at a much faster rate, receiving a $1.035 billion giveaway from the government. Title IX, Subtitle J provides $1.5 billion in direct payments to natural gas and oil corporations to drill in deepwater wells. According to *Public Citizen*, this provision was a pet project of Texas Republican House Majority Leader Tom DeLay. It designated a private organization, Sugar Land- based Texas Energy Center, as the "program consortium" that would give out taxpayer money to corporations. With strong ties to Tom DeLay, the Texas Energy Center's six different chief executives (Herbert W. Appel, Jr., Robert C. Brown, III, Phillip E. Lewis, Thomas Moccia, Ronald E. Oligney, and Barry Ashlin Williamson) gave a total of $8,000 to DeLay's campaign since March 2004. Additionally, three of the Center's executives gave a total of $4,500 to President George W. Bush's 2004 successful re-election campaign.

For us to better understand the tremendous impact of "Dollar Democracy", (the influence of campaign funding and lobbying dollars on the decisions of public officials that effect all of us), we need only to look a little further: at this time, the Texas Energy Center's lobbyist was Barry Ashlin Williamson. He had gone to work in 1988 for the Reagan administration and had become principal advisor on the creation and formulation of a national energy policy, to the U.S. Secretary of Energy. Williamson was later chosen by President George H.W. Bush to be the U.S. Interior Department's Director of the Minerals Management

Service, the agency that manages gas and oil exploration and production on the nation's 1.4 billion acre continental shelf. The Texas Energy Center was to "…play host to The Research Partnership to Secure Energy for America, whose members include Halliburton and Marathon Oil." (http://www.citizen.org/cmep/article_ redirect.cfm?ID=13980)

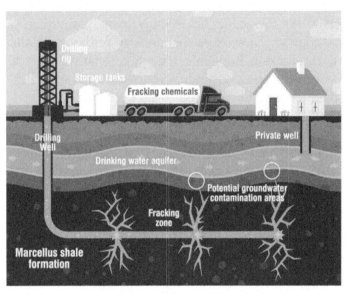

Image 2-2 | Illustration of Fracking | Image/Charles' Social Studies Journal

In addition to the $6 billion in corporate tax loopholes and subsidies given to the oil and gas industries by Cheney, Bush and the U.S. Congress, the energy bill rolled back many of the most important regulations in place on the oil and gas industry:

Called the "Halliburton Loophole", Section 322 exempts from the Safe Drinking Water Act a coal bed methane drilling technique known as "hydraulic fracturing" ("fracking"), which pollutes underground drinking water. Halliburton, for which Dick Cheney was the CEO in the 1990s, is one of the largest corporations engaged in widespread fracking. This exemption prevents lawsuits by Western ranchers and others who claim that fracking pollutes groundwater by injecting contaminated fluids underground. Sixteen companies benefit the most from the Halliburton Loophole, exempting them from clean water laws:

ChevronTexaco, BP, ConocoPhillips, Marathon Oil, Halliburton, Anadarko, Burlington Resources, Devon Energy, Dominion Resources, EOG Resources, Evergreen Resources, Oxbow (Gunnison Energy), Tom Brown, Western Gas Resources, William Cos, and XTO. Practicing "Dollar Democracy" these oil and gas corporations gave almost $15 million to federal candidates, more than three-quarters of it to Republicans. At the same time, they spent more than $70 million lobbying Congress. They reaped hundreds of millions of dollars in profits with their Halliburton Loophole. The American people reaped bloody noses, severe headaches, respiratory illnesses, other maladies, flammable faucets, polluted air and dangerous drinking water!

Section 323 of the Cheney-Bush energy bill exempts oil and gas companies from the Federal Water Pollution Control Act for their construction activities around oil and gas drilling. The bill abolished a host of other regulations necessary for the protection of human and environmental health.

The Cheney-Bush-Congress energy bill gave $9 billion in corporate tax loopholes and government subsidies to the heavily polluting coal industry. Section 1307 gives $1.612 billion in tax subsidies to invest in new coal plants. Section 401 appropriates $1.8 billion of taxpayers' money to support building a new set of coal power plants. Section 421 gave $3 billon of taxpayer money to "help build a new fleet of coal power plants." (http://www.citizen.org/cmep/article_redirect.cfm?ID =13980). These are just three of the $9 billion worth of giveaways to the coal industry through the practice of Dollar Democracy. In the 2004 election cycle alone, just before the 2005 energy bill became law, the Energy and Natural Resources industry (which includes coal), gave $54 million to federal candidates, and spent $186 million lobbying them (www.opensecrets.org). The coal corporations got the gold mine, and the American People got the shaft. The oil, gas, and coal corporations and their owners had the money to pay, and bought the right to play, in the game of Dollar Democracy.

The following are partial lists of wealthy special interest donors (mostly corporations and their owners) who have bought Congress and got the government to work for them:

NANCY PELOSI

Rolling Stone | Image 2-4

Nancy Pelosi
Speaker of the House of Representatives

Democrat – California

Total Contributions 2017-2018: $5,986,709

Top Campaign and Leadership PAC Contributors
2017-2018

Contributor		Industry PAC Contributor	
R&S Associates	$30,800	Retired	$743,739
Alphabet Inc.	$29,510	Health Professionals	$376,555
Salesforce.com	$29,200	Real Estate	$239,204
Akin, Gump et al	$27,500	Lawyers/Law Firms	$232,355
Puma Springs Vineyards	$25,800	Education	$170,647
Certain Software Inc.	$25,800	Electronics Mfg. & Equip	$159,850
American Health Care Assn	$25,000	Public Sector Unions	$151,475
Intel Corp	$24,500	Hospitals/Nursing Homes	$141,630
American Hospital Assn	$22,250	Securities & Investment	$141,006
Blue Cross/Blue Shield	$21,713	Insurance	$107,277
National Football League	$21,000	Non-Profit Institutions	$102,369
Lieff, Cabraser et al	$20,830	Internet	$99,972
Flynn Investments	$20,800	Misc. Finance	$93,542
PG&E Corp	$20,350	Building Trade Unions	$85,000
National Education Assn	$20,315	Lobbyists	$78,963
Delta Airlines	$20,219	Industrial Unions	$78,144
American Federation of State/Cnty/Municipal Empoyees	$20,080	TV/Movies/Music	$76,984
		Transportation Unions	$69,710
International Brotherhood of Electrical Workers	$20,075	Casinos/Gambling	$69,230
American Fed. of Teachers	$20,056	Women's Issues	$65,280
AFLAC Inc.	$20,040		

Source: http://www.OpenSecrets.org
Table 2-3

STENY HOYER

Steny Hoyer
House Majority Leader

Democrat – Maryland

Total Contributions 2017-2018: $9,124,449

Top Campaign and Leadership PAC Contributors
2017-2018

Contributor		Industry PAC Contributor	
Akin, Gump et al	$63,755	Retired	$494,895
Nai Michael Co.	$42,500	Health Professionals	$439,957
Blue Cross/Blue Shield	$40,626	Securities & Investment	$428,737
MacAndrews & Forbes	$40,100	Insurance	$388,006
Exelon Corp.	$37,750	Electric Utilities	$321,052
Metcor Ltd.	$34,500	Real Estate	$313,762
Northrop Grumman	$34,233	Pharmaceuticals/Health	
USAA	$31,015	Products	$227,255
Hanabusa for Hawaii	$30,000	Lawyers/Law Firms	$218,558
Medstar Health	$28,500	Lobbyists	$200,090
Eli Lilly & Co.	$27,500	Public Sector Unions	$189,142
KPMG LLP	$26,500	Health Services/HMOs	$179,445
Goldman Sachs	$26,000	Commercial Banks	$157,651
United Health Group	$25,021	Hospitals/Nursing Homes	$146,420
CTIS Inc.	$25,000	Transportation Unions	$142,758
Bayer AG	$23,000	Retail Sales	$130,109
Capital One Financial	$22,700	Accountants	$124,140
American Hospital Assn	$22,500	Air Transport	$118,371
UBS AG	$22,000	Pro-Israel	$106,246
Coca-Cola Co.	$21,750	Telecom Services	$101,326
		Building Trade Unions	$98,601

Source: http://www.OpenSecrets.org
Table 2-4

KEVIN McCARTHY

Kevin McCarthy
House Minority Leader

Republican - California

Total Contributions 2017-2018: $12,170,577

Top Campaign and Leadership PAC Contributors
2017-2018

Contributor		**Industry PAC Contributor**	
Goldman Sachs	$134,300	Securities & Investment	$1,272,267
Federated Investors Inc	$118,300	Real Estate	$958,682
Altria Group	$77,750	Lobbyists	$680,300
Oracle Corp	$77,000	Pharmaceuticals/Health	
Citigroup Inc	$66,600	Products	$609,550
Eli Lilly & Co	$64,900	Insurance	$588,458
MetLife Inc	$64,350	Oil and Gas	$576,136
Amgen Inc	$60,200	Health Professionals	$462,895
NHS Management	$60,000	Crop Production & Basic	
Blackstone Group	$52,900	Processing	$430,374
CGCN Group	$50,150	Commercial Banks	$330,400
NextEra Energy	$49,000	Electric Utilities	$317,500
Gilead Sciences	$47,900	Electronics Mfg & Equip	$289,790
Capital Group Companies	$45,700	Lawyers/Law firms	$286,365
MCNA Dental Plan	$38,900	Hospitals/Nursing Homes	$273,000
Jackson Family Enterprises	$37,400	Retired	$265,707
Pfizer Inc	$35,400	Misc. Finance	$243,450
UnitedHealth Group	$35,400	Food & Beverage	$208,162
Kirby Corp	$35,399	Misc. Manufact. & Distrib	$202,150
Western National Group	$33.856	Mining	$200,900
		Casinos/Gambling	$200,350
		Beer, Wine & Liquor	$198,539

Source: http://www.OpenSecrets.org

Table 2-5

MITCH McCONNELL

Mitch McConnell
Senate Majority Leader

Republican - Kentucky

Total Contributions 2013-2018: $30,929,404

Top 20 Campaign and Leadership PAC Contributors 2013-2018

Contributor		Industry PAC Contributor	
Blackstone Group	$223,700	Securities & Investment	$2,289,912
Altria Group	$156,050	Insurance	$1,212,575
Goldman Sachs	$123,225	Real Estate	$1,088,965
Blue Cross/Blue Shield	$117,350	Lawyers/Law Firms	$1,004,861
Elliott Management	$109,600	Health Professionals	$1,004,270
Alliance Resource Partners	$105,150	Oil & Gas	$964,764
NorPAC	$100,151	Pharmaceuticals/Health	
Comcast Corp	$99,850	Products	$935,986
DaVita Inc	$98,875	Lobbyists	$893,524
MetLife Inc	$98,550	Health Services/HMOs	$610,326
Humana Inc	$95,450	Hospitals/Nursing Homes	$519,870
Kindred Healthcare	$93,150	Leadership PACs	$504,962
BGR Group	$82,889	Misc. Finance	$481,905
FedEx Corp	$82,800	Commercial Banks	$476,214
Votesane PAC	$81,600	Electric Utilities	$470,900
Amgen Inc.	$81,100	Pro-Israel	$430,548
Brown-Forman Corp	$80,750	Misc. Manufact. & Distrib	$427,405
Eli Lilly & Co	$77,450	Air Transport	$397,379
General Electric	$75,955	Food & Beverage	$384,425
Massachusetts Mutual Life		Automotive	$832,350
Insurance	$75,750		

Source: http://www.OpenSecrets.org

Table 2-6

CHUCK SCHUMER

Chuck Schumer
Senate Minority Leader

Democrat – New York

Total Contributions 2013-2018: $28,257,115

Top 20 Campaign and Leadership PAC Contributors
2013-2018

Contributor		Industry PAC Contributor	
Paul, Weiss et al	$156,827	Securities & Investment	$3,619,553
Deloitte LLP	$132,259	Lawyers/Law Firms	$2,049,150
Lockheed Martin	$128,013	Real Estate	$2,011,822
PricewaterhouseCoopers	$124,010	Insurance	$1,044,077
NorPAC	$117,368	Lobbyists	$793,027
KPMG LLP	$115,300	Pharmaceuticals/Health	
Blackstone Group	$114,110	Products	$744,751
Alphabet Inc.	$105,722	Health Professionals	$723,685
Corning Inc	$104,600	Electronics Mfg & Equip	$680,349
Goldman Sachs	$103,950	TV/Movies/Music	$622,454
Lazard Ltd	$103,050	Accountants	$596,089
New York Life Insurance	$100,050	Hospitals/Nursing Homes	$593,625
Citigroup Inc.	$99,488	Misc. Finance	$555,019
Regeneron Pharmaceuticals	$93,313	Health Services/HMOs	$519,366
BlueCross/BlueShield	$92,014	Retired	$581,845
Ernst & Young	$91,600	Commercial Banks	$509,383
Cisco Systems	$88,940	Business Services	$489,385
MetLife Inc.	$87,200	Pro-Israel	$386,668
Fragomen, Del Rey et al	$85,300	Misc. Manufact. & Distrib	$358,709
Microsoft Corp	$85,265	Internet	$355,098
		Beer, Wine, Liquor	$355,014

Source: http://www.OpenSecrets.org
Table 2-7

About the Above Tables

(The data on the above pages is available from the Federal Election Commission as of March 6, 2019)

NOTE: All the numbers on this page are for the 2017 - 2018 election cycle and based on Federal Election Commission data released electronically on 03/06/19 for Fundraising totals, Source of Funds and Total Raised vs Average, and on 02/01/19 for Top Contributors and Industries.

These tables list the top donors to the House candidates in 2017-2018, and to the Senate candidates from 2013-2018.

The organizations themselves did not donate, rather the money came from the organizations' PACs, their individual members or employees or owners, and those individuals' immediate families. Organization totals include subsidiaries and affiliates.
at www.fec.gov

(The data for the above top five leaders of Congress was compiled by the Center for Responsive Politics from Federal Election Commission data, and can be found at www.OpenSecrets.org.)

The above is only a partial list of the thousands of wealthy, mostly corporate donors who have given tens of millions of dollars to just the top five members of Congress to buy influence/access to them. Wealthy donors have given billions of dollars in the last several years to the rest of Congress to buy access and influence policies that help them and often hurt the rest of America. We have a system of Pay to Play. The problem is that only the top 1% can afford to pay and get to play. The rest of America, the bottom 99%, can't afford to pay and don't get to play in the game of politics which effects many aspects of our lives: access to good jobs, quality affordable education, adequate health care, a clean sustainable environment, good roads and clean efficient public transit, safe neighborhoods, good parks and recreation, public libraries, dependable infrastructure, after school academic and arts programs, and leisure time, such as guaranteed paid vacations, to spend with our children, families, and friends.

After I won the 1994 Congressional Democratic Primary, the Democratic Party and the Democratic Congressional Campaign Committee helped sponsor a seminar in Sacramento for newly elected congressional nominees, such as myself, to attend and learn the ropes of how to run a successful professional campaign in the general election. My campaign manager arranged for me to attend. While he said that he respected my decision to not accept corporate political action committee money so I would not be beholden to wealthy corporate interests while in Congress, he insisted that we must raise the $500,000 in order to run a serious campaign and win in November. So I told him that we could try to raise the money from individual donors as well as from public interest groups such as environmental groups, labor groups, women's equality groups and any other groups pursuing the general well-being of the community and the nation. This would be a gargantuan task, especially considering that corporate political action committees and affiliated groups have deep pockets and raise and contribute the vast majority of campaign money to candidates for high office in America.

This is an inside story of what really goes on between politicians running for high office and their wealthy special interest donor groups.

Even Some Public Interest Groups Have Been Infected by Dollar Democracy

As a Congressional candidate once again for the 1996 Democratic primary election, I was called for interviews for endorsements by public interest groups as well, not just by special interest groups such as the oil companies. One of these public interest groups (groups that promote the public good, such as clean air, clean water, clean renewable energy, health care for all, healthy food, environmental sustainability, living wages, small business opportunity, public education, etc.) was the California League of Conservation Voters (CLCV). It was June 1995 and the Congressional Democratic Primary in my California district was in March 1996. The CLCV's issues platform was based on the foundation of environmental sustainability.

I was excited about the interview and expected to ace it and win the

65

group's endorsement hands down. I not only knew the technical aspects of environmental sustainability, but I held strong convictions and philosophical beliefs, that I could clearly articulate, about the need for strong environmental policies in Congress. I drove to the CLCV's West Los Angeles office full of enthusiasm. My interview with the CLCV endorsement committee was enjoyable, fulfilling, and went very smoothly. Unlike in the ARCO PAC interview, here I was with kindred spirits—people who thought and felt as I did politically, holding the same values as me. When the interview ended, the committee members greeted me warmly and thanked me for coming. The vice chair of the group walked me to the door, personally.

As I walked down the stairs to my car, I saw my Democratic Primary opponent entering the front door downstairs. As we crossed paths, I greeted him and wished him good luck in his interview. I knew his campaign had deep pockets because he was a corporate lawyer and a partner in his corporate law firm, one of the biggest in Los Angeles. It turned out that he ended up raising over $300,000, most of it from corporate sources, including (at that time) maximum donations of $1,000 each from his corporate law partners, all for the March Primary. Since I refused to accept corporate PAC money, I was able to raise $60,000 for my campaign.

When I arrived home later that night, I found that the vice chair had left me a message to call her so that we could discuss the CLCV interview and endorsement. I called her right away, certain that the news would be favorable. When she came on the line she went right to the point. She said "Peter, you did very well in the interview. You knew the details of environmental policy and we saw that your philosophical values regarding the environment are the same as ours. You would be a 100 per cent vote for us in Congress. Your opponent would probably vote for the environment about 60 per cent of the time. However, we decided to endorse your opponent. The reason is that he is 'financially viable', and you are not! It is nine months before the election and he already has $165,000 in his campaign account. You have only $5,000 in yours. We wish you luck, and if by any chance, you win in the March Primary, we the California League of Conservation Voters will support you 100 per cent in the November General Election against the Republican incumbent!

While refusing to accept corporate PAC money for my campaign, so that I would be free to serve the public interest in Congress, I had struggled to raise $60,000. My campaign volunteers and I had walked and talked door-to-door to 15,000 voters for 2 years and had enough money for only one mailing to only 40,000 of the 150,000 voters that needed to be reached with our message. We mailed our only brochure three weeks before the election. My opponent, with his campaign war chest of $300,000 was able to mail several brochures to targeted groups of voters. They contained multiple messages with specific appeal to each group of voters, telling them only what the specific group wanted to hear, based on expensive public opinion polls. These were all paid for by corporate special interests, and ironically also by the CLCV, a public interest group collaborating with them.

Because they feel the need to have some influence, no matter how little, the public interest group often endorses the candidate with more money, who is overwhelmingly funded by wealthy corporate special interests. Having big money makes her/him "viable", in their minds. That's why the best candidate who would best serve the public interest rarely wins. Instead, the wealthy special interests have been winning and the American People have been losing for the last forty-five years! Outspent 5-1, and unable to garner the support of the CLCV public interest group, I lost the election by a razor thin 51% to 49% margin. I have experienced this at times with other public interest groups such as labor and public education groups. One of the first questions they asked me in the endorsement interview was, "How much money do you expect to raise for this campaign?" and, "How much have you raised so far?" The important questions about my core beliefs and issue positions, usually come later, if I first satisfied them about my "financial viability." This is one pernicious effect of "Dollar Democracy."

My Inside View of American Politics and Dollar Democracy

After winning the 1994 Democratic Primary Election for Congress, I was invited to Washington, D.C. to meet with the Democratic

Congressional Campaign Committee (DCCC) leadership. They wanted to take a measure of the candidate and to strategize for the November General Election.

The office of the DCCC was not too far from the Capitol. I met with the leaders of the DCCC, including Congressman Martin Frost of Texas, as well as with other party leaders. I was told in no uncertain terms that in order to win in November I had to do only three things: RAISE MONEY, RAISE MONEY, and RAISE MONEY. I mentioned the example of Senator Paul Wellstone, who was outspent 7 to 1 and still won his first U.S. Senate campaign in Minnesota in 1990 based on ideas, issues, and the grassroots support of thousands of volunteers. The Democratic Party leaders in the room listened patiently. They must have been briefed about this naïve, idealistic Political Science Professor, Peter Mathews, who might try to quixotically follow Senator Wellstone's example. They immediately nipped in the bud any thoughts I might have had on trying to run my campaign the Wellstone Way: focusing on a grassroots campaign, meeting voters door-to-door, speaking to neighborhood groups and associations, holding town hall meetings with the voters, taking part in many debates, speaking on college campuses, to Kiwanis and Rotary Clubs, labor unions, small business associations, environmental organizations, etc., and recruiting hundreds of volunteers from them to campaign with me.

I was basically told, "You can't win the way Wellstone did. He was a fluke." I was told by these Party leaders and strategists that in order to win I had to follow the tried and true path: I must RAISE MONEY, RAISE MONEY, and RAISE MONEY. I must get the minimum of $500,000 (today it's $1.7 million) that it would take to win, from anywhere, as long as it was legal! They, the leaders, would arrange for my campaign to interview and hire experts in campaign strategy and management. These experts would include a professional political consultant, campaign manager, treasurer, scheduler, fundraising director, and a pollster. All of this would cost money, big money. As importantly, there would be a tremendous cost for hundreds of thousands of targeted mailers, hundreds of street signs and thousands of lawn signs, and money for TV and radio ads.

The cost to print, process, and mail out 15 mailers to over 200,000 targeted "high propensity" voters (those who have voted in 4 of the past 4 elections) in the district would be around $350,000 minimum. In 1994, a campaign consultant would charge a $50,000 fee plus a commission on each mailer. Today, in 2019, it is much more. The campaign manager's salary in 1994 was around $5,000 per month. Today, it is much more. The consultant, who works with more than one campaign at a time, designs the brochures and the messages in each, contracts mail house services for the campaign, and provides ongoing tactical and strategic advice. He helps the campaign manager find the polling company and works with him and the pollster to design each and every brochure based on the results of the "base line" poll that is taken at the start of a campaign. In 1994, pollsters were charging $20,000 for a base line poll. The subsequent "tracking" polls, conducted every month (or every week closer to the election) would each cost $10,000. The "cross-tabs" in the poll tell the pollster, campaign consultant, and campaign manager what the 5 or 6 issues of greatest importance were to each subset of voters. This information is crucial because it determines the content and design of the brochure/mailer sent to a set of voters.

For example, if the pollster's polling data showed that the top 5 issues for Democratic women voters in the district between the ages of 18 to 30 were 1) Education, 2) Health Care, 3) Choice on Abortion, 4) Jobs and Pay Equity, and 5) Child Care, then the campaign would mail 5 tailor made brochures, one on each issue to them. The beautiful high-resolution pictures and vacuous statements in them would appeal to many voters who are too busy to read detailed plans with too much writing from the candidate. The brochure on Education would have one picture showing the candidate engagingly speaking with college students on campus, and the other picture would show him answering questions from eager elementary school students in their third-grade classroom, with the teacher looking on approvingly. The vacuous written lines in the brochure will read something like this: "Candidate John Leader firmly believes that a good education is the birthright of every American child. As our Congressman, he will do everything in his power to ensure that our children are guaranteed the strong education that they deserve!" "VOTE FOR JOHN LEADER for OUR EDUCATION CONGRESSMAN on JUNE 3". Another brochure would be sent in similar fashion on the issues of Health Care, Choice on Abortion, and so on.

If the pollster's "cross-tabs" data showed that the top 5 issues for blue-collar Democratic male voters between the ages of 35 and 55 were 1) High paying Jobs, 2) Fair Trade, 3) Crime, 4) Pensions, and 5) Health Care, the campaign would target a brochure to thousands of these voters, covering one issue per brochure, with glossy pictures depicting the candidate at a Labor Day barbecue with these voters and their families, with some empty feel-good statements about being a "Fighter for Good High Paying Union Jobs and Against Free Trade, and a Congressman who will work to protect the American Dream!"

"Expert" campaign consultants have figured out that glossy campaign brochures, targeted to specific groups of thousands of voters in a particular Congressional district, with messages that appeal only to the individuals in that set of voters is an absolute necessity. Beautiful pictures of the candidate interacting with people in a warm and down-to-earth manner must dominate the brochure. The written words have to be catchy and vague on the issue being covered. I, as the candidate, was told that being specific, clear, and detailed about my stance on the issue would bore and turn off many voters and I would lose the election.

Politics has been reduced to the science and mechanics of winning elections. The heart, soul, and mind have been taken out of it. The expert advisors tell the candidate what to say when speaking, what message should go in the brochures, how it should be presented, what should be in the candidates' 30 second TV commercials, even what to say and not to say in public debates. When he is elected, this "rubber stamped" politician owes, not only his donors access, favors, and votes, but also the campaign experts who helped put him in office. The basic formula given him is: "Win the election so you can have power. Use your power to do some minimal good as you see it. But don't say anything or do anything that may alienate your (mostly wealthy, corporate) donors, even if it might promote the common good." Do not talk about raising taxes on the super-rich, or even closing their corporate tax loopholes, in order to fund schools, colleges, lower tuition, health care for all, and job creation through investment in small businesses and infrastructure such as roads, bridges, clean private and public transportation, renewable

70

efficient energy, public libraries and parks. No, don't anger the wealthy donors: because, once you are elected to Congress, you need their money to get re-elected every two years.

The very meaning of the word "politics" has been perverted. The word "politics" has its origin in the ancient Greek word "Polis", which meant "City/Community". The ancient Greeks, to whom we give credit for building the intellectual foundation of modern Democracy, said that it is a Citizen's duty to be "political". To be political means being involved fully in making decisions with, by, and for the Community. Today, as corporate sponsored politicians make many decisions that hurt the American Public, and very few decisions that help and strengthen the American Public, people think of politics as a dirty word signifying corruption, manipulation, greed, lies, and broken promises! Dollar Democracy is rampant and is spreading like a disease that threatens the health of working poor, working middle class, and even upper-middle-class Americans, the 99%. It is destroying the Middle-Class Dream and America itself, unless "We the People" rise up non-violently and fight peacefully for Economic and Social Justice by ENDING DOLLAR DEMOCRACY and replacing it with REAL DEMOCRACY! This book will help show the way.

Human Victims of Dollar Democracy

The naked truth has been exposed, and the emperor has no clothes: American Democracy has become Dollar Democracy, where policies made by elected leaders are bought and paid for by campaign contributions from wealthy special interest lobbyists and super rich individuals. In the 2016 federal elections alone, Congressional and Presidential candidates and their supporters raised and spent over $6.5 billion (opensecrets.org). The bulk of this money came from wealthy individuals and groups: the top half a percent of the U.S. population. As Will Rogers also said, "We have the best Congress money can buy." Rich individuals and corporations hire lobbyists to walk into the offices of Congresspersons to whom they donate and ask them to vote in favor of their corporate interests against the public interest. As a result, the U.S.

71

Congress and other elected leaders have made decisions that benefit wealthy corporations and super rich individuals, to the detriment of regular Americans such as Breanna Lane, Manny Arroyo, and Frank Greenthaler.

In a form of "legalized bribery", many politicians vote for tax cuts, tax loopholes, and corporate subsidies for their wealthy donors. This forces spending cuts in programs that help working Americans and the economy prosper and grow; for example, cuts in funding for small business, infrastructure, health care, teachers, firefighters, police officers, government employees, and research and development of new technologies. Congresspersons are choosing their rich donors over suffering working Americans. Here are some shocking examples:

Breanna Lane, a 22-year-old Utah woman loses part of her skull in a tragic auto accident. This is shocking enough. Worse still, the uninsured waitress, without private health insurance, is kept waiting for four months, with her scalp temporarily sown over the missing part of her skull, because the hospital and Medicaid cannot agree on who should pay the bill! After a painful and horrifying four months, she finally receives her surgery to reattach the missing part of her skull.

Manny Arroyo, a 62-year-old Nevada man, who worked decades for a large U.S. corporation, and has "full health care coverage", loses his wife to cancer and is stuck with approximately $10,000 in "co-payments." This crushing debt is a heavy enough burden on his life. Even more heartbreaking for him is his belief that his wife's death may have been unnecessary! He believes that if their healthcare providers had not delayed specialized diagnosis and treatment, her brain cancer may have been found and treated before it killed her.

Frank Greenthaler, an uninsured 29-year-old California college student and full-time worker starts bleeding internally from his intestine. He rushes to the nearest hospital. He waits for three hours before the treatment preparation begins. Barely able to stand, he makes it clear that he does not wish to drown in medical bills. He is kept at the hospital for 5 days and is "temporarily stabilized" by the doctors and nurses.

Stabilized but still in serious condition, he is told that he needs to find his way to a Los Angeles County hospital, so that his surgery will be paid for by the county instead of the private hospital! After major surgery and several days at the county hospital, Frank is discharged and is stricken with a $20,000 medical bill from the private hospital. As a working student who can barely make ends meet, he cannot pay the $20,000. This goes on his credit record. The young Californian makes a rapid recovery and is two semesters away from graduating with an engineering degree. Because of his mounting debt, he applies to become a police officer and passes all the tests except the financial credit test. His inability to pay the $20,000 medical bill shatters his dream of becoming a police officer and eventually a forensic psychologist.

As a professor of political science at Cypress College in Southern California, I've seen hundreds of students drop out of college in the last several years because they could not afford the skyrocketing tuition and textbook costs. One of my former students, **Tony Castro**, discovered his strong interest in the study of politics in my introductory American Government class. His enthusiasm for this subject was sparked by a discovery that politics does not have to be about money and power games but should be about making a positive difference in the world. Tony said his goal was to finish community college, earn his bachelor's, master's, and doctorate degrees in Political Science, become a university professor, and inspire young people to change the world for the better.

The tragedy is that this academically promising young man was side tracked from this meaningful goal. After a semester or two, because of unaffordable education costs, he dropped out of school and went to work full time to pay for the rising cost of living in Southern California. Tony recently told me that he was hoping to return to college to finish his degree once he retires as a senior citizen! Tony's experience is shared by hundreds of thousands of American youth today.

Dollar Democracy has cost us millions of well-paying middle-class jobs. In a pleasant middle-class neighborhood in Long Beach, in which Long Beach City College and a Boeing plant are located, signs of outsourcing are apparent. In recent years, many homes have been put up for sale. Boeing, which, a few years ago, employed 55,000 people, homeowners who earned a solid middle-class living, has exported most of its jobs and manufacturing to low wage states and low wage countries such as China. Only a few jobs are now left here. Policies of Free Trade, not Fair Trade, were imposed by many American political leaders who were influenced by corporate donors, lobbyists, and wealthy investors who benefited from cheap labor found in low wage states and countries.

The above tragic scenarios could have been avoided if American political leaders did not rely on the private financing of their campaigns, and private lobbying by wealthy corporate and individual donors. American campaigns and elections must reject this Dollar Democracy and replace it with Real Democracy based on Clean Money publicly financed elections as practiced in Maine, Arizona, and several other states (which I will discuss in detail in Chapter 10). In doing so, our elected leaders will be free to make decisions that benefit the public interest and promote the "general Welfare" as mandated in the preamble of our Constitution. They can then pursue policies of Fair Trade, creating high paying jobs, rebuilding the middle class, a universal health care system that covers every American, and a tuition free public education system from preschool through technical school, trade school, college and university.

They say you get what you pay for; the corporate lobbyists certainly do. In this book I will show you the connection between money and American politics in 21st Century America. I will expose the ways in which wealthy special interests donate big money to candidates who run for Congress and state legislatures, hire expensive lobbyists, and get laws passed that hurt the public, and block laws and policies that help average Americans achieve the "American Dream." I will include real life cases of real Americans in order to make the story alive and real.

What is the American Dream? I ask hundreds of my college students this question at the beginning of each semester. These students come from low income, middle class, and upper middle-class family backgrounds. They are a microcosm of 99% of America. Approximately 10 percent of them answer: "I want to become a multi-millionaire or billionaire so I can maximize my freedom". The rest, 90 percent of them, describe their American Dream in the following way:

"I want to pursue the career I enjoy, and that will allow me to make enough money to own my own home and pay my bills, have children and a family, free time to spend with them and go on vacations, pay for my children's higher education to give them a better life than I had, and to ensure a comfortable retirement". Is this unreasonable? Of course not! In fact, the American Declaration of Independence and Constitution seem to require government to create the opportunity and foundation for Americans to achieve the Middle-Class Dream.

In recent decades, the "Middle-Class Dream" has been shattered and has become the Middle-Class Nightmare for millions of formerly middle-class citizens. I will show how the buying of many politicians, by wealthy special interests and lobbyists, has destroyed the Middle-Class Dream and launched the dismantling of the American middle class, whose high paying jobs were exported. It has also destroyed the opportunity for the working poor to become middle class. These politicians have promoted policies that exported high paying manufacturing, high technology and even service jobs from the U.S. to low wage countries. In these low wage countries, anti-worker, free trade policies, are promoted by U.S. multi-national corporate interest in league with those countries corrupt leaders (Fulgencio Batista in Cuba, Anastasio Somoza in Nicaragua, Ferdinand Marcos in the Philippines, Suharto in Indonesia, Augusto Pinochet in Chile, Juan Orlando Hernandez of Honduras). When progressive, pro-worker, social justice leaders have arisen and been elected, U.S. corporate-led foreign policy has suppressed, discredited, and sometimes overthrown them. For example, Prime Minister Mohammad Mosaddegh of Iran, President Jacobo Arbenz of Guatemala, and President Salvador Allende of Chile.

Many politicians, from State Legislators and Governors to members of Congress and Presidents, dominated by corporate donors and their special interest lobbyists have promoted "outsourcing" based on "Free Trade". Money went in and favors went out: Corporate lobbyists and their politicians won the gold mine, while the American middle class and poor got the shaft.

I will examine the failing American Health Care system that left 54 million Americans uninsured, and 2 million losing their health insurance every year. I will also look at Americans who still have so called "full coverage," yet are stuck with back breaking co-payments and deductibles. Although "insured", many of them suffer inadequate care because the Health Industry places its profits above human needs. The Affordable Care Act (Obamacare) may be a step in the right direction, but falls short, leaving 20 million Americans uninsured, even when fully implemented. With no "Public Option" included, Obamacare also does little to rein in costs, leaving the U.S. as the country with the highest per person health care costs among all the modern industrialized nations: per person costs that are twice that of France, which is rated by the World Health Organization as the best (universal) health care system in the world.

We will see how Dollar Democracy has created broken schools and unaffordable colleges. There are great shortages in many public schools attended by middle class and poor children: a shortage of credentialed teachers, a shortage of updated textbooks, a shortage of learning resources, and a shortage of small manageable class sizes, etc. We will carefully evaluate the increasingly staggering costs of American Higher Education due to cuts in government subsidies. We will make clear that these cuts are due to corporate tax loopholes passed by legislators, many of whom were funded by wealthy donors and corporate lobbyists. These tax loopholes and corporate subsidies cost the government almost $1 trillion annually, some of which could be spent on American Public Education.

Under the influence of corporate campaign and lobbying money, Congress re-wrote the pension/retirement rules enabling large corporations to reduce their responsibility to American workers by cutting their pensions or shifting them away from defined benefits. Corporations like Enron engaged in corrupt business and accounting practices that allowed their CEOs and chairmen to sell their stocks at huge profits while encouraging their employees to hold on to, and buy new stocks, as the corporation was going bankrupt. The result was thousands of employees each losing thousands of dollars in retirement savings and pensions. In the 2008 Wall Street debacle which ushered in the Great Recession, very similar creative accounting and fraudulent business practices were engaged in by major financial institutions such as Goldman Sachs, AIG, Lehman Bros., and others. Because of the influence of big corporate and lobbyist money in American election campaigns, resulting in government deregulation and corporate bail outs, once again the top 1% (the owners of Big Corporations and Big Banks) got the gold mine, and the bottom 99% of Americans (those making less than $400,000 annually) got the shaft.

Dollar Democracy has resulted in a Reverse Robin Hood: the tax burden was shifted from the super-rich on to the backs of working Americans. Decades of government "tax reforms", have reduced federal income tax rates on the super wealthy from 91.0 percent on the highest portion of their income (under President Eisenhower) to 28.0 percent (under President Reagan), to 39.6 percent (under President Obama), to 37 percent today (under President Trump). Meanwhile, the government increased income taxes, and payroll taxes (under President Reagan) on working Americans (this, while cutting much needed social programs). Government has forced working Americans to pay more in college tuition fees, as their overall cost of living has gone up. This has also been a major cause of the middle class shrinking. Corporate funded politicians have shifted a large share of the federal tax burden from corporations to individual Americans. According to New York University economist Richard Wolfe, in 1945, for every $1 individuals paid in income taxes, corporations paid $1.50. Today, for every $1 individuals pay in income taxes, corporations pay 25 cents.

I will carefully examine the effects of corporate donations and lobbyist money on many politicians and the policies they made which resulted in environmental injustice, and under regulated, unhealthy food. Clean air, clean water, protection against harmful chemicals, and the availability of natural, uncontaminated food are all important for Americans' health and quality of life. I will look at the increased dangers to the ongoing health of Americans because of weak environmental and food regulation. We will examine the effects of big campaign contributions from corporate polluters and corporate agriculture, such as Monsanto Corporation, on policies that affect peoples' health.

One of the ingredients Americans need to help them achieve the American Dream is affordable, clean, efficient, and renewable energy. I will examine the effect of big campaign contributions and lobbying activity by the automobile, electric utility, coal, natural gas, and oil industries. I will look at the effects of campaign contributions and spending by corporate lobbyists to influence government policies regarding auto fuel efficiency (skyrocketing gasoline prices). This Dollar Democracy also has health related costs for Americans. Government deregulation has resulted in coal fired electric plants producing more dangerous mercury emissions. Because of the influence of corporate campaign contributions and lobbying on our politicians, our government has weakened pollution controls by allowing the buying and selling of pollution credits, causing increased asthma and cancer rates for Americans.

In conclusion, I will offer the reader possibilities for significant change in the American election system which will move us away from Dollar Democracy closer to a Real Democracy. These changes will reduce, if not eliminate, the overwhelming power of wealthy special interests in American government and society. We will carefully analyze the Clean Money/Clean Elections campaign finance system, versions of which have already been implemented in Arizona, Maine, Massachusetts, North Carolina, New Mexico, and Vermont. I will also provide a careful look at a successful grassroots campaign, U.S. Senator Paul Wellstone's, that refused wealthy special interest corporate lobbyist money, and still won a seat in the U.S. Senate. We will see that government leaders who are elected in either of these ways were able to work for policies that improve the lives of all Americans, not just the top 1%. If implemented, this system of Clean Elections will truly bring Liberty and Justice for All, and Reclaim the Middle-Class Dream for All.

Another structural reform that will have a major impact on shifting the United States from Dollar Democracy to Real Democracy is the **Move To Amend Coalition**'s strong push to adopt a **28th Amendment** to the U.S. Constitution. This amendment would **Void Corporate Personhood and declare that Money Is Not Speech** as understood by the 1st Amendment. The detailed goals and implications of adopting this amendment will be analyzed and discussed in Chapter 10, the concluding chapter of this book.

Image 2-8 | Goldman Sach's CEO Lloyd Blankfein's $32.5 million 8,000 square ft. mansion in the Hamptons | Photo/Wikimedia.org/commons/

Image 2-9 | Homeless Woman Lives in Shopping Cart
Photo/Wikimedia.org/commons/

CHAPTER 3

JOBS AND THE ECONOMY: THE RICH ARE GETTING RICHER, THE POOR ARE GETTING POORER, THE MIDDLE CLASS IS DISAPPEARING

"They say you get what you pay for;
The corporate lobbyists certainly do.
'We must replace Dollar Democracy
with real democracy!'"

--Peter Mathews

What is the American Dream? For 99% of us Americans, it is the dream of being able to have a good well-paying job that allows us to make enough money to buy our own home, raise children, have time to spend with our children, have enough income to afford a vacation every year with our families, have enough income to put our kids through college, so they'll have a better life than their parents, and enough money for a few niceties such as going to a baseball game, or on a ski trip. Most of us believe that this is the American Dream. In contrast, most of the top 1% and their supporters believe that the American Dream means becoming millionaires or billionaires, at all costs. This means, grabbing for all the opportunities that exist, even "creating your own opportunities" through hard work. It can also mean cutting corners and influencing politicians, through campaign contributions and lobbying money; all in order to re-write the rules of the game in their favor.

These rules include: tax cuts for themselves, the super-rich; tax loopholes and government subsidies for their big corporations; free-trade policies that allow them to ship well-paying American jobs to low wage countries; government deregulation of these big corporations that allows them to merge, lay off workers, act like monopolies, pollute our

80

environment, food and water, and make huge profits at the expense of our health. Most of those in the richest 1% want to privatize, or cut funding for: our public education, our public parks, our police forces, our firefighters, our teachers, our public hospitals, our public health programs such as Social Security, Medicare and Medicaid, even for our roads and other public infrastructure, such as government funded scientific research and development, and the arts. Many public opinion polls have revealed their views. Most of the top 1% support cuts to these important government programs so they can keep their taxes low and enjoy greater opportunities and luxuries for themselves and their children. To paraphrase the famous wealthy New York socialite Leona Helmsley, "We don't pay taxes. Only the little people pay taxes," as her former housekeeper recalled. A popular bumper sticker not so long ago reflected the mentality of many of the super-rich, "The One Who Dies with the Most Toys, Wins."

The American Dream was alive and well from the 1940s until 1980. The Dream became a reality because millions of working Americans in the 1930s and 40s, coming out of the Great Depression, were able to organize into unions and demand through collective-bargaining, that their employers pay them their fair share of the wealth they were creating for their employers. As a result, working Americans were able to gain income and afford a middle-class life. They could then buy their own homes and cars, educate their children in public schools, take summer vacations with their families, engage in recreational activities such as skiing and boating trips; all of this with just one income in the household.

Human Faces of the Disappearing Middle-Class

In the last 30 years the American Middle-Class shrank by a startling 10%. Now 40% of Americans consider themselves lower-middle or lower class compared to 25% in 2008. (Time.com).

Rob McGann, of Pensacola, Florida with an MBA (Master of Business Administration) degree, was a purchasing agent for Boeing. He was recently laid off and found part-time work at a Publix Supermarket.

Although he now works full-time at the supermarket, his present pay is much lower than his previous. He's not getting calls back from his job applications for higher paying professional work. His potential employers say he's overqualified. This huge drop in income has left him sliding precariously out of the American middle class. He says, "It's tough, it still is. It's something I think about not only all day and every day, but all the time."

Another example of the disappearing American middle-class is **Jeremy Horning**, a warehouse logistics worker. By working more than 70 hours a week, he made a decent living and was planning to get married in a couple of months. Like thousands of other Americans, he was suddenly laid off. It was one and a half months before his wedding, and he went from over 70 hours a week to nothing. Not giving up hope, Jeremy went back to school and got a part time job in a call center.

Today, the rich have gotten richer, the poor have gotten poorer, and the middle class is disappearing quickly. For example, in the current anemic economic recovery from the Great Recession, the top one percent have captured 52% of the real income growth that was generated in the first six years from 2009 to 2015. ("Striking it Rich" by Emmanuel Saez, UC Berkeley, June 31, 2016). To put this in perspective, in 1980, the income of the average CEO was 40 times the income of the average American worker; today however, the average CEO income is almost 361 times the average worker's income (Forbes.com, May 22, 2018).

Because of the outsourcing of American middle-class jobs by corporate CEOs to low wage countries, the American working middle class has lost income and purchasing power. That's why millions of middle-income Americans don't qualify to buy a home, and millions have lost their homes to foreclosure. Millions more have now become poor and can't afford enough food to eat. A presently middle-class Californian said he is buying potato chips instead of a full meal. Many American young people of the Millennial Generation are forced to live at home with their parents because they can't find jobs. Many of the same youth can't afford to go to college or technical and trade school, because the tuitions have been raised exorbitantly by state politicians. These very same politicians, themselves, benefited from tuition free colleges and universities in California in the 1960s and '70s.

When I started teaching at Foothill College and City College of San Francisco in the 1970's, my students, full time or part time, paid no tuition. They only paid a $6 service fee. Today, my students at Cypress College and all California Community Colleges are paying $46 per unit, for a total of $690 for 15 units full time.

Beginning in 1960, under California Governor Pat Brown's Master Plan for Higher Education, Community College, UC and CSU students paid a small service fee with no tuition charged for a full load of classes. I completed my Bachelors' and Masters' degrees in 1973 and 1975, and paid only $100 per semester for a full time load of 15 units at the University of North Texas. This solid educational foundation, paid for by We the People (the government) enabled me to obtain the middle-class American Dream of a well-paying job as a professor, home owner, and gave me the ability to raise a family. As a result, I have been able to give back to society by teaching over 30,000 college students in 33 years. If we would only give the same opportunity of tuition free/affordable education that I had, to our students today, they would give back their talent to society as the best doctors, engineers, computer programmers, scientists, aircraft mechanics, automotive technicians, and artists. The taxes they pay will fund the next generation. This is our moral obligation to "pay it forward." Instead, 44 million Americans have student debt, which has skyrocketed to $37,000 per college graduate (CNBC.com). It is a crime for our present crop of politicians, who got their tuition free education 30 or more years ago, to have burdened our young people today with so much debt. They did this by raising campaign contributions from wealthy corporate special interests, voting for corporate tax loopholes and tax cuts on the super-rich, which reduced government funding for public higher education, and made the students pay skyrocketing tuition fees instead.

Most politicians have failed the American middle class because they served the interests of their corporate donors most of the time. On almost every major issue that's important for the middle class, they have voted in the interests of their donors instead of the American people. The person who writes the paycheck is boss! In a presidential election year, the top ½ of 1 percent of Americans write the campaign checks worth 80 percent of all the campaign contributions.

As mentioned earlier, in a 2014 study of political inequality in America called "Testing Theories of American Politics: Elites, Interest Groups, and Average Citizens", political scientists Benjamin Page and Martin Gilens found that "economic elites and interest groups can shape U.S. government policy – but Americans who are less well-off have essentially no influence over what their government does." (*Washington Post*, May 23, 2016, by Martin Gilens and Benjamin Page).

Most Politicians' Campaign Money Comes from the Top 1%, Whom They Serve Most of the Time

Very, very few American politicians run their campaigns without money from corporate lobbyists and special interests and win. The late U.S. Senator Paul Wellstone of Minnesota was one of them. Paul Wellstone was a friend of mine and an inspiration as a politician with integrity. He once said, *"Politics is not about power. Politics is not about money. Politics is not about winning for the sake of winning. Politics is about the improvement of people's lives."* He won his elections to the U.S. Senate in 1990 and in 1996 by running grassroots campaigns supported by volunteers, individual donors, and the support of public interest groups. He refused to accept money from corporate political action committees and special interests. You will hear his story in greater detail in chapter 9. If all American politicians were like Senator Wellstone, the Middle-Class American Dream would still be an attainable reality for the working poor and the working middle class in America today.

Unfortunately, most of the members of both major parties, Democratic and Republican, have not followed Wellstone's example. They have engaged in Dollar Democracy which has resulted in Liberty and Justice for Some. This book will explain how this happened and provide three options that will help us make the American Dream a reality for all Americans, with Liberty and Justice for All.

Beginning in the 1980s with the election of Ronald Reagan and the popularity of Reaganomics, everything changed for the middle class and the Middle-Class American Dream. Ronald Reagan and his ideological followers argued that Americans must rely more on themselves and work for individual success. Reagan's idea was: Don't expect the government or society to provide resources and opportunity for you to make it. No matter where you begin on the economic ladder, for Reagan it was all about pulling yourself up by your own bootstraps. He and his followers considered the actions of government to be wasteful and in some cases unnecessary. Deregulation became the rage. Deregulation of businesses, particularly large businesses, lower taxes on mostly wealthy business people, and successful attempts at weakening unions. Collective bargaining was seen by Reagan and his friends as socialistic and not ruggedly individualistic.

The tax cuts brought in by Reagan gave huge benefits to rich Americans and big corporations and far fewer benefits to ordinary Americans. For example, a person earning $1 million a year received $27,000 from Reagan's tax cuts, while a person earning $40,000 a year received $300 in tax cuts from Reagan (Barlett and Steele, "America: What Went Wrong?"). This was called Supply-side Economics or "Trickle Down economics". And this is where everything changed for America: A wedge was driven between the American people and their government.

From the 1930s to the 1970s, an unprecedented era in which the American Dream was achieved by millions of Americans, the dominant idea was Franklin Roosevelt's belief that Government could be a positive instrument to create Equal Opportunity for All. This was a powerful American belief that gave rise to unprecedented prosperity and a large middle class. In direct contrast, the Reagan belief was that Government can do nothing right, is inefficient, wasteful, and needs to be starved in domestic policy areas and heavily boosted in spending on military defense. Reagan accomplished this through tax cuts mostly on the super wealthy, and heavy government borrowing, primarily from the same super wealthy investors in U.S. bonds. In this way, Reagan was the Reverse Robin Hood: taking from middle class and poor Americans and giving to the super rich.

Through this process, Reagan redefined the concept of Governments' duty to promote the "General Welfare" in the Preamble to the U.S. Constitution. Reagan's Supply Side Economic policies caused the dismantling of the American Middle Class and the loss of the Middle-Class Dream. The argument made by the Reaganites was that when wealthy people get tax cuts they will invest money in their businesses, expand their businesses, hire other people and produce a greater supply of goods and services. This will also produce more hiring by the wealthy. And, last but not least, it would generate overall growth in the American economy. So as the rich got richer by expanding their businesses and producing more, this increased wealth would trickle down to all of us middle class and poor folks. We get hired by the rich, get paid something, and go and spend some of our money in restaurants, shoe stores, and maybe even in automobile dealerships, and buy more things, expanding the economy.

The economy did grow to some extent but grew mainly at the top. Most of the new income generated went to the top 1% of the population, those who owned the bigger businesses and corporations. The federal deficit got larger because the tax cuts took money out of the federal budget. And the working middle class and working poor saw their wages diminish because the employers paid them less and made more profits. The rich got richer and the poor got poorer while the middle class began to disappear.

The ideology of "Reaganomics" was very skillfully put forward by the charismatic and good-natured Ronald Reagan. So much so that Reagan's thinking is still with us today. While it may be that Reagan was the most vociferous of Republican presidents, and acted the most forcefully to implement supply-side economics, even Democrats like Bill Clinton were influenced by Reagan's ideology.

Bill Clinton was the first Democrat to say, "the era of big government is over". Clinton practiced this idea by helping to dismantle many government programs and regulations that were instituted by President Franklin Roosevelt during the New Deal. For example, Clinton abolished the New Deal Aid to Families with Dependent Children (AFDC) program. Clinton also signed into law the bill that abolished the Glass-Steagall Act regulation of banking, which was brought in by FDR during the Depression, and worked very well to separate the commercial banks from investment banks. This act prevented commercial banks such as Bank of America, Wells Fargo and Chase, from investing their money in high risk areas.

The reason for this was because the Roosevelt administration believed that small bank depositors, meaning the majority of American people, should have their money safe in the commercial banks and not lost by reckless speculation. The Roosevelt administration also brought in FDIC, the Federal Deposit Insurance Corporation, which was established to insure deposits of up to $100,000 in commercial banks. With the abolishing of Glass-Steagall by Clinton and the Republican Congress these safety measures were abandoned. This was a major reason for the 2008 collapse on Wall Street and the advent of the Great Recession. Of course, we all know that the Great Recession has helped to devastate the middle class and the poor in America even more.

Another major cause of the disappearing middle class is the dismantling of the world-class American public education system, kindergarten through university. The United States is the country that invented public education. It's a shame that our policymakers have been dismantling it in the last 30 years.

The role of Reaganism cannot be over emphasized here. President Ronald Reagan rose to power arguing that government is corrupt, inefficient, wasteful, can't be trusted, and should be tremendously limited. Reagan said, "Government cannot solve our problems, because government *is* the problem". Reaganism urged Americans to be rugged individuals, pull themselves up by their own bootstraps, and not rely on government or its social programs.

The most beneficial government social program of the 20th century was American public education. Invented by pioneers such as Thomas Jefferson, Horace Mann, John Dewey, Susan B. Anthony, and others, American public education, kindergarten through university, was not only a gift to ourselves but to the whole world.

Most of the advanced industrialized countries took this American education system and ran with it. Under the Master Plan for Higher Education, while California extended tuition free education all the way to college and university from 1960 until the early 1980s, California has now reduced government subsidies drastically. That's why college and university students have to pay very steep tuition fees. Many of the advanced industrialized countries such as France, Sweden, Denmark, Germany, and Belgium have still maintained their tuition free trade, technical, college and university programs. There, students in a few cases pay a very small enrollment fee, no tuition. As a result, these countries can draw on a wide pool of talented potential trades people, technicians, and professionals such as scientists, engineers, architects, mathematicians, and doctors.

By cutting and under-funding public education in America, our leaders have prevented low income children and middle-class children from advancing. Low income children have difficulty getting a good education, graduating from high school, and going on to technical and trade school, college and university, and entering the middle class. Middle class students are finding the same difficulties in getting a good education and climbing the ladder to the upper middle class. By letting the Reagan ideology influence their thinking, these corporate backed politicians have basically sold out opportunity for working Americans, the bottom 99%. The rich have gotten richer the poor have gotten poorer, and the middle class has been disappearing.

The great irony of these developments is that wealthy corporate owners need to hire highly trained engineers, mathematicians, and scientists to invent and build new products. Yet these wealthy corporate owners have not been willing to pay their fair share of taxes in order to fully finance the high quality American public education, especially higher education, that this requires. Instead they have been willing to hire highly trained professionals from other countries such as India and China at much lower wages than their American counterparts. In the case of information technology, the American corporate interests are willing to let their new employees live in their own countries and accept the much lower wages, since the work is accomplished through electronic transfer. An Indian software engineer can live very well on a fraction of the wage of an American engineer. The second development is that these corporate technology giants import Indian software engineers to work in the United States for less than their American counterparts. And the Corporation and its owners refuse to pay the taxes that it would take to train and educate

American software engineers. Instead they are getting these Indian software engineers, who are trained in India, at no cost to the American-based corporate software company. This also helps to dismantle the American middle class.

Since the 1980s, in the United States we have gone in the opposite direction of other advanced countries. The Reagan ideology of rugged individualism was very cleverly and effectively propagated on the majority of voters and their corporate sponsored elected officials. Therefore, this thinking not only prevailed at the federal level, but was transmitted into policies at the state level. It's no wonder that the severe cuts to government funding at the state level for colleges and universities coincided with the 1980s, when Ronald Reagan and his ideas were at their zenith. Reaganism was so powerful and all pervasive in American society from the 1980s through the 2000s, that even Democratic Presidents and members of Congress seem to have been infected by it. Not every Democrat, but large numbers of them. There were exceptions who remained true to progressive ideals of social justice, equal opportunity, and fairness, all foundations of the American Dream. Examples include U.S. Senators Paul Wellstone, Elizabeth Warren, U.S. Representatives Dennis Kucinich, Marcy Captor, Jim McDermott, and Independent U.S. Senator Bernie Sanders, who ran for the 2016 Democratic nomination for President. Senator Sanders ran a strong grassroots-based, mostly small individual donor, non-corporate sponsored campaign against Hillary Clinton's corporate and big donor funded campaign. Despite his loss in 2016, Sanders' campaign had a major impact on the Democratic Party and American politics, moving both in a progressive left direction. Sanders was responsible for popularizing the ideas of tuition-free college and Medicare for All. Sanders' 2016 presidential campaign inspired new progressive populist candidates (mostly Democrats) such as Alexandria Ocasio-Cortez of New York, Ayanna Pressley of Massachusetts, Rashida Tlaib of Michigan, Ilhan Omar of Minnesota, to run without corporate money and win Congressional seats. Ocasio-Cortez and dozens of non-corporate grassroots candidates who won in 2018 are pushing Congress to implement tuition-free college, Medicare for All, and a Green New Deal to create high paying jobs to reduce greenhouse gasses and save us from the ravages of Climate Change/Climate Disruption/Global Warming.

(For ongoing, non-partisan, comprehensive reporting, documenting the pernicious influence of big money on American politicians, politics, policies, and government, visit OpenSecrets.org, MapLight.org, and FollowTheMoney.org.)

Public Education Is Defunded As the Need for An Educated Workforce Grows

Now we come to the issue of the need for an educated workforce in building a strong economy and prosperous American middle class. A highly educated workforce in the technical fields and in the arts and humanities will result in a strong and dynamic middle class and a vibrant, innovative society as a whole. Because, the more educated a nation's population is, the more productive and innovative the economy will be. Not only will the economy be more productive, scientifically and technologically, but this abundance of material production will be the basis of the nation's security in an insecure world. Here's how:

There are two aspects to securing the defense of a strong nation: the first is called soft power, a term invented by Harvard Political Science Professor Joseph Nye. By soft power Professor Nye was referring to the influence a nation has based on its ideas, its way of life, its cultural attributes, all resulting in important influence that this nation will have with other nations and peoples. Soft power means influence other than raw military might.

The second aspects of defending a strong nation is its hard power. This is the power that comes from being able to afford a strong military. It takes a highly educated workforce to create a highly productive economy that can invent and deploy the most necessary weapons for defense against possible attack from enemies. Since soft power and hard power are both necessary for the security of the nation, we must ensure that America's educational system is adequate to the task of building a productive economy. We need both guns and butter if we are to be realistic and safe in this world.

90

China Projects Soft Power
Around the World

An excellent example of a nation that is gaining enormous influence in the world today is China. China has been using a combination of hard power and, to a greater extent, soft power. China has not only sought natural resources and energy sources throughout the world, but also trade that is mutually beneficial to other countries. This trade and investment includes joint ventures in African and South American nations to develop those countries' resources, as well as Chinese activity to promote and develop those countries' social infrastructure. This includes China's efforts to build railroads, hospitals, and schools in many of these countries. Because of the size of the Chinese nation (1.4 billion people), the Chinese middle-class numbers in the hundreds of millions. It is the recent spectacular growth of this middle class, and the technology and scientific discoveries produced by it, which is the foundation for the projection of Chinese soft power and hard power in the world.

It seems that with the advent of Reaganomics and Reaganism and his right-wing rugged individualistic ideology, the United States has allowed its middle class to shrink while promoting the interests of its top 1% corporate owners who are millionaires and billionaires. This investing class has done very well, while the middle class and working poor have been sinking downwards. This is a recipe for disaster for any nation. To reverse this, America must rebuild its educational system and provide it free of charge to all of America's citizens and residents. Then we can rebuild the middle class, reclaim the American Dream, and make it a reality for all, once again. The American Dream is not just a pipe dream. Making the Middle-Class American Dream a reality for all will require the iconic American principle of equal opportunity for all. Then we can say with honesty, "One nation, indivisible, with liberty and justice for all", not just for some.

Another big reason for the outsourcing of middle-class jobs, and the dismantling of the middle class, is free trade. Both Democratic and Republican politicians supported and promoted free trade policies. The most prominent and glaring example of free trade was the North

American Free Trade Agreement or NAFTA. Promoted and supported by Democratic President Bill Clinton, and the majority of Republicans in Congress, and a minority of Democrats in Congress, NAFTA opened the floodgates to competition from cheap labor in Mexico. From 1994 to 2009, tariffs on products and services traded among Canada, the U.S. and Mexico were eliminated step-by-step, stage by stage. This encouraged big U.S. based multi-national corporations to close down factories in the U.S., move their factories to Mexico and hire cheap labor at a fraction of the cost of American workers. Using very low paid Mexican workers, these companies could produce their products for a fraction of the cost of producing them in the U.S. or Canada and make huge profits when these products were sold in the U.S. and around the world.

Because of NAFTA and free trade, millions of American middle-class manufacturing jobs that paid high wages were lost. When these jobs were taken to Mexico, the American-based corporate owners became very wealthy, Mexican workers remained poor or became poorer, and the former American workers who were in the middle class sank downward, with no jobs or with low-paying jobs, into the ranks of the working poor, the unemployed and underemployed. Ever since, in the United States, the rich got richer, the poor got poorer, and the middle class has been slowly and not so slowly disappearing.

There is an important link between the need to have an educated workforce and the growth of a prosperous middle class. The growth of the American middle class during the 1940s, 50s, 60s, and 70s was based on widespread access to a high quality American public education. As this access was curtailed by politicians who no longer made it a priority, educational opportunity and the middle class shrank.

Here is an interesting irony: while corporations, both high-tech and manufacturing, require and want educated workers, in recent decades they have been unwilling to pay a fair share of taxes to fund the public education of their workers.

For example, in 2012 Apple used the legal offshoring corporate tax loophole to avoid paying taxes on $44 billion of income. These taxes totaled $15 billion in 2012.

Facebook, using the stock option loophole reduced its corporate tax burden for 2012 to 0. It also received $429 million in government subsidies. This brought Facebook a negative tax burden of -40.4% in 2012 (CTJ.org, February 2014). As a result, hundreds of millions and billions of dollars are lost to the federal treasury.

In some cases, these loopholes also cost the state governments. California state government lost close to $10 billion in unfair and unproductive corporate tax loopholes in 2012 alone. We can see that corporate tax loopholes and subsidies, created by members of Congress and signed into law by U.S. Presidents, end up costing the federal treasury approximately $1 trillion a year. To put that in perspective, the tuition paid to public universities and colleges across the United States by undergraduate students and their parents totaled approximately $62 billion in 2012 (http://nces.ed.gov/pubs2013/2013183.pdf). The bulk of K-12 funding comes from the 50 states' governments. This funding is approximately $500 billion per year. (http://www2.ed.gov/about/ overview/fed/10facts/index.html?exp)

If the state corporate tax loopholes were closed and the federal corporate tax loopholes and subsidies were eliminated, the United States could provide the highest quality education, from kindergarten and preschool through university and college, free of tuition fees. This would go a long way toward providing equal opportunity for all Americans to develop their full human technical and intellectual potential and climb into the middle class and upper middle class. In fact, many Americans would make it to the affluent level of income and wealth while producing some of the best and newest technology products and services, restoring the American economy dynamically beyond its previous heights. If we once again funded education fully we would have a reappearing middle class, not a disappearing middle class.

Citizens for Tax Justice (www.ctj.org) has found that 155 of the Fortune 500 private corporations engaged in legal tax avoidance schemes based on corporate tax loopholes. These companies cost the 50 state governments a total of $14 billion in 2012. This was more than the 12.6 billion that was cut by state governments all over the U.S. in that year. (http://ctj.org/ctjinthenews/2013/06/truthout_why_our_schools_are_bro ke_five_years_of_corporate_state_tax_avoidance.php#.UcfRNj usjTo).

In the short run, by not paying taxes the large corporations are making and keeping huge amounts of profits. In the long run they are depriving the American education system of valuable resources that will create productive engineers, mathematicians, and scientists who can produce the products and services that will grow a strong middle class. Because of this, the large corporations themselves will not have highly trained engineers and scientists in the U.S. to produce the next generation of products that will make them competitive globally. It's time for the big corporations to wake up, pay their fair share of taxes, and to help fully fund public education in America. This will create a strong middle class, a strong economy, and a strong democracy.

From ancient theorists such as Aristotle to modern theorists of democracy such as Thomas Jefferson and Robert Dahl, the underlying truth has been found that democracy cannot flourish in a society of extreme concentrations of wealth and income, a society that lacks a broad and large middle class. Large corporations themselves need a vibrant, innovative, and dynamic economy with a large middle-class foundation so that they can function fully and freely in peace and harmony. Two of the most prominent Founders of the U.S., Alexander Hamilton and James Madison believed that they were creating, among other things, a "commercial republic". In order for the American commercial republic to function well and be long-lasting, it must have an extensive and large middle class as its foundation.

NAFTA Helps Dismantle the American Middle Class

The distinguished investigative journalists Donald Barlett and James Steele claim that the cumulative deficit in trade with Mexico had ballooned, in their words, to $698 billion by the end of 2011, and sometime in the next five years the total trade deficit with Mexico will approach $1 trillion. Barlett and Steele go on to say that "Rather than stimulate exports to Mexico, NAFTA triggered a rush of American companies to invest south of the border, and Mexican imports to the (United) States surged. In the five years before NAFTA, Mexican imports increased 51%. In the five years afterward, they jumped 91%. General Motors even built housing there for its new workforce. Indeed, it felt almost as if entire portions of the U.S. economy had, as it were, gone south. As for exports to Mexico, the growth rate actually declined, according to the Washington-based Economic Policy Institute (EPI)."

Barlett and Steele point out that in the five years before NAFTA the U.S. had an average trade surplus of $168 million with Mexico. In the subsequent five years, that number went in the other direction, to an average annual trade deficit of $12.5 billion. They also point out that by 2011 an estimated 1.5 million American jobs had been eliminated by imports from Mexico, according to EPI calculations. The same calculation estimated that exports to Mexico supported 791,900 jobs in 2010, meaning a net loss of about 700,000 jobs. In 2004 alone, EPI had estimated that lost wages from NAFTA job losses were costing American workers $7.6 billion a year. That's equal to the annual incomes of 150,000 American families. So, as Barlett and Steele point out, NAFTA has been a total disaster for many, many American middle-class workers with good middle class high-paying jobs, which they've now lost. It wasn't just Congress that was complicit in this, but every president, regardless of party, has been very supportive of Free Trade. You might think that American presidents just didn't know any better, or maybe they didn't study economics. However, I'm sure they had access to the Council of Economic Advisers (CEA), whom they get to appoint. The CEA is made up of three leading U.S. economists appointed by the president to give them advice on these matters. There are numerous economists who were critical of free trade and supportive of fair-trade policies. These economists published editorials, articles, and analysis in many leading U.S. newspapers. Presidents must have been aware of the arguments against unfettered free trade and of the warnings against it, with real evidence that was provided by the analysts. Instead presidents of both parties took the side of the wealthy corporate campaign donors, who overwhelmingly favor free trade over fair trade.

Fair trade would have required, before the U.S. signed agreements with Mexico, that Mexico must first raise its labor standards. That means raising the Mexican minimum wage, implementing stronger Mexican environmental regulations, in order to even out the playing field. In that way many U.S. based corporations would not race to cross the border and establish factories in Mexico, just to hire cheap labor. If, after thinking twice, they decided to set up shop in Mexico anyway, companies like General Motors will find themselves paying higher wages to Mexican factory workers and having to comply with stricter environmental standards. The higher wages paid to Mexican factory workers by their U.S. corporate employers such as General Motors would have provided a stimulus to American exports, because the Mexican employees of GM would use their higher wages and salaries to demand new technology products manufactured in the U.S. This would have created millions of more cutting-edge manufacturing and technology driven high-paying jobs in the U.S. When President Bill Clinton was asked to insist that Mexico raise its labor standards, strengthen its environmental safeguards, before he signed the NAFTA agreement, Clinton replied that he would negotiate side agreements with Mexico after NAFTA is signed into law. The side agreements were never really strong or firmly enforced. Instead NAFTA implemented free trade with Mexico without strong fair trade provisions that would have protected workers and residents on both sides of the border. Instead, as usual, the ruling corporate elites on both sides of the border benefited tremendously, made lots of profits and money from free trade, while workers on both sides of the border suffered tremendously with job loss and/or lower wages. This was a perfect recipe for a disappearing middle class. It's been reported that when NAFTA was implemented, many Mexican professionals such as doctors and engineers, who were paid handsomely at one time, were now moonlighting as taxicab drivers, and their wives had gone to work as low-paid sales clerks just to make ends meet. With free trade and NAFTA many Mexican family farmers were driven off their farms and out of business by American corporate farmers. American corporate agri-business dumped their U.S. government-subsidized corn on the Mexican market and undercut prices and income for the Mexican family farmer. So, free trade has damaged the prospects of middle-class people on both sides of the U.S.- Mexican border. And a major side effect of free trade with Mexico has been millions of formerly hard-working middle-class farmers in Mexico crossing the U.S./Mexico border, despite great peril, to seek a new livelihood and replace the one that was taken from them through Free Trade. The legacy of Free Trade with Mexico has been two-fold: a disappearing middle class in the U.S., because of the loss of well-paying manufacturing jobs here, and illegal immigration from Mexico to the United States.

TPP Would Have Been NAFTA on Steroids for the U.S. and Pacific Rim Nations

Free Trade and NAFTA worked very well for the top 1%, mostly super rich corporate owners. For the bottom 99% of Americans, mostly workers, Free Trade and NAFTA are a disaster, as we've seen. And yet, American corporate elites and their sponsored politicians are not content with the enormous riches they have gained from Free Trade and Globalization. They pushed hard to pass a Free Trade agreement among the United States and eleven Pacific Rim nations. This so-called Trans-Pacific Partnership (TPP) was led by President Obama, nearly all Republicans in Congress, and a large number of Democrats in Congress. What did they have in common? The bulk of their campaign contributions came from corporate and big business interests. They've also been heavily influenced by lobbying from big business and multi-national corporations. There are a few stalwart leaders in Congress, including U.S. Senator Elizabeth Warren (D-MA), U.S. Senator Bernie Sanders (D-VT), U.S. Senator Sherrod Brown (D-OH), U.S. Representative Donna Edwards (D-MD), U.S. Representative Rosa DeLauro (D-CT), U.S. Representative Keith Ellison (D-MN), and U.S. Representative Marcy Kaptur (D-OH) who vehemently opposed the TPP. Representative Rosa DeLauro put it bluntly, "Over the past 25 years, our country has signed trade deal after trade deal after trade deal, and each time, each and every time, we have been promised more jobs, increased wages, but the reality has been very different. What is insanity is doing the same thing over and over and over again and expecting a different result. We are headed to the madhouse with this agreement."

Before it was finalized, President Donald Trump shelved it. Let's look at some of its proposals. The TPP would have "allow(ed) foreign corporations to sue the United States Government for actions that undermine their 'expectations' and hurt their business, …" (Trans-Pacific Partnership Seen as Door for Foreign Suits Against U.S.", by

Jonathan Weisman, *New York Times*, March 25, 2015). Corporations and private investors would have been allowed to challenge local, state, or federal government rules, regulations, actions, and court rulings before tribunals, established by the World Bank or the United Nations, made up of unelected judges, many of whom were corporate lawyers. Corporations, not government, would be allowed to rule the people. No wonder the U.S. Business Coalition for TPP, including Apple Inc., strongly supported the TPP.

Because of NAFTA and other Free Trade agreements, the United States lost millions of high paying jobs, and is running a $500 billion annual trade deficit. TPP, "NAFTA on Steroids", would have caused us to lose even more jobs, run bigger trade deficits, and lose much of America's sovereignty.

TTIP is NAFTA on Steroids for the U.S. and the European Union

The Transatlantic Trade and Investment Partnership (TTIP) is just as nefarious as the TPP, only larger. While the 12 TPP nations compose 40% of global gross domestic product (GDP), the 29 TTIP nations compose 45% of global GDP. The TTIP consists of the United States and the 28 European Union (EU) countries. So, 40 out of 195 nations in the world make up over 50% of Global GDP, and multi-national corporations will be able to block the democratic decisions of the people of these countries.

A recently leaked chapter from the secretive TTIP agreement, which is currently being negotiated between the United States and European Union, shows that the "Free Trade deal is even a greater threat to environmental, labor, health, and human rights protections – including democracy – than we previously knew." ("Newly Leaked TTIP Draft Reveals Far-Reaching Assault on US/EU Democracy", by *Common Dreams*, April 20, 2015). Just as the TPP does, the TTIP also establishes international tribunals composed of unelected "judges", many of them corporate lawyers and pro-corporate bureaucrats. These tribunals can rule against national governments (representing the people) when multinational corporations sue them for making and implementing safety regulations regarding food, labor rights, industrial chemicals, pesticides, and other environmental regulations that may interfere with maximizing corporate profits.

The TTIP has been criticized by its opponents in the US and the EU who claim that "TTIP may give too much power to corporations, especially foreign investors, and that it could undermine food safety and environmental standards, lowering U.S. chemical regulations and forcing Europeans to consume genetically-modified (GMO) American foods and chlorinated chickens." ("Is Europe on board for a new trade deal with the U.S.?", by Bruce Stokes, Pew Research Center).

The EU admits that TTIP will cause European job loss to the U.S. since American wages and union rights are less. The proof for this is that one million U.S. jobs were lost in 12 years due to the North American Free Trade Agreement (NAFTA) between the U.S., Mexico, and Canada. ("What is TTIP? And six reasons why the answer should scare you.", by Lee Williams, *The Independent*, October 7, 2014).

Instead of correcting the above listed flawed aspects of TTIP, President Trump imposed hefty steel and aluminum tariffs on the European Union (and other countries), launching a destructive trade war.

Middle Class Race to the Bottom Is Caused by Corporate-Led Free Trade and Globalization with Low Wages

Free Trade and Globalization have been pushed by corporate elites in the United States and throughout the world. This has helped multi-national corporations, such as Apple, Nike, General Motors, Coca- Cola, and many more, to make huge profits by shifting production to cheap labor countries. Decades ago, Nike, which had its headquarters and production factories in Oregon, moved the production of its shoes and clothing to Indonesia and other low wage countries. Jobs that paid working middle class wages in Oregon were shifted to a largely female impoverished work force of Indonesian women who were paid 10 cents to 20 cents an hour. Today, they are paid 30 cents an hour. Jason Lemon wrote in *Newsweek,* September 6, 2018, "Nike called out for low wages in Asia amid Colin Kaepernick Ad Promotion." Using this cheap labor force, Nike is able to produce and ship a pair of shoes back to the U.S. store for $28, where they sell for $200. With the various free trade agreements in effect, multinational corporations such as Nike in many cases have greater powers than "sovereign" countries. Corporate elites and their sponsored politicians have successfully implemented corporate favored globalization and free trade agreements such as the North American Free Trade Agreement (NAFTA), the General Agreement on Tariffs and Trade (GATT), and the General Agreement on Trade in Services (GATS). Political Scientist Michael Parenti notes that these free trade agreements "endow anonymous international trade committees such as the World Trade Organization (WTO), established in 1994, with the authority to overrule any nation-state laws that are deemed a burden to the investment opportunities of trans-national corporations." (*The Face of Imperialism,* Michael Parenti). He further elaborates:

> These trade panels consist of "trade specialists" elected by no one and drawn from the corporate world. They meet in secret and often have investment stakes in the very issues they adjudicate, being bound by no conflict-of-interest provisions. Their function is to allow the trans-national companies to do whatever they wish without any regulations place on them by any country. Not one of GATT's 500 pages of rules and restrictions are directed against private corporations; all are against governments. Signatory governments must lower tariffs, end farm subsidies, treat foreign countries the same as domestic ones, honor all trans- national corporate patent claims on natural resources, and obey the rulings of a permanent elite bureaucracy, the WTO.
>
> Should a country refuse to change its laws when a WTO panel so dictates, the WTO can impose fines or

international trade sanctions depriving the resisting country of needed markets and materials. The WTO has ruled against laws deemed *barriers to free trade.* It has forced Japan to accept greater pesticide residues in imported food. It has kept Guatemala from outlawing deceptive advertising of baby food. It has eliminated the ban that various countries had imposed on asbestos and on fuel and emission standards for motor vehicles. ...

The European Union banned the importation of hormone-ridden US beef, a ruling that had overwhelming popular support throughout Europe, but a three-member WTO panel decided the ban was an *illegal restraint on trade.* The WTO decision on beef put in jeopardy a host of other food import regulations based on health concerns. The WTO overturned a portion of the US Clean Air Act banning certain additives in gasoline because it interfered with imports from foreign refineries, along with a portion of the US Endangered Species Act that forbade the import of shrimp caught with nets that failed to protect sea turtles.

In his recent excellent book, *The Face of Imperialism,* Michael Parenti succinctly and clearly reveals the chilling nature of corporate globalization. He calls globalization one of "...the measures contrived by international business to achieve dominion over the entire planet."

In an op-ed piece recently published in *Random Lengths News,* I made the connection between Dollar Democracy and corporate sponsored free trade agreements. I noted that the free trade agreement on steroids, the Trans-Pacific Partnership (TPP), was negotiated secretly and fully supported by the Obama Administration, almost all Republicans in Congress, and a large number of Democrats in Congress. What did these political leaders have in common? I noted that "The bulk of their campaign contributions came from corporate and big business interests. They were heavily influenced by lobbying from big business and multi-national corporations." ("TPP and TTIP Will Give Power to Multinational Corporations", Peter Mathews, *Random Lengths News*, April 30-May 13, 2015).

Corporate America's globalization agenda is dismantling the middle class and the story of Apple's phenomenal success illustrates this. We've all heard of how Steve Jobs and Steve Wozniak built the first Apple computer in Jobs' family garage, launching the personal computer industry. Soon, Jobs and Wozniak were building Apple computers and factories near San Francisco, in Fremont California, then in Elk Grove, California, and Fountain, Colorado. Opening in 1992, Apple's Elk Grove plant was followed to the Sacramento area by many other computer makers. The Elk Grove plant was open seven days a week with 1500 people working there. The factory in Fountain, Colorado turned out one million PowerBooks and desktop computers annually and was Apple's largest manufacturing plant.

Apple's early years illustrated classic American entrepreneurial success: someone invents a new and useful product, the market for it becomes larger and larger because of its value to the public, thousands of workers are trained and hired and paid well to produce the product, and the American entrepreneur makes enough profit to live a comfortable life, reinvest in new technology that advances the product, a new generation of products hits the market and basically everyone prospers, including the local community, the state, and the nation. This process was repeated thousands and millions of times all over America from the 1930s through the 1970s and early 1980s, creating the most dynamic and productive economic engine that the world has known. A major component of this process was the legalization of labor unions in the 1930s and the role played by them to demand a fair share of the value that workers produced, and better and better wages. During those decades, American employers felt an allegiance, practical and moral, to the American worker and his or her family. It was understood by American society and proclaimed by American leaders and public intellectuals, that without a well-paid, economically improving, middle class, with enough money in their hands to demand and buy the products that were produced, the economy would falter and crash. The memory of the Great Depression was not far from people's minds. With the push toward globalization, by the 1970s, American corporations sought more and more of their raw material and human labor in low- wage countries. American capitalism was no longer involved with just domestic supplies, the labor of American workers, and the American consumer market, but instead became fully global.

Free Trade, Not Fair Trade, Dismantles the Middle Class

In the relentless pursuit of more and larger profits, American-based multinational corporations started operating around the world, finding and using cheap labor, cheap resources, and producing products there with little regard for sustaining the environment or the overall economy. The mentality of the Gilded Age of the 1890s was back, along with a raw corporate capitalist mentality. This mentality was reflected very clearly by General Motors CEO Charles Wilson who said, "What's good for General Motors is good for America, and vice versa."

Just as in ancient Greek mythology the sailors could not resist the sirens' call, by the 1980s and the 1990s the vast majority of big American corporations had gone global, unable to resist the relentless drive to maximize profits by moving their manufacturing offshore in pursuit of cheap labor, cheap and abundant raw materials, and weak government regulation. Quite often the elite leaders of the cheap labor countries colluded with the American multinational corporation to provide them with cheap labor, raw materials, and weak government regulation. These local elites were rewarded well for protecting the corporate interests. They became richer and richer, as the workers and peasants in those nations suffered even more. Examples of these types of leaders were President Ferdinand Marcos in the Philippines, President Anastasio Somoza of Nicaragua, the Shah of Iran, Reza Pahlavi, the dictator Augusto Pinochet in Chile, and many others in the so-called "underdeveloped countries" of the global South.

Apple Incorporated was no exception. Just 12 years after it opened in 1992, Apple's Elk Grove plant was closed. Apple had already sold the

Fountain, Colorado plant in 1996. The well-paying jobs that provided a middle-class life for thousands of Americans in Fountain and Elk Grove are now in China. Within one generation all the American middle-class jobs involved with manufacturing almost every Apple product-- Macs, iPods, iPhones, and iPads are all in China today.

Apple was incorporated by Steve Jobs and Steve Wozniak on January 3, 1977 in Cupertino, California. This was the birth of today's largest publicly traded corporation in the world, measured by market capitalization. Apple had an estimated value (market capitalization) of U.S. $1 trillion as of August 2, 2018 (*Wall Street Journal*), becoming the first U.S. company to reach $1 trillion. Market capitalization is calculated by multiplying the company's share price by the number of shares issued on a selected day. Then the figures are converted into USD millions (using the rate from the selected day) in order to allow for comparison. Apple's market capitalization is larger than ExxonMobil, IBM, Microsoft, Royal Dutch Shell, and even Walmart. Apple's worldwide annual revenue in 2010 totaled $65 billion. In 2011 it totaled $127.8 billion. In 2012 it totaled $156 billion. In 2014, it total $182.8 billion. In 2018, Apple's revenue came to a total of 265.6 billion U.S. dollars (statista.com). Because of one of many corporate tax loopholes passed by Congress, the offshoring tax loophole, Apple was able to stash $44 billion of its income in low tax or no tax havens such as Ireland or the Cayman Islands, and avoided paying $15 billion that it would have owed the U.S. government.

The United States of America Bicentennial year, 1976, was the year Steve Jobs and Steve Wozniak founded Apple. It was also the year that I decided to move to California after completing my university education in Texas. I began my college teaching career in the summer of 1976 with political science classes at Foothill College, the sister to De Anza College and part of the Foothill—De Anza Community College District. Unlike Jobs and Wozniak, I had no aptitude, and at that time, very little interest in the technical field of electronics. Wozniak was the genius who knew electronics and engineering and almost single-handedly invented the Apple PC. Jobs' genius was in the area of product design and marketing.

If my calculations are correct, 1976 was the year in which America had her 200th birthday, Steve Jobs had his 21st birthday, Steve Wozniak had his 26th birthday, and I, Peter Mathews, had my 25th birthday. 1976 was a momentous year for all four of us, and even though I was teaching in the same college district where Jobs and Wozniak had attended De Anza College, and I was living just a few miles from where they were doing their genius work, our paths never crossed.

James Anderson, a student of mine at Foothill College, who became a friend for a while, before I lost touch with him, began his startup tech company a year or two later in the same area. I remember James Anderson showing me around his company's new headquarters in the late 70s in the San Jose area. Even the best dreamers and visionaries among us could never have predicted the modern day American high-tech industry's growth into a gigantic engine, driving the train of the modern-day post-industrial world economy. The last I saw of my former student and friend James Anderson was at his brother's wedding at the top of Lake Tahoe, where he introduced me to his grandfather, the world-famous television and entertainment personality Art Linkletter ("Kids Say The Darndest Things"). One of my lasting memories of that day was of Art dancing away at the reception in his plaid suit. Sadly, in 2010, at the age of 97 Art Linkletter passed away. A private family Memorial ceremony was held at his home in exclusive Bel Air, next-door to Beverly Hills. Later, a special memorial ceremony was held at the Bohemian Grove, north of San Francisco. It was one of Linkletter's most favorite places. He had attended and performed at the exclusive invitation-only gathering of the American (and world's) political, economic, social, and cultural elite. Active in Republican and conservative causes, Art Linkletter had served on Pepperdine University's Board of Regents and on the President's Council on Service and Civic Participation until 2008. Here was a man who was well off and well-connected politically, economically, socially, and culturally, and his grandson was my student in one of the most academically advanced California Community Colleges.

When Steve Jobs, Steve Wozniak, and James Anderson were students in the Foothill-De Anza Community College District, where I started my teaching career as a 25-year-old professor in California, Governor Pat Brown's 1960 Master Plan for Higher Education was still in effect. Under the Master Plan, the State of California was required to cover the full cost of a college or university education. That's why middle-class students such as Wozniak and Jobs, students from upper-income families such as James Anderson, as well as students from low income families, could each pay a $6 processing fee and receive their full-time education tuition free at De Anza College and Foothill College. From 1960 through the 1970s, tuition free education was the norm at all California Community Colleges, and at California State University, and University of California campuses.

It was this guarantee by the State of California, that any of its high school graduates who studied and worked hard would not be blocked by financial challenges from fully developing their technical and creative talents, and be able to excel in their fields of endeavor. For Jobs and Wozniak it was their solid K-12 public education, especially their schools' science and electronics teachers, that encouraged creative thinking, problem-solving, and project building, which helped produce the geniuses that they became. Under its former CEO, the late Steve Jobs and its present CEO Tim Cook, Apple has outsourced hundreds of thousands of manufacturing jobs to low-wage countries such as China. This has resulted in a loss of income to working middle class Americans, and a loss of tax revenue to the U.S. federal and state governments. As mentioned earlier Apple has also avoided paying billions of dollars in taxes by taking advantage of the offshoring corporate tax loophole passed for companies like it, by the U.S. Congress. This has been a blow to funds for public education: fully funded public education kindergarten through technical and trade schools, college and university. What an irony that Apple complains of the shortage of educated skilled labor in the U.S. and says it must go to other countries to find it.

In 2011, President Obama had dinner in California with Silicon Valley's top entrepreneurs. There, the president asked Steve Jobs, what would it take to make iPhones in the United States? Because the fact is that almost all of the 70 million iPhones, 30 million iPads, and 59 million other products that Apple sold in 2011 were made overseas. Jobs replied, "Those jobs aren't coming back." According to a *New York Times* investigative report, "How the U.S. Lost Out on iPhone Work", it isn't just that Apple can get much cheaper labor in other countries. Writing in the *MIT Technology Review* in 2016, Konstantin Kakaef showed that if the cost of labor were factored in and "even if every part (of the iPhone) was made in the U.S., an iPhone would cost just $100 more," an increase of about 10%. ("How Much Would the iPhone Cost If It Were Made In America?", by Emily Stewart, VOX, September 22, 2018). According to Apple's executives, the reason they make the phone overseas, in China for example, is because of the huge size of overseas factories, and the:

> flexibility, diligence and industrial skills of foreign workers, (which) have so outpaced their American counterparts that "Made in the U.S.A." is no longer a viable option for most Apple products.

> Apple has become one of the best-known, most admired and most imitated companies on earth, in part through an unrelenting mastery of global operations. Last year, it earned over $400,000 in profit per employee, more than Goldman Sachs, ExxonMobil or Google.

> However, what is apparent to Mr. Obama as well as economists and policymakers is that Apple -- and many of its high-technology peers -- are not nearly as avid in creating American jobs as other famous companies were in their heydays.

> Apple employs 43,000 people in the United States and 20,000 overseas, a small fraction of the over 400,000 American workers at General Motors in the 1950s, or the hundreds of thousands at General Electric in the 1980s. Many more people work for Apple's contractors: an additional 700,000 people engineer, build and assemble iPads, iPhones and Apple's other products. But almost none of them work in the United States. Instead they work for foreign companies in Asia, Europe and elsewhere, at factories that almost

all electronics designers rely upon to build their wares.

"Apple's an example of why it's so hard to create middle class jobs in the U.S. now," said Jared Bernstein, who until last year was an economic advisor to the White House.

"If it's the pinnacle of capitalism, we should be worried."

Apple executives say that going overseas, at this point, is their only option. One former executive described how the company relied upon a Chinese factory to revamp iPhone manufacturing just weeks before the device was due on shelves. Apple had redesigned the iPhone's screen at the last minute, forcing an assembly line overhaul. New screens began arriving at the plant near midnight.

A foreman immediately aroused 1000 workers inside the company's dormitories, according to the executive. Each employee was given a biscuit and a cup of tea, guided to a workstation and within half an hour started a 12 hour shift fitting glass screens into beveled frames. Within 96 hours the plant was producing over 10,000 iPhones a day.

"The speed and flexibility is breathtaking,' the executive said. 'There's no American plant that can match that."

Similar stories could be told about almost any electronics company-- and outsourcing has also become common in hundreds of industries, including accounting, legal services, banking, auto manufacturing and pharmaceuticals.

(*New York Times*, "How the U.S. Lost Out on iPhone Work")

This story shows us why the success of some large corporations through outsourcing has not produced large numbers of domestic jobs. It also raises questions about whether or not corporate America has a moral obligation to Americans as the national economy is increasingly affected by globalization. The counterargument from Apple executives is that their success has benefited the American economy by "empowering entrepreneurs and creating jobs at companies like cellular providers and businesses shipping Apple products. And, ultimately, they say curing unemployment is not their job.

" 'We sell iPhones in over 100 countries,' a current Apple executive said. 'We don't have an obligation to solve America's problems. Our only obligation is making the best product possible.'" ("Apple, America and a Squeezed Middle Class", *NYTimes.com*).

The Apple executive should have said, "... Our only obligation is making the best product possible, at the highest possible profit of $400,000 per employee." Of course, to do this Apple would have to have a compliant large-scale workforce, willing to work for just over $1 per hour, for 10 to 12 hours per day, six, sometimes seven days a week including overtime, for a total of 60 to 70 hours per week, despite the Chinese labor law maximum of 49 hours per week. It found this standing army of impoverished slave like workers who are treated like robots, not human beings, mostly in China, the world's largest country with over 1 billion people. No shortage of willing workers there, streaming in from the countryside where they were eking out a desperate living on not so productive farms. Perhaps to salve their conscience, but more likely to distance themselves from the terrible and obvious exploitation of these Chinese workers, the leaders of Apple decided not to hire the Chinese workers directly but to contract with companies such as Pegatron and Foxconn to manufacture Apple products such as the iPhone.

Just over a month before the iPhone was to make its debut in stores in 2007, Apple CEO Steve Jobs decided on one more innovation that would set Apple apart from the pack of cell phone makers. He demanded from his top executives the creation of a glass screen that could not be scratched, even by the keys in people's pockets. He said to them "I won't sell a product that gets scratched. I want a glass screen, and I want it perfect in six weeks." ("Apple, America and a Squeezed Middle Class", *NYTimes.com*). But where could a glass screen like this be produced within six weeks? This time the answer was in China.

As *New York Times* investigative journalists found, for over two years Apple had been working on a project -- code-named Purple 2 – that brought up the question each time: how can the cell phone be completely re-imagined? How do you design it with the highest quality innovations, for example with a screen that cannot be scratched, while guaranteeing that millions of them can be manufactured inexpensively and quickly enough to earn a huge profit?

> The answers, almost every time, were found outside the United States. Though components differ between versions, all iPhones contain hundreds of parts, an estimated 90 per cent of which are manufactured abroad. Advanced semiconductors have come from Germany and Taiwan, memory from Korea and Japan, display panels and circuitry from Korea and Taiwan, chipsets from Europe and rare metals from Africa and Asia. And all of it is put together in China.

But by 2004, Apple had largely turned to foreign manufacturing. Guiding that decision was Apple's operations expert, Timothy D. Cook, who replaced Mr. Jobs as chief executive in August 2011, six weeks before Mr. Jobs' death. Most other American electronics companies had already gone abroad, and Apple, which at the time was struggling, felt it had to grasp every advantage.

In part, Asia was attractive because the semiskilled workers there were cheaper. But that wasn't driving Apple. For technology companies, the cost of labor is minimal compared with the expense of buying parts and managing supply chains that bring together components and services from hundreds of companies.

For Mr. Cook, the focus on Asia "came down to two things," said one former high-ranking Apple executive. Factories in Asia "can scale up and down faster" and "Asian supply chains have surpassed what's in the U.S." The result is that "we can't compete at this point," the executive said.

The impact of such advantages became obvious as soon as Mr. Jobs demanded glass screens in 2007.

For years, cell phone makers had avoided using glass because it required precision and cutting and grinding that was extremely difficult to achieve. Apple had already selected an American company, Corning Inc., to manufacture large panes of strengthened glass. But figuring out how to cut those panes into millions of iPhone screens required finding an empty cutting plant, hundreds of pieces of glass to use in experiments and an army of mid-level engineers. It would cost a fortune simply to prepare.

Then a bid for the work arrived from a Chinese factory. When an Apple team visited, the Chinese plant's owners were already constructing a new wing. "This is in case you give us the contract," the manager said, according to a former Apple executive. The Chinese government had agreed to underwrite costs for numerous industries, and those subsidies had trickled down to the glass cutting factory. It had a warehouse filled with glass samples available to Apple, free of charge. The owners made engineers available at almost no cost. They had built on-site dormitories so employees would be available 24 hours a day.

The Chinese plant got the job. An eight hour drive from the glass factory is a gigantic high-tech industrial complex in Shenzhen, less than an hour from Hong Kong, the Longhua Science and Technology Park, also known as Foxconn City. It is owned by Taiwan-based Foxconn Technology Group, which is the largest manufacturer of electronics and computer components in the world, owning dozens of facilities in Mexico, Brazil, Asia, and Eastern Europe. In these low-wage countries, Foxconn assembles approximately 40% of the world's consumer electronics. Its customers include Samsung, Sony, the Kia, Motorola, Dell, Hewlett-Packard, and Nintendo.

"The (Apple's) entire supply chain is in China now," said another former high-ranking Apple executive. "You need a thousand rubber gaskets? That's the factory next door. You need 1 million screws? That factory is a block away. You need that screw made a little bit different? It will take three hours." ("Apple, America and a Squeezed Middle Class", NYTimes.com).

The epicenter of Apple's production in China is Foxconn City, just outside Shenzhen, although Apple has other suppliers with factories in China. According to Pulitzer Prize winning investigative journalists Donald L. Barlett and James B. Steele, Foxconn City

> is a massive, fortress-like compound surrounded by walls and protected by tight security where guards stop each vehicle at the entrance and check identities of occupants by using fingerprint-recognition scanners.

> Within the walled city are numerous factories, dormitories, support businesses, and an on-site television network, all humming around the clock....Longhua (Foxconn City) is home to as many as 300,000 workers.

> The workers labor in enormous factories, row after row of them bent over workstations that seem to stretch endlessly into the distance. They assemble iPods, iPhones, iPads, and products for other electronics makers. Occasionally photos surface showing workers, mostly young women, wearing spiffy white coats and caps, going about their work in what appears to be pleasant, well-lit surroundings, just as workers once did at Elk Grove (California) and Fountain (Colorado).

> But that's the only similarity with Apple's former plants in the United States.

Barlett and Steele found that,

> workers at Longhua and other Foxconn plants in China usually work from 10 to 12 hours a day, sometimes for seven days straight without overtime pay. They're not allowed to speak to each other on the job or to leave their workstations----not even to go to the bathroom-- without permission from guards. Some of them perform repetitive tasks for up to 10 hours of time without a break. Supervisors berate workers with foul language and warn that if they fall behind on production they will be replaced. Some have reportedly been beaten for mistakes they allegedly made on the assembly line. For this, they earn little more than a dollar an hour at most.

> SACOM (Students and Scholars Against Corporate Misbehavior, a courageous Hong Kong-based human rights group), which has documented these practices in numerous reports, describe working conditions at one Foxconn plant making iPhones: 'Workers frequently endure excessive and forced overtime in order to gain a higher wage. If they cannot reach the production target, they have to skip dinner or work on unpaid overtime shifts.' SACOM calls Foxconn's Apple workers 'iSlaves.'

Most young workers live on-site in cramped high-rise dormitories near the factories, where as many as a dozen workers squeeze into small rooms with three tiers of bunk beds. Most of them are peasants in their late teens or early 20s who have been lured to the city in hopes of earning money for themselves and their families back home, only to find themselves yoked to brutal production schedules that can become unbearable.

Upward of two dozen workers at Apple plants in China have become so desperate that they have taken their own lives, often by jumping to their deaths from their dormitories. The deaths were so common for a time the Chinese bloggers began referring to the Shenzhen plant as the "Foxconn Suicide Express." In its investigation of conditions at Longhua and other plants making Apple products, SACOM concluded that many of those who committed suicide were exhausted, overworked, verbally and physically abused by supervisors, or publicly humiliated when they failed to meet their production quotas. SACOM reports tell the story of some of these young victims:

- **Hou**, a nineteen-year-old woman from Hunan province, hanged herself in the toilet of her dorm room on June 18, 2007, shortly after she had assured her parents that she would soon be coming home.

- **Sun**, a 25-year-old college graduate from Yunan province, jumped to his death from his 12th floor room on July 16, 2009, after he was allegedly blamed for losing a prototype for a new iPhone. According to SACOM, Sun was detained by security officers, placed in "solitary confinement," subjected to "psychological pressures," and allegedly beaten. In a final chat with friends shortly before he killed himself, he described the relief he felt in planning to take his own life: "Thinking that I won't be bullied tomorrow, won't have to be the scapegoat, I feel much better."

- After **Feng**, a 23-year-old college graduate, jumped to his death from his fourteenth floor room on January 16, 2009, police found a suicide note: "Too much work pressure; unstable emotions."

- **Ma**, a 19-year-old native of Henan province, was found dead near a stairway of his dormitory on January 23, 2010. An autopsy concluded that he had fallen to his death. His sisters later insisted that their brother died from a beating he had suffered after he accidentally damaged equipment at work.(Donald Barlett and James Steele, *The Betrayal of the American Dream*)

After several suicides by Chinese factory workers who jumped to their deaths from the several story high buildings that were their dormitories, Foxconn put up nets to catch them before they fell to their deaths. It blocked roof access and balcony doors. Workers were encouraged to sign a statement promising not to kill themselves. Apple issued a report on "supplier responsibility" which they gave to shareholders saying they were saddened by the workers' suicides and started looking for suicide prevention specialists. Apple commended Foxconn for attaching the large nets to reduce the number of suicides. SACOM says that the number of suicides went down but working conditions pretty much remain the same at Longhua and other Foxconn factories. Although Apple has pledged to work with Foxconn to improve conditions for workers, SACOM says that Apple failed to follow through and insist on reforms, leaving many of the horrendous working conditions in place.

After taking over in 2011 Apple's new CEO Tim Cook said Apple would work to improve conditions at overseas factories that made its iPhones and other products. But for the second time in the summer of 2013, the New York-based nonprofit China Labor Watch (CLW), charged another iPhone factory with discrimination in hiring, poor living conditions for workers living in dormitories, and unpaid overtime. China Labor Watch said it found many labor violations at a factory in Wuxi, China. Owned by Florida-based Jabil Circuit the factory was thought to be manufacturing the cheap, plastic backs to Apple's rumored new line of low-cost iPhones (Huffington Post, 9/5/2013). Apple said that it had conducted three audits of Jabil Wuxi in the last three years. Apple told the *Huffington Post* that "while the factory has generally complied with Apple's standard of 60-hour work weeks and that Jabil has 'an excellent track record of meeting Apple's high standards,' it found that some factory employees work more than six consecutive days without rest.

Even with Tim Cook, Apple's CEO who appears more concerned about foreign workers' well-being, Apple has not made progress in some parts of its global manufacturing chain. China Labor Watch found similar abuses at another Apple contractor based in Shanghai. Even though Apple seems to be the prime target of criticism, other electronics gadget makers are no better. Still, Dino Grandoni, writing in the September 5,

2013 *Huffington Post*, points out these facts about the lives of iPhone workers in China:

- **Pregnant women and old people need not apply**: The factory in Wuxi only hires workers between 18 and 25 years of age and conducts a pregnancy test on female applicants.

- **Mandatory, unpaid overtime**: China Labor Watch reports that "110 hours of overtime per month is common, which is in excess of Apple's own code and even further in excess of Chinese statutory regulations on overtime hours." Much of this overtime is unpaid. According to China Labor Watch morning and evening meetings that don't count toward working time account for about $23 in lost wages per month. Jabil makes new workers sign a document saying that overtime is voluntary.

- **No time to sit**: 11 1/2 hours of standing work is often normal at Jabil Wuxi. Breaks aren't. The CLW report says "despite work intensity and continual standing, workers are given no breaks outside of meal breaks during a 12 hour shift."

- **No time to eat**: and even those meal breaks are insufficient. The following is a typical anecdote provided by CLW: when Ting leaves for her lunch break, she first needs to pass through security. In a production facility with 300 workers, Ting has to wait in line for three minutes before getting to the checkpoint. After passing security, Ting rushes to the factory cafeteria, which is on the third floor of another building. When she arrives at the cafeteria eight minutes later, she waits another three minutes to get her food. When Ting finally takes her seat to eat her lunch, she has just five minutes to eat before she needs to head back to the production floor.

- **No time to sleep**: imagine being in a dorm with seven other people, according to CLW. What's worse than this is that workers assigned to night and day shifts are put in the same room, which makes it hard for anyone to sleep properly.

- **No money to live on**: overtime (even when some is unpaid) is a fact of life for Jabil workers because the cost of living in the city is too expensive for their salary. According to the China Labor Watch report: "at Jabil Wuxi, the typical monthly base wage for a worker is 1500 RMB ($245), while the average monthly income in Wuxi is 2,890 RMB ($472) for private industry employees and 4615 RMB ($753) for non-private industry employees in 2012. The combined base wages for two adults working at Jabil (3000 RMB or $490 per month) is insufficient to raise a child in Wuxi, with basic expenses for such a family amounting to 4110 RMB ($671) per month.

Dino Grandoni asks "so, how excited are you for the new iPhone?"

CHAPTER 4

EDUCATION: DISMANTLING PUBLIC SCHOOLS AND COLLEGES FOR THE 99%

"All the scientific evidence says that the best indicator of an American child's success in life beginning in K-12 and in college is dependent primarily on her/his parents' income level."

--Peter Mathews

Rich Parent, Poor Parent: Inequality in American Education

An American child's chance of acquiring a quality education depends more on the parents' income than on almost anything else, including ethnicity.

Several years ago, I was walking my infant daughter in her stroller in our Long Beach Belmont Heights neighborhood. As I turned the corner, I saw a lemonade stand run by a mother, her children, and their friends. I thought the mom was teaching the kids how to become successful entrepreneurs!

Then I read the sign that said, "Lemonade for Fremont Elementary. Please support our fabulous science and computer labs!!" Another sign said, "Thank you Mrs. Phelps for your donations of lemons!!" I wanted to help in a small way, so I bought a couple of glasses of lemonade.

As I sipped the delicious fresh lemonade, the mother at the stand told me that for the last several years, the parents in the Fremont Elementary neighborhood had raised approximately $100,000 annually to help keep the labs open. They had been threatened with closure because of statewide budget cuts. I wondered how much lemonade it would take to raise $100,000? Too much! And that's why the parents from this affluent neighborhood had to raise and donate their own money; parents such as **Keith** and **Karen Vescial**, whose sons **Evan** and **Zach** were attending Fremont Elementary. Keith called this "a hybrid form of private/public education." Keith went on to tell me "in communities that can't or won't raise or donate private money, the kids suffer". Keith corroborated the lemonade mom's story and said that he got the details at a PTA meeting.

This got me thinking, how many parents in the low-income neighborhoods in the United States can raise or donate $100,000 annually to save their school's science lab, if they even have one? With the median household income in most of these areas lower than the national median of $61,372 in 2017, I would venture to say, not many of those parents, if any, can. As I walked my sleeping 2-year old daughter back home, it occurred to me, that something had to be done about the lack of resources in low-income neighborhoods. My daughter is now 7-years old, and the parents' annual fundraising continues.

The differences between low-income neighborhoods and high-income neighborhoods are clear when we compare two Long Beach High Schools, and two Long Beach Elementary Schools. Because Long Beach's Jordan High School and Wilson High School are both in the Long Beach Unified School District, they both receive similar levels of per pupil funding. Yet, the majority of Wilson students' academic achievement levels were higher than Jordan's. The majority of Jordan students' academic achievement levels were far lower than the majority of Wilson students' academic achievement levels. In this case, the students' academic achievement rates were correlated with the parents' income levels. Generally, the higher income levels of Wilson parents produce the social environment which enables their children to do better in school.

As we can see, it is the inequality of parental income that is the major factor: in Long Beach, California, and in the U.S., most high-income parents themselves have higher educational levels and more resources to provide their children with a rich, supportive learning environment resulting in higher student achievement. Adequate, equal per pupil funding is necessary but not enough. Inequality in parental income is a major factor in students' achievement because more affluent parents can provide all the needed support outside of school such as extra academic support including homework, outside tutoring, extra-curricular arts and science activities, "academic camps" and well-funded PTAs that can spend money as well. Also, higher income families enjoy the benefits of economically secure (home ownership) and physically safe environments, for example, with less crime and gang activity. Most low-income parents cannot afford these things. Many low-income parents, for no fault of their own, do not have resources or time to provide their children with the same rich, supportive learning environment. Many of these parents are forced to work overtime or hold down two jobs to make ends meet. Until low income parents' wages and resources are increased, public spending must be increased to provide their children with a similar, supportive outside-the-classroom learning environment as the children of the wealthy. I know this works because I experienced this type of program that was created by the city of Cambridge in England.

When I was teaching in the Semester Abroad program in Cambridge, England, I visited the Cambridge Youth Center. This center was open in the afternoons and evenings, and all day on weekends. It provided academic, arts, technical, trade, and mentoring programs for school age young people. These programs included tutoring in math, language and science, as well as fashion design and marketing, fashion show production, music lessons, battle of the bands, and so much more.

Jordan High School is located in a low to moderate income area of North Long Beach. Five percent of parents in the area make over $125,000, annually, and 75 percent of students are classified as socio-economically disadvantaged. Wilson High School is located in the middle to high income area of southern Long Beach, 15 percent of parents in this area make over $125,000 annually, and 48 percent of students are classified as socio-economically disadvantaged. This is why, despite the similar per pupil funding level, test scores at Wilson High school far surpass those at Jordan high school. (lbschools.net). Measuring academic performance for 2010-2011 by the percent of students who are proficient or advanced on standardized tests, Jordan's scores are less than half of Wilson's: 22% in English/Language Arts, 9% in Math, 23% in Science, and 23% in History/Social Science. In

120

comparison, Wilson's numbers are 50% in English/Language Arts, 22% in Math, 56% in Science and 49% in History/Social Science. (lbschools.net)

Jordan's numbers are much lower than Wilson's in other ways: For every 100 students in 9th grade enrolled in Jordan, 48 go on to graduate four years later, and only 13 pass the courses required to enter the CSU and UC systems. In contrast, for every 100 students in 9th grade enrolled in Wilson, 67 go on to graduate, and 36 pass the courses required. (California Education Opportunity Report, 2011, idea.gseis.ucla.edu/educational-opportunity-report).

The same differences that exist at the high school level also exist at the elementary school level. Fremont Elementary and King Elementary are both in the Long Beach Unified School District and receive similar per pupil funding. Fremont Elementary, which is in the same affluent Belmont Heights area of Long Beach as Wilson High School, produces excellent academic achievement results. Fremont, the school with its own Science and Computer labs now kept open by generous donations from affluent parents, jog-a-thons, and lemonade stands, produces high academic achievement results: in English, Math, and Science, 84 percent, 88 percent, and 88 percent of students scored in the proficient or advanced category, respectively. In contrast, King Elementary, in the same lower-income area of North Long Beach as Jordan High School, produces much lower academic achievement results than Fremont Elementary. King's achievement results were: in English, Math, and Science, 48 percent, 65 percent, and 41 percent of students score in the proficient or advanced category, respectively. (lbschools.net)

Why are these differences so great? Some would argue that the fault lies with the parents, others would blame the failing economy. The simple fact of the matter is that greater family income and wealth are correlated with greater student academic achievement. That fact has been proven in study upon study.

In a 1966 report to the U.S. Congress, sociologist James S. Coleman found that, regardless of ethnicity or race, students from low income families didn't perform as well academically as students whose parents were higher income. Coleman's findings have been confirmed over and over since then. In 2006, Douglas Harris, a University of Wisconsin economist found that in schools where more than half of the students were low-income, only 1.1 percent of those schools performed at a high level. In schools that were majority middle class, 24.2 percent of those schools met the "high" level standard. That's a huge difference.

The inequality in funding and student educational achievement is also great when we compare a wealthy California school district with a less affluent one. Palo Alto Unified School District is one of the most affluent school districts in California. Annually, 48 percent of parents of students in this district make over $125,000, ranking it high on the Neighborhood Affluence Rate, and per pupil funding is approximately $16,154. Compare that to Long Beach Unified School District (LBUSD), where parents earn significantly less and the per pupil spending is approximately $8,756. The test scores mirror what is happening in dollars. The average API score in Palo Alto is 925, ranking it in the highest 25 percent of California students. The average API score in Long Beach is 759, ranking it in the next to lowest 25 percent, much lower than Palo Alto. (June 2, 2011, Californiawatch.org).

The numbers are even more staggering at Palo Alto High School. For every 100 students enrolled as 9th graders, 92 graduated, and 92 passed the courses required for admission to CSU and UC. At Gunn High School in Palo Alto the numbers were even higher. For every 100 students enrolled as 9th graders, 96 graduated, and 96 passed the courses required for admission to CSU and UC. (California Education Opportunity Report, 2011).

As we have seen, California generally has very unequal funding among school districts. Despite former Governor Jerry Brown's recent success in getting the State Legislature to adopt his Local Control Funding Formula, the State still has not equalized per pupil funding, which is primarily due to wealthier districts raising more in property taxes. According to the California Department of Education:

> First, the State of California calculates each district's revenue limit using historical per student amounts that are adjusted annually, usually by a cost of living increase. The State then determines if each district generates enough local property taxes to reach   its

122

calculated revenue limit. If a district's local property taxes ARE NOT sufficient to meet the revenue limit calculated by the State, then that district is classified as a "Revenue Limit" district. For each "Revenue Limit" district, the State provides the remainder of funding needed to reach the revenue limit.

In a Revenue Limit district, the state provides additional (or less) funding as enrollment increases (or decreases).

If a district's local property taxes ARE sufficient to meet the revenue limit set by the State, then that district is classified as a "Basic Aid" district. The State provides only additional funding of $120 per student to that district. Any local property taxes beyond the revenue limit are retained by the district. This property tax base is a more stable funding source to Basic Aid districts than what the Revenue Limit districts receive from the state. For the 2011-2012 school year, there were 127 Basic Aid districts in California (with the majority located in wealthier Marin, San Mateo, and Santa Clara counties). (www.mpaef.org/www.cde.ca.gov as cited by the Menlo Park-Atherton Education Foundation.)

In other words, the State sets a minimum funding limit (This "revenue limit" is around $5,000 per pupil) which it provides. If the districts with higher property values raise more money in property taxes than the minimum funding limit, they get to keep the full amount of their high-level property tax funding. The districts with lower property values will collect less than the minimum funding limit, therefore the state makes up the difference to meet the revenue limit. As a result, these districts have much less funding than the high property value districts. For example, total per pupil funding is $16,154 in the Palo Alto Unified School District, a part of wealthy Silicon Valley. Former Governor Jerry

Brown's Local Control Funding Formula temporarily boosted average California per pupil funding by approximately $800. The low-income districts' share was more than $800, and the high-income districts' share was less than $800. As a result, the average per pupil funding for 2018 is $8,756 in the Long Beach Unified School District, while the wealthy Palo Alto Unified School District per pupil funding is $16,154. The per pupil funding in the affluent Shoreline Unified School District in Marin County is $28,073, and the low-income Lynwood Unified School District per pupil funding will be approximately just over $7,000. Federal funding is the least of the three sources of revenue and is only three percent of the total federal budget. (*edweek.org*).

As a result, the high-income Shoreline Unified School District in Marin County has small classes, with an average student to teacher ratio of 14:1, lower than the national average ratio of 17:1, and the 27:1 ratio of Long Beach Unified School District, which includes Fremont Elementary School with a 31:1 ratio, where my daughter attends first grade with 29 students to 1 teacher. Despite this high student to teacher ratio, the teachers that my daughter has had in kindergarten and first grade have been extremely hard working, diligent, and often inspiring to children such as my daughter. I can only imagine how much better the classroom experience would be for both the teacher and the students if the class size had a 17:1 student to teacher ratio, the same as the national average: greater individualized instruction, enabling each child to reach her or his full potential, with no child falling through the cracks.

Growing Income Gap in the U.S. Affects Our Schools

That's why the growing income gap, brought to our attention by the iconoclastic Occupy Wall Street Movement, between the super-rich (average CEO) and the average worker in America is obscene: it was 40 to 1 in 1980, and today, according to Forbes, it is almost 361 to 1. (Forbes.com, May 22, 2018). This is devastating to our schools and society. Let's further compare the two Long Beach, California High Schools.

The higher income levels of Wilson High School parents produce an environment which enables their children to do better in school. It helps a lot when your parents have more income to put you in private music, ballet and tutoring classes, and more time to help with your homework. Jordan High School parents love their kids just as much and want the best for them. Yet, their generally lower incomes and tougher work schedules make it harder for their children to climb the educational and economic ladder. Of course, there are exceptions to this: a low-income child may occasionally succeed by overcoming major hurdles because one parent stays home and is able to tutor and mentor her/him, while the other parent works grueling hours at two or three jobs to make ends meet. Or one grandparent is still at home to do the same. This is increasingly difficult because, with the outsourcing of jobs and depressing of wages, both parents, and even the grandparents have to work overtime to survive!

As we have seen earlier, academic achievement scores and graduation rates at Wilson far surpassed those at Jordan (lbschools.net). Education budgets have eliminated resources and classes across districts. But low and middle-income districts ($60,336 per household and less) have been hit the hardest. Those parents don't have the time and resources to compensate for the overall decrease in funding and cuts in programs. That's why places like the Cambridge Youth Center in England need to be established in low income neighborhoods in the U.S.

Even the U.S. Department of Education has found that "children raised in the bottom fifth of family incomes nationally have a 70 percent chance of remaining below the middle-income level as adults." Supporting research has found that students growing up in low-income communities fall behind their peers. They engage in early learning at much lower rates than wealthier students, they are less ready when they enter school, and they are more likely to drop out before graduating. For those who do graduate, poor students are less likely to go to college and graduate from college. Former President Obama's Department of Education noted that "This hurts young people, their families, and their communities, and damages America's economic strength and international competitiveness." In order "To ensure that all students have the opportunity to succeed in college and the work force, our nation must address the needs of students in low-income communities and low performing schools ...." (http://www.ed.gov/ladders) In order to accomplish this, President Trump, already in office for two years, needs to ask Congress to fully fund Cambridge style youth centers with extensive after school programs that would be based in every low-income neighborhood school, fully staffed with mentors and counselors. However, Dollar Democracy is the biggest obstacle preventing this from happening: Instead of closing unproductive corporate tax loopholes to bring in hundreds of billions of dollars to fund these valuable youth centers, President Trump and the majority of Congress would rather give their corporate campaign donors this money to finance their lavish lifestyles. The Trump/Congressional Republicans' $1.5 trillion tax cuts in 2017, mostly for the rich and big corporations, is proof of this.

In addition, the Great Recession has reduced public spending at many levels of government, including for education. However, the deterioration of our economy didn't happen in a tunnel and neither did the dismantling of California's great public education system. The following were the key culprits in this outrageous and pathetic tragedy:

First, the passage of Proposition 13 in 1978 in California, which removed billions of dollars from the public education system, was the start of the slippery downward slope that we are on. Ironically, two thirds of Prop 13 tax cuts have gone to big commercial property owners such as ExxonMobil, Chevron, and Bank of America, while only one third of the tax cuts have gone to home owners. Homeowners need it and should keep it. Big commercial property owners do not need the tax cuts, and their tax loophole should be closed. This will send billions of badly needed dollars to public education in California.

Second, drastic reduction in federal tax rates on the upper portion of the incomes of the super-rich: under Republican President Eisenhower the rate was 91%; under Republican President Reagan, 28%; under Democratic President Obama, 39.9%, and under Republican President Trump, 37%. Congress' Joint Committee on Taxation estimates the law delivers taxpayers who earn $1 million or more a tax cut of $37 billion in 2019 alone. This is over half the annual cost of bringing tuition-free college for all American students. This brought severe reductions in federal funding for effective social and educational programs such as CETA, Pell Grants, Americorps, Head Start, and after-school academic arts and sports programs that helped keep kids on the path of educational and life success. These cuts have made an already dire situation worse.

Third, since the Reagan right wing agenda of cutting taxes on the rich, immensely increasing defense spending, and severely cutting social programs such as public education, a cultural/ideological shift has taken place. Because of this shift, the gap between the rich and poor has grown substantially in the past 30 years. Rich corporate executives are making 361 times the income of the average American worker. In the first three years after the Great Recession the top 1 percent of Americans captured 93 percent of the total growth in income, according to UC Berkeley economist Emmanuel Saez. That left only 7 percent of the new income for 99 percent of Americans to share.

Much of Corporate America sees no problem with the increasing gap between rich and poor. Moreover, they feel that the growth in this gap is the natural outcome of their hard work, innovation, ingenuity, and the laziness of the rest of America. Their ideology of extreme rugged individualism says that we should each pull ourselves up by our own boot straps! Most of them would argue that they deserve huge tax cuts and corporate subsidies because they, the 1%, are creating jobs for us, the 99%, and we should be grateful to them. President Trumps' 2017 tax cuts disproportionately favored the wealthiest Americans.

Distribution of Trump Tax Cuts Favors Wealthiest
On average, in 2018, taxes declined for everyone, but top groups got the biggest benefit

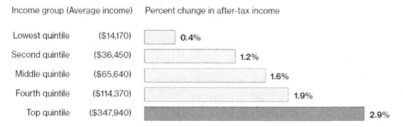

Income group (Average income)		Percent change in after-tax income
Lowest quintile	($14,170)	0.4%
Second quintile	($36,450)	1.2%
Middle quintile	($65,640)	1.6%
Fourth quintile	($114,370)	1.9%
Top quintile	($347,940)	2.9%

Source: Tax Policy Center estimates

Note: Average federal tax (includes individual and corporate income tax, payroll taxes for Social Security and Medicare, the estate tax, and excise taxes) as a percentage of average expanded cash income.

Graph 4-1

With success in education increasingly determining success in income and life chances, we face a dire future as Californians and

Americans: the well-educated, upper middle class and upper class will leave in the dust the less educated, deteriorating and desperate, working middle class and working poor. Universal public education, promoted by American educational reformers such as Thomas Jefferson, Horace Mann, Susan B. Anthony, and John Dewey, has served as a force to break down class barriers. Today, extremely unequal public education appears to be increasing class barriers!

What becomes clearly apparent from numerous studies conducted over time, is that most students from higher-income neighborhoods do far better in school than most students from lower-income neighborhoods. This sets most of them on the trajectory of high academic achievement in high school, college and university, and strongly positions them for high economic achievement on the American socio-economic ladder. On the other hand, most students from lower-income neighborhoods tend to have greater obstacles to overcome in their climb up the academic and socio-economic ladder in the United States. It does not and should not have to be this way.

We pride ourselves as being an exemplary democracy for the rest of the world to follow, a country which provides equal opportunity for all of its children to achieve their full human potential by studying and working hard. In order to live up to this ideal, we must undertake major socio-economic and political reforms. Socio-economic reforms must include reducing the gap between rich and poor, and rebuilding the middle class by implementing a strongly progressive income tax such as we had from the 1930s until the 1970s; closing unfair corporate tax loopholes and ending corporate welfare; increasing the wages of working Americans by strengthening unions and the right to organize; promoting Fair Trade, not Free Trade. Eliminating waste in the bloated military budget will produce revenue to invest in new green technology manufacturing jobs in the public and private sectors. We will also be able to invest in equal educational opportunity for all Americans, preschool through technical, and trade school, college and university.

None of the above will happen in any significant way until the majority of American elected officials are financed through a voluntary, publicly funded campaign system, not through the huge amounts of money donated to them by wealthy special interest lobbyists, and millionaires and billionaires. Clean Money Elections at the Federal level, following the example of states such as Maine and Arizona, need to be adopted through Federal legislation or a Constitutional Amendment. Then only will we be able to implement a system of educational and social justice, and move from a Dollar Democracy, with liberty and justice for some, to a Real Democracy with liberty and justice and equal educational opportunity for all!

"If you give a man a fish he eats for a day, if you teach him how to fish, he eats for a lifetime." This statement came from an ancient Chinese proverb. It also implies that one of the initial reasons for education is to provide ongoing skills that enable human beings to secure the basic economic needs of food, shelter, and clothing. Once those basic needs are met adequately, it enables the human being to continue on her or his quest for greater meaning in life. As the great psychologist Abraham Maslow came up with his hierarchy of needs, we learned that human beings don't just need food, shelter, and clothing, but are inclined to fulfill other needs such as love and belonging, esteem, and finally self-actualization.

Education is indispensable for achieving a society where the basic human needs are met. It is also a most valuable tool for helping human beings progress, develop, and meet their higher needs. Through education we will learn how to live in relationships and comfort, with a sense of belonging to each other in the community. Through education we learn to achieve; through achievement we gain self-esteem, confidence, and respect for others.

Through education we are able to develop the skills and understanding to live in that highest stage of human life called self-actualization. This is the place in which we understand what life is all about, where we learn about public morality, overcoming prejudice and engaging in spiritual and creative pursuits; pursuits such as the arts, sports, leisure time with others, literature, and other meaningful activities that make us truly human and sets us apart from other animals.

So, we see that education is important in two major ways. First to help us develop our physical, intellectual, and scientific skills in order to create the technology to make life easier to live. Technology reduces the drudgery of human labor. It makes it easier for us to travel, it gives us houses that provide physical comfort and safety, and it helps us develop the best medical treatment to help keep us alive. In other words, it helps us understand our physical environment and how to shape it in order to guarantee our physical existence and make it easier. The second major function of education is to enable human beings to develop critical thinking skills to help them learn how to treat each other and how to enjoy being with each other, and to understand the thoughts and ideas regarding this. The second function of education is to help take us to the truly human level; what Maslow calls self- actualization.

The truly good society which America has been striving to become since 1776 is one in which the conditions have been achieved to enable each American, by working hard, to meet her and his family's physical needs fully and be able to go further in helping develop her and his family's social, spiritual, intellectual, and recreational needs. In other words the Middle-Class American Dream includes a guaranteed trade, technical, or academic education that will enable a person to be able to get a good job with adequate pay that allows him or her to buy a home, to educate her or his children with skills to provide a better life for the next generation, to be able to have transportation, to be able to take a vacation and share time with his family, and to be able to secure a guaranteed income for old-age retirement.

If we look at the American Dream today, we find that this generation of young Americans will be the first who will do worse than their parents in achieving this dream. Matter of fact, the way our government and its leaders have been running the economy, it will be a miracle if many of the young people in America's working middle class will be able to achieve what their parents were able to do from the 1940s until the 1990s.

The reasons that the Middle-Class American Dream is fading and is slowly turning into the American Nightmare are several. First of all, the resurrection in the 1980s of an outdated ideology from the 1890s and the 1920s. An ideology based on the belief that each American should stand mostly on his own, without relying on the government or society to provide opportunity. This ideology, so brilliantly resurrected by Ronald Reagan, convinced many Americans that government mostly gets in our way with its policies of progressive taxation and spending on social programs. Reagan said that government cannot solve our problems because government is the problem. So, Reagan was able to push through large tax cuts that went overwhelmingly to the super wealthy, draining the government of necessary social spending on programs that were meant to teach people how to fish. Programs such as public higher education, job training, Head Start, investment in government research and development of technology, and social safety net programs such as AFDC, that enabled Americans who fell upon hard times to regain their footing after an average of two years of help from the government. Reagan didn't stop there. He went on to deregulate big business and industry and to launch an assault on labor unions and collective bargaining, the beginning of which was his firing of the unionized air-traffic controllers.

When he was governor of California, Ronald Reagan launched a direct attack on the University of California system of free public higher education. At that time, the University of California was the leading and most highly acclaimed public university in the United States. It's academic performance rivaled, and in some cases, outperformed even the Ivy League schools, both in technological and scientific achievement and in literary, philosophical, and humanities achievement. Before Reagan began his onslaught on the UC, California's system of tuition free college and university education made California the fifth largest economy in the world. This system laid the groundwork and training for the high-level groundbreaking achievements in computer technology of Silicon Valley, as well as other industries. California's higher education system became the envy of the rest of the world. Thousands of foreign students selected California as the place to seek their higher education. This not only helped increase California's technical and educational achievements but also promoted goodwill to the United States throughout the world, fostered by future leaders of the world who studied here. These achievements of California's public higher education system included the "soft power" concept developed by Professor Joseph Nye of Harvard. For a nation to have a great amount of soft power in addition to its hard military power, it means that this nation is able to win admiration and influence throughout the world based on the appeal of its ideas, and on its cultural, scientific, and technological strength.

Ronald Reagan Turned America Away from Franklin Roosevelt

In the 2008 presidential election, Barack Obama said that Ronald Reagan was the most influential president we've had since FDR. What he meant by that was that Reagan was influential in successfully turning the U.S. away from the ideals of President Franklin Roosevelt's New Deal. The ideal that government has the basic role of providing opportunity that enables Americans to achieve their right to Life, Liberty and the Pursuit of Happiness. The ideal based on the thinking that if you give a man a fish he eats for a day, if you teach him how to fish, he eats for a lifetime. The Roosevelt ideal that those Americans who suffer hardship, due to no fault of their own, deserve a government that would provide a cushion, that would not only soften the fall, but give them a hand up to help put them on their feet once again. In other words the ideals of FDR and his Democratic Party from the 1930s until the 1970s were based on the idea that government must be a positive instrument that provides equal opportunity for all who are willing to work hard and sacrifice for the future, while enjoying a meaningful life with some leisure time to enjoy with their families. Candidate Barack Obama was correct in 2008: Ronald Reagan was the most influential President in turning the American ship of state and society away from the ideals of FDR to something today based on rugged individualism, immediate gratification, profit-making at all costs, and a lack of understanding on the part of many leaders that we are all in the same boat together. And that for individual Americans to prosper, we must all prosper. This necessitates using our government to guarantee the truths that are self-evident that "all Men are created equal, that they are endowed by their Creator with certain unalienable Rights, that among these are Life, Liberty, and the Pursuit of Happiness--" in the words of the American Declaration of Independence. In order to do this our governmental leaders need to move away from the self-defeating and destructive ideals of Reaganism which have brought us to a downward spiral. By changing our ideas and ideals back toward the direction of FDR and the New Deal, a direction rooted in the U.S. Declaration of Independence and the U.S.

Constitution, we can and will rebuild the American public educational system, rebuild the middle class, and rebuild America itself with its inherent goodness and greatness. We need to go back to the future.

All the scientific evidence says that the best indicator of an American child's success in life beginning in K-12 and in college is dependent primarily on her/his parents' income level. This is a very important finding, because the gap in income ratios has grown tremendously since Ronald Reagan took office. In 1980 when Reagan was elected, the income ratio between the average CEO and the average American worker was 40 to 1. Today, it is 361 to 1 (*Forbes* May 22, 2018). In other words, the average CEO in corporate America is making 361 times the income of the average American worker. What are the chances of the children of average American workers doing as well in education and later in life, as the children of the corporate executive? Not very high. The children of the average worker attend less affluent schools than the children of the wealthy CEOs. The reason for this is that the American public school funding K-12 is still largely based on property taxes. The areas where the wealthiest people live are areas with high property values which bring in many more tax dollars to fund their schools. As noted earlier, areas such as Palo Alto California, the home of Silicon Valley, where per-pupil funding is $16,154 per year (nbcbayarea.com, by Kate Frankel, Apr. 7, 2018). Palo Alto Unified School District was recently ranked the number one public school district in California by *24/7 Wall Street*. Compare that with schools in southeast Los Angeles County in less affluent working middle class and working poor areas such as Long Beach California, where per- pupil funding is $8,756. The academic achievement scores of students in Palo Alto are much higher than the average academic achievement scores in Long Beach. The high school graduation rates are much higher in Palo Alto than in Long Beach. The parents in Palo Alto have far more income than the parents in Long Beach. This helps the Palo Alto parents provide many support programs, such as afterschool academic and arts programs for their children. These parents also have greater free time to help their children with homework or send their children to private tutorial programs. The parents in much of Long Beach have to work overtime and sometimes have two jobs to make ends meet. This does not leave them with extra resources to pay for private tutorial programs and the extra time to spend helping their children with homework and other academic requirements.

The economic disparity between the rich parents and poor parents is very detrimental to the full achievement of quality American education for all. The California Supreme Court ruled in *Serrano* v. *Priest* (1971) that unequal resources per child ends up with unequal educational opportunity per child and is therefore a violation of the equal protection clause of the U.S. Constitution. The Court ordered the California state government to come up with a more equitable funding mechanism. To this day the state's solution has been inadequate, leaving many less affluent school districts in California with a fraction of per-pupil spending than other more affluent districts.

There are three major problems which have weakened the American educational system and made it more difficult for the American middle class to prosper. As the middle class is weakened, America is weakened. The first problem is unequal funding for rich versus poor schools K-12. The second problem is making higher education unaffordable to the middle class and the working poor. The third problem is the dismantling of vocational, trade, technical and apprenticeship programs in high school as we exported American manufacturing jobs.

Let's begin with rich versus poor schools. There are two parts to this problem. First it is the unequal per-pupil funding. School districts in the low and moderate-income areas end up with far less per pupil funding, because funding is still mainly based on property values and property taxes. The second problem is the huge gap in the income of rich parents versus poor parents.

To reiterate, unequal per-pupil funding exists among school districts in a single state such as California. It also exists in average per-pupil funding among the 50 states. After Former Governor Jerry Brown and the California State Legislature recently implemented the Local Control Funding Formula, per-pupil funding in the Long Beach Unified School District is $8,756. In the more affluent Palo Alto Unified School District per-pupil funding is $16,154. The average per-pupil funding in California is $10,291, while the average per-pupil funding in the state of New York was $22,356 in 2016, 90 percent above the national average (U.S. Census Bureau), even though California has many, many more millionaires and billionaires than New York.

The large amount of extra money in more affluent districts allow them to provide up-to-date textbooks, smaller class sizes, higher salaries for the teachers, all the needed supplies including the latest technology, and after school academic, arts and sports enrichment programs. The enhanced positive atmosphere in the affluent school districts provide all the needed equipment and positive ambience that enhances learning and high academic achievement levels for those fortunate students.

The second part of this problem is the major disparity between high income parents and low-income parents. As I noted earlier, from the 1960s to the present day, research has repeatedly shown that in the United States the chance of a student's success in school depends more on his or her parents' income level than on any other factor. The affluent parents' high incomes enable them to privately pay for high quality private preschool, giving their children a head start. Since low and moderate-income parents cannot afford private preschool, their children start out with an early disadvantage. The government- sponsored Head Start preschool program is underfunded and therefore not available to all the low and moderate-income students who need it. The wealthy parents are also able to pay for additional afterschool enrichment activities for their children. Activities such as academic tutoring, theater, dance, and other arts programs which provide a stronger foundation to catapult their affluent children to success from kindergarten through high school and on to college and university. The children of low income and moderate-income parents cannot receive this additional foundation since their parents cannot afford to pay privately for the added academic and arts programs that provide the springboard for success for the children of the wealthy.

The children of low and middle-income parents find themselves at a disadvantage in such a competitive society, with such an unequal public education system. In general, public schools in wealthy areas of our nation such as Beverly Hills, Newport Beach, and Palo Alto in California, as well as wealthy areas such as the upper East side of Manhattan, and parts of Long Island in New York, see a much larger proportion of their high school graduates moving on to highly competitive private and public universities and graduate schools. These children are able to achieve as much and more than what their affluent parents have achieved, both academically and materially. The children of low to moderate income parents graduate from high school at far lower rates, enter college and university at far lower rates and at this time are scheduled to be the first generation of Americans since the Great Depression, who will do worse than their parents in their attempts to enter or remain in the middle class. These are the high school graduates who are finding it difficult and sometimes impossible to afford to go on to college because of the skyrocketing tuition fees and other educational costs due to severe cutbacks in government funding for state colleges and universities in recent decades.

$1.5 Trillion Student Debt and Lower Paying Jobs are Crippling the Younger Generation

The students from low and middle-income families are facing strong headwinds and hurdles in the form of huge tuition and textbook costs, fewer class sections offered, higher cost of living with stagnant wages, more hours of work to support their education, and many other obstacles that keep them from graduating on time. If and when they graduate, the moderate to low income bulk of this generation find it difficult to find employment, since much of the work for which they were qualified, has been outsourced to cheap labor countries in the global South or so-called "Third World". If any of them is fortunate to land a job it will be for less pay than their counterparts 50 years ago, in 1969 (naceweb.org). The starting salary for a college graduate in 2018 averages $50,004 per year (naceweb.org). The starting salary for a college graduate 50 years ago averaged $59,169 per year in today's dollars. In 1969, the average college graduates' income was $9,504. In 2018, it is $50,004, a 500% increase. In 1969, rent for a two-bedroom apartment was $70 a month. In 2018, it is $1,100 a month, a 1600% increase. Gasoline increased from $.20 a gallon to $2.79 a gallon in 2018. You can see why so many American college students today are doing worse than their parents!

The second major problem in American Public Education is the deadly combination of severe cutbacks in state and federal government funding for public higher education. This has resulted in skyrocketing tuition costs and has produced a generation of students which is heavily in debt from borrowing from private banks and the government.

The total U.S. college student debt is $1.5 trillion, larger than the nation's credit card debt. 44,000,000 student borrowers owe $37,172 each on average. Since many of these students have not been able to, or will not be able to find decent paying jobs, there is a real danger that the default rate on this debt will go up rapidly and cause the next financial crash. This may happen before the U.S. economy fully recovers from the Great Recession brought on by the Wall Street debacle of 2008. If it does, we could see America experiencing the second Great Depression in less than 100 years.

Politicians Dismantled California's Master Plan and Tuition-free Education

As the prime example of severe government cutbacks for public higher education, let's look at California. California's Master Plan for Higher Education, put into place by Governor Pat Brown and the state legislature in 1960, established a system of full government funding for California's Community Colleges, California State University, and the University of California. The students in each of these three systems were only asked to pay a small service fee. The student fee at the community colleges was $6 per semester for a full load of classes. The fee at Cal State and UC was around $37 per semester for a full load of classes.

When I started teaching at Foothill College and City College of San Francisco in the San Francisco Bay Area in 1976, my community college students were paying a $6 ($24 in today's dollars) service fee for all 12 units. Not $6 per unit. When Governor **Arnold Schwarzenegger** attended Santa Monica Community College in the early 70s, he paid the $6 service fee for 12 units, a full load of classes. Arnold Schwarzenegger went on to transfer to the University of Wisconsin and to earn his Bachelor's degree, promote his body building skills into a successful business, become a successful actor, and then become governor of California. When Governor **Pete Wilson** attended UC Berkeley law school, he paid a $37 ($204 in today's dollars) service fee for a full load of classes. He graduated with a law degree from UC Berkeley, became a lawyer, a U.S. Senator, and Governor of California. These are examples of Californians who were able to climb the economic and professional ladders and fully live the American Dream, because California's public higher education was tuition free and therefore affordable for Californians of low income, medium income, and high- income background.

This system of tuition free public higher education, that enabled any high school graduate in California to develop her/his full talent and pursue happiness and the American Dream by finishing their higher education, became a beacon to the world. It became the economic engine that powered California to the fifth-largest economy in the world. It also laid the groundwork for the development of advanced manufacturing and high technology, that became the foundation of a solid middle class and made California the truly Golden State.

There were many other examples, not as well-known as Governors Schwarzenegger and Wilson, but just as important in building the large middle class that a successful, dynamic, and democratic California needed. My friend Dr. **Paul Garver** attended and graduated from UCLA medical school in 1979. His service fees were $225 per quarter, in other words $675 per year to attend UCLA's world-class medical school full-time. Dr. Garver graduated with no student loan debt, unlike present California medical graduates, because California practiced the Master Plan for Higher Education at that time.

Political science professor **Mark Roessler** began his higher education at Long Beach City (community) College in 1977. Just as future Governor Arnold Schwarzenegger had done at Santa Monica (community) College a few years earlier, future professor Mark Roessler paid a $6 per semester service fee for a full load of classes
and attended LBCC tuition-free from 1977 until 1980. He then transferred to California State University Long Beach, paid $166 per semester for a full load of classes and graduated with a bachelor's degree in 1985. Mark Roessler earned his master's degree in 1990 and ended up with a $2000 student loan debt for all those years of California higher education.

When I attended the University of North Texas for my bachelor's

138

degrees and master's degree from 1969 to 1975, the tuition fees were around $100 per semester for a full load of classes. That is because the State of Texas, at that time, as did the State of California, heavily subsidized public college and university education, keeping the supply of classes and class sections high, and the cost of tuition low. That is why I could graduate with two Bachelors' degrees, one in Political Science and one in Psychology, and a Master of Political Science degree, as well as doctorate coursework in Political Science and Sociology, all in seven years. I, a middle-class student, emerged from university ready to work, with no student loan debt whatsoever!

The educational experience and its costs were so very different for Pete Wilson, Arnold Schwarzenegger, Paul Garver, Mark Roessler, and me, on the one hand, and students today on the other hand. Take for example **Gilbert Buchanan**, who runs his own small business planning and program management company. He graduated with a bachelor's degree in 1995, and a master's degree in 1998, from the State University of New York, Binghamton, with a $58,000 student loan debt. This huge debt was mainly due to the high tuition of $4,800 per semester at the State University of New York, Binghamton in the 1990s. If Gilbert Buchanan's tuition had been free, as in California in 1960 through 1980, and as in most of Europe today, he would have begun his career debt free. The $1.5 trillion American student loan debt is the next bubble waiting to burst and will rival the burst of the housing bubble driven by predatory lending and Wall Street greed, that caused the Great Recession.

Despite paying down his student debt for fifteen years, Gilbert Buchanan tells me he still has $48,000 remaining to fully pay off the loan. Sallie Mae, which used to be a public agency providing affordable loans to college students, has been privatized. Buchanan blames exorbitant interest rates charged by privatized Sallie Mae for the difficulty that he and millions of other American college students have in paying off their student loans. He calls this "legalized loansharking". We have let the private banks and our corporate bought government put our college students into indentured servitude. For many of them, it will take a lifetime of payments to get close to paying off their loans.

It is private banks that are primarily profiting off the misery of

America's college graduates and college students, today. This was not true of earlier generations of American college and university graduates, such as me, who were able to graduate debt free, just as today's graduates in Germany, France, and most of Europe do. Today, many American college and university graduates are drowning in student loan debt because of Dollar Democracy.

Harrison Wills, a former student at Santa Monica College in California, and recent Student Body President put it very clearly. He said to me:

> A massive generational injustice is occurring right now. The current student debt burden puts students on a perpetual life treadmill and the higher the interest rate and the more they borrow, the faster they have to run just to stay on the machine. At a certain point, we just have to step off and shut the machine down because it's not serving the interest of the public at large. Students have become mere commodities for Wall-Street banks/lenders and privatized educational institutions. The further states cut funding to public higher education, the more students end up borrowing. In other words, when tuition rises, oftentimes so do the profits of private lenders.

For Profit Colleges Grow Through Fraud

A growing player in Dollar Democracy has been the For-Profit Colleges. Although making up just 13% of student enrollment, American For-Profit Colleges account for almost 50% of federal student loan defaults. ("Reining In For-profit Colleges", *LA Times*, March 23, 2014). According to the Center for Responsive Politics, a 2011 National Bureau of Economic Research study found that "for- profit college students are more likely to have higher debt levels, default on their student loans, be unemployed and earn less compared to students that attend non-profits." The Government Accountability Office found in 2010 that fifteen for-profit colleges used deceptive recruiting tactics and encouraged prospective students to falsify their financial aid applications. Some for-profits have also been accused of inflating their graduation rates, misleading prospective students about the cost of their programs, paying for expensive marketing and advertising campaigns with their federal funds, and exaggerating salaries for graduates in certain job areas.

Playing the game of Dollar Democracy, campaign contributions to politicians from the for-profit college industry have been increasing almost every year since 1990.

Top 20 House of Representatives Members Receiving Campaign Money from For-Profit Education 2017-18

Rank	Candidate	Amount
1	Foxx, Virginia (R-NC)	$79,050
2	Murphy, Stephanie (D-FL)	$25,680
3	Hastings, Alcee L (D-FL)	$25,000
4	McSally, Martha (R-AZ)	$24,600
5	Stivers, Steve (R-OH)	$20,400
6	Guthrie, Brett (R-KY)	$19,000
7	Sinema, Kyrsten (D-AZ)	$16,721
8	Biggs, Andy (R-AZ)	$15,300
9	O'Rourke, Beto (D-TX)	$14,095
10	Curbelo, Carlos (R-FL)	$13,500
11	Scott, Bobby (D-VA)	$12,500
11	Coffman, Mike (R-CO)	$12,500
13	Bacon, Donald John (R-NE)	$12,000
14	Barletta, Lou (R-PA)	$11,500
15	Buchanan, Vernon (R-FL)	$10,800
16	Ryan, Paul (R-WI)	$10,550
17	Lesko, Debbie (R-AZ)	$9,900
18	Grothman, Glenn S (R-WI)	$9,700
19	Rokita, Todd (R-IN)	$8,900
20	Mast, Brian (R-FL)	$8,500

Source: Center for Responsive Politics, www.OpenSecrets.org

Table 4-2

Political action committees associated with, and individual employees of the for-profit colleges and universities donated $4.5 million to federal election campaigns in the 2011-2012 election cycle (www.OpenSecrets.org).

The dollars spent by this for-profit higher education industry on lobbying members of Congress, the White House, and the Department of Education skyrocketed from less than $2.7 million in 2009 to $7.4 million in 2010, and almost $12.5 million in 2011. The payoff was about $26 billion in student loans and $10 billion in Pell grants that go to for-profit college students annually with very little to show in terms of repaid loans and employed graduates.

Top 20 For-Profit Education Contributors to Candidates, Parties and Outside Campaign Groups 2017-2018

Contributor	Amount
Thompson Education Center	$710,000
Full Sail	$404,743
Bridgepoint Education	$229,990
Apollo Education Group	$106,054
Career Education Colleges & Universities	$106,000
Pima Medical Institute	$105,005
Medical Education Administrative Services	$83,900
Keiser University	$73,064
Herzing University	$63,295
Adtalem Global Education	$58,938
Capella Education	$47,713
Empower Schools	$46,250
Laureate Education	$44,357
Universal Technical Institute	$30,581
Career Education Corp	$27,687
Rasmussen Inc	$22,750
Leona Group	$22,363
Schoolhouse Development	$21,600
University of Phoenix	$20,795
IXL Learning	$15,695

Contributions to:
Democrats ■
Republicans ■
Liberal Groups ■
Conservative Groups ■

Source: Center for Responsive Politics,   www.OpenSecrets.org

Table 4-3

Today, because of Dollar Democracy, the majority of California and national politicians raise and spend millions of campaign dollars from big corporations, and their wealthy owners. Through an unwritten understanding, without a formal *quid pro quo* (because that would be bribery and illegal), these elected politicians often support the interests of their donors by voting them tax loopholes, tax reductions, and tax subsidies, costing the State and Federal Treasuries billions of dollars in revenue for valuable programs like K-12, College and University public education. These state and federal leaders refuse to close corporate tax loopholes or increase taxes on their super wealthy campaign donor friends and corporations owned by them. Instead, they force students to pay unaffordable tuitions, strangling them with unbearable debt.

Highly credible non-profit, non-partisan organizations such as CALPIRG, USPIRG, and Citizens for Tax Justice have found that tax loopholes, provided by elected politicians to both big corporations and super wealthy individuals, cost the 50 state treasuries billions of dollars and the Federal Treasury almost a trillion dollars in lost revenue annually, billions of which were cut from public education. (ctj.org). These tax loopholes include the stock option loophole, which enabled Facebook to avoid paying income taxes on $1.06 billion in profit they made in 2012. They even received a government subsidy of $429 million that year (ctj.org, February 2014). Apple avoided $15 billion in taxes on billions of dollars it had legally stashed in banks in low-tax havens such as Ireland or no-tax havens like the Cayman Islands. Corporate tax loopholes include the California oil severance tax loophole which costs the state $4 billion annually, because California has no 15% oil severance tax in place. Alaska's is 25%, Louisiana's is 12.5%, and California, the 3rd largest oil producing state has none. A 9% proposed oil severance tax got buried last year in a 2/3 majority Democratic California State Legislature. Just see which legislators and governors, Democratic and Republican took money from Oil Corporations for their campaigns: www.maplight.org or www.followthemoney.org.

If the majority of state and federal politicians were freed from the clutches of their mega-wealthy campaign donors, Public Education and other programs would be fully funded, helping bring Liberty and Justice for All.

Instead, California's Master Plan for Higher Education has been revised many times to allow cutbacks in government funding. The severe cutbacks by the California Legislature and Governor have resulted in skyrocketing tuition fees that have had to be paid by individual students and/or their parents. Cutbacks in government funding resulted in cutbacks in class offerings. This lengthened the graduation time from four years to six years for a Bachelor's degree.

Let's take California Community Colleges. From a $6 service fee for all 15 units in the 1960s and 1970s the fee was raised to $6 per unit in the 1980s. A few years later it was raised to $10 per unit. It was then raised to $13 per unit. A few years later it was again raised to $20 per unit. Once again it was raised to $26 per unit. Then again it was raised to $36 per unit. The most recent increase brought it to $46 per unit a couple of years ago, where it stands today. That is an 8300% educational inflation rate. During the same period, general inflation, which is the cost of all the goods and services, increased by 350%. As noted earlier the cost of tuition at UC rose from $37 for all 15 units in the 1960s to over $7000 per semester in 2019. That is over 1200% educational inflation. The situation was very similar at Cal State. In other words, the increased cost of public higher education in California has skyrocketed a lot faster and higher than the increased cost of everything else. Most outrageously, the incomes of working middle class Americans have stagnated, and their purchasing power has slowly but surely gone downward.

To get California and the rest of the U.S. to change course and make public higher education affordable and truly public once again, the politicians need to close the unnecessary corporate tax loopholes. This would bring in an extra $10 billion per year to the California state budget. If half of this amount were used to fully fund UC, CSU, and the California Community Colleges, they could be made tuition free once again. Or if Congress and the president were to close the unnecessary federal corporate tax loopholes, over half a trillion dollars would be produced in revenues. The tuition costs of all the undergraduate public higher education students in the United States is $62 billion annually. If the corporate tax loopholes were closed, the federal government could pay for tuition free public higher education for all American undergraduate college students nationwide. Then students would be able to compete on their ability and hard work, not on the size of their own or their parents' checkbooks. Closing corporate tax loopholes would also provide money to pay down the federal debt, and have money to invest in infrastructure, small business opportunity, scientific research, tax cuts for the middle class and poor, universal preschool, and quality childcare.

America's Advanced Industrial Competitors Provide Tuition-free Education

All of the advanced industrial countries in the world, including Germany and France, provide very low cost or tuition free public higher education, except the United States. This exception is costing us dearly. Our talent pool is being narrowed to include just the well-off and the super-rich. We may be losing those potential scientists who would have found a cure for AIDS, just because their parents could not afford to send them to college and University.

The third major problem which has weakened the American education system and the middle class is the dismantling of vocational, trade, technical, and apprenticeship programs in high school and community college. This is very critical because, as we dismantled these programs, manufacturing was relocated to the Global South (former "Third World") from the United States. This did not happen in Germany. The German government made the conscious effort to maintain and strengthen Germany's technical, trade, and apprenticeship programs throughout the last several decades. It has produced an industrial policy which calls for a true partnership between the government, business, workers, and the use of scientific technology. Since Ronald Reagan's era, the United States has emphasized only the rights and privileges of Big Business, and through benign neglect and conscious effort, the U.S. has ignored the role of workers and the need for scientific and technological research and coordination through government with the private sector.

Because of this conscious neglect to coordinate the roles of government, business, and workers in economic and social production, the U.S. has fallen behind countries like Germany in its ability to export goods and services produced in the United States. Instead, the extreme free-market capitalism promoted by Reaganites has resulted in government deregulation of big business and has encouraged big business to outsource American manufacturing. Today manufacturing accounts for only 9% of the American economy, down from 33% in the 1950s. Instead of encouraging and training highly skilled American workers and technologists to produce 21st century products in the United States for global export, the U.S. government, heavily influenced by large corporations, has subsidized the big corporations' export of American manufacturing jobs.

Furthermore, the U.S. government has created corporate tax loopholes for big business, which results in a zero income tax for the largest American corporations. (see Table 2-1) These large corporations are no longer helping to pay for the training of highly skilled American workers. The large multinational corporations based in the U.S. are shirking their responsibility for creating and keeping solid high paying jobs in the U.S., as they are shirking their responsibility for helping train and educate American workers for important jobs that would pay well. These are jobs in the vocational, technical, and trade fields, which would include solar and wind power, air-conditioning and heating technology, less polluting aircraft production and maintenance, the latest green electric car automotive technology and maintenance, wood making in carpentry and cabinet making, computer programming and computer science, interior design which includes green buildings, welding, auto body, and audio production. Many of these jobs pay solid middle-class wages of between $44,000 and $79,000 a year.

It's a crying shame that many elected officials in the U.S. government have aided and abetted in the downsizing of the American high-tech and manufacturing export economy. Companies such as Microsoft have opened up software parks in India where they hire Indian software engineers for a quarter of the wage that would be paid to well-trained American software engineers. Apple, using technology developed in the United States by highly skilled American technicians and scientists, has been producing its latest expensive products such as

146

the iPhone and the iPad in China, using extremely low wage workers. These expensive products are imported back to the U.S. and sold for huge profits to American and global consumers. U.S. political leaders need to find a way to discourage the wholesale export of these good jobs through corporate subsidies. American government policy should encourage these large companies to bring back some of these jobs and to create new jobs, using new technologies and fully trained American workers in the United States. Congress and the president need to use tax and regulatory incentives, the carrot and the stick, to get these huge corporations to do the right thing and help to rebuild the American middle class, with the Green New Deal, and assist other countries to do so, as China is doing.

In order to accomplish the above we must reinstate strengthened and modernized vocational, trade, and green technology programs in American high schools as well as in American community colleges. We can look at the German example. The Federal Republic of Germany is a country with an excellent economy today: 5.4% unemployment, billions of dollars in trade surpluses, and a technology juggernaut in specific technologies such as machine tools, automobiles, electronics, and chemicals, and Green Technology such as solar, wind, and tide power.

Germany's Industrial Policy Is Non-existent in the U.S.

This didn't happen out of accident. The German people had reached a consensus that their government has an important role to play in promoting an industrial policy that strengthens the overall economy and generates huge amounts of exports. The first thing the government has done is to ensure that every German young person will be able to develop their talent or talents fully, will be respected for it, and paid very well for using their talent to contribute to the economy. The auto mechanics, steelworkers, automotive technicians, engineers, architects, construction workers, solar and wind power workers, janitors, as well as managers and corporate CEOs are all viewed as having equal human dignity and as being necessary for the well-being, and productivity of the German economy and society. Even the pay scales reflect this philosophy.

Not only are German semiskilled and skilled workers guaranteed a tuition free education, but they are well paid once they serve their apprenticeships and finish their trade and technical training. These workers are paid 1 1/2 times the salaries of their American counterparts. They have no debt accumulated during their education.

Their salaries are more than enough to pay for a decent standard of living. Universal healthcare coverage is guaranteed to them and their families. Five weeks of paid vacation are guaranteed by law to them. One year of paid parental leave to bond with their newly born infant is guaranteed to them. These are some of the benefits that flow to the working middle class in Germany due to government's industrial policy. Professionals who come out of engineering school, medical school, managerial school, scientific academy and university, are all paid approximately 1 1/2 times the income of their American counterparts. On the other hand, German CEOs of large corporations take home approximately 1/2 to 2/3 the after-tax income of their American counterparts. Workers through their unions get seats at the management table by electing their representatives to help make major decisions regarding workplace and even some investment decisions, on an ongoing basis.

Vocational and Technical Education Was Dismantled in the U.S.

Instead of moving in this direction, the United States, and California in particular, has moved in the opposite direction. For example, Long Beach City College (LBCC) which is a California community college, recently saw its Board of Trustees vote to dismantle 10 vocational education programs in the areas of aviation maintenance, audio production, heating and air-conditioning technology, real estate, carpentry, interior design, including green buildings and ecological renovations, welding, and auto body programs. There was talk of LBCC dismantling its diagnostic imaging program after one year. These programs were very successful in training Californians for solid middle-class jobs. In fact, the aircraft maintenance program and the air-conditioning and refrigeration heating program were established to help many veterans starting with World War II to gain highly skilled solidly middle-class jobs. Thousands of them did from the 1940s until the 2000s.

My friend **Fred Cruz**, an 87- year-old World War II veteran, is a prime example. When he returned from serving in World War II and the Korean War, he was granted training in Long Beach City College's air-conditioning and heating program in which he earned a certificate and went to work. This allowed him to earn a middle class living, buy a home, raise a family, and see his children do better than what even he did economically. Educational Opportunity, an important part of the Middle-Class Dream, has been taken away from many in the current generation of Californians because of budget and program cuts. The principle reason is that politicians vote for corporate tax loopholes for special interests, who help fund their campaigns. After giving away part of the public treasury, these very same politicians cry that there is no money in the treasury and beg our students to understand why their future has been curtailed. This has got to stop. It has got to be reversed, and it can be changed. Part of the solution is to move away from Dollar Democracy and base our election system on Clean Elections campaigns and Clean Money funding, as pioneered by the States of Maine and Arizona. We will examine this system in detail in Chapter 10 of this book.

CHAPTER 5

HEALTH CARE: BANDAGING THE HEALTH CARE SYSTEM WITHOUT MEDICARE FOR ALL

"... the founders proclaimed that a major role for constitutional government is to promote the general welfare. The word 'welfare' means well-being."
--Peter Mathews

Today, in 2019, 44 million Americans have no health insurance, eight out of ten of these are workers or their dependents. Another 38 million have inadequate health insurance coverage! In the two years of the Trump presidency (2017-2018), the rate of Americans without any health insurance coverage has risen from 10.9 percent to 13.7 percent: an additional 7 million more people, mostly women, young adults, and low-income Americans are now without health insurance. (news.gallup.com, by Dan Witters, Jan. 23, 2019).

Healthcare is a fundamental human right to be guaranteed to all. It is not a privilege that has to be earned by the individual. The American Declaration of Independence states, "We hold these truths to be self-evident that all Men are created equal, that they are endowed by their Creator with certain unalienable Rights, that among these are Life, Liberty and the pursuit of Happiness.--" It goes on to say that governments are instituted among men in order to secure these unalienable Natural Rights. In other words, the main role of government is to guarantee these Natural Rights, with which we humans are born.

From here it's easy to see that without guaranteed health care for all, our very Natural Rights of Life, Liberty, and the pursuit of Happiness are in danger. Without guaranteed healthcare through which we can get treated when we are sick or in danger of dying, we will not live healthy, fulfilling lives, and we will not be able to pursue our Happiness (our full human potential and fulfillment). In fact, we might not only remain sick, but without healthcare we may actually die prematurely. In the preamble to the U.S. Constitution there is reference to the role of government in promoting the general Welfare (wellbeing) of the people. The Constitution states "We the People of the United States, in Order to form a more perfect Union, establish Justice, insure domestic Tranquility, provide for the common defense, promote the general Welfare, and secure the Blessings of Liberty to ourselves and our Posterity, do ordain and establish this Constitution of the United States of America."

In writing this, the founders proclaimed that a major role for constitutional government is to promote the general welfare. The word "welfare" means well-being. To promote the general well-being means the well-being of all the people in our society. What a righteous command! This command clearly implies that healthcare is absolutely necessary for promoting the well-being of the individual and the general well-being of the society. It doesn't take a rocket scientist to figure out that if someone has tuberculosis, especially if he happens to be the chef in the restaurant in which we are dining, he needs to be treated immediately. People with a sense of ethics would say this chef should be treated and cured of his TB, because it is the humane thing to do, and as importantly, it is the practical, sensible thing to do. We don't want to be infected and we don't want others to be infected by this chef with tuberculosis.

The United States of America is the only advanced industrialized nation without universal healthcare to cover all of its people when they get sick. Before the Affordable Care Act (Obamacare) became law in 2010 and began expanding coverage, 54 million Americans had no health insurance (*Huffington Post*, August 14, 2014). In fact, by May 2015, 16.4 million Americans had gained health care coverage from 2014 to 2015 due to Obamacare (Affordable Care Act) (obamacarefacts.com). In 2015, that still left 37.6 million Americans with no health insurance, no health coverage when they get sick (aspe.hhs.gov). New Gallup Polls survey show that health coverage has eroded because of Trump Administration policies. The uninsured rate for adults increased by 1.3 percentage points.

During 2018 alone, there were more than 3 million more people without health insurance.

Countries such as Canada, France, Great Britain, Germany, Japan, and Italy all have universal healthcare coverage while using different systems of delivery. Canada uses a single-payer universal health insurance system. Great Britain uses a national health system which is funded by the government and employs doctors, nurses and other healthcare professionals. Germany uses primarily an employer-based health insurance system, supplemented by government subsidies. Unlike in these countries, even if you have "full health insurance coverage" in the U.S., you may be denied the health care you need!

Shima Andre, who has hepatitis C, was denied critical care although she has Anthem Blue Cross health insurance. Her doctor recommended Harvoni, which "cures 99 percent of patients within 12 weeks." ("Sick and Denied a Cure", Susan Abram, *Press Telegram,* June 2015). Anthem Blue Cross says it will not pay for the medication until Andre is at Stage 3 of severity. By that time, she will be too sick "to work as a book editor, her liver will develop scar tissue and cirrhosis, and she may have to consider an organ transplant." (Susan Abram, *Press Telegram*). It does not have to be this way.

In All Advanced Countries, Except the U.S., Health Care and Dental Care Are Human Rights Guaranteed to All, Lowering Production Costs

Every one of the advanced industrial nations views full healthcare coverage, including comprehensive dental care, as a human right and a necessity, not an optional privilege that individuals have to earn on their own. Healthy teeth and gums are indispensable for a healthy body. Digestion begins in the mouth and promotes the full absorption of the nutrients in our food, strengthening our bodies, minds, and immune systems. This keeps us strong and healthy. Also, unhealthy teeth left untreated will cause infection, and in some cases, even death. That is why the advanced industrialized countries include the guarantee of universal dental care in their comprehensive health care systems. We Americans must do the same. Brett Covey knows this only too well.

About three years ago, due to a hit and run car accident while riding his bike, **Brett Covey** developed complications with the teeth in his upper jaw bone, and the bone itself. According to Brett, after two years, his jaw and teeth started hurting. The pain suddenly became worse, accompanied by severe swelling and flu-like symptoms.

Brett tried to see the dentist right away, but was told that his dental plan had elapsed, even though he was under the assumption that he had full dental coverage through "Medi-Medi" (Medicare--Medi-Cal) coverage. Sadly, his coverage had lapsed without him knowing that he had to re-register in 2014 for the dental portion of his coverage, although the medical portion carried on smoothly during the Affordable Care Act (Obamacare) transition.

At this point, Brett said his flu-like symptoms had become a full-fledged fever of 101 degrees. Brett's father drove him to the nearest hospital emergency room where he was diagnosed, treated and stabilized for an acute infection in his teeth/jaw area. Brett said, "the emergency room doctor explained that they don't treat dental problems and that I must see a dentist immediately, within three days." Brett proceeded to say,

> It actually took me a week to get an appointment lined up with a dentist outside my plan, and the antibiotics and pain medication they had given me were meant only to last a few days. In fact, the antibiotics worked so well, I didn't need the pain medication at all after the first day's treatment. I was examined by the dentist which I had to pay out of my own pocket, who explained to me the seriousness of this type of infection. The dentist told me there was a clear chance that if I let this infection persist over only a short period of time, it could become septic and literally kill me. I find it both irritating and ironic that the medical room doctors and nurses insisted that, aside from the

infection, the problem with my tooth was not a medical problem.

Brett would not have suffered any of these problems in treatment if we had guaranteed Universal Dental Care for all Americans, as other advanced nations have for their people, and as members of the U.S. Congress have, paid for by us taxpayers.

The practical benefits of these universal health care systems are clearly reflected in statistics regarding average life expectancy, rates of infant mortality, rates of communicable diseases, and other indicators of the efficiency and health of the healthcare systems in each of these countries. In the United States today we have the shortest average life expectancy, highest rates of infant mortality, and greater rates of communicable diseases and preventable illnesses than any of the other countries with healthcare systems that cover all of their people, and in many cases cover even visitors and guests. Also, the per capita cost of healthcare in the United States is one and a half times to two times that of the advanced industrialized countries with universal healthcare in place. Also, the cost of producing the same automobile in Canada is $1,000 less than producing it in the United States, because the Canadian government single-payer universal health insurance system, Canadian Medicare, pays for the auto workers' health coverage, saving the auto company the cost. In the U.S. the auto company has to pick up the tab and passes it on to the consumer in a higher priced automobile.

In the U.S. approximately one third of our healthcare is covered through government programs such as Medi-Cal, Medicaid, and Medicare. One half of Americans are covered by employer-based private health insurance. About 18%, or about 54 million Americans were without health insurance coverage before the Affordable Care Act ("Obamacare") kicked in (*Huffington Post*, August 14, 2014). Even after Obamacare was fully implemented, 20 million Americans, about 7%, did not have health insurance coverage. Even with the implementation of Obamacare, those who are covered by health insurance have copayments and deductibles to meet when they get sick and are treated.

Many Americans who became severely ill with diseases such as cancer found that their expensive treatments required them to meet their

154

co-payments of approximately $20,000-$30,000 out of their own pocket. In some cases, these people lost their life savings, lost their homes, and destroyed their credit, because they could not afford to make the co-payments, especially if they were recovering from such a dreaded disease and could not work. This problem has not gone away in spite of Obamacare. You will meet some of these people in this chapter. People whose lives were shattered or negatively altered because of the lack of a universal comprehensive healthcare system in the United States. President Trump eliminated Obamacare's individual mandate, and left Obamacare with the same problems it already had.

Many people have begun to wonder how this situation came about? Why don't Congress and the president fix this problem completely? The short answer is Dollar Democracy, which produces Liberty and Justice and Health Care for some. Campaign contributions and massive lobbying money spent by wealthy healthcare industry special interests, such as the pharmaceutical corporations, the health insurance corporations, and some of the HMO corporations, to influence members of Congress and to block comprehensive health care reform legislation, have been major obstacles to implementing a universal comprehensive healthcare system in the United States. Too many of these special interests are making millions of dollars in profit off of the current privately run, inefficient, and non-comprehensive healthcare system. They want to preserve the system that benefits themselves and not the American public.

The Affordable Care Act (Obamacare): A Small Step in the Right Direction, Without Single-payer Medicare for All

President Barack Obama was elected overwhelmingly in 2008 by making universal healthcare a major part of his campaign platform. The President never attempted to fight for a truly universal, single-payer, Medicare for All system, which would have been more efficient and easier to explain to the public; why not? Because he thought that he could never get it through Congress, many of whose members' campaigns are heavily funded by the special interests of the Health Care Industry: Big

Pharmaceuticals, Health Maintenance Organizations (HMOs), Private Hospitals, and private Health Insurance Corporations, all of whom oppose a single-payer system such as the non-profit Canadian Medicare for All System and our own Medicare System.

Instead, his plan was to work with the existing healthcare providers, regulate them, and add a few features, all of which was done to provide health coverage to the majority of the uncovered 54 million Americans. As noted earlier, this so-called Obamacare plan was not totally comprehensive and still allows 20 million Americans to remain uncovered, even after the plan is fully implemented. The Obamacare plan insisted that no health insurance company could deny any American coverage based on a pre-existing condition. It also guarantees that young people in college could remain on their parents' insurance until the age of 26, and not suffer dropped coverage at the age of 21. The Obamacare plan also requires that 80% of a health insurance company's revenues must be spent on care, and only a maximum of 20% can be spent on overhead costs including profits. But all insurers have to do to make more in profit is to raise their premiums on the consumer. And they are doing just that. Insurance premiums are increasing 5% per year under Obamacare, which is three times the cost of living. This is unsustainable and is preventing some employers from hiring workers full time. Although, before Obamacare, healthcare costs were rising by 12% per year. By 2019, health care inflation had risen to 8% to 10% per year. Obamacare could have avoided many of these problems and would have been much more effective if the President had been able to get Congress to pass a single-payer, Medicare for All system, such as Canada's. He tried to obtain a "public option" feature in his plan, which was a type of single-payer alternative that consumers could choose if they were not satisfied with their private insurance. This public option was defeated by health insurance industry lobbyists who had bought key members of Congress with campaign contributions. Today, Senator Bernie Sanders and Congresswoman Alexandria Ocasio-Cortez are leading sponsors of Medicare for All.

Obamacare required that all Americans who are working must buy health insurance if they are uninsured. Government promised to subsidize the cost of buying this private insurance if the individual's or family's income was moderate or low. For those who were uninsured, the individual mandate forced them to purchase private insurance for themselves or be fined by the government. Obamacare also mandated that medium to large businesses must pay for their employees' health insurance premiums (this mandate was delayed for a while). The Obamacare plan also established health exchanges. Each of the 50 states were required to establish its own health exchange system which would list several healthcare companies with comparative pricing. Consumers could go on the Internet, look up the health exchange listing and decide which of these companies would be most affordable and appropriate for the consumer's need. If the governors of several states refused to establish health exchanges as many Republican (Red State) governors have, then the federal government would establish health exchanges and provide this information to the prospective consumer. The argument here was that the health exchange listings would create competition among private health insurers and provide the best service for the lowest price.

Supporters claimed that this is a model based on free markets and competition that would be similar to shopping for shoes or automobiles. The consumer would go to the shoe store, select the most desirable pair of shoes at the most desirable price from among many, and buy the shoes on the spot. In this case at least, the shopper could make a rational choice, and government deregulation of the private economy has been the mantra. However, when shopping for health care, the choice is more restricted: Most employer-based health plans allow the consumer to change plans only once a year, and the consumer may already be sick while shopping for health insurance.

In the U.S. health care system, the principle of the Invisible Hand of the market place has created the most expensive, inefficient, price gouging, top-heavy, system that leaves millions without even minimal health coverage. It has left 54 million Americans without health insurance coverage. It has caused untold misery among them and for them. And yet the current American system, dominated by private health insurance, costs 1 1/2 times and more per person than the universal healthcare systems of the other advanced Western industrial democracies, and Japan. These other countries insure all of their residents and citizens at 1/2 to 2/3 the cost per person as the American system.

These include, as mentioned earlier, the Canadian health care system which relies primarily on a single-payer, nonprofit, government Medicare for All insurance. Canadians also have an option of buying private health insurance. Very few do because the government system of health insurance is so efficient and humane. Doctors and nurses and other health care providers are private professional entrepreneurs. They have associations and unions that bargain with the government Medicare insurance company for fee-for-service payment. Contracts are negotiated on an annual basis in many Canadian provinces. After the patient is treated, the doctor bills Medicare and is paid fully and directly by it. The Medicare for All system is funded by the Canadian federal government and administered and delivered by the Canadian provincial governments. In many provinces there are no co-payments and no deductibles. You can see a doctor quickly and in time. Because under Canadian Medicare for All, and American Medicare for the elderly, the systems are run on a nonprofit basis, the overhead costs average between 3% and 5%, and there are no private stockholders and CEOs sucking up the healthcare dollar in the form of dividends and profits and million-dollar CEO incomes. In the for-profit American health care system, the overhead costs are 20%, most of which goes to private profits, dividends, and millions of dollars in CEO salaries.

In Great Britain the health care system is called the National Health Service or NHS. It is a system that was implemented by the Labour Party with its victory in 1948. It is a government owned and run system in which the hospitals, doctors and nurses, and other health care workers are generally employed by the government and paid by the government. British patients can get treated fully by the National Health Service. Prescription drugs cost the British patient a $10 flat fee, regardless of the quantity or expense of production.

The universal health care systems in all of these Western industrialized countries and Japan use some combination of public insurance or public ownership and administration of the actual healthcare. France, whose system is ranked number one by the World Health Organization, even provides doctors who make house calls to the patient's home. The one common denominator of all the systems is the underlying value and belief that health care is a human right to be guaranteed to all, not a private privilege to be earned individually. All of these systems place the delivery of needed care above the ability of private individuals and corporations to make a profit off of sick people!

Once a Leader In Healthcare and Education, the U.S. Now Ranks 27th in the World

As the Institute for Health Metrics and Evaluation (IHME) noted in the *Business Insider*:

> US investments in healthcare and education haven't changed much in the last three decades — and it's putting the country far behind its peers, according to a new study from the Institute for Health Metrics and Evaluation (IHME) at the University of Washington. After ranking countries based on their levels of education and health, the study found that the US ranked 27th in the world on these metrics as of 2016, behind a host of top-ranking Nordic countries, including Finland, Iceland, Denmark, and the Netherlands.

> This comes as little surprise, given that healthcare services in these countries are universal and publicly funded. The US, by contrast, is one of the few developed nations that lacks universal healthcare, according to *The Atlantic*.

> When it comes to education, the nation fares even worse. The latest findings from the Pew Research Center have the US in 38th place out of 71 countries when it come to math scores and 24th place when it comes to science.

(*Business Insider,* September 27, 2018, "The U.S. Was Once a Leader In Healthcare and Education – Now It Ranks 27th In the World", by Aria Bendix)

In 1990, the U.S. ranked 6th in the world in education and health, that's 21 positions higher than now. One reason for the U.S. decline in position is the decline in U.S. spending on k-12 education. According to *U.S. News,* spending fell by 3% from 2010 to 2014 despite a population increase of 1%. In contrast, in developed nations such as the U.K. and Portugal, from 2008 to 2014, education spending rose by more than 25%. It's not just the spending level, but how the money is spent: The advanced nations spend money more equitably nationwide. As I noted earlier in this chapter, the gap in American per pupil spending among public school districts in the U.S., and among the states in the U.S. is gigantic. As in education, there is a tremendous gap in the quality and amount of spending on healthcare between well-off and poor Americans.

The glaring difference between the universal comprehensive healthcare systems of Europe, Canada, New Zealand, Australia, and Japan, and the lack of comprehensive healthcare in the United States is directly tied to the difference in the campaign and election systems of many of those countries and the campaign and election system in the United States. I will first speak in generalities and then will offer specific details.

In the American system of elections, private financing of campaigns has been legalized and legitimized. Candidates for public office raise huge amounts of money from private donors which are used for advertising to win the most number of votes. These private donors are mostly super wealthy individuals and well-heeled, well-funded organized groups such as big business corporations, labor unions, and professional interest groups made up of doctors, dentists, and lawyers. One study has revealed that in a typical presidential election year the top one half of one percent of the U.S. population, made up of super wealthy individuals and organizations, provide 80% of the campaign funding to national candidates. The top 12% provide almost 100% of the campaign funding to national candidates. According to www.opensecrets.org, in the 2016 presidential election, approximately $6.5 billion was raised and spent on behalf of, and directly by, the national presidential and congressional campaigns. In fact, the healthcare industry alone raised and spent and donated $260 million in the 2012 national elections. This money was not given out of the goodness of their heart. This money is considered an investment by these private companies. The return on this investment comes in the form of federal laws and policies which guarantee that these companies will make hundreds of billions of dollars in profit in the privately run and designed healthcare system already in place. The $6.5 billion was a record sum. It was a glaring example of Dollar Democracy, in which private interests finance public elections and in return gain favorable treatment for themselves, most of the time, from the elected officials that they support. The majority of elected officials either ignore the needs of the public interest or are actively undermining the public interest in favor of their private special interest donors.

The same phenomenon exists at the state level and at the local level of American government. The private financing of American elections has brought us Dollar Democracy, one whose policies favor private special interests and ignore or suppress the public interest, "the general Welfare" as our Constitution calls it. As this book points out, key policies that would promote the general welfare or well-being of the American people, are neglected while policies that favor the few wealthy interests are implemented to the detriment of a strong, vibrant, technically advanced, humanely based, and democratic American society. A society based on equal opportunity for all, has become a society based on opportunity for some, the well-off and wealthy few. Later in the book, we will look at ways in which we can turn America around in its true direction.

In many of the European democracies, election campaigns are based primarily on information provided to the public through mass media debates and discussions by the various candidates and political party representatives. Information is also carried by highly organized local parties and their representatives, including the youth wings, to the general public during and between election time. The representative listens to the viewpoints of members of the public in door-to-door face encounters. Each of the several parties in each of these countries is highly organized around a clearly defined set of ideas. These ideas and the issue positions coming from them are clearly understood by the voters at election time. The electorates are highly educated on political and social matters starting in high school and earlier. They are also educated by volunteers and other representatives of the various parties throughout the year, including in door-to-door efforts. Because of this and because the electoral districts are much smaller in population than American congressional districts, it is possible for the candidate and her or his party backers to conduct extensive grassroots and door-to-door campaigns, meeting the voters directly. Even though in some of those European countries political parties do receive financing from groups such as labor unions and businesses, the primary way of winning votes is not through direct mail or private television commercials, but instead through discussion and debate free of charge on television and radio, as well as through door-to-door campaigning, and massive outdoor political rallies and town hall meetings. In fact, in some of the European democracies, it is illegal for any candidates who run for public office to buy private television ads. In the United States, candidates for national and state office rely on private television ads, targeted mailing, signs and posters, and sophisticated polling data which tells the campaign what message to aim at which set of voters. All of this is paid for by private campaign contributions provided by wealthy private donors and organizations.

In addition to the above differences in the American and European election systems, in the American system big money is raised from wealthy private special interests far more than in European election campaigns. These wealthy special interest donors such as private health insurance companies, private Health Maintenance Organizations (HMOs), private hospitals, and private medical practitioners and their associations, have been able to block, and now weaken, any universal comprehensive healthcare system that the U.S. could have implemented. Because of the nature of many of the European countries' election and campaign finance systems, those countries were able to implement universal, comprehensive, affordable, and efficient healthcare systems and deliveries for their populations. It is time to overcome Dollar Democracy with Real Democracy by implementing campaign finance reform in the United States. There have been successful examples at the state level led by states such as Maine and Arizona. It is called Clean Money Elections: a type of voluntary public financing system of state elections in those states. These systems will be discussed in greater detail in the final chapter of this book.

U.S. HEALTH CARE RANKS LAST AMONG WEALTHY COUNTRIES

A recent international study compared 11 nations on health care quality, access, efficiency, and equity, as well as indicators of healthy lives such as infant mortality.

Overall Health Care Ranking

Source: K.Davis, K.Stremikis, D.Squires, and C.Schoen, *Mirror, Mirror on the Wall: How the Performance of the U.S. Heath Care System Compares Internationally, 2014 Update*, The Commonwealth Fund, June 2014

Graph 5-1 | U.S. Healthcare Ranks Last

The United States ranks last in health care system performance among the 11 countries included in this study (Graph 5-2). The U.S. ranks last in Access, Equity, and Health Care Outcomes, and next to last in

Administrative Efficiency, as reported by patients and providers.

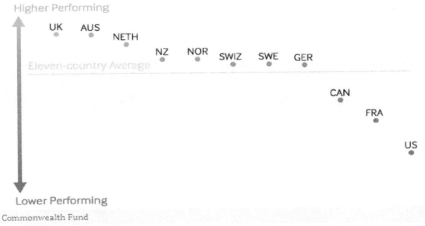

Higher Performing

UK   AUS

NETH

NZ   NOR   SWIZ   SWE   GER

Eleven-country Average

CAN

FRA

US

Lower Performing

Commonwealth Fund

(https://interactives.commonwealthfund.org/2017/july/mirror-mirror/)
Graph 5-2 | Healthcare Ranking Among 11 Nations |
Graph/Commonwealthfund.org

Medicare for All Act of 2019 is Being Blocked in the House by $43 Million in Campaign Contributions to 130 Democrats from Big Pharma and Insurance Lobbyists

Representative Pramila Jayapal (D-Washington) recently introduced the Medicare for All Act of 2019 (H.R. 1384) which would guarantee healthcare for all Americans. Jayapal's bill calls for a transition from the current system to her single-payer universal plan in two years. Jayapal's plan has no emergency room co-pays, no fees for doctor's visits, and covers long-term care and nursing services.

"We will be pushing it as hard as we can and as fast as we can," Rep. Jayapal said. "Enough nibbling around the edges. We really need to transform the system." ("Pharma & Insurance Gave $43M to the 130 House Democrats Not Backing Medicare for All", by Carl Gibson, healthoverprofits.org, March 7, 2019).

Gibson provides the list of the 130 Democrats who received over

$43 million from Big Pharma and health insurers for their campaigns, and are not co-sponsoring Medicare for All. House Republicans, who receive the majority of campaign money from Big Pharma and private health insurance companies, overwhelmingly oppose Single-Payer Medicare for All. 106 Democrats are co-sponsoring Jayapal's Medicare for All Act of 2019. Not one House Republican is co-sponsoring Representative Jayapal's Medicare for All Act.

As Gibson points out:

> Additionally, not one member of House Democrats' leadership has co-sponsored the (Medicare for All) bill. House Speaker Nancy Pelosi (D-California), House Majority Leader Steny Hoyer (D-Maryland), House Majority Whip Jim Clyburn (D-South Carolina), and House Democratic Caucus chairman Hakeem Jeffries (D-New York) have all received generous donations from pharma and insurance (Hoyer alone received more than $2.5 million in career donations) throughout their Congressional careers ("Pharma & Insurance Gave $43M to the 130 House Democrats Not Backing Medicare for All", by Carl Gibson, healthoverprofits.org, March 7, 2019).

Dollar Democracy is a bi-partisan phenomenon!

CHAPTER 6

DESTROYING OUR ENVIRONMENT FOR IMMEDIATE PROFITS

"We do not inherit the Earth from our ancestors; We borrow it from our children."

--Chief Seattle

Humankind has lost the ancient wisdom that acknowledged that we humans are part of the natural environment. If we do not preserve and sustain our natural environment we will not be able to preserve and sustain ourselves. Dollar Democracy has caused the dangerous destruction of critical aspects of our environment: our air, water, and soil. Let's first examine air pollution in the United States.

Air Pollution

Ninety percent of air pollution is produced by two major sources: automobiles and trucks burning fossil fuels, and power plants burning fossil fuels such as coal, natural gas, and oil. In the 2016 Presidential elections, the coal, oil and gas industry spent $115,901,054 on federal candidates. This includes $49,712,771 from individuals, $17,624,005 from Political Action Committees (PACs), and $48,564,278 from soft/outside money (www. open secrets.org). In the 2018 midterm congressional elections alone, coal, oil and gas spent $90,118,001. As a result, this fossil fuel industry maintains control and influence over policies passed by Congress and the President. The fossil fuel energy industry has been very influential in blocking and weakening regulations on their emissions. For example, when leading environmentalists argued

166

decades ago that the corporate average fuel efficiency, or CAFE standards, must be increased significantly as soon as possible, presidents and Congress took their own sweet time in increasing the CAFE standards, which means the average miles per gallon of gas burned by all vehicles in the fleet. The George W. Bush administration raised the standards by only a couple of miles per gallon. President Obama raised the standard to 54.5 miles per gallon by 2025. President Trump has called for a lower standard, freezing it at the 2021 level. On August 2, 2018, the Trump Administration announced it would allow automakers to keep fuel efficiency standards at 36.9 miles per gallon. It rescinds the Obama administration's standard of 54.5 miles per gallon. It would also revoke states' rights to set their own, more stringent standards. It would increase U.S. oil consumption by half a million barrels per day, increasing greenhouse-gas emissions. (TheBalance.com, Kimberly Amadeo, Feb. 29, 2019).

Trump received $2,675,000 from oil, gas and coal corporations for his inauguration: Chevron, Exxon, BP, Murray Energy, Citgo Petroleum, and Energy Transfer Partners, developer of the Dakota Access pipeline, and fracking company Continental Resources. In the 2016 Presidential election, Trump received $2,000,000 from coal, oil and gas interests. It's no wonder that President Trump has withdrawn the U.S. from the Paris Climate Accord to fight Climate Change. Trump has recently boasted that the U.S. has become the number one producer of oil and natural gas in the world.

Only when government forced the automobile and energy industries to adhere to significant CAFE standards did they begin to comply. Now, automobile producers for the U.S. market have applied new technologies to get the gasoline engines to produce far more miles per gallon than before. Many foreign and U.S. based auto companies that sell cars in the U.S. are also producing hybrid gasoline electric cars. These hybrid cars are capable of getting even better gas mileage than the high-technology pure gasoline engine. The newest of these hybrid cars are called plug-in electric extended hybrids. The hybrids switch back and forth between their electric engine and their gasoline engine. The extended hybrids also provide a longer range of electric- only driving. The Chevy Volt, the Ford C Max, and Toyota Pruis extended hybrids provide dozens of miles of electric only driving, and when this runs out, their gas-powered generators automatically switch on to charge the battery to power the engine.

The latest development in much cleaner automobile technology is the all-electric car. By 1900, electric cars accounted for around a third of all vehicles on the road (energy.gov, Sept. 15, 2014). But because of the power and political influence of the fossil fuel oil industry, and the auto manufacturing industry, electric cars were put on the shelf in America.

In contrast, the Japanese government's Ministry of Economy, Trade and Industry (METI), hired cutting-edge engineers and scientists, and paid them to research how electric engines could be combined with gasoline engines in the same car to produce a 21st Century automobile. The pioneers in this area were the Toyota Prius and Honda Insight. The Japanese government subsidized the building and export of these cars by Japanese auto companies. This is called "Industrial Policy." America produced early electric cars, but the Japanese corporations, supported by their government reinvented the early American electric car, whose battery had a very short range. They made the new Japanese hybrid electric cars totally viable, producing 50 miles per gallon or more, without the need to recharge them, since the gasoline engine and regenerative braking system recharge the battery automatically. Chinese manufacturers, with support from the Chinese government are producing electric cars and busses in China and around the world.

In 1992, when he visited my U.S. Government class at Cypress College, I asked Republican Congressman Steve Horn why the U.S. government does not have a comprehensive industrial policy, such as the Japanese, German, and Chinese governments do. He answered: "We don't believe in this. We are a free enterprise system in which private entrepreneurs should be left alone without governmental involvement in the production process." He argued, contrary to evidence, that this would result in a much more innovative production process and a more efficient and dynamic economy. Not only have the hybrid electric cars and fully electric cars reduced our consumption of fossil fuels that pollute our air, hurt our lungs, and produce "global warming" (climate change, climate disruption), but they have actually reduced fossil fuel emissions of carbon dioxide and other pollutants.

In order to make electric cars a viable option in the United States we need to find a way to extend the battery range from the current average of 110 miles per charge, to at least 300 miles per charge. Tesla has done this. Tesla, an American based company building all its automobiles almost entirely in the U.S., had received some government support, now reduced by the Trump administration: the electric vehicle subsidy was cut in half to $3,750 from $7,500 (finance.yahoo.com). We also need to build an infrastructure of charging stations on freeways and city roads as well as charging ports in parking places, as some other pioneering countries such as Denmark have begun doing. Denmark has gone one step further. They have built a few charging stations where the electric car owner can drive his car onto something like the old oil change bay, but instead of oil, the electric car owner gets his low battery pack exchanged for a fully charged battery pack in five minutes, and he's on his way. An American based high-end electric car company called Tesla Motors has already built a few fast charge stations (30 minutes) as well as a few Danish style battery pack exchange places. (Watch Tesla battery swap on YouTube: https://youtu.be/aaSuTPn5g-o. The problem is that there are too few of these to encourage potential electric car buyers to kick the gasoline habit. This is where the government could come in.

When Franklin Roosevelt was faced with the Great Depression, unemployment rates officially at 25% and real rates at 40%, he and his "brain trust" used visionary thinking to create a new, dynamic, and efficient role for government: they called it the New Deal. This was a grand experiment in American industrial policy; putting the American government to use in a positive way to hire millions of American unemployed workers, from construction workers to engineers and scientists, to build the next generation of American infrastructure. These newly employed Americans were paid by the federal government to build roads, sidewalks, highways, bridges, and hydroelectric dams across the U.S. The federal government, through its Tennessee Valley Authority hired Americans to produce electricity for the several states in the Tennessee Valley area. Roosevelt's New Deal also hired young unemployed, unmarried men in its Civilian Conservation Corps to work in America's forests, parks, and fields. FDR's New Deal hired artists, writers, poets, actors and directors to beautify buildings and inspire

Americans with the arts. The millions of employees in all of these areas earned a paycheck from the government for their hard work. They rebuilt the United States of America and provided the infrastructure on which the dynamic American economy could be built, grow, and flourish. Some critics of Roosevelt's visionary work argue that it was not the New Deal that brought us out of the Great Depression, but that it was World War II. These critics are wrong on the facts and short on the overall picture of things. From 1933 until 1937, when the New Deal was put in place and flourished, unemployment dropped from 25% officially to 15%.

When the reactionaries in Congress regrouped and blocked FDR's New Deal from continuing beyond 1937, the unemployment rates stopped dropping. Once government began to spend massively again as the war effort began and continued, unemployment was drastically reduced. It wasn't World War II *per se* that brought down the unemployment rate, it was the government spending in World War II that brought down the unemployment rate. If government could spend and grow the economy and production through war, government can spend and help grow the economy in peacetime. The most effective government spending in peacetime should be targeted to rebuilding, expanding, modernizing, and maintaining the infrastructure. Today this must include conventional and high technology transportation, sewer systems, water systems, power lines, alternative energy development in the forms of wind, solar, and tide power, full access to free education for all Americans in the trades, technical programs, apprenticeships, in K through 12, colleges, universities and professional schools. Government spending today must include updating public buildings with green energy efficient systems, and last but not least, government spending should be focused on providing small businesses the necessary capital at affordable interest rates to expand and modernize and generate more jobs; especially since small business employs two thirds of American workers.

The revenues necessary for this massive investment must come from the closing of unnecessary and unproductive corporate tax loopholes and reinstating a progressive tax on the portion of income over $1 million. This will provide approximately $1 trillion more annually, a portion of which should be used for public investment in these areas. A smaller portion could be used to pay down the national debt.

Building a complete infrastructure for electric cars and electric trucks is not enough. The federal government must invest some of this money in a public/private partnership to build a cutting-edge high-speed rail and maglev nationwide system, as other countries such as France, Germany, Japan, and China have done. China's government has built over 15,000 miles of High-Speed Rail (HSR). Its HSR trains travel over 200 mph, and are being exported to Turkey, and soon to South America and other countries. China's maglev, owned by the Shanghai municipal government, has reached speeds of 311 mph. Japan's maglev does 375 mph. The U.S. was the first to put a man on the moon; it should not be the last to build HSR and Maglev. This will not only help to clean up the air, it will create millions of well-paying jobs. The people in these jobs will spend their money in restaurants and coffee shops and other small businesses, generating more growth in the economy and more public revenue for public investment, which is the foundation for healthy growth in the private economy.

The other major cause of air pollution is emissions from fossil fuel burning power plants generated by coal, oil, and natural gas. Each of these fossil fuels alone, or in combination, produces huge amounts of air pollution in the form of mercury emissions and carbon dioxide emissions, among others. These are deadly for human health and for the health of the planet, and cause global warming, rising seas, and more devastating and frequent storms which result in property damage as well.

The 2008 study by the European Environment Agency found that all three fossil fuels used to fuel power plants produce varying degrees of emissions of carbon dioxide, sulfur dioxide, nitrogen oxides, carbon monoxide, non-methane organic compounds, and particulate matter. Coal was the highest polluter and natural gas the lowest polluter. In 2018, 27.4% of U.S. electricity was produced by coal fired power plants, 35.1% from natural gas fired power plants, 19.3% from nuclear generated power plants, 0.6% from petroleum generated power plants, all of which are dangerous and pollute the air or atmosphere in some way. Only 17.1% of U.S. electricity is generated by renewable energy sources, including wind (6.6%), solar (1.6%), hydro-electric (7.0%), and biomass (1.5%) power (U.S. Energy Information Administration {www.eia.gov}, March

1, 2019). In Germany, 50% of electricity is produced by renewable energy. At the beginning of 2019, German Chancellor Angela Merkel's government pledged to shut down all 84 coal-fired power plants in the next 19 years. Earlier, Germany decided to shut down all its nuclear plants by 2022. Twelve of nineteen have already been shut. (*Los Angeles Times,* January 26, 2019)

The Union of Concerned Scientists has studied air pollution in great detail. They found that emissions from coal-fired power plants include sulfur dioxide, which contributes to the formation of small acidic particulates that penetrate into human lungs and are absorbed by the blood stream. So2 also causes acid rain, damaging crops and some soils, lakes, and streams. Coal-fired plants produce nitrogen oxides which cause ground-level ozone or smog, can burn lung tissue, exacerbate asthma and bring about chronic respiratory diseases. Coal- fired plants also produce particulate matter that can cause chronic bronchitis, aggravated asthma, and premature death, as well as the haze that reduces visibility. Coal plants are responsible for more than half of the human-caused emissions of mercury in the U.S. Mercury is a toxic heavy metal that causes brain damage and heart problems. Other pollutants that are harmful to human beings from a typical uncontrolled coal plant include lead and cadmium, toxic heavy metals, and trace amounts of uranium. Seven hundred and twenty tons of carbon monoxide are produced by coal-fired plants annually. This causes headaches and stress on people with heart disease. Tons of hydrocarbons are produced, which are volatile organic compounds that form ozone which is really bad for human breathing and health.

Natural gas fired power plants, which produce harmful emissions, but far less than coal, are problematic in another way. In recent years with new technology, oil and natural gas companies have been extracting larger and more quantities of natural gas by using new technologies, equipment, and methods such as hydraulic fracturing, commonly known as fracking. This is a technique by which natural gas is extracted from deep underground wells, after the company applies chemicals in water to create explosions that break the rock which releases natural gas for capture. Research has shown in states like Pennsylvania, that when natural gas was extracted with the use of fracking, surrounding water supplies became polluted with the chemicals. A startling visual example was provided in the movie *Gasland*, which showed a resident in that area turning on his water faucet in the kitchen, lighting a match next to it, sending the water into flames. Many farmers in the area who had leased some of their land to oil or gas companies that used fracking, found themselves and many of their farm animals, such as cattle, getting very sick. The health of the farm animals was so impaired that one owner put the cows to sleep rather than sell them on the market.

As the pressure mounts for the U.S. to move away from coal fired power plants to cleaner natural gas generated power plants, the temptation will be to expand natural gas exploration and to use the dangerous technique of fracking, in order to provide natural gas to fuel the "cleaner" power plants. Instead the United States ought to be learning from Germany's example. We must use our technological and scientific genius to move rapidly and leapfrog into alternative energy production. Not only Germany, but now China, has started to do so. The Chinese rapid investment in solar panel production has allowed them to surpass Germany and become the number one solar panel producer in the world. We need to move rapidly in the direction of alternative energy production, which will create new high technology and well-paying green jobs in manufacturing. To do this the U.S. government will need to create an efficient industrial policy that funds research and development and subsidizes the manufacturing of alternative energy in the form of solar, wind, and tide power. Great Britain will soon be producing 20% of her electricity through tide power. This means placing electricity generators that can be powered by the waves and tide of coastal waters.

The Union of Concerned Scientists has carefully studied air pollution produced by cars, trucks, and diesel engine trains as well. They found that this air pollution was emitted during vehicle operation, refueling, manufacturing, and disposal. Additional emissions were associated with the refining and distribution of vehicle fuel. They then examined the major pollutants from motor vehicles. They found that particulate matter, which are tiny fine particles of soot and metals less than 1/10 the diameter of a human hair, pose the most serious threat to human health because they can penetrate deep in the lungs. Pollution produced by cars, trucks, and diesel engine trains include hydrocarbons. Hydrocarbons react with nitrogen oxides in the presence of sunlight to form ground-level ozone, which irritates the respiratory system causing coughing, choking, and reduced lung capacity. They also found that nitrogen oxides cause lung irritation and weaken the body's defenses against infections such as pneumonia and influenza.

These transportation sources also produce carbon monoxide. This colorless and odorless poisonous gas blocks the transport of oxygen to the brain, heart, and other vital organs of the body. Fetuses, newborn children and people with chronic illnesses are especially susceptible to carbon monoxide. Other pollutants produced by cars, trucks, and diesel engine trains include sulfur dioxide. Sulfur dioxide can react in the atmosphere to form fine particles and poses the largest health risks to young children and asthmatics.

Ask **Taylor Thomas**, a young woman in her twenties who has lived all of her life in Long Beach, California. She lived most of her life on the Westside. This part of Long Beach has some of the worst air pollution in the city because it is close to the main transportation corridor of the 710 freeway and the rail lines, where heavy trucks and trains carry goods to and from the Long Beach and Los Angeles Ports. This is the largest U.S. Port complex, and the residents of West Long Beach, Downtown Long Beach, Wilmington, Carson and the surrounding communities of Southeast Los Angeles County pay a heavy price with their health. Their air is also heavily polluted by the nearby incinerator and oil refineries.

Based on data from the USC Children's Health Study, researchers at the University of Southern California have found that "heavy traffic corridors in the cities of Long Beach and Riverside are responsible for a significant proportion of preventable childhood asthma, and the true impact of air pollution and ship emissions on the disease has likely been underestimated." (*American Journal of Public Health*). The Southern California Environmental Health Sciences Center reports that the USC Children's Health Study shows that "current levels of air pollution have chronic, adverse effects on lung growth leading to clinically significant deficit in 18-year-old children. Air pollution affects both new onset

174

asthma and exacerbation.

Living in close proximity to busy roads is associated with risk for prevalent asthma. Residential traffic exposure is linked to deficit in lung function growth and increased school absences."

As quoted in *ScienceDaily*, "the USC study found that ship emissions from the Los Angeles-Long Beach port complex contributed to the exacerbation of asthma. For example, approximately 1,400 yearly episodes of asthma-related bronchitis episodes in Long Beach (21 percent of the total) were caused by the contribution of ship emissions to nitrogen dioxide levels in the city." (ScienceDaily.com, Nov.5, 2009).

Taylor Thomas was diagnosed with asthma early in life. She was six or seven and playing in her yard at her West Long Beach home when she had her first full-fledged asthma attack. She told me "It was really scary. I couldn't breathe and was gasping for breath!" Taylor's mother took her inside, lay her down and gave her the Albuterol inhaler. She has had several asthma attacks since then, but not any when she lived in another part of town with cleaner air, Bixby Knolls, from 1998-2001 and 2004-2007. When she lived on the Westside of Long Beach once again from 2001-2004 she had some attacks.

Taylor Thomas has been involved with theater productions depicting the connection between air pollution and asthma. Let's hope that some of the corporate sponsored politicians will see these plays about air pollution and its human costs. Would they then vote for stricter regulation of oil refineries in the area, and for electric trucks, cranes, and trains to transport goods to and from the ports? Or would their campaign funding and control by corporate lobbyists and political action committees be too great for them to bring Environmental Justice to people like Taylor Thomas, and clean air to children in air polluted neighborhoods such as West Long Beach?

Dollar Democracy is Accelerating Climate Change (Climate Disruption)

Diesel and gasoline burning cars, trucks, and trains also produce other hazardous air pollutants such as toxics. These chemical compounds have been linked to birth defects, cancer and other serious illnesses. The transportation sector, made up primarily of cars, trucks, and diesel engine trains, accounts for over one quarter of all U.S. greenhouse gas emissions, including carbon dioxide. These greenhouse gases are primarily responsible for global warming (climate change, climate disruption) and its accompanying phenomenon of rising oceans, unusual and severe storms, including hurricanes and tornadoes, floods, and severe drought, which brings more intense and numerous fires including forest fires.

Global warming, which has driven climate change (better called "climate disruption"), has been found by 95% of the world's leading scientists to have accelerated tremendously in the last hundred years. This was caused by the Industrial Revolution and its excesses. These scientists, while acknowledging warming and cooling trends in the past eons of time, are absolutely certain that the current global warming pattern has been caused primarily by human beings and our out-of-control, lack of environmental sensitivity, way of thinking and behaving.

Dollar Democracy, the massive amounts of money spent by special interests, in this case, the oil, natural gas, and other fossil fuel industries, on political campaigns and lobbying, have had a tremendous effect on the actions taken by large numbers of politicians in the U.S. at the state and federal levels. According to www.opensecrets.org, from 1990 to 2018, the Energy/Natural Resources Industry spent $639,972,579 on congressional candidates to influence their decisions through legalized bribery. According to current campaign law, this is legal because there is no direct and immediate exchange between the donor for his money and the Congressman for his vote. However, we all know that in politics, as in much of life, there's no such thing as a free lunch. Even without a *quid pro quo* the Congressman knows that he is going to have to work for his donors to a large extent. According to the same source, from 1998 to 2018, the Energy/Natural Resources Industry spent $5,633,910,000 in lobbying the government to act in their favor, quite often against the American public's interest (opensecrets.org).

The term "lobbying" originally referred to the actions of a person who wanted to influence the thinking of a Congressman or State Representative by grabbing him by the collar in the lobby of the Capitol

176

to ask him to vote a certain way. Lobbying today includes working vacations, in places such as Hawaii, with legislators, paid for by the industry and its lobbyists. ("Legislators and lobbyists bonding over Mai-Tais on Maui", David Horsey, *LA Times*, Nov. 14, 2014).

In order to change detrimental policies made by these corporate backed and financed politicians, we must change the Dollar Democracy in our current bankrupt campaign election system. We must move toward real democracy which would have to be based on Clean Money campaigns and elections, as discussed in the last chapter.

Water Pollution

It takes a lot of water to grow and produce food. Because water can be scarce where we often grow food, water is often moved long distances for irrigation. This is especially true in the country's most productive region in agriculture, California. Eighty percent of all water used by humans in California is for agriculture. Often, this water is "returned to water ways contaminated with pathogens from livestock, pesticides, nitrates in groundwater, trace metallic elements and emerging pollutants, including antibiotics and antibiotic-resistant genes excreted by livestock." (www.watercalculator.org/footprints/water-energy-food-nexus/)

Also, according to the Sierra Club, coal-fired power plants are the largest source of toxic water pollution in the U.S. In "Compass, Pointing the Way to a Clean Energy Future," the Sierra Club states the following facts: of the 274 coal plants that discharge coal ash and scrubber wastewater into our lakes and river basin streams, nearly 70% have no limits on the toxics most commonly found in these discharges, for example arsenic, boron, cadmium, lead, mercury, and selenium. Of these 274 coal plants, more than one third have no requirements to monitor or report the discharges of these toxic metals to government agencies or the public. A total of 71 coal plants surveyed discharge toxic water pollution into rivers, lakes, and streams and bays that have already been declared impaired due to poor water quality. And, last but not least, nearly half of the coal plants surveyed are operating with an expired Clean Water Act permit.

Why is this allowed? Is it the results of Dollar Democracy once again? How many Senators and Congress members have taken big-money contributions for their campaigns from the coal industry? In the 2016 election cycle, the coal industry spent over $13,524,427 in federal elections. In the 2018 election cycle, the coal industry spent $7,712,514. The Clean Water Act is one of the nation's greatest achievements, and because of it rivers are no longer catching on fire, and our waters are safer and healthier than they were decades ago. But even 40 years after the Act was passed, the coal industry still pollutes because of a loophole no other industry enjoys. The U.S. Environmental Protection Agency (EPA) has proposed a national standard to reduce power plant wastewater pollution, because the multiple options that are offered include some that are strong and some that are weak.

According to the Grace Communications Foundation, industrial agriculture is one of the leading causes of water pollution in the United States today. In the Environmental Protection Agency's 2017 National Water Quality Inventory, 46 percent of the nations' streams and rivers are in "poor biological condition," and 21 percent of the nation's lakes are "hypereutrophic", which means that high levels of algae and nutrients are degrading the water quality. Water pollution caused by industrial agriculture can negatively affect both the environment and people.

From huge corporate industrial farms comes the storage of disposable animal waste. Manure and other farm wastes are stored in gigantic tanks holding millions of gallons of manure and urine. The gigantic tanks often leak and during large storms they rupture or overflow. Raw manure is up to 160 times as toxic as raw municipal sewage. The leaking manure and urine release antibiotic residues in harmful bacteria which can enter the water supply.

Many industrial farmers spray the stored waste onto their fields as fertilizer, and the extra waste that is sprayed ends up as runoff and goes into nearby water systems. It's been found that the most common form of water pollution in the United States is excessive levels of nitrogen or phosphorus coming from fertilizer runoff. This runoff can include some very toxic substances in the livestock excretions; substances such as pharmaceuticals or bacteria. The water pollution from manure and synthetic fertilizer causes severe environmental damage as well as harm to human health. Two hundred thousand to 250,000 fish were killed when manure spilled from a ruptured tank on a New York State dairy farm in 2005, because 3,000,000 gallons of cow manure poured into the Black River.

Excessive levels of nitrogen and phosphorus, which are minerals and fertilizers that promote plant growth, cause Algae bloom, which can cause fish kills. Nitrogen can also hurt ecosystems by making water more acidic and killing some plants while increasing the growth of other plants. Excessive nutrients such as nitrogen can also cause dead zones. According to the U.S. Department of Agriculture "as much as 15% of the nitrogen fertilizer applied to cropland in the Mississippi River basin makes its way to the Gulf of Mexico." This pollution has helped cause a dead zone in the Gulf of Mexico, which is an oxygen deprived area of 8,000 square miles, almost the size of the state of New Jersey. In this area no fish can survive. Livestock manure is high in ammonia. Dissolved ammonia in water is highly toxic to fish and dangerous to humans. High levels of nitrate in drinking water are definitely highly poisonous to humans and can cause potentially fatal oxygen levels in babies, spontaneous abortions, and possibly cancer.

In a sample of wells that were surveyed by the U.S. geological survey from 1993 to 2000, 9% of domestic wells in rural areas, and 2% of public supply wells, had nitrate concentrations higher than the EPA maximum allowed. "EPA estimates that about 1.3 million households in counties with industrial livestock facilities get their water from wells with dangerously high nitrate levels." (GRACE Communications Foundation).

There's a high level of disease-causing microorganisms in midyear. When the manure is applied to fields, these pathogens can be transferred to local water supplies during irrigation or rainfall. There is severe impact of pathogens from livestock manure. For example, according to the Center for Disease Control, in every waterborne disease outbreak from 1986 to 1998 in the U.S., when the pathogen was identified, it most likely came from livestock. Some of these pathogens don't originate on farms but they come about because of a high level of nutrients. For example, it was found that Pfiesteria Piscicida thrives where algae blooms grow. It causes lesions in fish as well as large-scale fish kills. According to the Grace Foundation's research it can also cause a "range of symptoms in humans, including respiratory and eye irritation, gastrointestinal problems, fatigue, as well as skin problems and cognitive symptoms such as memory loss and confusion."

Corporate Agriculture (Agribusiness) Is a Leading Cause of Water Pollution in the U.S.

Corporate industrial farms often use antibiotics and artificial growth hormones injected into the livestock or added to their food. These animals excrete large amounts of both substances and, together with everything else in the waste of livestock, pollute our water. Some hormones continue functioning in manure almost 300 days after excretion, and there are many documented cases of hormones discovered miles downstream from the farms. These hormones have been shown to negatively affect the reproductive processes in fish. It's still uncertain of their effects on humans. It's been estimated that 75% to 90% of the antibiotics given to livestock are excreted. These antibiotics bring about the development of antimicrobial resistant bacteria. The Grace Foundation claims that some studies have suggested that waterways with high levels of antibiotics have begun to promote the growth of these resistant bacteria. The Foundation goes on to claim that numerous studies have demonstrated that waterways are an important means of transmitting this dangerous bacteria to humans.

Even though some heavy metals, such as copper and zinc, are important nutrients for growth, especially for cattle, swine, and poultry, such metals are often present in far higher concentration than is necessary in animal feed. The feed also has included heavy metals such as chromium, lead, arsenic and cadmium. Livestock and industrial farming excrete heavy metals such as these, spreading them as fertilizer, which leads to soil and water pollution. For human beings, exposure to these heavy metals in water results in kidney problems, exposure to lead results in headaches and nervous system disorders, and exposure to arsenic causes cardiovascular and nervous system problems. Arsenic is also known to cause cancer. Many of the salts present in large amounts of manure increase the salinity in waterways. This leads to changes in aquatic ecosystems, and leaves water unfit for drinking.

In addition to the organic matter in manure, animal bedding, wasted feed, soil, dust, hair and feathers are quite often mixed with manure and storage and end up in waterways. The decomposition of the substances also affect the color, smell, and taste of water.

Ground water is the source of drinking water for almost half of the U.S. population and for 99% of the rural population. Even though public drinking water systems are regulated by the Environment Protection Agency, private drinking water wells are not regulated and are not required to meet EPA clean water standards, according to the Grace Communications Foundation. And the private wells are not required to undergo routine testing by experts, whereas public water systems are. It's clear to see why families that rely on private drinking water wells are most vulnerable to the harmful effects of water pollution from factory farms. The staggering fact is that, of the U.S. counties that have industrial farms, domestic drinking water wells are the source for approximately 13.5 million households.

As pointed out by the Grace Foundation, industrial factory farm corporate agriculture uses a huge amount of water annually. For example, in the year 2000, 41% of all freshwater used by humans in the United States was used for agriculture. Water overuse is a major problem on industrial farms that do not implement their water usage on a case-by-case basis. A dairy farm that uses automatic flushing systems to clean out its animal houses uses an average of 150 gallons of water per cow per day compared to an average of 5 to 10 gallons used by farms that monitor their water use in order to conserve it, according to the Grace Foundation. Water overuse not only hurts the environment but is also very expensive. The USDA estimated that increasing water use efficiency on irrigated farms by just 10% could save almost $200 million per year. The EPA considers agriculture to be "the most widespread source of impairment on the nation's assessed lake acres."

Oil and Gas Campaign Dollars and Fracking

Hydraulic fracturing, or fracking, not only helps create air pollution and global warming leading to climate disruption, by tapping huge amounts of fossil fuels, it is also devastating to our water supply. This process allows the oil and gas companies to mix chemicals with highly pressurized water. This is then used to fracture or break up shale rock far below the ground, release natural gas, and provide greater access to oil. Through the modernization of this technology, the oil and gas companies, which in many cases are one corporation, have been able to vastly increase the production and refining of oil as well as the capture of vast amounts of natural gas. This natural gas from the U.S. is made into liquefied form and exported around the world today. Not only is crude oil production in the U.S. increasing, in 2018 the U.S. became the world's number one producer of greenhouse gas producing, climate disrupting fossil fuels of oil and natural gas. (https://www.api.org)

In his 2019 State of the Union address, President Trump accurately boasted that "The United States is now the No. 1 producer of oil and natural gas anywhere in the world." (*Washington Post*, Feb. 6, 2019). As greater amounts of oil and gas are extracted in the U.S., the U.S. is vastly increasing its exports of these two fossil fuels to the world market.

Fracking is a Major Source of Water Pollution in America

Fracking has become a major source of water pollution in America. The chemicals used in the fracking process find their way into groundwater, well water, and rivers and streams. These important sources of water used for drinking, bathing, washing, and brushing your teeth become heavily polluted with chemicals and other unwanted items that are products of the fracking process.

Vast territories of states like Pennsylvania, Texas, and New York

182

are sitting on oil and gas sources such as the Marcellus Shale in New York and Pennsylvania, the Barnett Shale in Texas, and the Monterey Shale in California. States such as Oklahoma and Arkansas are also located on oil and vast gas reserves. The results of fracking in these states (for which there are studies) have clearly shown that people's health in Pennsylvania, Texas, and New York have been compromised and devastated from the fracking chemicals in their water and that of their livestock. Many suffered bloody noses, bloody coughs, breathing difficulties and worse symptoms. Arkansas and Oklahoma have experienced earthquakes in areas which never had earthquakes before.

For example, since September 2013, when fracking began and was stepped up in Arkansas, there were 1100 earthquakes recorded. In Oklahoma, earthquakes of magnitude 4.7 were experienced, the largest in the recorded history of Oklahoma.

We don't know the extent of fracking or its effects in California for one major reason. For a hundred years the state of California's government did not require the oil and gas companies to report where they were fracking and what chemicals they were using while fracking. AB 7, which would have required companies to disclose the chemicals that they use in fracking was defeated in the California State Assembly in 2013.

Senate Bill 4 (SB 4) was passed by the California State Assembly and signed into law by Governor Jerry Brown at the end of 2013. This was the first attempt to try to regulate fracking. Because of strong lobbying by oil and gas companies and major campaign contributions from them to the California Governor and the state legislators of both parties, the bill was amended several times at the last minute, which made most environmental groups remove their support for it. Yet the Governor signed it into law in late 2013. SB 4 made California Environmental Quality Act (CEQA) review of fracking permits optional and prevents imposing a moratorium on fracking for 15 months. Big Oil strongly supported the amended version of SB 4 that Brown signed. Brown had received at least $2,014,570.22 from fossil fuel interests for his campaigns since he ran for California Attorney General in 2006. (Counterpunch.org). Although the law required that fracking sites be revealed publicly by oil companies and the state beginning in 2014, as late as May 2014, dozens of fracking sites had not been publicly listed on the website of the California Division of Oil Gas and Geothermal Resources (DOGGR), contrary to the law. Many of the regulations in SB 4 will not take full effect until January 2016. Even though it will require the oil and gas corporations to disclose the chemicals they use in a particular fracking job, many other dangerous well-stimulation projects "will be exempt from environmental review, groundwater monitoring, and the public notification process." ("What the Frack is Happening Under Long Beach?" by Joshua Frank, *OC Weekly*, April 24 to April 30, 2015).

Dr. Tom Williams, a retired geologist who worked with Parsons Oil and Gas for more than two decades and with the government of Dubai for 10 years, claims that much of the well-stimulation taking place in my home town of Long Beach, California, won't be regulated by California Senate Bill 4. Other than fracking, two of these well-stimulation methods used in Long Beach are gravel packing and acidizing. Gravel packing, which is not regulated by SB 4, is a technique that uses dangerous chemicals to get the oil out of rocks. This process produces air toxins and vapors, making nearby residents vulnerable. Many of the same chemicals used in fracking, such as biocides and benzene (both are carcinogens and kill living organisms) are used in gravel packing. According to investigative reporter Joshua Frank of the *OC Weekly*, gravel packing "has been used offshore at least 90 times in Long Beach in the past three years." Acidizing is the most common method of drilling in Long Beach. Acidizing has occurred at least 150 times in Long Beach since 2012, and some of it will be regulated under SB 4. Just as in fracking, acidizing utilizes hydrogen fluoride (HF), which is a colorless gas which dissolves in water. Although not visible, HF is extremely dangerous. Being exposed to HF can cause chronic lung disease, skin damage, permanent visual defects and even death, according to the U.S. Centers for Disease Control. The neighboring North Orange County city of Huntington Beach has also been a victim of gravel packing and acidizing 31 times since 2012. (*OC Weekly*, April 24 to April 30, 2015).

Large parts of North Orange and South Los Angeles Counties are situated on top of a major aquifer that provides water to local communities including 60 percent of Long Beach's water. The risk to this precious water supply is extremely high from fracking, gravel packing and acidizing. The citizen activist group called Stop Fracking Long Beach (SFLB) already has almost 300 members on its Facebook page. In February 2015, the California Environmental Protection Agency admitted that state regulators permitted more than 2,500 fracking wells to dump polluted waste water into protected underground aquifers. According to state documents obtained by the Center for Biological Diversity "almost 3 billion gallons of oil industry wastewater have been

Image 6-1 | Fracking Water Injection Well | Photo/Creative Commons

illegally dumped into central California aquifers that supply drinking water and farming irrigation. The wastewater entered the aquifers through at least 9 disposal injection wells used by the oil industry to dispose of waste contaminated with fracking fluids and other pollutants." The state documents also show that "Central Valley Water Board testing found high levels of arsenic, thallium and nitrates – contaminants sometimes found in oil industry wastewater – in water supply wells near these waste-disposal operations." Thallium is a highly toxic chemical that is used in rat poison quite often. Arsenic can cause cancer and even low-level exposure to arsenic in drinking water can weaken the immune system's ability to fight against illness. (Center for Biological Diversity).

Assembly Bill (AB) 1323 which would have placed a moratorium on fracking in California, while its safety and dangers were studied, was also defeated in a vote in the California State Assembly. Since 2004 the oil and natural gas industry donated over $700,000 in campaign contributions to Democratic legislators in the California State Assembly and State Senate. Since 2004 the oil and natural gas industry donated over $860,000 to Republican legislators in the California State Assembly and State Senate. According to campaign finance data from www.maplight.org, a majority of the members of the California State Assembly who voted against the moratorium, or abstained to assure its defeat, were bought and paid for with thousands of dollars of campaign contributions by pro-fracking oil and gas interests. (http://maplight.org/content/73261)

Campaign Dollars Influence Votes on Fracking

Data: MapLight analysis of **campaign contributions to members of the California State Assembly and Senate from interest groups in support of or opposition to bills related to hydraulic fracturing from January 1, 2011—December 31, 2012.** Contributions data source: *National Institute of Money in State Politics*

- Interest groups opposing AB 1323 have contributed
- 7.1 times as much money as groups supporting it.
- Member of the Assembly voting "NO" on AB 1323 received, on average, 31 times as much money from opposing groups as from supporting groups.
- Seventeen members of the Assembly "Not Voting" on AB 1323 received 5 times as much money from opposing groups as from supporting groups.

- Eight of the 12 bills identified by MapLight* as relevant to fracking were opposed by the Western States Petroleum Association, whose members include ExxonMobil, Valero, BP, and Chevron.

Organization	Campaign Contributions to California State Legislature
British Petroleum (BP)	$28,450
Chevron	$292,700
ExxonMobil	$72,000
Valero Energy	$71,300
Total	**$464,450**

Table 6-1 | Campaign Contributions to State Legislature

SB 1281, passed in 2014, somewhat improves the regulatory regime for fracking (lao.ca.gov, December 1, 2016).

At the federal level the influence that the oil, gas, and coal industries buy with the government is staggering: in the 2012 federal elections alone these fossil fuel industries contributed $150 million to federal campaigns, including the House and Senate. This election- related money buys a lot of influence even between elections, when the time comes for the politicians elected, with the help of their money, to make policy regarding the safety of our air, drinking water, and soil. One of the most egregious examples of the use of money to buy influence over policy decisions has to do with the so-called Halliburton loophole.

Halliburton Corporation and Fracking

The Halliburton Corporation is the major producer of fracking equipment. The fossil fuel industry has spent $747 million in lobbying money to gain and keep its exemption to the federal Safe Drinking Water Act. It is the only industry whose activity, such as fracking and its effects, is exempted from the stringent requirements of the Safe Drinking Water Act.

Campaign contributions are solicited by candidates from wealthy special interests in order to finance the candidates' election activities, such as TV and radio campaign commercials, targeted mass mailing, expensive public opinion polling, paying for campaign consultants and management, posting of political signs and banners, and investing money in expensive fundraising banquets and events. Ninety-five percent of the time the candidate with the greater amount of money, usually the incumbent, wins the election. These days the average winning candidate for a congressional House of Representatives seat raises and spends $1.7 million every two years to get elected and reelected. Once these candidates are elected, candidates that include state representatives and senators, state governors, U.S. Representatives, U.S. Senators, and U.S. Presidents, they will obviously owe their financial benefactors something in terms of the policies they make.

Legalized Bribery

The big donors do not expect to be obliged by the elected officials one hundred percent of the time. But they expect to be rewarded for their sponsorship between 60% to 80% of the time. Some political science studies in the 1980s have shown an 80% correlation between big campaign contributions from specific industries, for example tobacco, and the way particular candidates who receive lots of money from them, vote on issues pertaining to the tobacco industry. There have been other more recent studies in the 2000s indicating similar, if not greater correlation between campaign contributions and votes. It is not legal for an elected official to promise a direct *quid pro quo* vote on a specific bill in return for specific campaign contributions. Both the elected official and the donor would be convicted of bribery, if there is evidence of a direct bargain made by the donor for his donation, in exchange for the elected official's vote on specific legislation. However, what we have today is this pay to play atmosphere of money in politics in America. This was perfectly characterized by former U.S. Congressman Cecil Heftel of Hawaii as "legalized bribery."

In addition to millions of dollars in campaign contributions, there are hundreds of millions spent on lobbying activity by wealthy special interests such as corporate lobbyists for the large oil companies, pharmaceutical companies, tobacco companies, agribusiness corporations, wealthy defense contractors, and many others of their kind. Why would the special interests spend millions of dollars between elections on paid professional lobbyists, former members of Congress, high-powered lawyers, former executive branch members, and anyone who has the expertise and/or inside connections to be able to open doors for them? That's how these wealthy special interest groups buy "access" to powerful members of the executive and legislative branches of our state and federal governments! "Access" means a "hearing" at some key decision-making point. Access pays very handsomely. To gain and successfully use access, a wealthy special interest group employs lobbyists on Capitol Hill and influences the way laws are written in order to provide them with financial advantages. This explains why the fossil fuel industry spent $747 million in lobbying money to gain and keep the Halliburton loophole exemption to the Safe Drinking Water Act. It allowed this industry to continue making billions of dollars a year in profit, quite often tax-free, because of corporate tax loopholes passed by Congress, without being limited by the regulations of the Safe Drinking Water Act. You invest millions to make billions. Legalized tax avoidance and regulation avoidance are not victimless acts. When hundreds of billions of dollars are lost by the federal and state governments because of corporate tax loopholes (see Table 2-1), and when corporations are exempt from safe drinking water regulations, the American people pay with cuts in education funding, and the endangering of our health with unhealthy water.

CHAPTER 7

BIG AGRIBUSINESS, PESTICIDES, AND GMOS SICKENING OUR FOOD

"There are now just a few colossal companies reaping profits from their control of every link of the food chain, Hyper-consolidation raises consumer prices while lowering the prices farmers receive. It eliminates choices for both farmers and eaters and undermines the resiliency and sustainability of the food system."

–Wenonah Hauter,
Executive Director of Food & Water Watch

Agribusiness, consisting of corporations such as Monsanto and Cargill, is the dominant sector in American agriculture today. We have moved from farm and food production by small family farmers in the 19th century to food production, processing, packaging, and sales involving huge agricultural corporations today. These corporations use industrial farming including automation, mass production, use of pesticides, and chemical fertilizers. Today, less than 2% of the U.S. workforce is engaged in agriculture. With the advent of industrialized agriculture, came the use of tractors and other industrial equipment, the use of chemical fertilizers and pesticides, the popularity of processed and packaged food with inferior nutrients, and last but not least, the advent of genetically modified organisms (GMO foods) that have been proven to be detrimental to human health.

190

How did we get here? Once again through the lobbying and campaign contribution power of the wealthy special interest corporate agribusinesses, their owners, and their associations. I call it Dollar Democracy: a campaign finance system in which campaigns are bought and paid for by wealthy individual and corporate donors. These donors are able to wield enormous influence on the decisions of many elected officials such as members of the U.S. House and U.S. Senate, and the executive branch, including sometimes the U.S. President. We have to acknowledge that some of the formerly small and medium-sized farmers, successful in buying out or driving out their competitors, grew into fewer and fewer, larger and larger corporate farmers and related businesses, all of which I refer to as "agribusiness" or "corporate agriculture".

Corporate Monopoly of Food and Agriculture

According to the November 1, 2018 article in *Food and Water Watch*, "Over 200 Farm, Food and Rural Groups Endorse Agribusiness Merger Moratorium Bills", a diverse coalition of groups are urging Congress to block further consolidation of food and agribusiness corporations. They are urging Congress to pass the Food and Agribusiness Merger Moratorium and Antitrust Review Act of 2018 companion bills this year (S.3404/H.R.6800).

As Food and Water Watch claim in their November 2, 2012 issue, the agriculture and food sector is highly concentrated with just a few companies dominating in each link of the food chain. In most sectors of the U.S. economy in comparison, the four largest companies control between 40% and 45% of the market. In contrast, according to data by the University of Missouri, Columbia in 2012, in the agriculture and food sector, the four largest corporations controlled 82% of the beef packing industry, 85% of soybean processing, 63% of pork packing, and 52% of broiler chicken processing. This high concentration can have a negative effect on farmers and consumers. For example, farmers in Canada have to pay more for their supplies when just a few firms sell seeds, fertilizers, and tractors to them. The farmers also sell into a very highly consolidated market, and the few firms that bid for crops and livestock can drive down the prices that farmers receive. Consumers have fewer choices at the supermarket, and food processors and retailers can raise their prices when farm prices rise, but the same forces are slow to pass savings on to the consumers when farm prices fall. This is the direct result of the rising concentration of farm ownership in the hands of fewer and fewer gigantic agricultural corporations.

According to Food and Water Watch, the rising economic concentration of farm ownership has led to the decline in the number of farms and an increase in the size of the farms that remain. Also, communities "with more medium and smaller size farms have more shared prosperity, including higher incomes, lower unemployment and lower income inequality, than communities with larger farms tied to often distant agribusiness." Huge agribusiness corporations end up moving income from small farmers and rural economies to Wall Street investors. For decades the U.S. Department of Agriculture and the U.S. Department of Justice have taken a deregulated hands-off approach to the consolidation of food companies into huge agribusiness corporations.

As we investigate this further, we will find that campaign money and lobbying money's influence over the politicians who make food policy, and the bureaucrats who carry out food policy, has played a major role. Good policy that was in place in the form of strict and scientifically based regulations has been weakened or abandoned entirely. Deregulation did not stop with banking and industrial manufacturing. It has also heavily affected food production.

How has the quality of life of Americans been affected by the transformation of agriculture from small family farms to a few huge corporate agribusinesses? The impact of this transformation has been huge. For example, no longer does food come from local farmers who have a smaller energy footprint for transporting the food short distances. Now, most food that Americans buy is produced by giant food corporations and arrive in the grocery stores from thousands of miles away, much of it shipped from foreign countries, which also uses up more energy. The food is not as fresh. The food is mostly processed and packaged and sold in boxes on the shelf. The food is not as carefully regulated or inspected, which increases the frequency of food borne illness.

The Dangers of Genetically Modified (GMO) Foods

Most ominously the transformation to multinational factory production has resulted in the growing and promotion of genetically modified organisms (GM or GMOs), also known as genetically engineered (GE) food, both plant and animal.

Image 7-1 | Genetically Engineered Salmon | Photo/newfoodeconomy.org

The rapid growth rate of a genetically engineered AquaBounty salmon (left) is obvious when compared to a non-GE salmon (right) of the same age.

Let's focus on the development of genetically modified foods. In order to create new and specific traits in crops, genetic engineering changes the DNA of the crops. For example, by modifying the crop's DNA, scientists can make the crop resistant to pesticides and herbicides. These GMO or bio-engineered crops opened the door for approval of genetically modified animals such as salmon. Recently, the FDA approved genetically engineered salmon, which is the first GMO animal approved for human consumption. This fish is genetically modified to "contain genes from Chinook salmon and an eel-like creature called an ocean pout, which allows it to grow twice as fast, on less food, than a normal Atlantic salmon." It grows twice the size in the same amount of time. Senator Lisa Murkowski of Alaska "continues to 'have serious concerns about splicing DNA from two animals to produce a marketable fish,' and adds that the 'bioengineered' labels (USDA required), which don't require the disclosure of that information – just like they don't require the disclosure of how GMO corn or soy is made – do not 'suffice as giving consumers clear information.' " (newfoodeconomy.org).

The approval of GE salmon now opens the gates for GE cows and pigs, which the major biotech corporations are waiting to finally commercialize for huge profits. The USDA has been busy approving even more GE crops. In 2010, the USDA decided to allow unrestricted growing of alfalfa that has been genetically modified. The problem is that the U.S. farmers who grow GMO alfalfa are blocked from marketing it to many countries in the world. These countries won't accept GMO alfalfa because of fear it will contaminate their other crops. The USDA has also partly deregulated genetically engineered sugar beets and approved a new type of jagged corn that is designed to facilitate the production of ethanol. The USDA is currently considering approving GE crops that are designed to resist even more aggressive types of herbicides. There's been one more ominous development. Chemicals used on GMO crops are creating what's called dangerous super weeds which harm the farmers and the environment.

Influence of Agribusiness and Biotech Corporations Such as Monsanto, on Our Food and on the U.S. Government

No discussion of GMOs, genetically engineered foods, would be complete without an assessment of one of the most influential corporations in agribusiness, the Monsanto Corporation. Once, Monsanto was a saccharine and plastics manufacturer. Today Monsanto is a chemical company that produced Agent Orange during the Vietnam War. It also produced recombinant growth hormone, also known as rBGH. This hormone was injected in cattle to help them grow faster, larger and softer, and to produce more milk rapidly. Food and Water Watch calls Monsanto a bio-technology powerhouse, noting that it specializes in GMO seeds and herbicides such as Roundup. The Monsanto Corporation has become an octopus with 1000 tentacles reaching over the globe into our food supply. For example, 80% of corn and 93% of soybeans in the U.S. are grown from Monsanto patented seeds. These two crops form the basis of most processed food on our grocery store shelves.

According to Food and Water Watch, GMO seeds have been altered "with inserted genetic material to exhibit traits that repel pests or withstand the application of herbicides." FWW claims that Monsanto's extensive patents on GMO seeds and traits will guarantee the company a legal right to sue farmers for any assumed patent violations. Also, farmers are not allowed to save any leftover seeds for commercial use and the Corporation "reserves the right to visit farmers' land any time." The latest GMO action on seeds is the development of Terminator seeds which are patented and owned by Monsanto. Because of the limited suppliers of these seeds, and farmers' contracts with Monsanto, these seeds are purchased from Monsanto on a one-time basis by the farmers and can be planted only once. When the crop is harvested, the farmers have to go back to Monsanto to buy a new set of Terminator seeds.

According to the Institute for Responsible Technology (IRT) the FDA has non-regulation of GMO foods, and the FDA covers up health risks posed by GMO foods. GMO foods are inherently unsafe, and a GMO diet shows toxic reactions in the digestive tract. GMO diets cause liver damage, GMO fed animals had higher death rates and organ damage, higher reproductive failures and infant failures, and infant mortality. GMO fed livestock suffered sterility and deaths, according to farmers. GMO crops trigger immune reactions and may cause allergies. BT toxin produced GMO corn and cotton may cause allergies. Government evaluation misses most health problems. The IRT proceeds to describe the FDA's fake safety assessments. The IRT claims that company research is secret, inadequate, and flawed, and claims that unscientific assumptions are the basis of approvals by the FDA and other government agencies, and studies are rigged to avoid finding problems. The IRT convincingly provides a case study of flawed research involving Roundup ready soybeans. The Institute for Responsible Technology claims that toxic GMO foods could have been approved and that industry funded research favors the funders. The IRT also points out that promoting and regulating are contradictory roles for the FDA. The IRT's research reports on the manipulation of public opinion by supporters of GMOs and the Bio-Tech Industry. The report points out that critics of GMO foods and independent scientists have been attacked. Finally, the IRT points out that we consumers are the guinea pigs. I will examine and detail these claims in the following section of this chapter.

According to the Institute for Responsible Technology there are several reasons why the genetic engineering of our food presents certain dangers. IRT states:

> The first is that the *process* of genetic engineering itself creates unpredicted alterations, irrespective of which gene is transferred. The gene insertion process, for example, is accomplished by either shooting genes from a "gene gun" into a plate of cells or using bacteria to infect the cell with foreign DNA. Both create mutations in and around the insertion site and elsewhere. The "transformed" cell is then cloned into a plant through a process called tissue culture, which results in additional hundreds or thousands of mutations throughout the plants' genome. In the end, the GMO plant's DNA can be a staggering 2% to 4% different from its natural parent. Native genes can be mutated, deleted, or permanently turned on or off. In addition, the insertion process causes holistic and not-well-understood changes among large numbers of native genes. One study revealed that up to 5% of the natural genes altered their levels of protein expression as a result of a single insertion.

> The Royal Society of Canada acknowledged that "the default prediction" for GMO crops would include "a range of collateral changes in expression of other genes, changes in the pattern of proteins produced and/or changes in metabolic activities." Although the

FDA scientists evaluating GMOs in 1992 were unaware of the extent to which GMO DNA is damaged or changed, they too described the potential consequences. They reported that "The possibility of unexpected, accidental changes in genetically engineered plants" might produce "unexpected high concentrations of plant toxicants." GMO crops, they said, might have "increased levels of known naturally occurring toxins," and the "appearance of new, not previously identified" toxins. The same mechanism can also produce allergens, carcinogens, or substances that inhibit assimilation of nutrients.

Most of these problems would pass unnoticed through safety assessments on GM(O) foods, which are largely designed on the false premise that genes are like Legos that cleanly snap into place. But even if we disregard unexpected changes in the DNA for the moment, a proper functioning inserted gene still carries significant risk. It's newly created GM(O) protein, such as the Bt-toxin, may be dangerous for human health (see below). Moreover, even if that protein is safe in its natural organism, once it is transferred into a new species it may be processed differently. A harmless protein may then be transformed into a dangerous or deadly version. This happened with at least one GMO food crop under development, GMO peas, which were destroyed before being commercialized.

FDA scientists were also quite concerned about the possibility of inserted genes spontaneously transferring into the DNA of bacteria inside our digestive tract. They were particularly alarmed at the possibility of antibiotic resistant marker (ARM) genes transferring. ARM genes are employed during gene insertion to help scientists identify which cells successfully integrated the foreign gene. These ARM genes, however, remain in the cell and are cloned into the DNA of all the GMO plants produced from that cell. One FDA report wrote in all capital letters that ARM genes would be "A SERIOUS HEALTH HAZARD," due to the possibility that they might transfer to bacteria and create super diseases, untreatable with antibiotics.

Although the biotech industry confidently asserted that gene transfer from GM(O) foods was not possible, the only human feeding study on GM(O) foods later proved that it does take place. The genetic material in soybeans that make them herbicide tolerant transferred into the DNA of human gut bacteria and continued to function. That means that long after we stop eating a GM(O) crop, it's foreign GM(O) proteins may be produced inside our intestines. It is also possible that the foreign genes might end up inside our own DNA, within the cells of our own organs and tissues.

Another worry expressed by FDA scientists was that GMO plants might gather "toxic substances from the environment" such as "pesticides or heavy metals," or that toxic substances in GM(O) animal feed might bioaccumulate into milk and meat products. While no studies have looked at the bioaccumulation issue, herbicide tolerant crops certainly have higher levels of herbicide residues. In fact, many countries had to increase their legally allowable levels — by up to 50 times — in order to accommodate the introduction of GM(O) crops.

The overuse of the herbicides due to GM(O) crops has resulted in the development of herbicide resistant weeds. USDA statistics show that herbicide use is rapidly accelerating. Its use was up by 527 million pounds in the first 16 years of GM(O) crops (1996-2011). Glyphosate use per acre on Roundup Ready soybeans was up by two or 227% while use on non-GMO soy acreage decreased by 20% over the same period. The rate of application is accelerating due in large part to the emergence of herbicide tolerant weeds, now found on millions of acres. According to a study by Charles Benbrook, the incremental increase per year was 1.5 million pounds in 1999, 18 million in 2003, 79 million in 2009, and about 90 million in 2011. And as Roundup becomes less effective farmers are now using more toxic herbicides, such as 2-4D.

The pesticide-producing Bt crops do reduce the amount of (sic) sprayed on insecticides, but the total amount produced by the crops is far greater than the

Image 7-2 | Roundup Weed Killer | Photo/Creative Commons

amount of displaced spray. For example, Bt corn that kills the corn rootworm produces 1 to 2 pounds of Bt toxin per acre but reduces sprayed insecticides by only about 0.19 pounds. SmartStax with eight genes produces 3.7 pounds of Bt toxin per acre, but displaces only 0.3 pounds of sprayed insecticides.

All of the above risks associated with GM(O) foods are magnified for high- risk groups, such as pregnant women, children, the sick, and the elderly...." (http://www.respons ibletechnology.org/posts/wp-content/uploads/2013/01/State-of-the-Science-of-GMO-Health-Risks-sm-.2013.pdf).

Californians for GE Labeling led an effort, which began in 2014, to get California legislators to become cosponsors of legislation to label GMO foods. The following food-safety organizations also led this effort: Californians for GE Food Labeling is a coalition of organizations, businesses, and networks, including **Biosafety Alliance, Californians for Pesticide Reform, CALPIRG, Center for Food Safety, Consumers' Union, Environmental Working Group, Food Democracy Now!, Food and Water Watch, Friends of the Earth-US, Good Earth Natural Foods, LabelGMOs.org, Moms Advocating Sustainability, Organic Consumers Association, Pesticide Action Network North America** and **Pesticide Watch**, dedicated to giving California families informed choices about their food. This grassroots food safety movement wanted a GMO food labeling bill passed by the California Legislature as Vermont did, becoming the first state to do so.

Earlier, after campaigning and organizing across the state for a couple of years, the California Right to Know group was able to place Proposition 37 on the California ballot in the November 2012 general election. I met the lead organizer for Prop. 37, **Pamm Larry**, at the organizational kickoff at Santa Monica College in 2011. This organizing effort at Santa Monica College involved a couple dozen of us at the center of campus speaking in support of labeling Genetically Modified Foods in grocery stores. Pamm Larry's words were a powerful mixture of heart and mind. Surrounded by a grove of trees, her words captured their spirit and connected with the many people passing by. It was a call for basic honesty to guide our food choice; label GMOs so we can make the choice. In my talk, I clearly stated that we should not allow big agricultural corporations, such as Monsanto and DuPont, to undermine our health for huge immediate profits. Our efforts at Santa Monica College and those of millions of food safety advocates across the state were not in vain. Over a million voters signed the initiative and qualified Prop. 37 for the California ballot. According to the polls in early October 2012, Prop. 37 was leading by a 3 to 1 margin with California voters. It was finally defeated by a close margin because $45.6 million was spent against it by huge agricultural and bio-tech corporations. Monsanto and DuPont together gave $13.5 million of the $45.6 million. The pro-GMO labeling side had only $8.7 million to spend. Once again Dollar Democracy was victorious even in the initiative process. Ironically, a hundred years ago, California Governor Hiram Johnson and other Progressive Movement reformers had implemented the initiative process in order to give regular people the power to pass legislation. They saw that the California legislature had been heavily controlled by big corporations such as the Southern Pacific Railroad.

In the summer of 2013 the State of Maine Legislature, (70% of the Maine General Assembly and 86% of the Maine State Senate consists of Clean Money Legislators who won with publicly financed campaigns), overwhelmingly passed a bill that requires the labeling of GMO foods, when neighboring states also do so. A federal judge recently ruled against Monsanto in its challenge to Vermont's GMO labeling law. Monsanto agribusiness corporations were not deterred by the judge's ruling. Instead, they decided to continue their fight in Congress. Their millions of dollars in campaign contributions and lobbying with members of Congress finally paid off. These huge agribusiness corporations were able to persuade Congress to pass the Safe and Affordable Food Act in 2016. Opponents dubbed this the Deny Americans the Right-to-Know Act (DARK Act). The DARK act blocked Vermont's 2014 GMO labeling law two weeks after it took effect in 2016 and stopped any other state from passing one. Instead the USDA was to set national labeling standards, which are turning out to be weaker and ineffective.

Scott Faber, senior vice-president of government affairs for the Environmental Working Group, said the final (Trump Administration

USDA) rule "will allow the genetically engineered ingredients in many foods to remain hidden from consumers" because it doesn't include all genetically engineered foods and doesn't use terms that consumers understand. (https://www.fooddive.com/news/usda-issues-final-gmo-labeling-guidelines-for-food/544944/). Big Agribusiness Corporate Lobbyists have won again, at this time.

Meanwhile, the www.labelgmos.org has become gmofreeca.org. They had urged people to contact and comment on the USDA.gov site to let the USDA know that they want clear and proper GMO labeling. As importantly, GMO Free California are urging the public to help them expand the number of GMO-Free Zones beyond the six Northern California counties that have already done so. GMO Free California continues to educate the public on GMO foods by providing important information:

> 1996: GE (aka: GMO, genetically modified organisms) foods were introduced into the U.S. food supply by the biotech industry without adequate testing for human health or environmental risks and we've been eating them without labels ever since.

> 64 countries around the world-- including the EU (since 1998), China (since 2001), Russia, and Japan-- label GE foods. What do they know that Americans don't know?

> American children under the age of 19 have been on a steady diet of GE foods since birth.

> The FDA says foods that have been genetically engineered are as safe as conventional foods and don't require any special labeling. If biotech industry and big food believe their GE foods are safe, we Americans say, "label them now."

FDA's own scientists, many scientists, and doctors around the world, urge GE labeling.

Independent GE feeding studies on rats, pigs, and human breast cancer cells show causation for health risks.

"Bt" corn, soy, canola and cotton crops, a GE variety, are classified by the EPA as "insecticides" because every cell of the plant produces the poison Bt pesticide. So, why are they approved for human consumption in food products?

RoundUp, the herbicide most commonly sprayed on GE crops-- has been shown to have toxic effects on human health. But without labels there is no traceability, no accountability, and no liability. Labels will give Californians the information we need to choose for ourselves what we want to eat and feed our families.

Founded by **Zen Honeycutt, Moms Across America** is an activist group of mothers who are "committed to empowering millions to educate themselves about GMOs and related pesticides, get GMOs labeled, and offer GMO free and Organic solutions." (www.Moms AcrossAmerica.com). Their excellent website, which receives an average of 47,000 hits per week, is worth visiting for anyone concerned about the dangers of GMOs and what to do about them. Zen Honeycutt spoke to me passionately about the cause of labeling GMO foods because of the health dangers associated with them. Speaking at the California Rally for GE (GMO) Labeling, January 6, 2014 on the State Capitol steps in Sacramento, Zen Honeycutt rallied the troops:

Thank you! Good Morning!

How many of you have been volunteering since Prop

37? How many of you marched in the Moms Across America Marches on the 4th of July? How many of you care about what you eat?

First of all, I want to say I am truly honored to be here today with all of YOU. Whether you have just started or have been doing this for years, you are what makes America great. You are America's heroes. Also, without you who came before me, the health of my family Todd, Ben, Bodee and Bronson, would not be what it is today. So, we thank you very, very much.

I am here today because of love. We are all here because we love our families, our communities, our freedoms, our environment, our dogs and cats, our bees and butterflies. We love our farmers and we have FAITH in our farmers. We have faith that they can and will farm as has been done for thousands of years, without GMOs containing foreign proteins and the use of toxic chemicals. We have faith in Californians. Californians do not back down! We will not give up. Our love for our families will never end. We insist on GMO labeling now!

Some may say that it is not likely, but that doesn't concern us. After Prop 37, which was a win in so many ways…my son Ben said "Mom, even Star Wars took six episodes." And they had Yoda! Our children are our inspiration and that will never end!

My son went GMO free and organic for 4 months and his life-threatening allergic reactions were drastically reduced. This past year, his nut allergy decreased from a 19 down to a .2 (2 10ths). This is not just about an allergy; this is about LIFE and the people we love.

It is not enough that our family eats organic, however. My son's future spouses are out there somewhere and if they want to, I want them to be able to experience the profound love that it is to have their own child someday. Today, young couples have a 30% "failure to conceive" rate. That is the lowest in recorded US history. Everyone needs to know about GMOs!

I asked myself what could I do? Inspired by Jeffrey Smith's "Tipping Point Network" and Robyn O'Brien's "Patriotism on a Plate" I thought of 4th of July Parades. We could reach thousands locally and millions nationally in a single day. And it would be fun! With the partnership of the CA State Grange and support of Pamm Larry, Kathleen Hallal and many more, I founded Moms Across America and the March to Label GMOs in 4th of July parades. What happened was amazing.

Leaders from all across America emerged. Moms and supporters said, "I am the one who will have a group march in my 4th of July parade and educate my whole town about GMOs." And they did. In 172 parades in 44 states, generous, committed people made banners, signs, and floats and sang as they marched down Main streets all across America. We directly reached an estimated 1.5 million people and tens of millions more through the 120 media venues: radio, websites   and newspapers, which picked up the story including CNN and Fox News. It was an empowering gathering of community which has helped to grow our cause and raise awareness about GMOs. Our food system may be broken but the people are not. We are   creative, courageous and committed and we make a huge contribution to others by sharing with love.

Since the 4th of July parades we have received hundreds of stories, such as: Karen's son went from daily use of an inhaler to never having to use an inhaler again after switching to an organic diet. Cindy's son switched to organic for two years (and she is a single Mom who makes 40K so this was not easy, but it was important) and this year when he entered high school, NOT ONE of his new high school teachers could tell he was ever severely autistic. His life is dramatically improved. Who knows how our country will benefit by the contribution this one person will make? He has, WE have a NEW future because his Mom found out about GMOs.

The projected level of autism is predicted to be 1 out of 2 of our children in the U.S. within the next 20 years or sooner. That is half our children. What kind of society will we have? What kind of future and economy will we have if our children's futures are compromised? We Moms say, not on our watch! We will not stop! The love for our children will never end. We want a new future NOW!

We demand GMO labeling now so that the millions of people who still don't know about GMOs can have the ability to take care of the families they love. Moms see that GMOs ARE substantially different and our kids get better when we get them off GMO foods. We demand that people of ALL economic backgrounds have access to GMO free and pesticide free solutions and we have faith in our farmers that they can provide them.

How many of you think that most people really don't

want to know about GMOs and pesticides because it's too inconvenient? Let's check in. How many of you know someone with diabetes, obesity, asthma, auto immune disorders, allergies or autism? Look around. I assert everyone really wants to know about GMOs because everyone knows someone in America who is sick.

1 out of 2 of our children have some form of chronic condition. 1 out of 2 of our American men and 1 out of 3 American women are expected to get cancer...so everyone WANTS to know about GMOs and pesticides because we have enough problems & we want solutions! We want a new future now!

So, what can we do? Be a leader and inspire leaders! Join us in the celebration and sign up to host a 4th of July parade by Feb 14th "Share the Love, Sign Up your Parade Day" so we can have sponsors support the printing of the GMO flyers to pass out at the parades. Be the one to say, MY TOWN WILL KNOW about GMOs. Give them a new future. Go to momsacrossamerica.com and host one of the 75 parades in California and 589 parades on our list across the USA. Adopt a "Sister City", another town with a parade, and call and connect with other, moms in the Moms Club, La Leche League or Holistic Moms Network, share about GMOs and support and foster new leaders! When we get outside of our comfort zone, we will win. We can reach 600,000 in California and 5 million people in the USA in a single day. We are called "consumers" AND we are also the creators of our future. The future belongs to YOU. The future belongs to me. The future belongs to US. This is OUR time for health and freedom in California and America! Thank you! Go to www.momsacrossamerica.com for more information.

Thank you.

I have spoken on several occasions with Kathleen Hallal, a co-founder of Moms Across America. She is the mother of three sons who were diagnosed with food allergies and autoimmune issues. She says that none of these conditions run on either side of her family. She told me that as she began to research nutrition, she discovered what GMOs really are, and largely ended them in her family's diet. As a result, she saw improvements in her children's health. She continued to say:

> Since beginning on this journey, I have met many nutritionists, ecologists, doctors, farmers, and scientists who are all speaking out about problems that they are seeing with GMOs for the environment, animals, and humans. I co-founded Moms Across America with my friend Zen Honeycutt, another mother who was concerned about her children's food allergies. We were both frustrated with the fact that Prop 37 did not pass. We are connected to networks of mothers of children with what is known as the "4-A's": Allergies, Autism, Autoimmune, and Asthma, all of which are skyrocketing in our children's population. Cancer is the number one cause of death for children today. We want to raise awareness about how our food is being produced and how that process may likely be contributing to our nation's health epidemics. Together we planned 173 parades last summer on July 4, and this summer we are shooting for participation in 400 parades. We support labeling of GMOs so that consumers can know what they are buying, and they can decide whether they wish to consume GMOs in their daily diet. Or not.

In June 2014, Moms Across America and Californians for GE Food Labeling conducted a full court press to get the California Senate Agriculture Committee to approve and support SB 1381, the GMO

Labeling bill in the California Legislature. I fully supported their efforts to get millions of California voters to contact their state Legislators and obtain their support for SB 1381. Because of push back from Agribusiness lobbyists and special interest campaign donors SB 1381 fell short by two votes and failed to pass.

On April 9, 2014, Congressman Mike Pompeo (R-Kansas) (today, Trump's Secretary of State) introduced agribusiness supported legislation dubbed the Deny Americans the Right-to-Know Act (DARK Act) which would deny consumers the right to know if there are genetically engineered ingredients in their food. The DARK Act would make the current failed voluntary GMO labeling system permanent. Not a single company has disclosed the presence of genetically engineered ingredients in their products since the program was put into place in 2001. The worst part of this bill, as if denying us the right to know were not bad enough, is that it would prevent the FDA (Food and Drug Administration) from ever requiring labeling of GMO foods in the future! Companies would be able to label food products containing GMOs as "natural." Dollar Democracy also buys deception and lies.

Through Kathleen Hallal, I had the pleasure of meeting and speaking with **Howard Vlieger**, a farmer from Iowa who is campaigning nationally about the dangerous effects of GMOs on soil and farm animals. He recently spoke at an event that I attended in Irvine, California, organized by Kathleen and hosted by her community ladies group, and it was a very powerful presentation. Here was a farmer with complete integrity, a man of the soil, telling us his firsthand experiences about the havoc that GMOs are wreaking on our farm animals, grains, and vegetables. Howard Vlieger says, "There has been a fundamental change to the food supply as a result of ingredients from GMO crops ending up in 70-80% of the food. In addition, the ever-increasing amount of chemical residue (glyphosate) in the food and water is very concerning and very damaging to the health of all people who are exposed to this." We both agreed that We the People must take back our food supply from the devastating control of the big Agribusiness corporations!

CHAPTER 8

THE GREAT RECESSION: WALL STREET GETS THE GOLDMINE, MAIN STREET GETS THE SHAFT

"The abolition of the Glass-Steagall Act and its replacement with the Wild West deregulation of the Graham-Leach-Bliley Act was the most blatant example of the victory of Wild West cowboy capitalism over common sense"

--Peter Mathews

The bottom 99% of Americans are still staggering from the blows we took from the Great Recession of 2008-2009. This was the Greatest Recession since the Great Depression in terms of intensity, scope, and duration of effects. However, the top 1% (the super wealthy) have done extremely well in the so called "Recovery" beginning in 2009.

Although other actors such as the insurance and real estate industries could share some of the blame, the Great Recession was caused primarily by the reckless and greedy behavior of the biggest investment banks and credit rating agencies on Wall Street. Practicing Dollar Democracy, these huge financial corporations had bought influence with much of Congress, and even with U.S. Presidents, through billions of dollars of campaign contributions for decades. From 1990 to 2018 the Finance, Insurance, and Real Estate (FIRE) industry made $5,995,129,820 in campaign contributions to federal candidates, political parties, and outside groups, that spend to influence the elections. According to the Center for Public Integrity, "The financial sector is far and away the largest source of campaign contributions to federal candidates and parties, with insurance companies, securities and investment firms, real estate interests and commercial banks providing the bulk of that money."

Wall Street Associated Finance, Insurance, and Real Estate (FIRE) Industry Donors to Federal Candidates, Parties, Outside Groups: Top 20 Contributors, 2017-18

Rank	Contributor	Total Contribs
1	Bloomberg Lp	$95,660,416
2	Paloma Partners	$25,575,800
3	Citadel LLC	$19,482,756
4	Soros Fund Management	$18,433,207
5	Euclidean Capital	$16,418,900
6	National Assn of Realtors	$16,404,167
7	Renaissance Technologies	$15,744,022
8	Blackstone Group	$15,491,694
9	Marcus & Millichap	$9,676,295
10	Bain Capital	$8,941,698
11	Susquehanna International Group	$7,799,372
12	Baupost Group	$7,080,185
13	Elliott Management	$6,831,962
14	Wicklow Capital	$6,501,535
15	Beal Bank	$6,238,927
16	TD Ameritrade	$5,152,522
17	Franklin Resources	$5,126,854
18	Stephens Inc	$4,541,111
19	GH Palmer Assoc	$4,395,072
20	Goldman Sachs	$4,287,896

(https://www.opensecrets.org/industries/contrib.php?cycle=2018&ind=F)

Table 8-1 | Wall Street FIRE Industry Donors

Thousands of Americans Lose Their Homes and Jobs in the Great Recession

With the 2008 crash of some of the biggest financial houses on Wall Street and the resulting Great Recession, millions of Americans lost trillions of dollars' worth of equity in their homes. Thousands actually lost their homes. The country is still reeling and struggling to dig out of the ditch of this Great Recession. As I mentioned earlier, the so-called recovery has primarily benefitted the super wealthy owners and investors of Big Business.

In May 2019, the official unemployment rate was 3.6%. The real unemployment rate which includes the officially unemployed, the underemployed, temporarily employed, part-time workers who want to work full-time, and the long-term unemployed who have given up looking for work because of years of being rejected, all adds up to at least 8.1% unemployment. The American full-time workforce has shrunk by several percent. The labor force (workforce) participation rate was 67.3% in January 2000 and has dropped to 62.8% in April 2019 (tradingeconomics.com, May 3, 2019). Millions of Americans are uncounted in the workforce because they have stopped looking for work or cannot find full-time work. Annual worker productivity has gone up by 3.6%, yet workers' wages have gone up by only 1.3% after inflation is factored in (U.S. Bureau of Labor Statistics). Many small businesses cut back or were driven out of business. This didn't help matters any because small business hires two thirds of American workers. As more and more workers were laid off, there was less money for them to spend, and consumer demand went down, dampening the economic recovery. Two thirds of the jobs created since the so-called recovery began, have been low-paying jobs, forcing a downward spiral in median income. The American median household income of $51,000 today is 8.3% less than it was seven years ago just before the start of the Great Recession. The number of families, who had to take in unemployed relatives and children, has skyrocketed.

What happened? What caused the Wall Street crash and the ensuing Great Recession which caused such economic, social, emotional, and psychological devastation for millions of Americans? The reason this is referred to as the "Great Recession" is because it is far deeper, and its effects have been far longer-lasting and devastating than the periodic normal boom and bust cycle of the capitalist economy. Accompanying the Wall Street crash and its effects was also the trend starting earlier involving outsourcing of high-paying American manufacturing jobs to low-wage "Third World" (Global South) countries. These ranged from small countries with dependent economies such as Honduras, to larger countries such as Mexico, Indonesia, the Philippines, and Vietnam. Well-paying American manufacturing and high-tech jobs, such as Apple's iPhone and Microsoft's computer software production, were also exported to giant countries with cheap labor such as China and India. As these big corporations that took our jobs overseas made larger and larger profits on the cheap labor, they and the Wall Street banks invested in each other.

Before we begin looking at the Wall Street crash and the 2008 Great Recession, let's take a look at the tragic story of **Kevin Flanagan** who grew up in Long Beach, California and studied computer science and philosophy at California State University Long Beach. Kevin's story was told by authors Donald Barlett and James Steele in their recent book, *The Betrayal of the American Dream.* On the last day of his job Kevin packed a few boxes of his personal items for the back of his pick-up truck, after leaving the building where he worked for seven years. He got into his pickup truck, put a gun to his head, pulled the trigger, and killed himself. Kevin was a 41-year-old computer programmer. He had done computer programming work all his adult life. Then his job was outsourced to programmers from a low-wage country.

The practice of outsourcing has affected millions of American manufacturing and high-tech workers. For American business elites and the Wall Street titans that organize and maintain business stocks, exporting good American high paying jobs to cheap labor Third World countries is the best way to generate new and huge profits.

The increased value of corporate stocks on Wall Street provides huge profits and dividends for investors and CEOs. Outsourcing allows them to pay highly trained professionals, such as computer programmers and software engineers in China and India, one fourth the wage that an American computer science college graduate would have to be paid to write programs and produce software in the United States. Barlett and Steele call Kevin "a casualty of the new American economy". They point out that "only a few years before, programmers like him were seen as some of the brightest lights of a modern American workforce as technology became the backbone of so many corporate operations." Educated and hard-working, Kevin had an impressive resume with his last employer, Bank of America in Concorde, California and other jobs in the San Francisco Bay area and Los Angeles. His friends called him a "programming god." Another friend said that every time he got stuck on a computer program, Kevin would get him unstuck in a few seconds.

His employer Bank of America told him one day that he was being replaced, despite many years of loyal service. Thousands of high-tech workers and other high skilled workers are being replaced across United States because their corporate employers, with the help of federal policies, can hire a replacement worker for a lot less money.

According to Barlett and Steele, Kevin's replacement was a computer programmer from India who came to the United States under a U.S. government program implemented by Congress, because of lobbying by big business. The corporate lobbyists claimed this type of programmer was needed because of a shortage of American programmers and computer specialists. But in reality, it was a way for corporations to reduce salaries. The bitter reality was that Kevin was ordered to train his replacement worker or lose his small severance package. The situation must have torn him apart emotionally. He had studied hard, worked hard, abided by the rules, and still got fired.

After graduating from Cal State Long Beach, Kevin had worked as a programmer at McDonnell Douglas, and when Douglas was bought out by Boeing, he moved to the San Francisco Bay Area and worked as a computer programmer for two companies before joining Bank of America. Kevin worked as part of a unit at the bank's Concorde technology center in the East Bay, where computer programmers wrote code on money transfer transactions. Kevin's father Tom Flanagan told authors Barlett and Steele that Kevin was happy where he was, with his fellow workers, with his job, and with a small house that he had bought in nearby Pleasant Hill. Until Bank of America began shipping some of its work offshore and bringing programmers from India to the U.S. as guest workers, thanks to the visas issued by the U.S. government on the behest of Congress. Bank of America made an agreement in 2002 with a provider based in India to supervise part of this work transfer. Kevin even had to fix some of the mistakes coming in from overseas workers.

As time went on Kevin saw the disappearance of a small group of programmers. As more and more foreign guest workers came one by one, his longtime fellow programmers were laid off. Eventually he was the only one left. Although Kevin expected to be laid off eventually, what probably tipped him over the edge, as his father said, was the order that Kevin received to train his replacement worker.

Kevin's parents knew that he had felt betrayed by Bank of America, a company to which he had given so much time, commitment, and energy. What drove Kevin to such a desperate act of suicide? At least part of the responsibility must be shared by those politicians in power who voted for free trade, not fair trade, which resulted in the export of good meaningful jobs for Americans like Kevin. The uncontrolled profit motive of those who own the corporations, and of the Wall Street Stock Market to which they belong, has played a major role in the tragedies that have befallen thousands of individuals like Kevin.

The collective tragedy for the shrinking American middle class is that high paying manufacturing and technology jobs have been lost to low-wage "Third World" countries. The statistics are staggering: according to the Bureau of Labor Statistics, in 1950 manufacturing jobs made up 30% of the U.S. workforce. In the year 2000 this number had dropped to 11%. In 2011 manufacturing jobs, at one time the road to the American Dream, made up only 9% of the workforce. In 2015, manufacturing had dropped further to 8.7%. For this, the majority of the blame can be laid on shortsighted corporate business owners and their Wall Street stock market affiliates who have relentlessly pursued maximum profits, without consideration for human needs. The ethical question aside, the shrinking of the American middle class and its purchasing power has been a factor in this most recent Great Recession and our inability to decisively and strongly climb out of it. This will continue, until the U.S. government and the politicians in it (many of whose campaigns are sponsored by corporate interests and lobbyists) recognize that a market economy cannot prosper fully unless it's working people get paid well, in newly developed manufacturing and technology jobs; because consumer demand drives healthy growth in the economy and ultimately in shared prosperity. Our corporate and political leaders have a lot of rethinking to do regarding their policies of free trade, unregulated markets, and unfettered globalization of the American and world economy.

The Bi-partisan Dismantling of Glass-Steagall, the 2008 Wall Street Crash, and the Great Recession

As unregulated free-trade and the outsourcing of American manufacturing jobs skyrocketed in the 1990s, the stock value of publicly traded companies on Wall Street surged. The tech boom of the 1990s added increased value in the stock market. But what really blew up the bubble in the 1990s and early 2000's was the ultimate deregulation of the American financial sector. Under lobbying pressure and campaign contributions from the Big Banks and Wall Street, both Democratic and Republican politicians agreed to dismantle the Glass- Steagall Act. This Act, in response to the stock market crash and the banking fiasco in the Great Depression, was passed by Congress and signed by President Franklin Roosevelt to place a solid wall of separation between commercial banking and investment banking.

After the recession of 1920-21, the U.S. began a period of economic prosperity known as the Roaring Twenties. During this period there was tremendous innovation in products such as radio, refrigeration, and the auto industry. To encourage demand for these new products, consumer credit and banking were expanded. Banks such as Chase Bank and National City Bank began selling securities along with the more traditional banking products such as loans and deposits. As the 1920s went by, there was a boom in the stock market which eventually developed into a speculative bubble. Together with the bubble there was a tremendous amount of market manipulation. For example, there were well-organized purchasing pools which intentionally drove up the price of stocks and then sold these overvalued stocks to unsuspecting buyers just before it collapsed. Banks joined the roar of the 1920s by offering stocks of companies involved in leveraged pyramid-like schemes and other types of securities backed by questionable assets. To a large extent because of this, the stock market crashed in 1929 and the Great Depression arrived. As the following investigation showed, a tremendous amount of fraud in the financial and banking sector had preceded the crash.

In 1933 Congress passed and President Franklin Roosevelt implemented the Glass-Steagall Act to address the fraud and abuse in the banks and the stock market. The Glass-Steagall Act separated commercial banking and investment banking for the next 66 years. During this time no major financial crisis occurred. No Great Depression, no Great Recession. There was a reason for this. Glass- Steagall allowed commercial banks, where the vast majority of Americans kept their checking and savings accounts, to accept deposits and make loans that were conservative and safe. Both federal agencies, the FDIC and the FSLIC, insured these accounts. These banks were prevented by Glass-Steagall from making highly leveraged, risky, and speculative investments in areas such as commercial real estate. On the other hand, Glass-Steagall allowed large investment banks on Wall Street, whose money came from large private investors, who were willing to risk big and win big, to invest in high risk and high reward ventures such as stocks and speculative real estate and commodities. Unlike the millions of accounts in the commercial banks, the private investors' big-money in the Wall Street investment houses was not insured by the federal government. The attitude of government leaders, just after the Great Depression began, was that commercial banks, holding millions of regular Americans' hard-earned money, must be extra careful with it. The investment banks, funded primarily by extremely wealthy investors, would have much more leeway to make risky investments and reap risky rewards. Sounds like common sense governmental policy. It was. In the late 1990s this common-sense governmental policy, which had worked so well for over 60 years, was thrown out of the window by bipartisan agreement.

Let's now investigate the repeal of the common-sense-based Glass-Steagall Act in 1999. The Depression-era Glass-Steagall Act was made law by President Franklin Roosevelt and the Democratic Party dominated United States Congress. The main reason for it was to stabilize the American financial system by separating commercial banking from investment banking. The commercial banks, in which the vast majority of Americans kept their checking accounts and savings accounts, were prohibited from making risky investments that could fail and cause tremendous losses of working Americans' hard-earned money. These risky investments included speculation in real estate as well as risky investments in the stock market. Glass-Steagall prevented the commercial banks also from lending money to investors in the stock market. The government also agreed to insure these individual accounts of millions of Americans up to a set dollar amount. On the other hand, the investment banks were allowed to take part in riskier activity such as stock investments, speculative activity in real estate and commodities, etc. The government felt that investment bankers were taking risks with very, very rich people's money with their approval. The risks were very high, but so were the payoffs for mostly wealthy people willing to risk their private money. Government would not insure these investment banks accounts.

Some of the major players in the repeal of Glass-Steagall by the passage of the Financial Services Modernization Act, also known as the Gramm-Leach-Bliley Act of 1999, included Democratic President Bill Clinton, Republican U.S. Senator from Texas Phil Gramm, his wife economics professor Wendy Gramm, and Robert Rubin, President Clinton's former Secretary of the Treasury. Robert Weissman, the president of Public Citizen, claims that "among a long list of the regulatory moves large and small over the last two decades, Graham–Leach–Bliley was the signal piece of financial deregulation". He goes on to say, "repeal of Glass-Steagall had many important direct effects but the most important was to change the culture of commercial banking to emulate Wall Street's high-risk speculative betting approach". Nobel prize-winning economist Joseph Stiglitz says that "commercial banks are not supposed to be high-risk ventures; they are supposed to manage other people's money very conservatively. It is with this understanding that the government agrees to pick up the tab should they fail. Investment banks on the other hand, have traditionally managed rich people's money – people who can take big risks in order to get bigger returns. When repeal of Glass-Steagall brought investment and commercial banks together, the investment bank culture came out on top. There was a demand for the kind of high returns that could be obtained only through high leverage and big risk taking."

In addressing lessons that should be learned from the Wall Street debacle Robert Wiseman claims that Glass-Steagall's key insight was "in the need to treat regulation from an industry structure point of view." In other words, Wiseman says that Glass-Steagall authors did not try to establish a regulatory system that oversaw companies that combine commercial and investment banking, instead they simply banned the combining of these two separate types of banking systems. And Wiseman claims that to clean-up the current mess from the Wall Street debacle of 2008 and the ensuing Great Recession, we need to have strategies that would focus on the structure of industry, meaning that we must break up the big banks and have more traditional regulation.

Second, Wiseman says that we need to return to Glass-Steagall's specific understanding: depository institutions such as the commercial banks, backed by federal insurance, should not be involved in risky and speculative betting as practiced by investment bankers. Wiseman says that we should not just reinstate Glass-Steagall but "infuse its underlying principles throughout the financial regulatory scheme." In other words, commercial banks should not be engaged in speculative activities. The job of the commercial banks must be limited to providing credit for the real economy. They should not be engaged in betting on derivatives and other exotic financial instruments.

Third, says Wiseman, too much political power is exercised by giant financial institutions and for this reason alone these "too big to fail" banks must be broken up. Just over 100 years ago the same sentiment was echoed by leaders of the Progressive Movement such as President Teddy Roosevelt and California Governor Hiram Johnson. The Progressive Movement reformers of the early 1900s decided to break up the economic and political power of the big corporate monopolies in steel, railroads, oil and other industries. Progressive reformers made up of both Republicans and Democrats believed that increased competition and some regulation in the economy would result in a more level playing field among business owners, and between them and working Americans, including laws prohibiting child labor. Modern corporate leaders either had historical amnesia or they never fully understood the connection between the supply-side economic policies of the 1920s, 1980s, and the 2000s and the immediate crashing of our economy that followed these policies.

Shared prosperity and widespread economic growth are not produced by trickle-down economics but instead by economic expansion from the ground up. The American capitalist economy has enjoyed widespread prosperity only when government played a major and efficient role. A large American middle class was born and grew only when government provided opportunity for those at the ground-level. It provided free and affordable public education, skills training, the right to unionize, investment in public infrastructure, including roads, highways, bridges, public libraries, and research and development in technology, especially high-tech, public health, and the arts.

The abolition of the Glass-Steagall Act and its replacement with the Wild West deregulation of the Graham-Leach-Bliley Act was the most blatant example of the victory of Wild West cowboy capitalism. It was a victory over common sense, ethically-based, regulated, humanistic, and sustainable capitalism as practiced at varying levels in Western Europe, Canada, and Japan. In order to fully understand the causes and possible solutions to this Great Recession and its aftermath, from which millions are still suffering, we must take a very close look at the abolition of Glass-Steagall, and its effect on the Wall Street Crash of 2008.

Listening to the voices of Big Bank and Wall Street lobbyists, who wanted to remove the wall of separation between commercial banking and investment banking, bipartisan political and financial leaders such as Democratic President Bill Clinton, Republican U.S. Senator from Texas Phil Gramm, his wife economics professor Wendy Gramm, Treasury Secretary Robert Rubin, Deputy Treasury Secretary Lawrence Summers, and many Democratic and Republican members of Congress, led the effort to repeal Glass-Steagall and implement Gramm-Leach-Bliley. This Act removed the Glass-Steagall firewall between commercial and investment banking and allowed mergers and combining of banks in both fields. Glass-Steagall was finally abolished and replaced by Graham-Leach-Bliley, passed with bipartisan support in a Republican led Congress, with Democratic President Bill Clinton signing it into law in 1999. The wishes of the Big Banks and Wall Street were implemented by the votes of 155 Democrats and 207 Republicans in the U.S. House of Representatives.

The supporters of abolishing Glass-Steagall, allowing commercial banks to make high-risk investments while merging with investment banks, argued that Glass-Steagall's strict regulations were outdated and that a 21st Century banking model was needed. The model they called for was one based on deregulation, and mergers that created huge banking and investment firms as with the merger of Citigroup and Travelers Insurance. They argued that by the government allowing this to occur, United States banking and investment would grow, and the large powerful units could compete on the world market. Senator Graham and Larry Summers argued that the deregulation and merging of commercial and investment banking was helping to allocate resources where they belonged in the investment market. These men and their anti-Glass-Steagall allies did not understand, or completely ignored, the tremendous risk to the American financial system that their policies were bringing.

Nobel prize-winning economist Joseph Stiglitz noted "when repeal of Glass-Steagall brought investment and commercial banks together, the investment bank culture came on top. There was a demand for the kind of high returns that could be obtained only through high leverage and big risk-taking."

Stiglitz was talking about the risk-taking and fraudulent activities engaged in by huge banking/investment corporations on Wall Street after the repeal of the Glass-Steagall Act and the implementation of the Graham-Leach-Bliley Act by Democratic President Bill Clinton and the Republican led Congress in 1999. These huge banking/investment companies on Wall Street such as Goldman Sachs, Citigroup, Lehman Brothers, Morgan Stanley, JP Morgan Chase, Bank of America, and Countrywide, and AIG, an insurance company that was allowed to deal in securities, all promoted predatory lending in the home mortgage business. Most of these commercial/investment banks played a key role as sellers and buyers of mortgage-backed securities, such as collateralized debt obligations (CDO's), as well as credit default swaps and other dangerous financial derivatives. Had Glass-Steagall remained in place, commercial banks would have been banned from engaging in these activities. Commercial banks would not have merged with investment banks to engage in the risky activity of creating such exotic financial instruments.

Collateralized Debt Obligations (CDOs), Predatory Lending, and the Wall Street Crash

Let's examine one of these most risky financial instruments that helped cause the Wall Street crash of 2008: collateralized debt obligations (CDOs).

The abolishing of Glass-Steagall allowed commercial banks to engage in risky financial activity like investment banks, such as buying and selling CDOs, or to merge with investment banks and engage in this activity. Kimberly Amadeo (About.com) has defined and explained Collateralized Debt Obligations (CDOs), their relationship to derivatives, mortgage-backed securities, and subprime mortgages, all of which played a major role in causing the great recession. Amadeo says that CDOs are "sophisticated financial tools that banks use to repackage individual loans into a product that can be sold to investors on the secondary market. These packages consist of auto loans, credit card debt, mortgages or corporate debt. They are called collateralized because the promised repayment of loans are the collateral that gives the CDOs value."

CDOs are a type of derivative. A derivative is a financial product that derives its value from an underlying asset. There are several types of derivatives including put options, call options, and futures contracts. These have been used for a long time in the commodities and stock markets. If the CDOs consist of corporate debt they are called asset-backed commercial paper. If the CDOs consist of mortgage loans they are called mortgage-backed securities. If the mortgage loans are made to people with less than perfect credit history, they are called subprime mortgages.

Amadeo is absolutely correct when she says that banks sold CDOs for three reasons: 1) the funds they collected provided them with more cash to make new loans, 2) it moved the loan's risk of defaulting from the lending bank to the investors, 3) CDOs gave banks new and more profitable product to sell, which boosted share prices and bank managers' bonuses.

As the housing market heated up and expanded in the early 2000s, mortgage-backed CDOs were being bought and sold like hotcakes. As the demand for them skyrocketed, even subprime mortgage loans were made and sold as high value CDOs, since the higher interest rate required on subprime mortgages produced more investment income for the holder of subprime CDOs. That is, as long as the subprime borrowers were making their house payments. Presidents Bush and Clinton had pushed Congress to make laws and policies that made it easier to get a mortgage even if you did not have the best of credit.

Not only were subprime loans made in record numbers but so were adjustable rate mortgages (ARMs). Homebuyers with poor and even decent credit were offered these mortgages. For example. ARMs provided "teaser" low interest rates for the first three years, at which time the loan would reset to much higher rates. With home values skyrocketing, many buyers purchased homes with a very low three-year interest rate, hoping to sell and make a profit before the ARM loan reset at the much higher rate. Some of them did not meet their deadline, and instead lost their homes to foreclosure.

As subprime mortgages, including ARMs, became more popular, more CDOs were produced and sold. As the red-hot housing market got even hotter, CDOs produced even more money and the demand for them increased further. As Kimberly Amadeo points out, a CDO's value cannot be ascertained by seeing or touching it. Instead its value is based on a computer model. Thousands of college graduates started working on Wall Street as "quant jocks." They wrote computer programs that would configure the value of the bundle of loans in the CDO. As the demand for more sophisticated CDOs grew, the quant jocks made more complicated computer models. They segmented the loan into slices or tranches. For example, they designed different CDO tranches to hold different parts of the adjustable rate mortgage (ARM): one tranche would hold the low interest portion of the ARM, for example the first three years of the loan. Another CDO tranche would hold the portion of the loan that had higher interest rates during the years after the interest rate reset at a higher level. If you were a conservative investor you could buy the low interest rate, low risk tranche. If you were a daring investor, you could buy the higher rate, higher risk CDO tranche. As long as the economy and housing prices grew, everything seemed to go well, at least on the surface. However, danger lurked beneath the surface: not only was an asset bubble growing in housing, credit card debt, and auto debt, but the dangerous deregulation of banking and Wall Street with the abolition of Glass- Steagall and the deregulation of the housing industry brought about the subprime mortgage and housing crash, and the related collapse of large banks such as Bear Stearns and Lehman Brothers on Wall Street.

The repeal of the Glass-Steagall Act, and its replacement by the Graham-Bliley-Leach Act in the late 1990s, was, as we've seen, financial deregulation in its worst form. This allowed the commercial banks, which held millions of dollars in the modest checking and savings accounts of working Americans, to make risky investments, including in financially unsound home mortgage loans. Many of these loans were made by predatory lenders to many people who could not afford them. In some cases, the mortgage brokers and banks that arranged and approved these loans, including subprime loans, knew that these borrowers were not financially qualified and could very well default on them. Yet they gave out these loans, in many cases using fraudulent methods. For example, they created no-document loans. For this type of loan, the lender did not ask for any information and the borrower did not provide it. In some cases, even underemployed and unemployed people, and those with poor credit, received home loans for hundreds of thousands of dollars.

Lenders no longer had to worry about the risk of the borrower defaulting, because the lender immediately sold these loans to other banks and Wall Street investors, by packaging them as CDO mortgage-backed securities. In many cases these mortgage-backed securities were given AAA ratings by professional rating agencies such as Moody's and Standard & Poor's. And the ratings agencies were paid by big commercial/investment banks on Wall Street. This was as if I, a college professor, were paid my full salary directly by my students, while I was teaching them and grading them. Of course, there's a great probability that the grades I was issuing to my students would be influenced by the money (my salary) they were directly paying me. The grades that I then issued them would not be very credible, would they? The ratings agencies grading the big banks who paid their salaries were not very credible either. This arrangement played a big role in the crash of the Big Banks and Wall Street.

Many of the CDO mortgage-backed securities contained bad loans within them. When some home mortgage borrowers defaulted on their loan because their ARM interest rate reset at a much higher rate, or they lost their jobs to outsourcing, or the payments on the subprime loan were higher than expected, then the securitization food chain suffered a chain reaction. Since the original lenders and banks had sold the bad loans, they were off the hook. But the banks and investors who bought those loans became liable and started to lose millions of dollars. By 2008 investment banks such as Lehman Brothers were forced to declare bankruptcy, and Bear Stearns started to go bankrupt but was bought by J.P. Morgan through U.S. government pressure and support.

By 2007, in addition to the normal home foreclosure rate, skyrocketing rates of foreclosure had occurred in the subprime and ARM markets. As millions of foreclosed homes flooded the market, overall housing values started dropping precipitously. The home building industry suffered a severe downturn. At this time, the housing crisis caused many of the commercial banks to stop lending money to each other, for fear of being stuck with subprime mortgages on which many homeowners were defaulting. With the money supply tightening up, people could not borrow as easily to finance the purchases of automobiles and other goods, and businesses could not borrow as easily to hire more people and expand. The federal government desperately promised to address the subprime crisis by guaranteeing $75 billion in subprime debt to help the banks continue their borrowing and lending to each other and the public. This was totally ineffective. The Great Recession struck with a vengeance in 2008.

The Great Recession of 2008-09 was the worst recession since the Great Depression. The economy shrank in five quarters, including four quarters in a row. It was the longest recession since the Great Depression, lasting 18 months. Its effects have been devastating for the economy and millions of Americans in many ways. As I write today, in 2019, middle-class and working-class Americans are still struggling to overcome the negative effects of the Great Recession: at 3.6% official unemployment, millions of Americans are still out of work (tradingeconomics.com, May 3, 2019). Many of them are not counted as unemployed because they have stopped looking for work, not being able to find full-time jobs. According to the U.S. Department of Labor's Bureau of Labor Statistics, the Labor Force Participation Rate has plummeted from 66.4% in January 2007 to 63.2% in January 2019 (thebalance.com, "Labor Force Participation Rate and Why It Hasn't Improved Much", by Kimberly Amadeo, Feb. 6, 2019). In January 2019, the real unemployment rate (known as U-6) was 8.1%, which includes those who have given up looking for work, those who cannot find full-time work, those who cannot find permanent work, and others who have missed being counted on the unemployment rolls; a huge portion of those who found work, during this anemic "recovery", are earning much less than they were in their previous job.

The Great Recession has left millions of young Americans behind. Large numbers of them cannot find work despite graduating with a college degree. When they do find work their annual starting salary is $2,042 less than it was for their counterparts before the recession. The inflation adjusted average starting salary for a college graduate in 1969 was $59,169; In 2007 (just before the Great Recession started), it was $52,046; In 2015, it was $50,219 (naceweb.org). In 2018, the average college graduate's salary was $50,004 (naceweb.org). High paying manufacturing jobs that were outsourced to low-wage countries have not been replaced by high paying new technology manufacturing jobs. During the last few years of recovery from the recession, the top 1% of the population has captured 93% of the new income generated, according to UC Berkeley economist Emmanuel Saez. Wall Street and the big banks are sitting on over $2 trillion, the majority of it parked in the Federal Reserve, drawing interest income. Instead, this money should have been used in low interest rate loans to small businesses and entrepreneurs to create millions of new technology well-paying jobs, producing products and services for domestic consumption and export.

The Government Bailout Gave Wall Street the Goldmine and Main Street the Shaft

The Wall Street Bailout based on the Emergency Economic Stabilization Act of 2008 has been a great benefit to the big Wall Street banks. It is the reason that those Big Banks are sitting on $2 trillion. The plan was for the U.S. Treasury to "buy $700 billion of troubled mortgages from the banks, and then modify them to help struggling home owners. Section 109 of the act, in fact, specifically empowered the Treasury secretary to 'facilitate loan modifications to prevent avoidable foreclosures.' (Matt Taibbi, "Secrets and Lies of the Bailout", January 24, 2013, *Rolling Stone*). However, the Fed and the Treasury Department almost immediately decided to directly inject billions of dollars in cash into Wall Street banks such as Citigroup and Goldman Sachs. As Matt Taibbi points out, that what was sold as a 'bailout of both banks and homeowners' instantly became a bank-only operation...." As a result, working middle class Americans such as **Rossana** and **Arturo Cambron** lost their home because they could not obtain a loan modification. The irony is that Arturo was a Real Estate agent whose income dropped when the housing market was devastated by the Great Recession.

Another Californian, **Sherry Hernandez**'s new bank would not honor the temporary loan modification agreed to by her previous bank and decided to foreclose on the home owned by Sherry and her husband **Alfredo**. She had won a Stay of Eviction while her case was being appealed. Here is Sherry's poignant story as she formats it in her own words:

227

Exhibit 8-2 | Transcript

* The following names of people and entities used herein have been changed in order to protect their privacy:

WE ARE NOT DEADBEATS

Our story, like so many thousands of others, is about the greed of the corporation and their need for avarice that far exceeded their inclusion into a humane society. They could cultivate this inhuman treatment of their customers through the implementation of corporate policy and enforcing this policy by using their employees. They do not allow their employees to make any decision that would deviate from the corporate policies and procedures, no matter what exceptions or deviations they may encounter.

The officers of the corporation who implement the corporate policies and procedures never have to look into the eyes of their customers and see the damage they cause, nor do they have to hear their case if there is an exception or hardship that varies from the norm.

Our country, our families, are not being attacked by the atom bomb as we had feared back in the 50's. A bomb shelter will not save us from the enemy. The enemy comes from within. We have sold out our birthright as Americans, our constitutional amendments to the corporate powers.

The corporations are holding the people to the letter of THEIR laws, while the laws of the United States and laws of morality and ethics are being ignored.

Fifth Amendment – due process, double jeopardy,

self- incrimination, eminent domain.

*No person shall be held to answer for a capital, or otherwise infamous crime, unless on a presentment or indictment of a Grand Jury, except in cases arising in the land or naval forces, or in the Militia, when in actual service in time of War or public danger; nor shall any person be subject for the same offence to be twice put in jeopardy of life or limb; nor shall be compelled in any criminal case to be a witness against himself, **nor be deprived of life, liberty, or property**, without due process of law; nor shall private property be taken for public use, without just compensation.*

The mortgages corporations have foreclosed on homes they do not own, homes they do not have the paperwork for, and even homes that are not in arrears, yet still the madness is allowed to continue. They are using an electronic registration system (MERS) instead of the actual note to foreclose, thereby creating multiple errors in foreclosures and still this has been allowed to continue.

The government has given them bailout money to assist distressed homeowners and still they persist in their fraudulent behavior. They have covered their crimes in excess bureaucracy and red tape, buried so deep beneath their employee stockpile that the CEO's of these corporations feel safe to continue.

OUR CASE:

We knew we had a problem one month after we had obtained our loan and our "opt out" policy had expired. Our-Bank* raised our interest rate on the 1st by 1.25% and on the 2nd by 5%, immediately increasing our monthly payment by over $600.00 per month.

They had set the standard by which we could not "qualify" for a 30-year fixed rate. They had set the standard which said we could only afford 'X' amount in interest payments. Then after squeezing us in as tight as we were willing to go, they raised the bar once the trap was set…and we get the blame.

At least we had not agreed to a 3-year prepayment penalty.

It was on March 29, 2006 that we found ourselves in a restaurant in the evening signing papers in the presence of a notary. We called Gerald R* while we were seated at the table and reminded him that the prepayment penalty was supposed to be waived. The documents were being signed only three days prior to closing and we were already working under an escrow extension. It was not nice to pull this kind of switch on us at the last minute.

Gerald R* told us that he couldn't get it through without that and asked us to at least agree to a one-year prepayment penalty. "Just go ahead and sign it," he said, "I will promise you that we will only hold you to one year." We did not want to sign something that did not reflect that, so we adjusted the document to reflect his words. We crossed out 36 months and hand wrote in "12 months" and it was notarized with the changes.

We asked the notary if we could do this and he told us that he could notarize anything, but if it were not acceptable, we would have to notarize the entire contract again. So we signed it and had it notarized **with the changes**.

We were already in our new home for one week, when Gerald R* sent home a 3-year prepayment addendum with my daughter, whom he saw at work. The date was April 11th, thirteen days after we signed the contract. "We need this in the file temporarily", he said. "Don't worry, I see you every day at work, I wouldn't cheat you. We will honor the one year, but we just need this for now."

He was the General Sales Manager for Our-Bank*, who else could we have checked with. We believed him, in spite of our doubts, because of the position he held with the corporation.

One month into our new loan, Our-Bank* raised their rate by 1.25% on the 1st, and 5% on the 2nd and we were shocked. We didn't even know that was legally allowed. We did not know somewhere on Wall Street executives were busy adjusting the Libor rates for their convenience are our demise. This sort of interest manipulation was not legal when we had gotten a loan over 18 years ago.

The interest was already high, but 8.85 on a jumbo loan was unbelievable. We had a family meeting and agreed that we would have to pay the option payment for nine months, although that was never our intent. We paid the full amount the 1st 3 months and then agreed to pay the option payment on the 1st mortgage and pay down extra on the HELOC to lower our principle, until the one-year prepayment penalty was up and we could opt out of our loan and get a 30-year fixed. Our credit was good and property rates were rising at that time.

We had a new loan in place and ready to go prior to the year end date, but the broker informed us it would be approximately $25,000, more than the original loan, because of the 3 year prepayment penalty. We corrected him and informed him that we only had a one-year prepayment penalty and he assured us that we were mistaken.

A single phone call should have corrected the problem, but the corporate machine does not work like that. You see, Our- Bank's* corporate policy was that all loans should have a 3- year prepayment penalty. The disclaimer that they inserted inside the loan docs that state we can negotiate for another loan without a prepayment penalty is bogus, because inside the corporate mill, there is only one type of loan.

Twenty years ago, a single phone call would have fixed the problem. If we had been related to a senator or someone famous they might have heard us, and worked toward fixing the error, but what we did not know was that our loans had been sold out as securities and they did not want to lose a single investment. They had ceased to be humane and had become the machine.

We did not know what was going on behind the scenes then. All we knew was that we had only agreed to one year, and even that was under duress. We called Our-Bank* and thought the problem would be resolved. It was not.

Meanwhile, we lost our refinance loan and had to seek out another only to find that Our-Bank* did not pay our taxes, either, although we had an impound account; the payoff was now $35,000 more than the total of the loan. They added the penalties and interest onto our loan also. The new lenders would not lend us money over 80% of the property value, so we lost another chance to escape the 8.75% interest on the Our-Bank* loan.

On April 26, 2006, the Department of Corporations sent out a News Release to all its members with the following paragraph:

> **Mortgage Fraud.** *Predatory mortgage lending involves a wide array of abusive practices and usually takes place in the subprime market, targeting borrowers with weak or blemished credit records. **The most common lending abuses include excessive fees, abusive prepayment penalties....***

Although, Our-Bank* must have had this memo in their possession at the time, in February of 2007, they still would not release us from the fraudulent prepayment penalty. They sent us back a letter along with a copy of the adjusted, notarized prepayment addendum that reflected the changes we had made at the table. It was proof that they had the one-year prepayment addendum in their files. I thought they would have to honor it now, and I wondered why they would send it to me, but I soon learned that in a corporation, "the left hand doesn't know what the right hand is doing."

I faxed them back the copy of the prepayment addendum that they sent me, along with a letter asking them to release us. They still refused. I asked them to roll our loan over into a 30-year fixed at the new lower interest rate. They would not answer my calls. I went into an Our- Bank* office and saw a loan officer about refinancing our loan. He took my information, assured me he could help and then never returned my calls. Time and time, attempt after attempt was rejected. A loan modification was not even a question at that time, we just wanted to be refinanced at a reasonable rate.

Every month that we were held hostage to the fraudulent prepayment penalty, we went into debt $2,500 more.

Each government office referred us to another, but none of them did anything by way of investigation.

Meanwhile, time passed, and our debt increased, and we realized that if we didn't do something, we would be stuck in the toxic loan that was dragging us under. We were put into the position of taking money out of our income property to pay down the prepayment penalty and pay our loan down. No one was going to have sympathy for a family that owned two homes. It didn't matter that we had been cheated, we couldn't find anyone to listen. We had to borrow $130,000 against our income property at 8.5% interest in order to have enough to pay the 2nd, and loan fees, and an attorney if we were to need one.

We wrote the BBB (Better Business Bureau) back, and forwarded the letter to Our-Bank*, we also wrote the Department of Corporations in our further quest for help. Our debt was increasing daily and our property was dropping rapidly in value.

On July 28th, 2007, Our-Bank* sent us their "final" ruling on our request to waive the prepayment penalty. They would NOT release us from the 3-year prepayment penalty, regardless of the fact they had the notarized 1-year prepayment addendum in their file. They had somehow managed to find the 2nd prepayment addendum. The one that was NOT notarized and NOT supposed to make it to our file.

This is where the beauty of a corporation comes into play. Erica R*, didn't have to live in our home, she didn't have to suffer the injustice, rejecting our petition was just a job to her and she was just following orders. Patty M* does not have to accept responsibility for her actions, she is part of a corporation and she is simply following orders. We will never get to meet the personnel responsible for ruining our lives, they are well hidden in their luxury homes in enclosed communities, away from the pain that they have inflicted through their depraved indifference.

As we struggled to save our new home, we had to listen to the bad press about homeowners being greedy, that we were the ones who were the deadbeats. While Our-Bank* held us to the faulty prepayment penalty addendum like a bulldog to a bone, they dismissed their own incompetence by blaming the consumer.

After refinancing our income property, and after Our-Bank* refused to honor the one-year prepayment addendum, we sought out legal help. We still believed that the 7th Amendment was a right that we could use in our favor. We still believed justice would prevail. We sought out an attorney and told him we wanted a jury trial.

So, with our limited resources we attempted to take on one of the largest richest corporations in the United

States. We had hoped that justice would prevail.

On August 28, 2007, Our-Bank* received a notice from the Department of Corporations. Because of this notice, Our- Bank* decided to release us from the 3-year prepayment penalty, a mote point considering that they had already made up the difference by delaying the release and property values were now dropping making it more difficult to find another loan. They took NO responsibility for the six months that they illegally held us to the prepayment penalty, nor did they offer to refinance or give us a financial stipend for the money they had already extorted from us. Our attorney tried to negotiate for them to return the money that they had taken from us or rewrite our loan. They denied that Gerald R* had ever worked for them and denied responsibility for his actions.

I sent our attorney copies of e-mails from the Our-Bank* office listing Gerald R* as General Sales Manager. They still denied that the corporation was responsible. They tried to lay the blame in the lap of their ex-employee.

While the executives of these large banking institutions were collecting bonus money for a job well done, families like ours were losing their homes and being ridiculed for our poor financial judgment. Banks were getting bailouts and accusing the homeowners of looking for an easy way out.

During all this time and the subsequent months, we pleaded with Our-Bank* for relief, they were not even willing to consider it. Their final offer of settlement was $2,000. Yet in October 2008, Our-Bank*/The-Bank-That-Took-Over-Our-Lender* (now merged into a single entity) agreed to a settlement with the State of California, for 8.4 billion dollars to help distressed homeowners, they have yet to honor it.

The attorneys had numerous meetings with the judge as we awaited trial. As they met in the judge's office we were permitted to sit outside in the courtroom, if we chose to attend. Even though it was our trial and our home, we had to place our trust in an attorney we had only just met. He was personable and forthcoming with information, but we were not allowed to be privy to what was said behind closed doors.

In January of 2010, The-Bank-That-Took-Over-Our-Lender* filed 'in limine's' to petition the court to have our evidence removed from trial. Our attorney seemed discouraged. He told us that he could only argue them in court, but the judge had implied that he was inclined to grant The-Bank-That-Took-Over-Our-Lender's* request.

We could not believe that the court could eliminate evidence that was included in signed notarized documents that were part of our file and mailed to us by Our-Bank*. The judge ordered us to mediation to be paid for by Our- Bank*.

During this lengthy waiting period I tried to contact my government officials, to see if I could get help for my family as well as other homeowners in this toxic situation. Our rights, the rights I had been raised to believe were available to all citizens, were being stripped from us. I could not believe that after three years we were still not going to trial. So, I began writing our government representatives for help, I was disappointed in the responses that I received. They were generic and did not relate to my individual situation and although they talked about reform, no true reform was being implemented.

This is quoted from an e-mail from U.S. Senator Diane Feinstein's office:

> *"As part of President Obama's efforts to reduce foreclosures, the Administration is using $75 billion of Troubled Asset Relief Program (TARP) funds to finance a mortgage modification program, known as Making Home Affordable. Specifically, this program requires that in cases where refinancing is more cost effective than foreclosure, mortgages be modified to make monthly payments more affordable. Additionally, the Making Home Affordable initiative includes a systematic program through the government sponsored enterprises Fannie Mae and Freddie Mac to refinance loans into more affordable interestrates. This program targets homeowners who have lost equity due to the housing market decline, yet have not defaulted on their payments."*

U.S. Senator Barbara Boxer's office sent me the following e-mail:

> *"Thank you for taking the time to write and share your views with me. Your comments will help me continue to represent you and other Californians to the best of my ability. Be assured that I will keep your views in mind as the Senate considers legislation on this or similar issues."*

A spokesperson from U.S. Representative Dana Rohrabacher's office told us that it was a shame all of the homeowners were in trouble. Reform was needed, but there was nothing their office could do to help. He recommended we get a lawyer. When I told him we had a lawyer, but we couldn't get a court date, he told me to talk to my lawyer about that and see what he could do.

The State Attorney General took a copy of our letter and informed us that they could do nothing to help us legally, but they would use our letter to go after the Corporate Executives at Our-Bank*.

I didn't put much stock in what the State Attorney General office had to say but in May of 2010, **they sent us a letter informing us we had been named as witnesses in the lawsuit against the Our-Bank* executives.**

After three years, as we still awaited a trial date, we sent a letter to Governor Arnold Schwarzenegger's Office asking for help in getting our trial on the calendar with our evidence included, and amazingly his office tried to help. They sent our correspondence to the Department of Corporations, however, the Department of Corporations never even opened and read our letter, they just forwarded it on to the The-Bank-That-Took- Over-Our-Lender* Attorney's, which was inappropriate since we were in a lawsuit with them. The the-Bank- That-Took-Over-Our-Lender* Attorney called our attorney, and it did nothing toward moving our court date forward.

We had filed the lawsuit and hired an attorney so that we could save our home and our reputation. As we suffered through delay after delay, The-Bank-That-Took-Over-Our- Lender* pushed us toward the depletion of our resources
while they spent recklessly and with abandon an amount that far exceeded the amount it would have taken them to settle with us or release us from the

prepayment penalty after one year as agreed.

In February of 2010, Judge John S* sent us into mandatory mediation, after implying that he would grant   The-Bank-That-Took-Over-Our-Lender's* motion to remove our evidence from trial. Why was the court trying to disarm us before we even had a chance to state our case? We do not know, but we were finding it more and more difficult to find someone who would tell us the truth. What is happening to our country? What is happening to our laws?

We agreed to a meager settlement because, quite frankly, we were afraid. When they sent us the agreement to sign they had already violated and changed the agreement.

We felt as if we had been kicked in the gut, once again. Not only had they cheated us on the prepayment penalty, they were callously trying to cheat us again. They had little or no regard the hardship they had caused us. They were playing us like a game of chess and they had just called "check".

Moreover, our own attorney had just forwarded us the agreement without reading it or going over it with us. He was tiring of the case and wanted to move on and we felt trapped in a perpetual web of deceit.

There was a meeting of the attorneys on March 3rd, telling the court it was settled, however, after they reneged on the settlement, our attorney went back to court and informed the judge that there would be no settlement.

The judge gave us what he claimed was our final trial date of December 6th, 2010.

Our attorney had already been paid $30,000 thus far and it was becoming apparent he was tiring of the fight. He did not give us updates unless we called, and often we had to make repeated calls before receiving a response.

In April of 2010, our new lender, Xyzmortgage*, told us we qualified for a modification and they would take 30 to 45 days to complete the final processes. We were relieved, since our expenses were mounting, however the time came and went and they began to stall and lose our paperwork, as is so often the case. We knew that we were being forced into a position where we no longer would have a choice.

We were confident that we had a good case and that the jury would find in our favor. If we could make back the money that we had lost we could pay it toward our home and we could lower our payments without any further help, but it seemed that we were not going to get to see that day in court in time to salvage our home. In August of 2010, over 5 years after buying our home, we missed our first payment. We were losing hope in ever seeing justice. Xyzmortgage* called and told us they were almost at a point of decision regarding our modification, only 30 to 45 more days, but as we neared the date of our trial, they had still not made a decision.

In December 2010, we missed our 2nd payment as we used the money to pay our attorney in anticipation of court costs, **but our attorney lied and told us that the judge vacated our trial date.**

(We later discovered that our attorney had told the judge we would accept the previous settlement, something we did not agree to do.)

In January of 2011, Xyzmortgage* issued us a 3-month temporary Modification starting in Februray 2011. In March 2011, Xyzmortgage* sold our mortgage to Our- Latest-Bank*. Our-Latest-Bank* has already told us that they will not honor the modification. Our-Latest-Bank* originally stated that they wanted to go into business by buying risky loans at pennies on the dollar so that they could help distressed homeowners.

Our-Latest-Bank* is headed by the same executive that headed up Our-Bank* Home Loans. To date, their reputation has been as a company that is in the business of foreclosing.

They had sold our loan to the same executives we were scheduled to testify against in court.

As, June 10, 2011, we had yet to see the inside of the courtroom and our trial date had now been vacated with no future date on the calendar. Our attorney has grown weary of the battle and no longer answers our calls. **No doubt, we would later discover, because he had worked behind our back to shut down our case.** Our increased debt, due to this fiasco has risen to over $300,000.00 and we still have no resolution.

Our loan has been sold back to the same monsters that we fought so hard to escape. **These are the same executives that we had been slated to testify against, so we do not expect to see fair treatment**

from them.

So as we, the hard-working middle class homeowners are marched out of our homes and onto the streets, the executives who orchestrated this fiasco are rewarded with new ventures and bonuses.

Billy S* - former executive of Our-Bank Home Loans* recently named in a California lawsuit that settled for 6.5 million dollars now works as head of The World of Lending Group*: The-Bank-That-Took-Over-Our-Lender Corporation*.

Larry P* – former executive of Our-Bank Home Loans* recently named in several lawsuit by investors, **including the FHFA**, for millions of dollars – currently works as CEO for Our-Latest-Bank*... **He is being sued by our government who also has allowed him to open an IPO and new corporation to prey on the same homebuyers his former company sold fraudulent loans to.**

Jeffrey N* – CEO of The-Bank-that-took-over-our-Lender* received a 9 million dollar bonus for 2010. The-Bank-That- Took-Over-Our-Lender* represents the same corporation, Our-Bank*, that would not release us from a 3-year prepayment penalty that we did not agree to. To release us would have cost them $25,000 in money that they did not already have.

Justice apparently, is not for those who foot the bills.

We managed to find another lawyer to take our case against Our-Bank* and 3-days before our scheduled jury trial, in January 2013, we reached a settlement with Our- Bank*. Our-Bank*/The-Bank-That-Took-

Over-Our-Lender*, had kicked their correspondent and employee, who had been Sales manager for two of their offices to the curb in our lawsuit, and the individual lost on fraud and two counts of bad faith for an amount he will never be able to pay.

A part of our reason for settlement was the fact that Our- Latest-Bank* was foreclosing on our home and we could not afford to fight two battles at the same time.

As part of our settlement agreement we required that Our-Bank* write us an apology letter.

So the question is, where are we today? We are in litigation with Our-Latest-Bank*. They have foreclosed on our home using questionable documentation comparable to the same documentation that brought about the National Mortgage Settlement...As banks remove the predatory mortgages from their books and 'sell' them to secondary lenders, they improve their bottom line so they can come into regulatory compliance and the secondary lender makes a fortune foreclosing on loans that have no hope of recovery once they have burdened the borrower with additional charges and obligations. Or as Neil Barofsky described it in his book, Bailout; we have become 'foam on the runway to foreclosure', while the ones who created the mess are raking in the money 'hand over fist.' We do not yet have a court date. We just recently won a stay of eviction pending our appeal...so our saga and our expenses continue.

I spoke with Sherry Hernandez at the beginning of April 2015, and she told me that she and her husband Alfredo have finally lost their home and had to move out of it.

Only 1% of the Federal Bailout Money of $767 billion has been used to help working middle class Americans keep their homes. The overwhelming majority of the hundreds of billions in bailout funds went to the Big Banks. This enabled the big Wall Street banks, the main cause of the Great Recession, to survive and prosper, and pay their executives and stockholders millions of dollars in bonuses, severance pay, and exorbitant salaries. The effects of the Great Recession continue to linger because the Big Banks did not use their bailout money to increase lending to small businesses to create jobs, or to homeowners to save their homes and strengthen the housing market.

The bailout gave the Big Banks on Wall Street the Goldmine while small businesses and homeowners on Main Street got the Shaft.

CHAPTER 9

PENTAGON WASTE, FRAUD AND ABUSE; U.S. INTERVENTION ABROAD, AND GLOBALIZATION

" *Every gun that is made, every warship launched, every rocket fired signifies...a theft from those who hunger and are not fed, those who are cold and are not clothed."*

--President Dwight D. Eisenhower

In his farewell address on January 17, 1961, President Dwight D. Eisenhower warned us that "*In the councils of government, we must guard against the acquisition of unwarranted influence, whether sought or unsought, by the military-industrial complex. The potential for the disastrous rise of misplaced power exists, and will persist.*" These words of President Eisenhower, a former World War II general, have been ignored by the political, economic, military-industrial elites who have ruled America since World War II.

The "military-industrial-congressional" complex as it was called in a draft of Eisenhower's speech, consists of the Pentagon, large defense contractors (e.g. Lockheed Martin, Boeing, Raytheon, General Dynamics, and Northrop Grumman), and powerful members of Congress who are lobbied and funded by them. For example, between 2007 and 2018 these top five defense contractors spent $409.2 million in lobbying and campaign contributions to federal politicians. In return, "they received $629.8 billion in contracts and $480 million in other federal support. This is equal to $1,540 from the government for every dollar they spent influencing the government." (November 20, 2014, Project On Government Oversight, POGO.org).

During the Cold War with the Soviet Union, these corporate military-industrial elites promoted the development of a gigantic weapons industry, one whose "unwarranted influence" President Eisenhower had warned us against. Trillions of dollars were spent on weapons systems, some not needed, to block a perceived Soviet expansionary thrust into central and western Europe after World War ll.

Today, in 2019, with the Cold War long over and no more Soviet Union, President Trump's defense budget is $716 billion. This is its' base defense budget. That is more than the combined spending of the next 7 nations, and five times as much as second place China! When all Military/Defense/Security related spending is included, the United States spends $1 trillion annually. This is equal to the military budgets of the rest of the world's countries combined. Yet, many of our soldiers are woefully neglected in the areas of medical and mental health care (PTSD treatment and suicide prevention), paycheck accuracy, transition to civilian life and civilian employment, and housing support.

For fiscal year 2019, President Trump requested $1.19 trillion. For 2019 Military/Defense spending, President Trump requested $727 billion, which was 61% of the discretionary federal budget. Congress gave him $719 billion, about 60% of the discretionary federal budget. He asked for 5% for Education, and 2% for Science (nationalpriorities.org, source: Office of Management and Budget). It costs the American taxpayers $250 billion annually to maintain 1,000 American military bases in 150 countries, out of a total of 195 countries in the world. Additionally, the U.S. is the world's number one exporter of weapons, and it's military-industrial complex has a tremendous amount of unwarranted influence over U.S. military spending, because it engages in Dollar Democracy involving campaign donations and lobbying. These corporate defense contractors are huge in size and small in number, allowing them monopolistic power over the U.S. economy and over political decision-makers. From 1990 to 2018 individuals, political action committees (PACs), and soft/outside money groups from corporate military/defense industry contractors spent to elect and contributed $287,694,051 to Senate and House Congressional campaigns (www.opensecrets.org). From 1998 to 2018, these defense contractors spent $127,545,097 on lobbying Congress. Here is what they got in return: According to the Project on Government Oversight (POGO), the United States Defense Department has 96 major weapons programs. Citing data from the Government Accountability Office, POGO claims that the cost of these weapons is $1,580,000,000,000. (www.POGO.org) That's a windfall of $12,388 in federal defense contracts for every $1 invested in campaign spending and lobbying by corporate defense contractors! Which of these weapons systems is really needed for a robust and efficient military defense, and which weapons systems are mainly huge profit-generating programs for the corporate defense contractors? Which ones are overly expensive, unnecessary and plagued with malfunctions? Which of these had to be discontinued midway in development, because of a lack of performance, costing the taxpayers billions of wasted dollars?

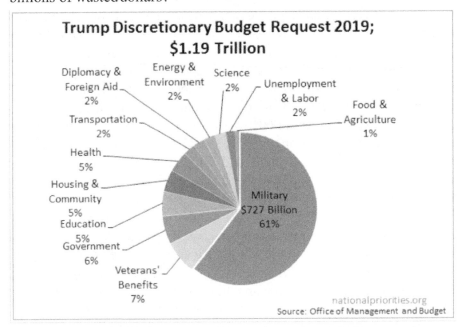

President Trump's 2019 budget request, left largely intact, was passed by Congress and signed by him in February 2019. Military/Defense received $719 billion, approximately 60% of the discretionary budget. Trump had requested 5% for Education and 2% for Science.

Chart 9-1 | Trump's Discretionary Budget Request 2019

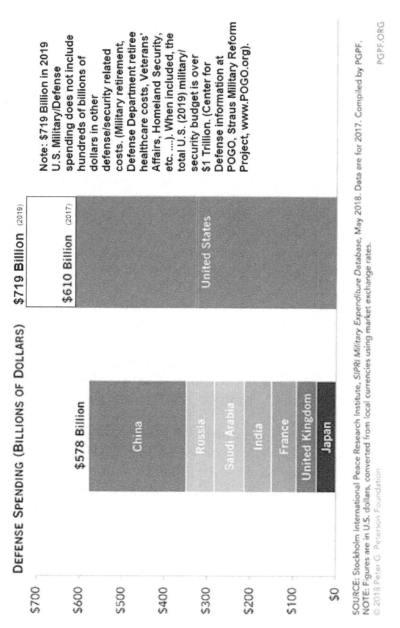

DEFENSE SPENDING (BILLIONS OF DOLLARS)

$719 Billion (2019)

$610 Billion (2017)

United States

$578 Billion

China
Russia
Saudi Arabia
India
France
United Kingdom
Japan

Note: $719 Billion in 2019 U.S. Military/Defense spending does not include hundreds of billions of dollars in other defense/security related costs. (Military retirement, Defense Department retiree healthcare costs, Veterans' Affairs, Homeland Security, etc. ....). When included, the total U.S. (2019) military/security budget is over $1 Trillion. (Center for Defense information at POGO, Straus Military Reform Project, www.POGO.org).

$700
$600
$500
$400
$300
$200
$100
$0

SOURCE: Stockholm International Peace Research Institute, *SIPRI Military Expenditure Database,* May 2018. Data are for 2017. Compiled by PGPF.
NOTE: Figures are in U.S. dollars, converted from local currencies using market exchange rates.
© 2018 Peter G. Peterson Foundation

PGPF.ORG

Chart 9-2 | Defense Spending comparrison with other nations

After World War II, U.S. leaders refused to see the Soviet Union's move to create friendly and compliant states on its western border (which lacked natural barriers such as mountains, oceans or rivers) as a historically defensive action to prevent any repeat of several major and destructive invasions from the West, such as the devastating invasions of Napoleon, Kaiser Wilhelm, and Adolf Hitler within a short 130 year period. Instead U.S. foreign-policy elites viewed the Soviet action in Eastern Europe as if it were based on its earlier internationalist Communist ideology that espoused world socialist revolution, promoted by leaders such as the first Soviet Foreign Minister Leon Trotsky. The view of elite U.S. leaders was that the Soviet Union was inherently an aggressive expansionist nation, basing its support for worldwide communism on the Marxist slogan "workers of the world unite, you have nothing to lose but your chains!" These American Cold Warriors, and their intellectual supporters, conveniently left out a crucial fact that explains Soviet fears of another attack from the West and post-World War II Soviet attempts to create a "buffer zone" in Eastern Europe: in January, 1918, Great Britain and the United States led 13 countries in an invasion of the Soviet Union on the side of the anti-Communist White Guard against the Soviet Communist Bolshevik government's Red Guard, during the Russian Civil War. This was done in a conscious attempt to, in Winston Churchill's words, "strangle the infant Bolshevism in the cradle."

According to University of Louisiana Professor of history Carl J. Richard, U.S. President Woodrow Wilson continued the intervention for a year and a half after World War I had ended in order to overthrow the Bolsheviks. (*When the United States Invaded Russia: Woodrow Wilson's Siberian Disaster*, by Carl J. Richard, December 1, 2012). According to Vasilis Vourkoutiotis of the University of Ottawa, the Allied military presence of 150,000 troops included thousands of American soldiers and was aimed at eradicating the Bolshevik regime. ("Allied Intervention in the Russian Revolution"). Cypress College Professor of history, Bryan Seiling called it an "attempt to thwart communism." While conducting research at the University of Southern California, I found that, beginning with the Britain-U.S. led intervention in 1918 against the Soviet

250

revolutionary government, whenever outside forces were perceived to threaten its survival, the Soviet Communist Party and government leaders became more dictatorial and intolerant of varying viewpoints. Whenever outside forces, particularly the U.S. led Western alliance, were less threatening and willing to develop more cordial relations, the Soviet Communist Party and government leadership allowed greater discussion and diversity of viewpoints among themselves and in Soviet society. These were the periods of "thaw" in the Cold War, détente, and arms control/arms reduction. This occurred during the Kennedy-Kruschev, Nixon-Brezhnev, and Reagan-Gorbachev eras. This was the case despite the fact that the U.S. had a much larger economy and could support a more technologically sophisticated and diversified military.

Since the 1940s during the Cold War, the United States was almost always the first nation to invent and implement major new weapons systems-- from the atomic bomb, to the hydrogen bomb, to the MX multiple warheaded missile-- with the Soviet Union spending a larger proportion of its smaller GDP to play catch-up. As the Soviet Union started behind us, they ran faster to catch up. To American Cold War elite leaders, it appeared that the Soviets had caught up militarily by the 1980s, by reaching an asymmetrical balance, and might forge ahead if their pace were to continue.

The U.S. had emerged relatively unscathed by World War II compared to the tremendous destruction of the Soviet Union's infrastructure and economy. Therefore the U.S. was able to hold a significant lead in arms race technology and military might, until the Soviets caught up by achieving a rough balance by the 1980s. Because the Soviet economy was smaller than the U.S. economy, it spent almost 20% of its GDP on the military to catch up with the U.S., compared to 7% of GDP spent by the U.S. This heavy spending by the Soviet military was certainly a factor in the demise of the Soviet economy.

The insistence of American foreign-policy leaders, and their military-industrial complex corporate allies, that the U.S. should always maintain its military technology and new weapons superiority over the Soviet Union fueled a gigantic American military buildup and costly arms race with the Soviet Union. This was the problem President Eisenhower was addressing when he warned us against the "unwarranted influence... by the military-industrial complex."

An excellent example of an unwanted and unneeded weapons system which cost taxpayers billions of dollars consisted of 10 additional C-17 transport planes to be added to the 200 already in the U.S. arsenal. This plane was initially designed and built during the Cold War with the Soviet Union, in case hundreds of thousands of troops and thousands of tanks had to be quickly airlifted to central Europe to block a Soviet ground invasion. With the fall of the Soviet Union, many defense experts, Defense Secretary Robert Gates, and President Obama concluded that 200 C-17s were adequate for transporting thousands of American troops, tanks, and other equipment to military hotspots and battlefields around the world, if necessary. That's why, by 2009, President Obama and Secretary Gates insisted on eliminating $2.5 billion in added spending to purchase 10 additional C- 17 planes.

However, Congress insisted on spending the money to purchase the planes because thousands of jobs and billions of dollars of profit for Boeing were at stake: over 40 states were involved in production of the C-17. At least 80 Senators and hundreds of Representatives sat in Congress from those states. Foremost of these was Congresswoman Laura Richardson of Long Beach, California, where the C-17 was assembled. During her career in Congress from 2007 until 2012 Congresswoman Laura Richardson received $35,000 in campaign donations from the Machinists/Aerospace workers union that represents Boeing workers, and $25,500 from Boeing corporation. (www.opensecrets.org)

From the 2008 through the 2012 election cycle Boeing corporation donated approximately $7.6 million to federal election campaigns. This was the time that Boeing and its interests were lobbying federal officials, including many members of Congress across the country, on behalf of building more C-17 transport planes. It took less than $8 million in campaign contributions, for Boeing, its corporate owners, and its workers to get $2.5 billion of taxpayer money to build 10 more C-17's, even though President Obama and Defense Secretary Gates had told Congress not to waste the taxpayers' hard-earned money!

During the George W. Bush presidency the U.S. was spending $200 billion more annually on defense, than during the heights of the Cold

War. U.S. military spending that included major waste, fraud, and abuse did not begin nor end with George W. Bush. We've all heard about the $604 toilet seats paid for by the Navy and the $7600 coffee makers paid for by the Air Force in recent decades. Add to that present boondoggles such as the F-35 joint strike fighter which costs up to $337 million per plane (for the Navy version) and is plagued by cost overruns, delays, poor planning, inadequate technology, and poor performance. It was temporarily grounded for the 13th time since 2007, when one of the planes caught fire on June 23, 2014. The Lockheed Martin built F-35 "can't turn, can't climb, can't run," said John Stillion and Harold Scott Perdue of the RAND Corporation think tank. Major reasons are: the single engine design on a 35-ton airplane that requires two engines to perform adequately, and multiple contradictory performance requirements from a single plane, which pull the design requirements in contradictory directions.

In order to take off and land vertically like a helicopter or a Harrier Jet, the plane must have only one engine and not be too long and sleek. To perform efficiently as a fighter jet, it needs to be longer, sleeker, and have two powerful engines. The lobbyists and contractors from Lockheed Martin apparently did not care about these contradictions. They just wanted the contract and the Pentagon gave it to them on a low bid. That's largely why the plane's cost has skyrocketed to an average of $178 million in 2015 from the initial Lockheed Martin bid of $69 million in 2001.

"The F-35 has a maximum speed of Mach 1.6, compared to Mach 2 to 2.5 for the F-16 and F-15, respectively. Its service ceiling is fifty thousand feet, compared to sixty thousand for the other models. In 2015, the Air Force tested the F-35 in a short-range dogfight with an F-16D mounting external fuel tanks, and the test pilot complained that it was simply out-turned and less energy efficient than its more agile opponent." (NationalInterest.org, April 21, 2018, "Is the F-35 Really Worth the $1,500,000,000,000 Price Tag? or a giant mistake?", by Sebastein Roblin).

How has this military misspending fiasco come about and remained in place for decades? It's due to what I've been saying all along, "Dollar Democracy": the buying of influence over our government by super-wealthy corporate special interests, through lobbying and huge campaign donations to politicians who make decisions that benefit their corporate donors. In this case it's the huge military/defense contractors such as Lockheed Martin, Boeing, Raytheon, General Dynamics, and Northrop Grumman. We should ask Congress, "Who's your Daddy? Are you wasting our hard-earned tax dollars to primarily benefit your wealthy donors, or to 'provide for the common defense' in the Public Interest, as the Constitution requires?

Pentagon's Antiquated, Dysfunctional Accounting and Computer Systems Produce Waste, Fraud, and Abuse

Another major reason for waste, fraud, and abuse in military spending is the antiquated, dysfunctional accounting and computer systems used by the Pentagon for tracking weapons procurement and spending as well as for producing accurate paychecks for our women and men in uniform. While she worked at the office of the Defense Finance and Accounting Service (DEFAS), the Pentagon's main accounting agency, Linda Woodford monthly inserted phony numbers in the U.S. Department of Defense accounts. Just a couple of days before the deadline, the Navy would dump numbers on the Cleveland, Ohio office ("Special Report: The Pentagon's Doctored Ledgers Conceal Epic Waste", by Scott J. Paltrow, *Reuters*, November 18, 2013). Using the data received by her and her fellow accountants, Woodford would prepare monthly reports to reconcile the Navy's books with the Treasury Department's books, which is required of all military services and Pentagon agencies. Every month numbers were missing, wrong, or arrived without explanation of how the money had been spent, or which Congressional appropriation it came from. (*Reuters*, 2013).

When faced with these major discrepancies between the Treasury's numbers and the Military's, Woodford's superiors told her and her fellow accountants to enter false numbers called "plugs", to make the numbers match. According to a *Reuters* investigative report, "At the DFAS offices that handle accounting for the Army, Navy, Air Force and other defense agencies, fudging the accounts with false entries is standard operating procedure. And plugging isn't confined to DEFAS. Former military service officials say record-keeping at the operational level throughout the services is rife with made-up numbers to cover lost or missing information." (*Reuters*, 2013). Plugs are symptoms of a major problem says Scott J. Paltrow of *Reuters*: "the Pentagon's chronic failure to keep track of its money – how much it has, how much it pays out and how much is wasted or stolen." In the November 22, 2018 issue of *The Nation,* Dave Lindorff says,

> The plugs can be staggering in size. In fiscal year 2015, for example, congress appropriated $122 billion for the US Army. Yet DoD financial records for the Army's 2015 budget included a whopping $6.5 trillion (yes, trillion) in plugs. Most of these plugs 'lack[ed] supporting documentation,' in the bland phrasing of the department's internal watchdog, the Office of Inspector General. In other words, there were no ledger entries or receipts to back up how that $6.5 trillion supposedly was spent. Indeed, more than 16,000 records that might reveal either the source or the destination of some of that $6.5 trillion had been 'removed,' the inspector general's office reported.
>
> In this way, the DoD propels US military spending higher year after year, even when the country is not fighting any major wars, says Franklin "Chuck" Spinney, a former Pentagon whistleblower. Spinney's revelations to Congress and the news media about wildly inflated Pentagon spending helped public outrage in the 1980s. 'They're making up the numbers and then just asking for more money each year,' … (*The Nation,* "Exclusive: The Pentagon's Massive Accounting Fraud Exposed", by Dave Lindorff, November 22, 2018)

In fact, Congress spent a record $716 billion for the Pentagon in fiscal year 2019, $24 billion more than fiscal year 2018's $692 billion, up by $6 billion from fiscal year 2017's $686 billion. That's why the U.S. Military/Defense spending is higher than the next ten countries combined. (see Charts 9-1 and 9-2)

In her Nov. 16, 2018 *Defense Systems* article, "Financial Audit Spotlights DOD IT Woes", Lauren C. Williams claims that "the Department of Defense has a long way to go before it can account for its estimated $2.7 trillion in far-flung assets ….

"The information technology portfolio of the military services, the joint commands and the various defense agencies is proving particularly nettlesome for auditors. Some of the IT flaws and vulnerabilities released in the Nov. 15 report on the audit were identified years prior. Material weaknesses in the financial management systems and IT were named in fiscal 2017 inspector general report. Antiquated military pay systems, which lacked audibility framework and required manual manipulation, were first identified in fiscal 2011."

Lauren Williams' assessments seem to indicate that many of the problems with DEFAS as well as auditing of the Defense Department, that existed in 2013, appear to still exist today.

In 2019 the United States will spend between $700 billion and $1 trillion on military defense while sustaining almost 1000 military bases in 150 countries out of 195 in the world. This is over half of the discretionary U.S. federal budget, and roughly equal to the military budgets of all the other nations of the world combined. How much bang for our buck are we getting? U.S. Senator Charles Grassley of Iowa estimated that the taxpayer gets about 30 cents of defense for every dollar the Pentagon spends. (*The Pathology of Power*, by Norman Cousins)

In addition to "Dollar Democracy" there is a revolving door, through which many former high-ranking government officials and retired military leaders enter and become highly paid lobbyists for the weapons industry. This type of legalized corruption has brought us a bloated, inefficient, and overly expensive military defense system in which taxpayers' hard-earned dollars are squandered on weapons systems such as the boondoggle F-35 Joint Strike Fighter ($337 million each for the

Navy version), plagued by cost overruns, delays, poor planning, inadequate technology, and poor performance (the Rand Corporation's simulation warfare study showed the F- 35 losing an air war against Chinese fighter planes).

To stop the Military-Industrial-Congressional Complex from bankrupting America, we must not only end the "unwarranted influence...by the military-industrial complex" that President Eisenhower warned us of, we must end the buying of Congress and our politicians by Big Corporations, their lobbyists, and their super-wealthy owners!

This "dollar democracy", a form of legalized bribery, has produced a bloated, inefficient, and overly expensive military defense/security system. It squanders taxpayers' hard-earned dollars on many unneeded, overly expensive, and inefficient weapons; for example, the $337 million F-35c joint strike fighter plane (Navy version), the Littoral Combat Ship (LCS), the M-1 Abrams tank, of which the Army has 2,300 with another 3,000 in storage. Regarding the hundreds of millions of dollars being spent on the M1, Army General Ray Odierno claimed "If we had our choice, we would use that money in a different way." According to the Congressional research service the LCS cost $813 million, up from its estimated cost of $220 million in 2001. More taxpayer money ($14 million) was wasted in a failed attempt to replace the M-4 carbine, which is the standard issue carbine used by troops in Afghanistan.

F-35 Joint Strike Fighter: Historic $1.5 Trillion Disaster

Let's take a closer look at the wasteful, inefficient, and expensive F-35 joint strike fighter, of which there are three versions: the F-35A for the Air Force, the F-35B for the Marine Corps, and the F-35C for the Navy. The cost to build and operate the F-35 over its 55-year lifetime is $1.5 trillion. This combat aircraft is the most expensive Pentagon weapons program ever. After winning the contract, Lockheed Martin began developing the F-35 in 2001. Each plane was to cost the Pentagon $69 million of taxpayer money. The cost of the plane has ballooned in

2015 to an average of $178 million each.

Winslow Wheeler is an expert on the F-35 Joint Strike Fighter. He has served for many years on the staff at the Project on Government Oversight (POGO), a nonprofit, nonpartisan research think tank. It focuses on military budget reform and is a watchdog organization against government waste. Wheeler had also worked for many years on national security issues for the United States Senate and the Government Accountability Office (GAO). Wheeler's research details the empirical, real world costs for the government to buy (but not to test or develop) an F-35 in 2015. He puts the production price per plane at $148 million for the Air Force's F 35A, which can take off and land on conventional runways; $251 million for the Marine Corps' F-35B, which can fly like a plane and also hover and land like a helicopter; the cost is $337 million for the Navy's F-35C, which can land on, and take off from, aircraft carriers.

Wheeler used recent numbers from the Senate Appropriations Committee. These numbers do not include research and development costs, which if included would raise the cost of each F-35. In his July 29, 2014 article "How Much Does an F-35 Actually Cost", Wheeler notes that "The cost of an F-35B grew from $232 million in 2014 to a bulging $251 million by 2015. The cost of the Navy's F-35C grew from $273 million in 2014 to a wallet busting $337 million by 2015." According to the July 3, 2014 Business Insider, "The F-35 Joint Strike Fighter Jet is a historic $1 trillion disaster, has had several years of delays, setbacks, and cost overruns of $167 billion before a single plane has flown a single mission."

After being grounded several times for mechanical malfunctions, of which one of the latest was in 2014, the Air Force temporarily suspended all flights of the F-35 after one of the planes caught on fire before takeoff at Elgin Air Force Base in Florida. The plane was grounded twice because of electrical problems in 2011. In August 2012 the F-35 suffered a complete failure of its integrated power package, which combines functions performed by an emergency power system, environmental controls, and an auxiliary power unit. The plane has also had major problematic issues with its software. Although it's supposed to escape enemy radar with its stealth capabilities, its stealth coatings have been found peeling off. One version of the F-35 has shown cracks beneath its fuselage, causing questions about its capabilities in rigorous air combat.

"The Pentagon's central F-35 Joint Program Office (JPO) announced the (latest) grounding on Oct. 11, 2018. The inciting incident occurred on Sept. 28, 2018, when an F-35B from Marine Fighter Attack Training Squadron Five Zero One (VMFAT-501) crashed at Marine Corps Air Station Beaufort in South Carolina. The pilot of that aircraft was able to safely eject, but the stealth fighter was a total loss." ... a fleet-wide stop in operations is ... a significant development for an aircraft that is in use, at least at some level, across three major U.S. military services and nine foreign countries. (thedrive.com, October 11, 2018, "U.S. Military, Foreign Operators Ground Their F-35s to Look for Faulty Fuel Tubes", by Joseph Trevithick).

Another major problem faced by the F-35 was its advanced helmet which was supposed to allow pilots to view data from all the plane's sensors. This should have allowed the pilot to look through the floor and all around the plane. But the helmet showed big problems with night vision, delays in displaying data, and jitter under certain conditions. Pilots even noticed a green glow at the edge of the helmet's visor, and problems with alignment. (Business Insider, July 3, 2014).

Once again, the F-35 was expected to be delayed for over a year beyond its scheduled mid-2015 delivery date. If things go the way they are, the Pentagon will be spending $400 billion for a total of 2,457 jets, and over $1 trillion for the expense of operating and supporting them. William Hartung, the director of the Arms and Security Project, at the Center for International Policy, notes that with a price tag of $1.5 trillion to build and operate over its 55-year lifespan, the F-35 Joint Strike Fighter is the most expensive weapons program ever built by the Pentagon. He claims it is overpriced, underperforming, and unnecessary. Because it is being asked to do too many different things, from serving as a bomber and fighter plane, to landing on the deck of an aircraft carrier, to doing vertical takeoff and landing, the F-35 does none of these assignments well. Each of these assignments requires different physical designs, preferably in different types of planes. Despite this, in the December 2014 spending bill, Congress approved almost half a billion dollars more for the F-35 than what the Pentagon had asked for.

(William Hartung, "Can the F-35 be Stopped?", *Huffington Post*, January 12, 2015). Even though a RAND Corporation study found that the F-35 has "inferior acceleration, inferior climb, and inferior sustained turn capability", in other words it "can't turn, can't climb, can't run." (Cited in Nick Schwellenbach's "Cancel the Flawed F-35 and Free Up Billions for Better Aircraft and Domestic Needs," Center for Effective Government, September 10, 2013, available at http://www.foreffectivegov.org/cancel-flawed-F-35-and-free-up-billions-better-aircraft-and-domestic-needs).

In his article, "F-35 Stealth Jet 'Will Not Be Able to Fire Its Guns Until 2019' ", David Millward says that William Hartung, of the Centre for International Policy, has even questioned whether the basic design is fit for purpose.

The F-35B Lightning II was to be the star turn of the Farnborough International Airshow

Image 9-1 | F-35B Lightning II | Photo/The Telegraph

Hartung warned that the plane would be too small to function as a bomber, too cumbersome in dogfights and too vulnerable to support ground troops.

In 2014, the F-35 was supposed to be the star attraction at the Farnborough Air Show in Hampshire, but it failed to appear after the entire fleet was grounded following a fire at a Florida airbase in June. (https://www.telegraph.co.uk/news/worldnews/northamerica/usa/1

1319455/F-35-stealth-jet-will-not-be-able-to-fire-its-guns-until-2019.html)

Because of the F-35's huge engineering and financial problems, the Congressional Budget Office (CBO) offered Congress a plan to cancel the program in order to reduce the budget deficit. The CBO estimated that replacing the F-35 "with upgraded Lockheed Martin F-16s and Boeing F/A -18s would save $48 billion between FY 2014 and FY 2023. It notes that while this option would reduce the stealth capabilities of the fighter force, those could be made up for with stealthy unmanned systems, long-range stealth bombers, or with a new aircraft design that lacks the drawbacks of the F-35. Most importantly, the CBO notes that 'new F-16s and F/A-18s would be sufficiently advanced -- if equipped with upgraded modern radar, precision weapons, and digital communications -- to meet the threats the United States is likely to face in the foreseeable future.' " (http://www.ciponline.org/research/entry/promising-the-sky-pork- barrel-politics-and-the-f-35-combat-aircraft).

Despite the F-35's huge engineering and cost problems, the Pentagon planned to fund 50% more F-35 fighter jets in fiscal 2016. That was 57 jets, an increase from 38 jets in 2015. (Andrea Shalal, "The Pentagon Will Spend Nearly $400 Billion for Thousands More Warplanes Over the Next 20 years", *Reuters* in *Business Insider*, February 5, 2015).

President Trump signed the 2019 Defense Authorization Bill in which Congress allocated $3.4 billion to purchase 29 more F-35 Joint Strike Fighters. (https://news.usni.org/2018/08/13/35764). (*U.S. Naval Institute News*, August 13, 2018, "President Trump Signs FY 2019 Defense Authorization Bill", by Ben Werner). Why and how does this boondoggle waste of taxpayer dollars continue? Let's take a closer look at how this happens.

Once again, we find that Pentagon waste, fraud, and abuse are the direct result of "Dollar Democracy" in the American elections and lobbying system. The maker of the F-35, Lockheed Martin, employs 95 lobbyists to get Congress and the Pentagon to do its bidding. Lockheed Martin's board includes Joseph Ralston, the former vice chair of the Joint Chiefs of Staff (the revolving door). Most importantly, Lockheed Martin is routinely one of the top donors of campaign money to members of Congress who have the most important roles in funding Lockheed

Martin's weapons contracts with the government.

Also, in the 116th Congress (2019-2020), more than one in six members of the U.S. House of Representatives is part of the "F-35 Caucus" -- yes, there actually is one in Congress! By compiling data from OpenSecrets.org, the website of the Center for Responsive Politics, William Hartung points out that in the 113th Congress (2013-2014), 39 members of the F-35 Caucus received over $1.9 million from F-35 weapons contractors in the last two election cycles -- not just from the four most important F-35 contractors: Lockheed Martin, BAE Systems, Northrop Grumman, and United Technologies but also from other key suppliers such as Alliant Techsystems, Elbit, Finmeccanica, Harris, Honeywell, L-3 Communications, Raytheon, and Rolls Royce. Those Caucus members who received the biggest contributions from F-35 contractors were Caucus co-chair Rep. Kay Granger (R-TX), $195,950; Caucus co-chair Rep. John Larson (D-CT), $137,450; Rep. Jack Kingston (R-GA), $85,000; Rep. Tom Rooney R-FL), $84,500; and Rep. Trent Franks (R-AZ), $75,800.

The F-35 Joint Strike Fighter Caucus had doubled in size to 70 members by 2016. Collectively, they received $17,899,233 in campaign contributions through the 2017-2018 election cycle from defense contractors such as Lockheed Martin and others. As a result, members of the House Joint Strike Fighter Caucus have faithfully lobbied fellow members of Congress hard for continued funding of the nation's most expensive ($1.5 Trillion) weapons program in U.S. history.

In spite of all the above criticism of defense technology experts, and the expensive problems and intermittent failures of this "boondoggle" weapons program, the F-35 House Joint Strike Fighter Caucus penned a letter with glowing remarks, requesting additional taxpayer money for the continuing production and purchase of the F-35 that Rand Corporation researchers said, has "inferior acceleration, inferior climb, and inferior sustained turn capability", in other words it "can't turn, can't climb, can't run." (Cited in Nick Schwellenbach's "Cancel the Flawed F-35 and Free Up Billions for Better Aircraft and Domestic Needs," Center for Effective Government, September 10, 2013, available at http://www.foreffectivegov.org/cancel-flawed-F-35-and-free-up-billions-better-aircraft-and-domestic-needs).

DEFENSE CONTRACTORS BUY KEY MEMBERS OF CONGRESS, INCLUDING THE HOUSE JOINT STRIKE FIGHTER (F-35) CAUCUS

Campaign Contributions to the 70 Members of the House Joint Strike Fighter (F-35) Caucus from Defense Contractors, through the 2017-2018 Election Cycle, Totaling $17,899,233 (source:OpenSecrets.org)

NOTE: Defense contractors gave a total of **$17,899,233** to the 70 members of the Joint Strike Fighter (F-35) Caucus through the 2017-2018 election cycle.

Kay Granger	$1,543,363	Hank Johnson	$120,500
(Caucus Chair)		Walter Jones	$429,390
John Larson	$690,994	Peter King	$435,900
Pete Aguilar	$248,225	Adam Kinzinger	$187,877
Rick Allen	$37,260	Ann Kirkpatrick	$23,042
Brian Babin	$52,748	Steven Knight	$304,200
Joe Barton	$358,665	Ann Custer	$150,467
Rob Bishop	$337,500	Barry Loudermilk	$47,500
Sanford Bishop	$383,600	Kenny Marchant	$146,240
Robert Brady	$109,750	Jeff Miller	$609,150
Jim Bridenstine	$171,000	Patrick Murphy	$72,252
Julia Brownley	$35,493	Grace Napolitano	$43,050
Cheri Bustos	$29,581	Richard Neal	$357,200
Andre Carson	$138,550	Donald Norcross	$103,510
Buddy Carter	$86,225	Pete Olson	$165,537
Mike Coffman	$457,125	Bill Pascrell Jr.	$261,800
Chris Collins	$83,525	Scott Peters	$410,087
Doug Collins	$70,850	Ted Poe	$47,012
Joe Courtney	$776,250	Martha Roby	$496,150
Rosa DeLauro	$387,175	Tom Rooney	$318,150
Mike Doyle	$114,350	David Schweikert	$98,100
Elizabeth Esty	$24,306	Austin Scott	$273,986
Blake Farenthold	$8,250	David Scott	$67,500
Paul Gosar	$22,500	Pete Sessions	$486,363
Tom Graves	$277,800	Kyrsten Sinema	$161,394
Gene Green	$80,900	Scott Tipton	$70,400
Frank Guinta	$92,250	David Valadao	$124,250
Richard Hanna	$34,800	Marc Veasey	$324,639
Alcee Hastings	$54,500	Filemon Vela	$45,800
Jody Hice	$26,000	Jackie Walorski	$340,500
Brian Higgins	$111,250	Lynn Westmoreland	$102,000
Jim Hines	$189,760	Roger Williams	$126,700
Duncan Hunter	$857,392	Joe Wilson	$798,215
Bill Johnson	$103,750	Robert Wittman	$1,111,686
Sam Johnson	$468,442	Rob Woodall	$22,500

Table 9-3 | Defense Contractors Buy Congressmembers

Exhibit 9-4 | Letter from Congressmembers supporting the F-35

Congress of the United States
Washington, DC 20515

October 4, 2016

The Honorable Rodney Frelinghuysen
Chairman
House Defense Appropriations Subcommittee
H-405, The Capitol
Washington, D.C. 20515

The Honorable Peter Visclosky
Ranking Member
House Defense Appropriations Subcommittee
H-405, The Capitol
Washington, D.C. 20515

Gentlemen:

As you head into conference, we write in strong support of the F-35 Joint Strike Fighter and urge you to continue supporting increased production rates at this critical juncture for the program. The F-35 is essential for U.S. national security and that of our closest allies like Israel.

As you are aware, the F-35 is the nation's only 5th Generation stealth aircraft currently in production. It is the backbone of future air superiority for all three US Services and many of our most important allies. The F-35's advanced capabilities are critical to maintaining air superiority in future surface-to-air and air-to-air threat environments without sustaining significant losses. Events around the globe continue to demonstrate the urgent need for the F-35's capabilities. The program is gaining momentum with the Marine Corps declaring initial operating capability (IOC) last year and the Air Force declaring IOC this summer. We believe it is essential for Congress to provide the funding necessary to continue increasing F-35 production at a rate sufficient to meet future threats and to reach full rate production of at least 120 US aircraft per year as quickly as possible.

Both the House and Senate Defense Appropriations bills support increasing the production rate for the F-35 program. The House bill added 11 F-35s (five F-35As, four F-35Cs and two F-35Bs) for all three Services to fulfill their unfunded requirements, while the Senate bill added four (two F-35Bs and two F-35Cs). Increasing the production rate is the single most important factor in reducing future aircraft unit costs. Additionally, significantly increasing production is critical to fielding F-35s in the numbers needed to meet the expected threats in the mid-2020s. Furthermore, the Senate bill added $100 million to significantly increase F-35A advance procurement to help the Air Force increase its ramp rate in Fiscal Year 2018. We strongly encourage the conferees to support the 11 aircraft added by the House and the $100 million in additional F-35A advance procurement included in the Senate bill.

Finally, we are concerned with the significant cuts to Follow-On-Modernization (FOM) included in the Senate bill. These cuts would delay critical FOM capability upgrades needed to ensure the F-35 stays ahead of increasing future threats. We urge the conferees to restore as much of this funding as possible.

Thank you for your continued steadfast support for the F-35 program and leadership on behalf of our nation's armed forces.

Sincerely,

Tom Graves

Sam Johnson

Reb A Brady

265

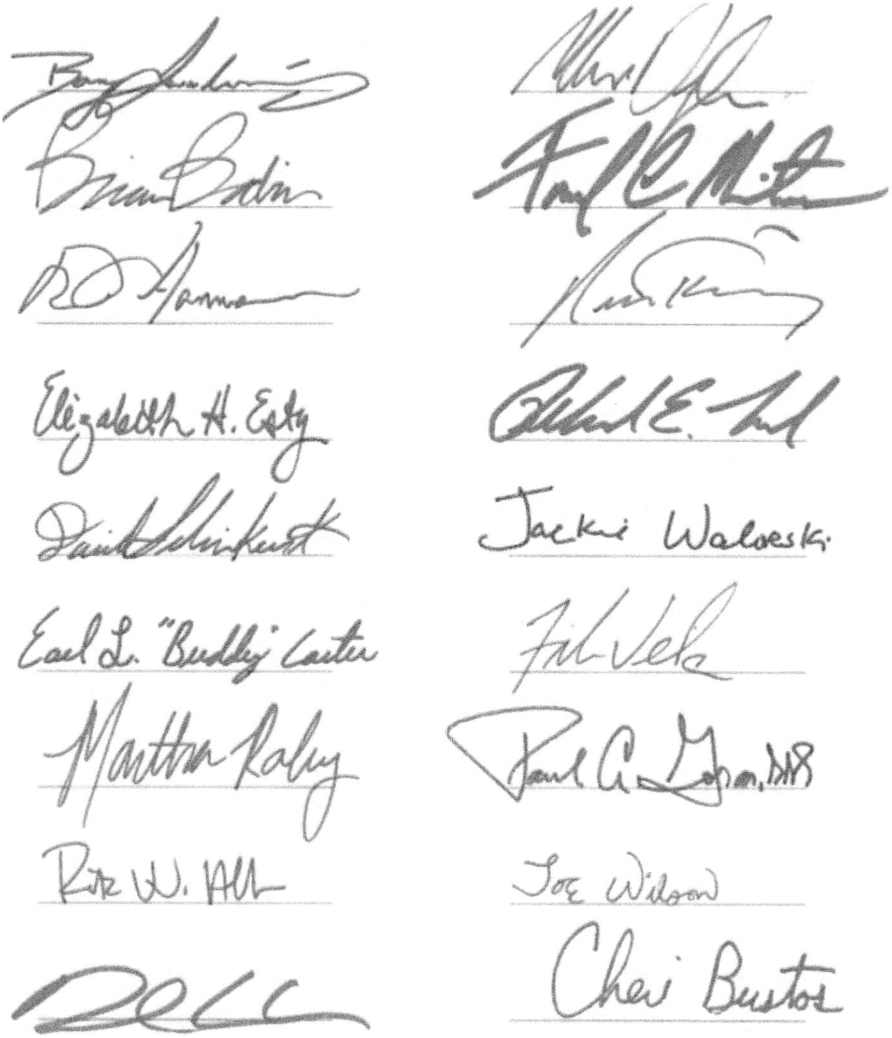
Elizabeth H. Esty
Jackie Walorski
Earl L. "Buddy" Carter
Joe Wilson
Cheri Bustos

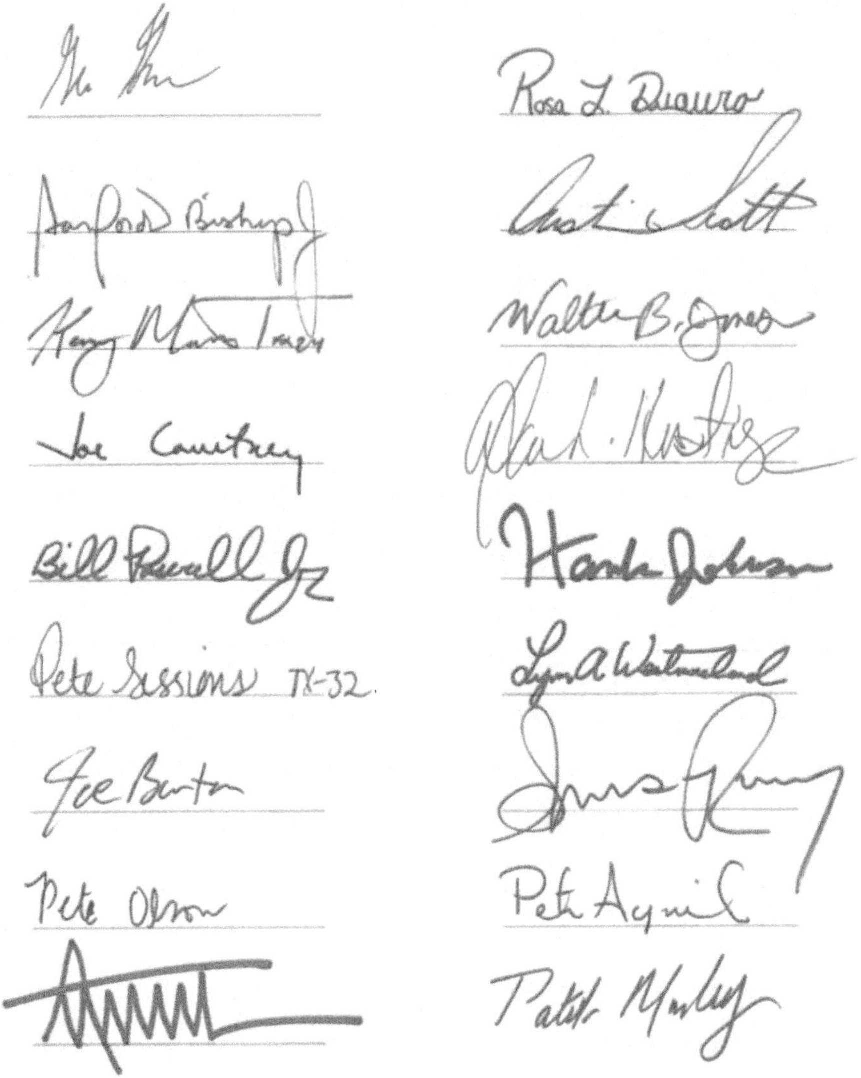

Rosa L. DeLauro

Sanford Bishop

Walter B. Jones

Joe Courtney

Hank Johnson

Bill Pascrell Jr

Pete Sessions TX-32

Joe Barton

Pete Olson

Pete Aguilar

Kay Granger
John Larson
Pete Aguilar
Rick Allen
Brad Ashford
Brian Babin
Joe Barton
Rob Bishop
Sanford Bishop
Robert Brady
Jim Bridenstine
Julia Brownley
Cheri Bustos
Andre Carson
Buddy Carter
Mike Coffman
Chris Collins
Doug Collins
Joe Courtney
Rosa DeLauro
Mike Doyle
Elizabeth Esty
Blake Farenthold
Paul Gosar

Tom Graves
Gene Green
Frank Guinta
Richard Hanna
Alcee Hastings
Jody Hice
Brian Higgins
Jim Himes
Duncan Hunter
Hank Johnson
Bill Johnson
Sam Johnson
Walter Jones
Peter King
Adam Kinzinger
Ann Kirkpatrick
Stephen Knight
Ann Kuster
Barry Loudermilk
Kenny Marchant
Jeff Miller
Patrick Murphy
Grace Napolitano

Richard Neal
Donald Norcross
Pete Olson
Bill Pascrell
Scott Peters
Ted Poe
Martha Roby
Tom Rooney
David Schweikert
Austin Scott
David Scott
Pete Sessions
Kyrsten Sinema
Scott Tipton
David Valadao
Marc Veasey
Filemon Vela
Jackie Walorski
Lynn Westmoreland
Roger Williams
Joe Wilson
Robert Wittman
Rob Woodall

Source: (https://www.documentcloud.org/documents/3144751-10-4-2016-Letter-to-Conference.html#document/p1)

In addition to buying influence with members of the influential F-35 Caucus in Congress in the 2011 to 2014 election cycles, the four most important F-35 contractors made $11.1 million in campaign contributions, overwhelmingly to powerful members of the Armed Services or Defense Appropriations Committees in the House and Senate, or to members with F-35 work being carried out in their states or districts. (Data on campaign contributions is from the Open Secrets database maintained by the Center for Responsive Politics).

The Center's figures include contributions by company Political Action Committees (PACs) and individuals associated with the company in question. Contributions by major companies are most easily accessed via the following page: (http://www.opensecrets.org/industries/contrib.php?ind=D&cycle=2014). The four campaign contributors and their contribution amounts were Lockheed Martin ($4.1 million), BAE Systems ($1.4 million), Northrop Grumman ($3.5 million), and United Technologies, the parent company of Pratt and Whitney, the maker of the F-35 engine ($2.1 million).

The largest recipient of campaign contributions from these four defense corporations from 2011 to 2014 has been Rep. Howard P. "Buck" McKeon (R-CA), the powerful House Armed Services Committee Chair, who retired at the end of 2014. McKeon received $218,650 in those four years from the big four F-35 weapons contractors. His top contributor in 2013-2014 was Northrop Grumman with $28,700, and in 2011-2012 it was the F-35 prime contractor Lockheed Martin with $75,700. Thinking long-term in their own interest, the F-35 contractors have been donating heavily to the campaigns of Rep. Mac Thornberry (R-TX), the new chair of the House Armed Services Committee. From 2011 to 2014, Thornberry received $162,500 from ten F-35 contractors, led by Northrop Grumman ($32,500), Honeywell ($32,000), and Lockheed Martin ($25,000). (Contribution data are taken from the Center for Responsive Politics' website www.OpenSecrets.org. Figures include both direct contributions to the members' campaigns and contributions to their Leadership PACs, which are used to donate to other members in an effort to increase the political leverage of the member operating the Leadership PAC)

What do these huge weapons manufacturers/defense contractors such as Lockheed Martin, BAE Systems, Northrop Grumman, and United Technologies get for their hundreds of millions in lobbying and campaign contributions to powerful members of Congress? The very members who decide how much taxpayers' money to spend, and how to spend it, on America's military defense and security? First, they get hundreds of billions of dollars in massive defense contracts to produce everything from sophisticated nuclear weapons, to jets like the F-35 Joint Strike Fighter, to potato chips and Pepsis from PepsiCo for our women and men in uniform in Iraq and elsewhere. Many members of Congress own stock in these defense corporations. These defense corporations make hundreds of billions of dollars in often wasteful profits, quite often with delayed deliveries, based on government contracts that include "cost plus overruns" provisions. These provisions have allowed them to increase charges and overcharge the taxpayer, based on their claims that the cost of their materials increased. In 2008 the Government Accountability Office (GAO) found that "95 major weapons systems have exceeded their original budgets by a total of $295 billion, bringing their total cost to $1.6 trillion, and are delivered almost 2 years late on average." (from the *Washington Post* as quoted in the April 2, 2008 *Orange County Register* Editorials). According to the same *Orange County Register* Editorials page, in the year 2000, 75 weapons systems came in at an average of 6 percent over original budget, but in 2007, the increase was 26 percent, and during the same time the cost of the F-35 joint strike fighter rose by 36 percent.

From 2001 to 2015, the cost of the F-35 Joint Strike Fighter has skyrocketed by 140 percent, from $69 million each to $178 million each. Some of this added cost has been due to failures in engineering, fabrication, and abysmal quality control over the decades in development and production. This included lack of strict oversight by members of Congress who were lobbied and sponsored by F-35 defense corporations such as Lockheed Martin, as well as government agencies such as the Joint Program Office (JPO) and the Defense Contract Management Agency. The best assessment of this is found in the Department of Defense (DoD) Inspector General's (IG) report entitled, "Quality Assurance Assessment of the F-35 Lightning II Program", published on September 30, 2013. Winslow Wheeler, who is also the director of the

Straus Military Reform Project, at the Center for Defense Information at Project on Government Oversight (POGO.org) has analyzed the DoD IG's report. According to POGO, "The goal of the Straus Military Reform Project is to secure far more effective military forces and much more ethical and professional military and civilian leadership at significantly lower cost." In his article "Interesting Findings in the DoD IG's F-35 Report", Wheeler summarizes and evaluates the key points of the Department of Defense Inspector General's report:

The "Findings" section states on p,i:

> *"The F 35 program did not sufficiently implement or flow down technical and quality management system requirements to prevent the fielding of nonconforming hardware and software. This could adversely affect aircraft performance, reliability, maintainability, and ultimately program cost. Lockheed Martin Aeronautics Company (Lockheed Martin) and its subcontractors did not follow discipline AS9100 Quality Management System practices, as evidenced by 363 findings, which contained 719 issues.*

The Joint Program Office did not:

- *Ensure that Lockheed Martin and its sub-contractors were applying rigor to design, manufacturing, and quality assurance processes.*
- *Flow down critical safety item requirements.*
- *Ensure that Lockheed Martin flowed down quality assurance and technical requirements to subcontractors.*
- *Establish an effective quality assurance organization.*
- *Ensure that the Defense Contract Management Agency perform adequate quality assurance oversight.*

In addition, the Defense Contract Management Agency did not:

"Sufficiently perform Government quality assurance oversight of F-35 contractors."

To summarize in plain English and as the text of the report bears out:

-The work of Lockheed Martin and five of its major subcontractors (not including engine manufacturer Pratt and Whitney, which was not included in this report)

-was sloppy up through 2012;

-Lockheed's oversight of its own subcontractors was inadequate, and most important and significant,

-the oversight performed by the F-35 Joint Program Office (and the Defense Contract Management Agency) over Lockheed and its subcontractors was narrow, shallow, and sometimes nonexistent

Throughout the text of the report both the Joint Program Office and Lockheed Martin are singled out for particularly serious failings.

Under the title "Overall Findings and Recommendations," the report reads on p. 55:

"The F-35 Program [Office] did not sufficiently implement or flow down technical and quality management system requirements to prevent the fielding of nonconforming hardware and software. This could adversely affect aircraft performance, reliability, maintainability, and ultimately program cost. Lockheed Martin as subcontractors did not follow disciplined AS9100 Quality Management System practices, as evidenced by 363 findings,

which contained 719 issues."

And below that, under the title "Insufficient Rigor in Design, Manufacturing, and Quality Assurance Processes, "the report reads on page 55:

"The F-35 JPO, Lockheed Martin, and its subcontractors were not ensuring that the necessary quality assurance process controls and disciplines where in place to produce a consistent and reliable product. This lack of process discipline and attention to detail creates an elevated risk of delivering nonconforming aircraft to the war fighter."

Under the heading "ineffective quality assurance organization," the report states on page 65:

"JPO's quality assurance organization did not have the appropriate resources and authority to effectively manage DOD's largest acquisition program. The lack of a strong and effective quality assurance organization contributed to the program's cost, schedule, and performance issues."

That is further explained by the statement on page 66:

"As evidenced by our assessment that identified 363 findings, JPO appeared to rely on Lockheed Martin and DCMA to identify, report, and address quality assurance issues. This indicates a lack of quality assurance and technical expertise within JPO to recognize F-35 supply chain issues."

The criticism of the JPO notwithstanding, Lockheed Martin is singled out for particularly revealing descriptions in Appendix C on page 77:

274

"On average, at final assembly each aircraft has 200+ corrective actions requiring rework or repair. The DOD IG team's overall conclusion is that LMA's, Fort Worth, Texas quality management system and the integrity of the F 35 product are jeopardized by lack of attention to detail, inadequate process discipline, and a 'we will catch it later' culture. We believe the quality assurance culture at LMA, Fort Worth, Texas must improve and that robust technical oversight by the government [found elsewhere in the report to be lacking] is required to ensure program performance and mission success."

(http://www.pogo.org/our-work/straus-military-reform-project/weapons/2013/interesting-findings-in-dod-ig-f-35- report.html).

As part of his conclusion, Winslow Wheeler makes an extremely important point. He says that since the Inspector General's report was published on September 30, 2013, the Joint Program Office and Lockheed Martin have said that most of the findings and recommendations have been addressed. This allows the supporters of the F-35 Joint Strike Fighter in Congress the excuse to continue voting to waste huge amounts of taxpayer money on this seriously flawed, inadequate, and unnecessary boondoggle of a fighter jet. The $1.5 trillion F-35 Joint Strike Fighter program is just the most glaring example of Dollar Democracy and waste, fraud, and abuse in the Military-Industrial Complex that is weakening our nation.

Winslow Wheeler, for many years an expert on the F-35 joint strike fighter at the Project on Government Oversight, provides a summary overview of its capabilities. He says:

"This grotesquely unpromising plan has already resulted in multitudes of problems-- and 80% of the flight testing remains. A virtual flying piano, the F-35 lacks the F-16's agility in the air- to-air mode and the F-15 E's range and payload in the bombing mode, and it can't even begin to compare to the A-10 at low altitude close air support for troops engaged in combat. Worse yet, it won't be able to get into the air as often to perform any mission-- or just as importantly, to train pilots-- because its complexity prolongs maintenance and limits availability....

"The bottom line: the F-35 is not the wonder it's advocates claim. It is a gigantic performance disappointment, and in some respects a step backward. The problems, integral to the design, cannot be fixed without starting from a clean sheet of paper." ("The Jet That Ate the Pentagon", *ForeignPolicy.com*, April 26, 2012).

The Littoral Combat Ship: Another Wasteful Boondoggle

A second glaring example of Dollar Democracy causing much of the waste, fraud, and abuse in America's Military-Industrial complex is the Littoral Combat Ship (LCS). Similar to how the F- 35 joint strike fighter was sold to the American public, the LCS was sold as the high-tech, multipurpose answer to the Navy's 21st Century needs. Writing in Atlantic Media's August 25, 2014 digital publication *Defenseone.com*, defense and arms control experts William Hartung and Jacob Marx claim the LCS is supposed to be "fast, maneuverable and able to operate in shallow water. And it is built to adapt to different tasks through a system of exchangeable weapons and equipment, known as 'mission packages.' " The Navy says that the LCS should be able to sail to port and head back to sea in 96 hours, refitted with a whole new payload. This would've given the LCS the capability to replace at least 56 small and medium warships. At a projected cost of $450 million for one seat frame and three mission packages, it seemed to provide three ships for the price of one. Sounds quite a bit like the F-35 Joint Strike Fighter, doesn't it, one plane in three different versions, to suit the needs of the Air Force, the Marine

Corps, and the Navy?

As we found, and noted by Hartung and Marx, "Designing a weapons system for a dozen missions makes it good at none of them. Such inherently flawed requirements balloon costs, in this case to a staggering $780 million for one sea frame with two mission packages. This, for a ship that is too big to be a corvette (usually costing around $200 million each), too lightly armed or armored to be a destroyer (costing around $1 billion each) and too overweight to be upgraded through a full-service life." In one war game the mission packages of the LCS took several weeks to exchange, because of the time required to get the appropriate equipment and personnel to the dock. We don't know the complete extent of the problems with the LCS. Despite the fact that 11 years have passed and six ships were built, the U.S. Navy still hasn't conducted formal testing for the LCS's ability to withstand an explosive shock, to operate in rough water, or to totally survive. (http://www.defenseone.com/ideas/2014/08/its-time-to-sink-lcs/92378/).

Littoral Combat Ship

Image 9-2 | Littoral Combat Ship | Photo/Creative Commons

The two baseline versions of the LCS were developed by one design team led by Lockheed Martin and another design team led by General Dynamics. The original cost estimate of $220 million for the LCS sea frame skyrocketed to $670 million for the first LCS, and $813 million for the second. Some defense procurement experts see a pattern of defense contractors winning government contracts to build the weapons at unrealistically low costs in the early stages of a proposed weapons program, and then jacking up the prices based on the "cost plus overruns" clause in the contract that I had mentioned earlier. Despite the staggeringly high cost per Littoral Combat Ship in the range of $780 million, and many problems with performance and physical quality, it's military-industrial complex backing by corporate defense contractors and their lobbyists, members of Congress sponsored by them, and powerful forces in the Pentagon, seems to be guaranteeing the continuation of this inadequate and unnecessary boondoggle of a ship.

For 2019, the Navy has requested funding for only one Littoral Combat Ship (LCS). Congress, under the pressure of the National Defense Industrial Association (NDIA-the lobbying arm for the large defense contractors), passed the 2019 defense budget which was signed into law by President Trump and included funding for three LCSs (https://news.usni.org/2018/09/28/36944). (U.S. Naval Institute News, September 28, 2018, "Pentagon to Start FY 2019 With Defense Spending Bill Signed into Law", by Ben Werner). The two extra LCSs cost the taxpayers approximately an extra $1 billion.

According to the January 30, 2015 Congressional Research Service report "Navy Littoral Combat Ship (LCS)/Frigate Program: Background and Issues for Congress", by Ronald O'Rourke, Specialist in Naval Affairs, the first LCS was funded in FY 2005, and a total of 23 have been funded through FY 2015. The Navy's proposed FY 2016 budget is expected to request funding for the procurement of three more LCSs. O'Rourke admits, "The LCS program has been controversial due to past cost growth, design and construction issues with the lead ships built to each design, concerns over the ships' survivability (i.e., ability to withstand battle damage), concerns over whether the ships are sufficiently armed and would be able to perform their stated missions effectively, and concerns over the development and testing of the ships' modular mission packages."

Other major problems with the Navy's Littoral Combat Ship that make it an unreliable, wasteful boondoggle, include the first LCS, USS *Freedom* developing a 6-inch long crack in its hull during trials, and taking on five gallons of water every hour. The Navy's blaming a welding error does not obscure real concerns about the ship's durability. In a simulated war game by Kyle Mizokami, involving a naval engagement between an LCS and Chinese warships, "...the LCS got shellacked." (https://medium.com/war-is-boring/heres-how-the-military-wasted-your-money-in-2013-ec86786aae30).

The Pentagon is apparently aware of the ship's shortcomings. In a 2013 report, J. Michael Gilmore, a top Pentagon weapons tester said, "LCS is not expected to be survivable in that it is not expected to maintain mission capability after taking a significant hit in a hostile combat environment." At high speeds the ship's 57-millimeter gun wobbles and its air-defense radar is not adequate. More seriously, for a Littoral ship, its sonar can't detect mines-- a major danger in shallow waters. (https://medium.com/war-is-boring/heres-how-the-military-wasted-your-money-in-2013-ec86786aae30).\

Why is the tremendous waste of tax payer dollars on the boondoggle Littoral Combat Ship allowed to continue? William D. Hartung and Jacob Marx offer three main reasons for this. First the U.S. Department of Defense issued contracts with unworkable and often conflicting requirements. There is no real need to have a ship the size of the LCS be able to travel at 40 knots. Traveling at that speed uses up too much fuel, does not make the ship safer from missiles or torpedoes, and presents balance and weight problems. The second reason for this fiasco is the lack of adequate Congressional oversight. Congress should do two things: require that all major capabilities of a ship are adequately tested before it goes into full scale production and require that contractors bear a larger burden of the financial risk if the systems don't work. The third reason is the common practice in the weapons industry of putting in unrealistically low bids in order to win major government contracts. If the DOD would carefully scrutinize those initial bids, Congress and the public can make better decisions as to whether the weapon is necessary and worth the cost. (http://www.defenseone.com/ideas/2014/08/its-time-sink-lcs/92378/).

I believe that as long as Dollar Democracy, the big-money campaign contributions and lobbying from the defense contractors of powerful members of Congress continues, it will be virtually impossible to address the second and third reasons as stated by Hartung and Marx above. Wasteful, inadequate, and unnecessary boondoggle weapons such as the F-35 Joint Strike Fighter and the Littoral Combat Ship will continue to drive America toward economic, technological, social, and national-security bankruptcy, the devastating result of the unwarranted influence of the Military-Industrial-Congressional Complex and Dollar Democracy.

From the time the first Littoral Combat Ship was accepted by the Navy from Lockheed Martin on September 18, 2008 until it went into dry dock in the summer of 2011-- less than 1000 days later-- "there were 640 chargeable equipment failures on the ship. On the average then, something on the ship failed on two out of every three days." (http://www.pogo.org/our-work/letters/2012/ns-lcs-20120423-littoral-combat-ship-cracks.html?print=t). Yet the Navy told Congress that all was well on LCS-1.

Despite the many LCS failures listed above, Navy Secretary Raymond Mabus told Congress that everything was fine on LCS-1, the *Freedom*. In December 2010, Secretary Mabus told the Senate Armed Services Committee that both versions of the LCS (the Lockheed Martin and General Dynamics versions) "were performing well, and that 'LCS-1, the *Freedom*, demonstrated some of the things we can expect during her maiden deployment earlier this year.' Then-Chief of Naval Operations Admiral Gary Roughead echoed this praise for the LCS-1, stating 'I deployed LCS earlier than any other ship class to assure we were on the right path operationally. It is clear to me that we were.' "

Mabus and Roughead failed to mention that during the approximately two-month deployment when the ship traveled from Mayport, Florida, to its home port in San Diego, California, there were more than 80 equipment failures on the ship. These failures were not trivial and placed the crew of the ship in undue danger. For example, on March 6, 2010, while the ship was in the midst of counter-drug trafficking operations and reportedly 'conducted four drug seizures, netting more than five tons of cocaine, detained nine suspected drug smugglers, and disabled two "go-fast" drug vessels,' there was a darken ship event (the electricity on the entire ship went out), temporarily leaving the ship adrift at sea."

(http://www.pogo.org/our-work/letters/2012/ns-lcs-20120423-littpral-combat-ship-cracks.html?print=t).

Writing in POGO.org on April 23, 2012 and in the *U.S. News & World Report* on February 12, 2014, Dr. Benjamin Freeman points to additional failures and problems with the Littoral Combat Ship. After over six months in port, on its first two outings: "several vital components on the ship failed, including, at some point in both trips, each of the four engines. In addition, there were shaft seal failures during the last trip, which led to flooding. ...the ship appears to have even more serious problems with critical ship-wide systems, including rampant corrosion and flooding." Dr. Freeman also notes that "according to the DoD's DOT&E FY 2011 Annual Report, the LCS is 'not expected to be survivable in a hostile combat environment.'"

Because of the many problems and failures of the LCS, the original $32 billion plan to purchase 52 ships was cut back, by Obama's Defense Secretary Chuck Hagel, to $23 billion to buy 32 ships. Since less than a handful of the ships have been built, Congress and the Pentagon will waste over $20 billion of hard-earned taxpayer money to buy 28 ships from Lockheed Martin and Austal Ltd. (General Dynamics). Writing in *Bloomberg Business* on January 8, 2015, Anthony Capaccio claims that the Littoral Combat Ship's upgrades, that were approved by former Secretary of Defense Chuck Hagel, won't significantly reduce its vulnerability to battle damage, according to the Pentagon's top weapons tester. Michael Gilmore, the Pentagon's director of operational testing, said "the minor modifications to the LCS will not yield a ship that is significantly more survivable."

Gilmore's assessment of the LCS in his annual report of major weapons could have been used by critics of the ship, such as the late U.S. Senator John McCain, Chair of the Senate Armed Services Committee. However, as Dollar Democracy continues, more members of Congress who are part of the Military-Industrial Complex, and are supported and influenced by its millions of dollars, will vote to squander our hard-earned taxpayer money on the wasteful and unnecessary boondoggle that is the Littoral Combat Ship, referred to by critics inside the Navy as the "Little Crappy Ship."

The M1 Abrams Tank: Hundreds of Millions of Dollars Wasted on a Weapon the Military Doesn't Want

According to the February 9, 2015 *DoD Buzz, Online Defense and Acquisition Journal*, after years of telling Congress that it did not need more money for the M1 Abrams tank, the U.S. Army succumbed to pressure from members of Congress whose campaigns were heavily funded by the M1's primary defense contractor, General Dynamics. Army officials reversed direction and requested $316 million for upgrades to the M1 tank in its latest budget proposal. This request was for 50 percent more funding than last year for the M1 Abrams tank. Last year the Army asked for $237 million. ("Army Asks for More Money to Upgrade Abrams Tanks", by Michael Hoffman, *Military.com*)

M1 Abrams Tank

Image 9-3 | M1 Abrams Tank | Photo/Creative Commons

Because the Army currently has more than 2,300 M1 Abrams tanks-- with another 3,000 in storage in the California desert-- and about 9,000 tanks in its force, Army Chief of Staff General Ray Odierno told *Associated Press* in April 2013, "If we had our choice, we would use that money in a different way." Gen. Odierno and other Army leaders had felt for many years that millions of dollars for more M1 tanks and their upgrades were not needed, at present. Their plan was to wait until 2017 to build upgraded tanks, saving $3 billion. Their reasons seemed to be twofold: first, the probability of a massive ground war with the defunct Soviet Union, for which the tanks were primarily built, no longer existed; second, the M1, in use since 1980, was proving increasingly vulnerable to IED's (improvised explosive devices) in counterinsurgency wars in the Middle East.

Given the M1's vulnerability to asymmetric tactics such as this, the tank's usefulness in counterinsurgency wars of the future has been questioned. In his February 17, 2012 testimony before the House Armed Services Committee, General Ray Odierno said that the U.S. has more tanks than it needs for a strong defense. He stated, "Our tank fleet is in good shape and we don't need to [make repairs] because of the great support that we have gotten over the last two years." (Sean Kennedy, *Waste Watcher*, January 2013, cagw.org).

And yet, the 2015 spending plan, approved by Congress and signed by former President Obama, provided $120 million for the M1 Abrams Upgrade Program. According to Citizens Against Government Waste, since 1994, Congress approved 31 "earmarks" worth $519.2 million for the Abrams Program ("You're Paying Billions for Weaponry the Military Doesn't Even Want", Chris Brady, *Standard Journal*, January 6, 2015). Earmarks are money provided by Congress for specific projects or programs, while avoiding a competitive or merit-based allocation process and applies to a limited number of entities or individuals, in this case the private defense contractors who make the M1 Abrams tank. Is it the private defense contractors and their sponsored politicians in Congress, who play the game of "Dollar Democracy" and lobbying, who are most responsible for the humongous waste, fraud, and abuse in the Military-Industrial Complex?

In the case of the M1 Abrams tank, the overwhelming evidence seems to point that way. The Lima, Ohio plant facility is owned by the federal government but operated by the land systems division of General Dynamics, the prime contractor for the M1 Abrams tank. It is one of the top five U.S. defense contractors, a major part of the U. S. Military-

Industrial Complex. According to the Center for Responsive Politics, during the 2014 election cycle General Dynamics spent $21,787,897 in lobbying Congress, and in the 2012 election cycle it spent $22,348,085 doing the same. In the 2014 election cycle General Dynamics made $1,974,599 in campaign contributions to Congressional candidates and members of Congress, including thousands of dollars to the campaigns of Republican U.S. Senator Rob Portman, Democratic U.S. Senator Sherrod Brown, and Republican U.S. Congressman Jim Jordan, all representing the state of Ohio and the congressional district where the M1 Abrams is manufactured. For the 2012 election cycle General Dynamics made $2,373,054 in Congressional campaign contributions. In the 2018 election cycle, General Dynamics made $2,690,944 in congressional campaign contributions.

The M1 plant is Lima's fifth-largest employer with approximately 700 employees. General Dynamics has estimated that there are more than 560 subcontractors throughout the U.S. involved in the M1 Abrams program, employing approximately 18,000 people ("Abrams Tank Pushed by Congress Despite Army's Protests", Richard Lardner, *Huffington Post*, June 28, 2013). According to OpenSecrets.org, General Dynamics assembles "virtually every type of military machinery engaged in modern combat. The company builds warships, nuclear submarines, tanks and combat jets, not to mention the command-and-control systems that link all of these technologies together. The company has lobbied hard to encourage lawmakers to step up appropriations for the Navy, one of the company's biggest clients."

Members of Congress and the Government Become Lobbyists by Going Through the Revolving Door

Through a revolving door, 96 out of 133 General Dynamics lobbyists in 2013-2014 had previously held government jobs (opensecrets.org). When they became lobbyists, their pay was much higher than as a member of Congress, quite often doubled, tripled, or quadrupled.

This raises an interesting point: many high placed government decision-makers, including some members of Congress, groom themselves to become high paid corporate lobbyists by doing the bidding of their future corporate employer, even while they are in the government. Take for example former Republican Congressman Billy Tauzin of Louisiana. After serving two dozen years in Congress-- first as a Democrat, and then as a Republican-- Tauzin is a living example of the bipartisan takeover of Congress by corporate interests. Although I must say there are a few non-corporate Democrats remaining, who fight for a progressive-populist agenda that would benefit the bottom 99% of Americans, such as Congresswoman Alexandria Ocasio-Cortez of New York, Congressman Ro Kahanna of California, Congresswoman Barbara Lee of California, Congresswoman Ayanna Pressley of Massachusetts, Congressman Raul Grijalva of Arizona, Congresswoman Maxine Waters of California, Congressman Rashida Tlaib of Michigan, Congresswoman Pramila Jayapal of Washington State, Congresswoman Ilhan Omar of Minnesota, Congressman Peter DeFazio of Oregon, Congressman Jim McDermott of Washington, Senator Bernie Sanders of Vermont, and Senator Elizabeth Warren of Massachusetts.

Unlike them, while still a congressman in 2003 and Chairman of the House Energy and Commerce Committee, Billy Tauzin wrote the law creating Medicare's prescription drug benefit, a giveaway to the pharmaceutical industry and its lobbying arm, PhRMA. In 2004 he left his $165,000 a year job as a member of Congress and became head of PhRMA, continuing to serve the special interests of Big Pharma. As CEO of PhRMA, Tauzin received $2.06 million. His compensation increased to $4.48 million in 2008, $4.62 million in 2009, and as he left in June 2010, he was paid $11.6 million. (*Bloomberg Business*, November 28, 2011).

Let's return to General Dynamics and the revolving door. Of the 96 General Dynamics lobbyists in 2013-2014 who had previously held government jobs, let's examine a handful. The most famous is probably former U.S. Senator from New York Republican Alfonse D'Amato. He served in the U.S. Senate from 1981 to 1998 and on the following powerful Senate Committees: Appropriations; Banking, Housing and Urban Affairs; Finance; and Select Intelligence Committees. D'Amato then went through the revolving door and became a lobbyist for Lockheed-Martin, General Dynamics, United Technologies, General Atomics, and Mercury Enterprises, from 1999 to the present.

Democratic Congressman Norm Dicks of Washington state served on the House Appropriations Committee. When he retired he went to work as a lobbyist for General Dynamics for $240,000 year, a slight raise from his $175,000 congressional salary.

Patrick Pettey was Chief of Staff for Republican U.S. Senator Bob Smith of New Hampshire. During this time, since his boss was on the Senate Armed Services Committee, Pettey must have made some excellent contacts which served him and General Dynamics well when he switched professions and became a lobbyist for a subsidiary of General Dynamics.

Robert W. Helm, from 1984-1988, served as the Department of Defense Comptroller, National Security Council Aide/Staff, and the Senate Budget Committee's Senior Defense Analyst. After leaving government work, in 1989 he went through the revolving door and became Corporate Vice President of Northrop Grumman, one of the five largest U.S. defense contractors. According to opensecrets.org Helm is also a lobbyist for General Dynamics.

Susan Sweat, from 2001-2011, was Legislative Director for Republican U.S. Senator Roger Wicker of Mississippi, who sat on the powerful Senate Armed Services Committee and Senate Budget Committee. After enhancing her resume by making valuable contacts in government service, she walked through the revolving door, and became a corporate lobbyist for General Dynamics, Boeing, Visa Inc. and other entities.

David Morris, from 2005-2012 was the U.S. Senate Armed Services Committee Minority Staff Director. While in this position he garnered important technical and procedural information on how defense bills were written and approved. In 2012 Morris began working as a lobbyist for the gigantic defense weapons producer General Dynamics, prime builder of the M1 Abrams tank.

Adam Paulson, from 2001-2012, was Legislative Director for

Republican Congressman Peter King of New York. As a long-term, highly visible, and powerful member of Congress, King served for many years on the House Financial Services Committee and the House Homeland Security Committee. Paulson, as King's Legislative Director, became well-versed in the nuances of the legislative process, in other words on how a bill becomes law. Since his boss served on these two crucial committees, dealing with issues of banking and homeland security, Paulson must have been well-acquainted with many of the movers and shakers on Wall Street as well as in the weapons industries. It's no wonder that he could not resist the revolving door, but instead went right through it to become a major lobbyist for General Dynamics.

Military Generals Become Lobbyists by Going Through the Revolving Door

In an earlier version of his "Military-Industrial Complex" speech, President Eisenhower had warned us of the creation of a "permanent, war-based industry," with "flag and general officers retiring at an early age (to) take positions in the war-based industrial complex shaping its decisions and guiding the direction of its tremendous thrust." The President said that steps need to be taken to "insure that the 'merchants of death' do not come to dictate national policy." ("Eisenhower's Neglected Warning", Melvin A. Goodman, *consortiumnews.com,* January 11, 2011). President Eisenhower was ignored.

The revolving door is not just for recent members of the government, such as members of Congress, their high-level staff, and top decision-making bureaucrats, who've now gone to work for big defense corporations who funded their campaigns and lobbied them for spending on weapons, through bloated and sometimes unnecessary weapons contracts. It is now the retired generals who are going through the door to work for the big weapons contractors such as the five largest-- Lockheed Martin, Boeing, General Dynamics, Raytheon, and Northrop Grumman. A recent report by Citizens for Responsibility and Ethics in Washington (CREW) and the Brave New Foundation discovered that 70 percent of retired three-and- four-star generals went to work for defense contractors or consultants. It cited General James Cartwright, who advised the Pentagon while serving on the Defense Policy Board at the same time he was elected to a paid position on Raytheon's Board of Directors. Admiral Gary Roughead also served on the Defense Policy Board while joining the board of Northrop Grumman, which paid him $115,000 annually.

The CREW- Brave New Foundation report found that in 2011 government spending on weapons from the "five largest defense contractors-- Lockheed Martin, Boeing, General Dynamics, Raytheon, and Northrop Grumman totaled $100 billion, with at least nine retiring top generals and admirals taking positions at the firms." (" Report: 70 Percent of Retired Generals Took Jobs with Defense Contractors or Consultants", Luke Johnson, *Huffington Post*, November 20, 2012). A recent *Boston Globe* study looked at the careers of 750 of the highest-ranking generals and admirals who retired in the last 20 years and found that most of them moved into what many in Washington refer to as the "rent-a-general" business.

The Globe study found that from 2004 to 2008, "80 percent of retiring three- and four-star officers went to work as consultants or defense executives. That compares with less than 50% who followed that path a decade earlier, from 1994 to 1998." *The Globe* found that:

- Dozens of retired generals employed by defense firms maintain Pentagon advisory roles, giving them unparalleled levels of influence and access to inside information on Department of Defense procurement plans.

- The generals are, in many cases, recruited for private sector roles well before they retire, raising questions about their independence and judgment while still working in the military. The Pentagon is aware and even supports this practice.

- The feeder system from some commands to certain defense firms is so powerful that successive generations of commanders have been hired by the same firms or into the same field. For example, the last seven generals and admirals who worked as Department of Defense gatekeepers for international arms sales are now helping military contractors sell weapons and defense technology overseas.

• When a general-turned-businessman arrives at the Pentagon, he is often treated with extraordinary deference-- as if still in uniform-- which can greatly increase his effectiveness as a rainmaker for industry. The military even has a name for it-- the "bobble head effect."

Retired General Robert "Doc" Foglesong, who was the second ranking Air Force officer in 2006, commented "we are changing the perception and maybe the reality of what it means to be a general. The fundamental question is whether this is shaping the acquisition system and influencing what the Pentagon buys. I think the answer is yes." ("From the Pentagon to the Private Sector", Bryan Bender, *Boston Globe*, December 26, 2010).

A case in point is Air Force General Gregory "Speedy" Martin who retired in 2005 after a 35-year career. An hour after his official retirement ceremony, the general was dressed to play golf. As soon as he was ready to hit the golf course, his phone rang. An executive at Northrop Grumman asked him if he would like to work for the B-2 stealth bomber's manufacturer, as a paid consultant. The Pentagon called General Martin a few weeks later, asking him to be part of a top- secret Air Force panel that was studying the future of stealth aircraft technology. General Martin accepted both offers, despite the apparent conflict of interest-- "pitting his duty to the U.S. military against the interests of his employer, (Northrop Grumman)-- not to mention a revolving-door sprint from uniformed responsibilities to private paid advocacy." (*Boston Globe*, December 26, 2010).

It is apparent that the powerful defense contractors, who are also our weapons manufacturers, are practicing a new principle of "Dollar Democracy": why stop at hiring just government bureaucrats, congressional staffers, and members of Congress? You get a bigger bang for your buck if you hire retired generals and admirals with the right connections, to capture weapons contracts with millions and billions of taxpayer dollars, whether or not these weapons are really needed, delivered decades late, function as promised, or end up bankrupting our economy and educational systems, which are the twin pillars of a strong and vibrant 21st Century nation and society.

While Congress Lines the Pockets of the Military Contractors, the Pentagon Picks the Pockets of our Soldiers

While Congress lines the pockets of the giant defense corporations and private military contractors, it allows the Pentagon to pick the pockets of many of our soldiers in uniform. The U.S. Constitution charges Congress with the responsibility of "raising and supporting armies." (Article 1, Section 8). In the last few decades members of Congress have voted to spend trillions of dollars on weapons and other military contracts that enriched their corporate campaign donors such as Lockheed Martin, General Dynamics, Northrop Grumman, Boeing, Raytheon, and Halliburton. A Pentagon investigation found "evidence that a subsidiary of the ... Halliburton Company (KBR) overcharged the government by $61 million for fuel delivered to Iraq under huge no- bid ... contracts.... (NY Times, Dec. 12, 2003). Halliburton truck drivers made $125,000 compared to the $30,000 made by a military truck driver. While funding the Pentagon and security-related agencies to the tune of $1 trillion annually taken from the taxpayer, Congress allowed the Pentagon to neglect the needs of our most precious and important resource: our women and men in uniform.

For example, after two tours of combat duty left him with traumatic brain injury, severe PTSD, chronic pain, and a hip injury, U.S. Army medic **Shawn Aiken** was shocked when he received his October 2011 paycheck for only $2,337 instead of his regular monthly take-home pay of $3,300. For December his pay dropped to $118. Because of a lack of help or answers from the staff, Aiken and his young family went through hell and back to survive, going to church- run food pantries, borrowing money for rent, and even pawning their jewelry, games, iPhone, and his medic bag which he had used to save lives in Afghanistan. The real outrage is that the money the military had taken from Aiken's paychecks was the result of "accounting and other errors, and it should have been his to keep." (*Reuters*, July 10, 2013).

The Pentagon agency in charge of accurately paying America's 2.7 million active-duty and Reserve soldiers, sailors, Marines, and airmen is the Defense Finance and Accounting Service (DFAS). Headquartered in Indianapolis, Indiana, it has approximately 12,000 employees and a $1.36 billion annual budget. DFAS often fails to pay our women and men in uniform accurately, according to a *Reuters* special report. ("Special Report: how the Pentagon's payroll quagmire traps America's soldiers", Tuesday, July 9, 2013, by Scott J. Paltrow and Kelly Carr). The report reviewed individuals' military pay records, government reports and other documents. The investigators also interviewed "dozens of current and former soldiers and other military personnel"... And found that Aikens case was not the only one. Errors in pay in the military are widespread. As quoted earlier, Democratic Senator Thomas Carper of Delaware, chairman of the Homeland Security and Government Affairs Committee said, "too often, a soldier who has a problem with his or her pay can wait days, weeks or even months to get things sorted out. This is simply unacceptable."

If this is "simply unacceptable" then why doesn't Congress, the president, and the Pentagon fix this problem immediately? Is it because our all-volunteer military recruits come primarily from working middle class and working poor families? ("The Evolution of the All-Volunteer Force", *Rand Corporation*). These American families cannot afford well-paid lobbyists and large campaign contributions to influence members of Congress and the U.S. president. Do many of our men and women in uniform suffer the stress of inaccurate paychecks because powerful members of Congress pay more attention to their wealthy donors such as defense contractors and other corporate lobbyists? Don't these politicians realize that lining the pockets of weapons manufacturers, while allowing pay errors for our soldiers, sailors, and airmen to continue, is not only unethical and immoral, but "may pose financial hardship for the soldiers and detract from their focus on mission." (*GAO Report*, December 2012). Waste, fraud and abuse in the Military-Industrial Complex are hurting many of our women and men in uniform, hurting their morale, and endangering our military defense. No wonder official army survey data show "more than half of about 770,000 soldiers are pessimistic about their future in the military, and nearly as many are unhappy in their jobs. … more than half reported poor nutrition and sleep." (*USA Today*, April 17-19, 2005). More than 21 veterans and 1 soldier are committing suicide daily.

There are some veterans and soldiers support groups that do not have the huge resources of the corporate defense contractors. Groups such as **Military Families Speak Out** (MFSO) whose present mission statement is "to end the US military fighting in Iraq and Afghanistan, bring our troops home now, take care of them when they get here, and end the policies that allowed these wars to happen."

I recently met with **Pat Alviso**, MFSO National Coordinator, and with some of the MFSO Steering Committee members including **Ed Garza**, and **Lorna Ramos Farnum**. Pat's son has been in the military for several years and has served two tours of duty in Iraq and three tours of duty in Afghanistan. Lorna's daughter served in the military, and Ed Garza's two nephews are in the military. Ed, also a veteran, was a recipient of the Purple Heart.

As we all sat around the dining room table in Lorna's home, Pat poignantly said, "We military families are on the front lines every day because many of our children are directly involved. We speak from our hearts when we talk to our leaders about the need for greater support of our soldiers in many ways: Medical and mental health care, treatment of Post-Traumatic Stress Disorder (PTSD), the need for housing for homeless veterans, and the need to end unnecessary wars, preemptive wars, wars of aggression, and wars that break international law."

With their millions of dollars in campaign contribution lobbying activity, the defense corporations have a thundering voice that many members of Congress hear clearly. The voices of Military Families Speak Out, while holding the moral high ground and pressing forward, will have difficulty being heard by members of Congress, until this Dollar Democracy is transformed into Real Democracy.

The Pentagon: The Only Government Department, Until Now, Not Subject to Full Audit, Failed the First Attempt at a Full Audit In 2018

Because the Pentagon had not ever been subject to a full audit, it had allowed its main accounting agency, the Defense Finance and Accounting Service (DEFAS) to "(fudge) the accounts with false entries...." (*Reuters*, November18, 2013). Scot Paltrow claimed in 2017 that the Pentagon was "unable to accurately track it's $591 billion annual budget and experiences billions of dollars in accounting gaps and errors each year despite two decades of reform efforts. (Reuters, April 13, 2017, "Government watchdog: Trump wants extra $54 billion on defense, but Pentagon can't track the $591 billion it already has", by Scot Paltrow). Taken together, the reports show that many of the endemic accounting problems exposed in (the) 2013 Reuters investigative series remain in place." Despite these problems and the inability of the Pentagon to meet audit requirements and track the $591 billion it already had, President Trump called for an extra $54 billion for the military budget. At the same time, he called for deep cuts in important non-military areas in his proposed 2018 military budget. As Paltrow notes, Trump called for cutting the State Department's budget by 28 percent ($10.1 billion). U.S. support for the United Nations would be cut. The Environmental Protection Agency (EPA) would be cut by Trump by 31 percent ($2.6 billion).His budget would eliminate more than 50 EPA programs and cut EPA research and development by 52 percent ($233 million). The budget for lead cleanup to states would be cut by 30 percent to $9.8 million. (Paltrow, 2017). In 2017, the Pentagon still lacked a unified, functioning accounting system.

The Pentagon relies on 2,200 different, obsolete, and largely incompatible accounting and business management systems, many of which were built in the 1970s and use ancient computer languages such as COBOL on old mainframes. That's why the Pentagon can't keep track of its money-- how much it has, how much it pays out, and how much is stolen or wasted. This has produced disastrous results in two critical areas: first, in paycheck errors for the women and men in uniform, burdening them with financial hardship, sapping their morale, and detracting from their focus on mission.

Second, the Pentagon has difficulty managing its finances, human resources, logistics, property and weapons acquisition, which makes it harder to deploy men and women in times of war, and also causes it to waste millions of taxpayer dollars in extra sets of spare parts that it already has. For example, Navy Vice Admiral Mark Hartnicheck the director of the Pentagon's Defense Logistics Agency says, "We have about $14 billion of inventory for lots of reasons, and probably half that is excess to what we need."

According to Scott J. Paltrow's and Kelly Carr's excellent investigative report in *Reuters*, because the Pentagon "has come to rely on an accounting system of antiquated, error-prone computers... these thousands of duplicative and inefficient systems cost billions of dollars to staff and maintain; (while) efforts to replace these systems with better ones have ended in costly failures;... it all adds up to billions of taxpayer dollars a year in losses to mismanagement, theft and fraud." ("Special Report: How the Pentagon's payroll quagmire traps America's soldiers", *Reuters* Tuesday, July 9, 2013). There are also serious security implications: "officers complain that the difficulty of keeping track of personnel makes it harder to deploy men and women in times of war. Retired four-star Navy Admiral William J. Fallon says that while serving in 2007 and 2008 as chief of the U.S. Central Command, overseeing joint military operations in Afghanistan and Iraq, he had to maintain 'an incredibly bloated staff' from each of the services to keep him informed of the number and availability of troops. 'It is an incredibly inefficient, wasteful way of doing business,' he says." (Paltrow and Carr).

Despite passage by Congress of the Chief Financial Officers Act of 1990, which required that all government agencies achieve audit readiness, 29 years later the Pentagon remains non-auditable. The Pentagon's dependence on an accounting system of error-prone and antiquated computers made it nearly impossible for it to be fully audit-ready by September 30, 2017 as mandated by the Defense Authorization Act of 2010. Despite this, the fiscal 2017 inspector general report cited

"Antiquated military pay systems, which lacked audi(ta)bility framework and required manual manipulation." (Nov. 16, 2018 *Defense Systems* article, "Financial Audit Spotlights DOD IT Woes" by Lauren C. Williams). Roy Wallace, an Army assistant Deputy Chief of Staff, said the outdated accounting system has "7 million lines of COBOL code that hasn't been updated" in over a dozen years, and important parts of the code have been "corrupted." It's harder to maintain as it gets older. (Paltrow and Carr). "In 1958, the DoD's first contracting software was launched, using an early computer language called COBOL. As of 2017, that software still manages Pentagon contracts." (businessinsider.com, "The Pentagon Still Uses Computer Software from 1958 to Manage Its Contracts.", March 30, 2017). Could this be part of the reason that "the Pentagon has failed what is being called its first-ever comprehensive audit, (as) a senior official said on Thursday, finding U.S. Defense Department accounting discrepancies that could take years to resolve"? (Reuters.com, "Pentagon Fails Its First-Ever Audit, Official Says", by Indrees Ali and Mike Stone, November 15, 2018). Ironically, the Deputy Secretary of Defense Patrick Shanahan said, "We failed the audit, but we never expected to pass it." President Trump has recently appointed him Acting U.S. Secretary of Defense. Shanahan added that the audit findings showed the need for greater discipline in Pentagon financial matters.

The Defense Science Board--corporate executives and senior military leaders who advise the Pentagon on technology-- called the Pentagon payroll system "obsolete" and claimed that it "damage(s) the morale and welfare of the Service members and their families." The board called for scrapping the current system and advocated a "single, all-Service and all- component, fully integrated personnel and pay system, with common core software." (Paltrow and Carr).

As a result, the Pentagon started designing and building a new system, the Defense Integrated Military Human Resources System (DIMHRS). Almost immediately, cost overruns and delays began. After more than 10 years of development and more than $1 billion spent, a consensus was reached in January 2009 by Deputy Secretary of Defense Gordon England, the secretaries of the Army, Navy, and Air Force and their top-ranking generals and admirals, along with DIMHRS personnel, to kill the project. They felt that the only way to make the project work would be to "pull a four-star general from the wars in Iraq and Afghanistan to manage what they saw as a bookkeeping project. (According to) Tina Jonas, the Pentagon's chief financial officer from 2004 to 2008, and other officials overseeing the project... It wasn't a top priority among top brass, who left implementation to lower-level managers, rarely checking in on progress." (Paltrow and Carr). Why was it so difficult for the top military brass to see that without the solid foundation of a single, all-Service and all component, fully integrated personnel and pay system, with common core software, the morale and welfare of our Service members and their families would be damaged, possibly weakening the most important, crucial, and precious component of a military defense system, its human resource.

And where are most of our leaders in Congress while all of this waste, fraud, and abuse in the Military-Industrial-Congressional complex is bankrupting our economy and endangering our society? Many of them are dialing for campaign dollars from and kowtowing to the demands of lobbyists from the corporate weapons manufacturers, the true leaders of our Military-Industrial-Congressional complex.

Where are most of our congressional leaders and ranking members of the military defense-related committees of Congress, such as the Senate Committee on Armed Services; the Senate Committee on Appropriations; the Senate Committee on the Budget; the Senate Committee on Veterans' Affairs; the Senate Committee on Homeland Security and Governmental Affairs; and the House Committee on Armed Services; the House Committee on Appropriations; the House Committee on the Budget; the House Committee on Homeland Security; the House Committee on Veterans' Affairs; and the House Committee on Ways and Means, which has tremendous power over taxation in order to raise the money for military/defense/security spending? Many of them are raising hundreds of millions of dollars in campaign contributions from the major military/defense/security corporations and voting for hundreds of billions of dollars in private contracts and weapons purchases from them, generating billions of dollars of profits, and multi-million-dollar salaries for their corporate CEOs. Some of these exorbitant profits are then used to further buy influence from Congress through lobbying and more campaign contributions, in an endless, wasteful, and debilitating cycle, for our country's economy, society, and true defense.

To stop the Military-Industrial Congressional Complex from bankrupting America and hurting American soldiers like Shawn Aiken, we must not only end the "unwarranted influence... Of the military-industrial complex" as President Eisenhower warned us. We must end the buying of Congress and our politicians by Big Corporations, their lobbyists, and their super-wealthy owners! President Eisenhower knew that too much military spending would weaken the economy and national security. Eisenhower, a military man, said, **"Every gun that is made, every warship launched, every rocket fired signifies...a theft from those who hunger and are not fed, those who are cold and are not clothed."** ("Eisenhower's Neglected Warning", Melvin A. Goodman, January 16, 2011, consortiumnews.com).

When we beat some of our unnecessary "swords into plowshares", the United States of America will have a streamlined, efficient, and adequate defense. This will include only necessary military hardware and personnel, civilian economic vitality, as well as "soft power." Harvard professor Joseph Nye coined the term "soft power" to mean the ability to attract and persuade. This ability arises from the attractiveness of a nation's culture, political ideas, and policies.

Instead of succumbing to the unwarranted influence of the military-industrial complex and its overindulgence in military hard power, we must expand the use of our soft power. This will help us address critical global issues that require multilateral cooperation among countries: interrelated issues such as national security and defense, poverty and inequality in the U.S. and world, educational, health, and infrastructural development, and the use of green technology to save our nation and our planet and advance the human condition. Redirecting our military, foreign, economic, and diplomatic policies in this way will make us truly safer. However, an enormous first step toward this life-changing goal and that of rebuilding the American middle class, and expanding the middle class throughout the world, is to require that the Pentagon obey the law and finally become fully audit ready. This is the only way to know exactly how much taxpayer money the Pentagon is receiving, is spending, and is losing through waste, fraud, and abuse. If the Pentagon had complied with the 25-year-old law requiring all government agencies to be audited annually, we could have prevented hundreds of billions of dollars of squandered spending on boondoggle, overly expensive and duplicative parts and weapons. We could have prevented billions of dollars from disappearing into thin air, unaccounted for.

The way Congress and the Pentagon are moving, prospects for a course correction do not seem bright. On March 23, 2015 the Department of Defense (Pentagon) Inspector General withdrew "a clean audit report it gave the U.S. Marine Corps in 2013, an embarrassing snag for the Defense Department's endeavor to become auditable..., after learning of Marine Corps transactions in U.S. Treasury 'suspense accounts,' setup for transactions where some piece of missing information prevents it from being posted properly." ("USMC Reversal a Hitch in DoD Audit Plans", by Joe Gould and Hope Hodge Seck, *Defense News*, March 30, 2015). Since 1995, the Government Accountability Office (GAO) has put the Pentagon "on its 'high risk list' of poor performing programs or agencies because it cannot account for inventory that's 33 percent of the federal government and includes $1.3 trillion in property, plants and equipment." (Gould and Hope).

As part of the original goals of being audit ready by 2017, the armed services had difficulty in submitting complete statements of budgetary resources. So, what did the Pentagon do? It lowered the bar. It stopped requiring complete statements from the services, which are called SBR's, but started accepting more limited, "less comprehensive, single-year schedules of budgetary activity, called SBA's-- which each service has since submitted." (Gould and Hope). As I predicted, at this rate, the Pentagon was not fully audit ready by 2017. In the November 27, 2018 issue of *The Nation,* Dave Lindorff's article, "Exclusive: The Pentagon's Massive Accounting Fraud Exposed", notes that

> On November 15, Ernst and Young and other private firms that were hired to audit the Pentagon announced that they could not complete the job. Congress had ordered an independent audit of the Department of Defense, the government's largest discretionary cost center—the Pentagon receives 54 cents of every

dollar in federal appropriations—after the Pentagon failed for decades to audit itself. The firms conclude, however, that the DoD's financial records were riddled with so many bookkeeping deficiencies, irregularities and errors, that a reliable audit was simply impossible.

As noted earlier, responding to the Pentagon's abysmal failure, failure of it's first-ever Full Audit in 2018, Trump's Acting Secretary of Defense, Patrick Shanahan said, *"We failed the audit, but we never expected to pass it"*! (italics and exclamation mark are mine.) Since the Pentagon failed the 2018 audit, it is the only government department or agency defying the law once again, and Congress will play along. Only a handful of members of Congress of both parties have the integrity and strength to attempt to penalize the Pentagon for its noncompliance. At the beginning of 2015, Democratic Congresswoman Barbara Lee of California was joined by Republican Congressman Michael Burgess of Texas, and Democratic Congresswoman Jan Schakowsky of Illinois in introducing the bipartisan Audit the Pentagon Act of 2015 (HR 942). It would impose a small penalty on Pentagon accounting units that are not auditable. However, the bill does exempt accounts that are related to personnel and those that are deemed critical to national security by the Secretary of Defense. According to Govtrack.us, the prognosis for HR 942 being enacted is 0 percent !

I will ask this question for the last time: why is it so difficult for the Pentagon, the single largest, richest unit of government, which invented the Internet, which uses advanced high technology in its military weapons and defense systems, to qualify as the largest, most advanced war machine in the history of humankind, unable to even meet the conditions of an audit? Why does it continue to spend the most money of any country on earth, and much more than the next 10 countries combined, on its weapons, military bases, and sometimes unjustified wars, and is as yet not responsible, or fully accountable, for every taxpayer dollar it receives and spends? Is a major part of the answer "DOLLAR DEMOCRACY"? If so, then it is the most glaring example of Dollar Democracy on Steroids: With Liberty and Justice for Some.

We must defeat Dollar Democracy in order to bring Liberty and Justice for All and Reclaim the Middle-Class Dream for All, as well as build a better world for Humankind. The next chapter points the way to reversing this disaster and reaching our lofty goal of a **Real, Deep, and True Democracy for All.**

Image 9-4 | Homeless Veteran
photo/Vietnam Veterans of America

It's unconscionable and outrageous that so many of our veterans are sleeping on the streets or in front of the locked gate at the Westwood (Los Angeles) VA, when that land was granted for the use of veterans. We're pretty quick to send them out to war, but not motivated to care for them when they return.... What we owe them more than anything is to respect them enough to not squander their lives in wars that make no sense. Yes, we need to be aware of dangers that beset our country around the world. But at the same time, if you can't care for those who wear the uniform and serve and risk their lives, then what kind of country is this?....

--Vietnam Veteran Ron Kovic
Author of *Born on the Fourth of July*

Excerpts from Steve Lopez column in the *Los Angeles Times,* November 9, 2014.

CHAPTER 10

WITH LIBERTY AND JUSTICE FOR ALL: TAKING BIG DOLLARS OUT OF DEMOCRACY WITH PAUL WELLSTONE'S EXAMPLE, CLEAN MONEY ELECTIONS, AND WITH MOVE TO AMEND AND WOLFPAC

" Politics is not about power. Politics is not about money. Politics is not about winning for the sake of winning. Politics is about the improvement of people's lives. "

--U.S. Senator Paul Wellstone

We will not realize President Lincoln's vision of government "of the people, by the people, and for the people", until we drastically reduce or fully eliminate the heavy influence of private, corporate, and special interest money in American Politics and Government. This heavy influence of private, corporate and special interest money in American Politics and Government is grounded in four major U.S. Supreme Court decisions: *Southern Pacific Railroad v. Santa Clara County* (1886); *Buckley v. Valeo* (1976); *Citizens United v. Federal Election Commission* (2010); and *McCutcheon v. Federal Election Commission* (2014). These four Supreme Court decisions, for which there is no basis in the U.S. Constitution or Declaration of Independence, have created the modern day American/multi-national corporation.

The very nature and actions of this post-1886 multinational corporation, whose allegiance is not to the American people but only to its major stockholders and CEOs, has undermined American democracy and is turning the Middle-Class Dream into the Middle-Class Nightmare for the bottom 99% of Americans and the world.

The 1886 *Southern Pacific Railroad* decision stated that the corporation is a natural person protected by the Bill of Rights and the 14th Amendment to the U.S. Constitution. The Supreme Court was wrong because corporations, unlike persons, do not breathe, eat, sleep, have emotions, have a conscience, or any other human attributes. The 1976 *Buckley* decision stated that money is equivalent to speech. The Supreme Court was wrong: money is not speech; money is a megaphone that can amplify speech for the well-funded candidate, while drowning out the speech of the lesser funded candidate. The 2010 *Citizens United* decision gave corporations, labor unions, and other large organizations the ability to raise and spend unlimited amounts of money, including their own, to "independently" support or oppose political candidates and public policy issues, based on the faulty argument that money is equivalent to free speech.

In the 2014 *McCutcheon* ruling, the Supreme Court removed all limits on aggregate campaign donations given by a super wealthy individual to Congressional candidates and political parties. This decision was also based on the erroneous notion that money equals free speech. Before *McCutcheon*, a super wealthy person was limited to donating only $123,200 of her/his own money to candidates for Congress and to the political parties. After *McCutcheon*, a super wealthy individual can give up to a total of $3.6 million of her/his money to all the candidates running for Congress and to the political parties in each election cycle, and buy enormous influence with and access to them. Before *Citizens United and McCutcheon* we had a Dollar Democracy with Liberty and Justice for Some. After *Citizens United* and *McCutcheon* we have Dollar Democracy on Steroids, with Liberty and Justice for the top ½ of 1%: the mega-rich giant corporations and their multi-millionaire and billionaire owners. This has made a mockery of the Equal Protection provision in the U.S. Constitution and its promise of Equal Opportunity for All. In the rest of this chapter, I will show how we can and must change direction, Reclaim the Middle-Class Dream and Make it a Reality for All.

Before Clean Money Elections, Senator Paul Wellstone's Clean Elections Legacy: People Power, Not Corporate Power

Just before he tragically died in a plane crash on October 25, 2002, my friend **Paul Wellstone** explained how his refusal to accept corporate lobbyist money for his campaigns allowed him to truly represent the people of Minnesota and America in the U.S. Senate: "I don't represent the big oil companies, the big pharmaceuticals, or the big insurance industry. They already have great representation in Washington. It's the rest of the people that need representation." This statement was absolutely true and backed by the solid evidence of the progressive positions he took on the key issues of the day.

In his 1990, 1996 and 2002 election campaigns for the U.S. Senate, Paul Wellstone, a college political science professor and community organizer, refused campaign donations from big corporate interests and their political action committees (PAC's). He won in 1990 and 1996. He was leading in the polls when he was tragically killed in a plane crash a few days before the 2002 General Election. Wellstone believed that if he accepted campaign money from special-interest corporate lobbyists, he would be obligated to serve their interests most of the time. He would not be able to address the needs of regular people and serve the public interest. Because he only accepted donations and support from individuals and public interest groups such as environmental, labor, educational, gender equity, and other social justice groups, he could fight in the Senate for regular Americans, what we would call today the 99%, not for the corporate elite and its allies, the top 1%. In other words, Wellstone saw himself as the David of America battling the corporate Goliath who held most of the power and wealth. He said, "I'm for the little fellers not the Rockefellers". Wellstone was not a traditional liberal but a Progressive Populist who believed in and worked for economic and social justice, including fairness and equal opportunity for all.

Wellstone was only able to live his life and practice his politics in the cause of social justice because he refused to be controlled by corporate special interests and their funding. One of my favorite quotes of his is:

"Politics is not about power. Politics is not about money. Politics is not about winning for the sake of winning. Politics is about the improvement of people's lives."

Paul Wellstone taught political science at Carleton College in Minnesota from 1969 to 1989. Wellstone believed in walking his talk. So, while teaching, he also got involved in community organizing for social change. He also encouraged his students to do so. One of them, Jeff Blodgett, who later was the campaign manager in Wellstone's three Senate races, was helped by Wellstone to get a job as a community organizer working with family farmers in Minnesota.

While a professor at Carleton College, Wellstone was arrested at a Vietnam War protest, and also at a local bank while protesting farm foreclosures. He publicly opposed the college's investments in companies doing business in South Africa. He picketed with striking workers at a meatpacking plant. Instead of crossing the picket line of striking Carleton custodians, Wellstone taught his classes off campus.

Even without the job security of tenure, Wellstone had the courage of his convictions and always sought to connect thought with action. Because of his political activism the college administration tried to fire him. They backed down because many Carleton students protested on behalf of keeping Wellstone hired. As a result, Wellstone received his tenure one year early. Wellstone joined the Minnesota Democratic Farmer Labor Party, and in 1982 ran for Minnesota State Auditor. Even though he lost that election, he decided to co-chair the 1988 Minnesota Jesse Jackson presidential campaign. He went on to work for the presidential campaign of Michael Dukakis in the general election.

Wellstone fully understood what I call the "Inside-Outside Strategy" for social change. As Jeff Blodgett, his former student and campaign manager, clearly puts it, "Paul believed that it was important to integrate community organizing and electoral politics. Organizing without electoral politics could marginalize social movements." (quoted by Peter Dreir, In These Times, Oct 25, 2012). Paul Wellstone also believed that American electoral politics has been tainted and corrupted by the influence of wealthy special interest corporate campaign money donations. That's why in 1990, Professor Paul Wellstone decided to run a grassroots, people oriented campaign for U.S. Senate while refusing special interest PAC money from corporate lobbyists. An inspiring and detailed account of this successful campaign story is provided in the book, *Professor Wellstone goes to Washington*.

Image 10-1 | Paul and Sheila Wellstone with supporters in front of the grassroots campaign's iconic bus | Photo/Wellstone.org

Having inspired and recruited hundreds of volunteers, including union workers, students, professors, poor people, including some on welfare, environmental activists, women's equality activists, teachers,

306

and others whom he met during his years of teaching and community organizing, Wellstone ran in the midterm 1990 election against U.S. Senator Rudy Boschwitz, a prolific fundraiser and two-term Republican who outspent Wellstone 7 to 1. He crisscrossed the state in an old green and white school bus with a speaker's platform on the back, which made Wellstone's campaign loosely resemble Harry Truman's whistle stop campaign from the platform of the train. Paul Wellstone spoke to regular voters at hundreds of house parties and diners. At the diners he would always go to the back in the kitchen and speak with, and listen to, the cooks, busboys, and waitresses, and hear their concerns. His mother had been a cafeteria worker and his father a federal employee.

Wellstone's campaign team also ran low-budget humorous campaign ads on television that caught the voters' attention. In the first commercial, "Fast-paced Paul", he speaks rapidly, introducing himself to voters, saying that he had to talk fast because he could not afford much airtime for lack of big money. In another allusion to big money in politics, a Wellstone commercial featuring young children writing big campaign checks to Senator Boschwitz had a voiceover that said, "if children could write big checks to Rudy Boschwitz then maybe he would fight in the Senate for education and afterschool programs for kids."

Despite the odds, Wellstone won the 1990 election against Boschwitz with 50.4% of the vote. The need to distinguish himself as a people funded, people supported candidate, who would fight for the common person in the Senate, as opposed to politicians like Rudy Boschwitz who would not, because they were bought by big money, was an important theme in Wellstone's campaigns and his political and governing strategies. Even as a U.S. Senator on the inside, Wellstone continued to be an organizer fully connected with the people on the outside. He often took part in rallies and protests sponsored by environmental, community, labor, and other progressive groups.

Because Wellstone was not bought by wealthy corporate special interests, he was able to champion progressive causes that benefited the public and the public interest. For example, in 1991 the first vote he cast in the Senate was in opposition to U.S. military action in the Persian Gulf War. In 2002 when Congress overwhelmingly voted to authorize the use of military force against Iraq, Wellstone, who faced a very tough reelection challenge, voted no. He said he opposed President Bush's, "preemptive, go it alone strategy." His vote of conscience paid off, and a few weeks before election day in November 2002, the polls showed him gaining a few percentage points, putting him ahead of Republican opponent Norm Coleman. Then just 11 days before the election, as I was driving home from a coffee shop near my home in California, I heard the devastating news on my radio, that Senator Paul Wellstone, his wife Sheila, and their daughter Marcia, had died in a plane crash in northern Minnesota.

News of their untimely death was devastating. I and my wife Toya had met Senator Wellstone and his wife Sheila, in 1998, at a reception for them in Beverly Hills, also attended by Senator Barbara Boxer.

When the Los Angeles County Democratic Party services director Gloria Alves, who had invited us, introduced us to Paul and Sheila, we had a lot to talk about. Two items topped the conversation: the first was Paul's remarkable 1990 and 1996 grassroots campaigns without corporate financing, and the freedom it gave him to work for public interest issues of peace and justice; the other topic I remember well was about Sheila's work for over 10 years championing the cause of battered women and children. Sheila had been a strong and inspiring advocate for helping battered women and children survive, recover, and flourish after escaping their horrible conditions. Sheila had not only worked to raise awareness in society, and help from the private sector, but also to involve legislative action championed by Paul Wellstone in the Senate.

When Paul heard that I had won the Primary Election and the Democratic Party nomination for the U.S. House of Representatives, and that I was campaigning against the incumbent Republican Congressman Steve Horn in order to win the upcoming November General Election, he became quite interested. When I mentioned that I was running a grassroots campaign, relying primarily on hundreds of community volunteers and individual donors, and especially when I mentioned that I refused to accept campaign contributions from corporate PACs and lobbyists, Senator Wellstone's interest peaked. When I told him that our campaign had purchased an inexpensive, medium-sized school bus as a voter education, voter registration, traveling headquarters, Paul Wellstone was delighted. I felt that I'd met a political soul mate.

Later in the evening at the hotel in Beverly Hills where we were, Wellstone made his speech to the guests. He highlighted his fight for economic fairness and social justice inside and outside the Senate, principles that were the foundation for specific issues on which he was working; issues such as universal single-payer healthcare, an economy that benefited the working poor and middle class, not just the rich, as well as a clean and sustainable environment that would benefit all of us. Of course I was quite pleased when he mentioned during his speech that there was a candidate for Congress in the audience named Peter Mathews who was running a grassroots campaign without corporate money, right here in Southern California, and that those in the audience, who would like to, should support him.

That evening in Beverly Hills in 1998 Senator Wellstone's words rang as an authentic, clarion call to put America back on the track of economic and social justice that would provide equal opportunity for all, not for just the top 1%. As Toya and I drove home that night, the Senator's words were an added inspiration in my efforts to join him in Congress and help turn America around in the right direction.

After I and my mostly volunteer campaign team knocked on thousands of voters' doors, and had spoken to many groups in the district, having refused special interest corporate PAC money, we were outspent by our Republican opponent 5 to 1. In the final two weeks, the most critical campaign period, we didn't have enough money to put up signs, mail enough brochures to voters with our message, or buy campaign TV or radio ads in order to reach as many voters, as many times as we needed to, in order to withstand the Republican candidate's onslaught of half a million dollars in campaign spending against us. Our grassroots, non-corporate, people-sponsored campaign, still made a strong showing, winning 45% of the vote to the incumbent Republican opponent's 52%.

The second time that I met Paul Wellstone was at a fundraiser in the Brentwood neighborhood of Los Angeles, California. I donated $100 to his exploratory campaign for President for the 2000 election.

Unfortunately, because of a back injury that he had suffered as a wrestler in his younger days, Wellstone came to find that he could not comply with the rigorous physical requirements of a nationwide presidential campaign. He decided to continue the fight for social and economic justice in the U.S. Senate. Of course, his physical death in 2002 has not destroyed the vision of a more fair and just world for which he lived and fought.

Once again, I cannot over emphasize Wellstone's belief that American politics had become more about big money and power games, run by wealthy corporate elites. Paul Wellstone believed that politics must be about improving people's lives. He was determined to change the direction of American politics by practicing what he preached. His refusal to raise campaign money from corporate special interests, but to rely instead on the volunteer work and campaign contributions from individual Americans and public interest groups, guaranteed his independent voice in the U.S. Senate; a voice that he used in order to speak up for the underdog and the little people, a voice that was used to block bad policy that would hurt the majority of Americans, and a voice that was used to champion, write, and push good policy and legislation through the Senate that would improve people's lives.

He worked to block oil drilling in Alaska's Arctic National Wildlife Refuge. He worked hard for a Canadian style universal single-payer healthcare system (Medicare for All) compared to President Clinton's more limited healthcare proposal. Wellstone opposed the North American Free Trade Agreement, which he felt would result in the loss of hundreds of thousands of well-paying manufacturing jobs in the U.S. In order to reduce the influence of big special interest money in politics, he worked hard for campaign finance reform and lobbying reform. He opposed President Bush's attempts to restart a version of President Reagan's Strategic Defense Initiative boondoggle and waste billions of dollars on it. He criticized President Clinton for not obtaining the consent of Congress before sending troops to Haiti.

Unlike other corporate sponsored Republican and Democratic senators, his hands were not tied by wealthy corporate campaign contributions. As a result, both his passion for social justice and his personal integrity could shine on issues of economic fairness: he was the only Democrat in the Senate to oppose lowering the inheritance tax. As the public record shows, he almost single-handedly temporarily blocked bankruptcy legislation that would have further burdened the poor while benefiting the credit card companies, banks and retailers. Paul Wellstone

310

was the only senator up for re-election in 1996 to vote against the Republican-led, Clinton-backed, welfare reform bill that became law. Wellstone claimed in a speech on the Senate floor that the law would hurt low income children. He said, "They don't have the lobbyists, they don't have the PACs." In Wellstone's 2002 Senate re- election campaign, he criticized Bush's tax cuts for the wealthiest 1% of Americans in his TV ads. Since his campaign contributions did not come from wealthy corporate special interests in the top 1%, Wellstone was free to criticize and oppose President Bush's tax cut policy that benefited the super-wealthy few at the expense of the rest of America.

Wellstone's freedom from the control of wealthy corporate interests and their "Dollar Democracy," enabled him to preserve his political integrity and fight for justice and fairness in social policy as well: as I mentioned earlier, Paul's wife, Sheila, became a passionate fighter for the rights and well-being of battered women and children. Sheila Wellstone played a major role in generating support for passage of the Violence Against Women Act in 1994, co-sponsored by Senator Wellstone and Senator Joe Biden. According to Professor Peter Dreier, "The law fundamentally changed the way our society responds to domestic violence, dating violence, sexual assault and stalking. It provides funding to create a comprehensive support system for survivors and their families." (*In These Times*, Oct. 25, 2012).

Wellstone's freedom from funding by corporate insurance companies, his personal integrity, compassion, and personal experience (Wellstone's brother suffered deeply from depression) made him a champion for mental health parity. In 1995, Wellstone cosponsored a bill, with New Mexico Republican Senator Pete Domenici, that would force insurance companies to provide the same care for mental health patients as they provide for patients with physical illnesses. The Wellstone/Domenici Mental Health Parity Act was pushed through Congress by Senator Ted Kennedy and Representative Patrick Kennedy in 2008, six years after Senator Paul Wellstone's death.

While we await Clean Money Elections at the federal level, United States Senator Paul Wellstone was a shining example of what American Politicians should do immediately: free themselves from Corporate Special Interest campaign funding, so they can truly fight for America's

Public Interest, or as the Constitution says, "the general Welfare" or wellbeing. Beside Senator Paul Wellstone, three high profile candidates who have not ever accepted corporate PAC money and were elected on Grassroots People Powered campaigns are U.S. Senators Elizabeth Warren and Bernie Sanders, and U.S. Representative Alexandria Ocasio-Cortez. They serve as living inspirations for the right way to win public office. In fact, Bernie Sanders showed this can be done in his remarkable 2016 Presidential Democratic Primary campaign.

Representatives Ro Khanna, Pramila Jayapal, Tulsi Gabbard, David Cicilline, Ilhan Omar, Rashida Tlaib, Jahana Hayes, Ayanna Pressley, Mark Pocan, and Raul Grijalva have also said they'll reject corporate PAC money. Support for the movement is more scarce among Republicans — Reps. Phil Roe of Tennessee and Francis Rooney of Florida are the only party incumbents who don't take corporate or Super PAC money, according to End Citizens United, a political action committee focused on campaign finance reform (https://theintercept.com/2018/12/02/public-campaign-finance-hr1/).

Also, two states have pioneered the way for publicly financed, non-corporate sponsored elections. The state of Maine in 1996 and the state of Arizona in 1998 adopted Clean Money Elections by passing citizen initiatives. The details vary slightly in each state, but the principles on which Clean Money Elections are based are the same in both states, and in several other places where they have been introduced. At present, Clean Money Elections are being used fully, or in some elections, in the following places: in Maine, Arizona, North Carolina, Connecticut, New Mexico, Hawaii, Vermont, and West Virginia.

Maine's Pioneering Clean Election System

In 1996 the voters in the state of Maine passed the Maine Clean Elections Act in order to free elected state officials from the clutches of private special interest money. For example, in order to qualify as a Clean Money Elections candidate for the Maine State House of Representatives, a candidate has to raise five dollars each from 65 registered voters in her district. As soon as the $325 is deposited in the

Maine Clean Election Fund, and the candidate meets the other normal qualifications of age, citizenship, and residency, the candidate is officially declared a Clean Money Candidate. She is allowed to raise a maximum total of $500 of seed money from individual private donors, with strict and low contribution limits per "seed donor" in order to start her campaign. As a Clean Money Candidate, she is not allowed to accept any more money from private sources, including her own. Instead, the state of Maine will provide $1429 for her campaign to spend in a contested primary, and $4724 for her campaign to spend in a contested general election. This money is used to reach the approximately 8700 registered voters in her district. This encourages grassroots campaigning through personal contact with the voters in door-to-door campaigning, at town hall meetings, and at forums and debates in front of interested and active voters. Approximately 70% of Maine's House of Representatives and 86% of Maine's State Senate, including Republicans and Democrats, were elected as Clean Money Candidates.

Those of us who believe in Clean Money Elections feel that campaigns for public office should not be financed by wealthy private interests. This is not a radical new idea. Just over 100 years ago, President Teddy Roosevelt and other Progressive Era reformers advocated publicly financed elections. Our argument goes like this: when we, the people in a democracy, elect public officials such as state legislators, members of Congress, state governors, and U.S. Presidents, we are electing leaders who are charged with making laws and policies in the public interest, also known as the common good, or "general Welfare" (the words in the Preamble to the U.S. Constitution). We should not be electing leaders whose campaigns for public office are heavily funded by wealthy private special interests to whom they will owe favors once they are in office: favors such as corporate tax breaks and subsidies, as well as financial and environmental deregulation, all of which generally harm the well-being of the vast majority of Americans.

Private Campaign Money in American Elections Thwarts the Constitution's Requirement That Government "...promote the general Welfare...."

The Preamble to the United States Constitution states that "We the People of the United States, in Order to...promote the general Welfare, and secure the blessings of Liberty to ourselves and our Posterity, do ordain and establish this Constitution (foundation of government) for the United States of America." There are two major thoughts expressed in this portion of the U.S. Constitution: the first is that government has a central role to play, and not just a role, but a duty, to promote the general Welfare or well-being of the people in society; the second is that government has an obligation to help one generation pass on its blessings of Liberty (including the freedom and opportunity to make a good meaningful living) to the next generation of Americans. Today we Americans are having a difficult time translating these two major Constitutional thoughts into action that will benefit this and future generations. The reason is "Dollar Democracy": campaigns and government financed by wealthy private special interests such as Big Oil companies, Big Pharmaceuticals, Big Agribusiness, Big Manufacturers, Big Banks, Big Chemical companies, Big High-tech firms, and other Big Corporations and their owners.

Clean Money Candidates for the Maine State Senate qualify and campaign the same way as their counterparts in the Maine State House of Representatives. As in the case of the House, the prospective candidate must first register with the Ethics Commission. She or he can then raise up to $1500 in seed money from private sources. State legislators may not accept seed money contributions from lobbyists and their clients when the legislature is in session. As in the case of the State House, seed money donations are limited and must be documented and publicly reported. Since the Senatorial districts are much larger in population and voters, the Maine Clean Election Act requires Senate candidates to gather five dollars from each of 175 registered voters in his or her district. As soon as the $875 is deposited in the Maine Clean Election Fund, the Senate candidate, after meeting other legal requirements is officially declared a Clean Money Candidate. As an official Clean Money Candidate, she or he is not allowed to accept any money from private sources, including his or her own, beyond her or his seed money. Instead, if she or he is running in a contested election, the state of Maine will provide him or her with $7359 in the primary, and $21,749 in the general election. The candidate and his or her campaign can decide how to use this public money in order to reach the approximately 11,000 registered voters in the State Senate district. In Maine, Clean Money Elections are funded by three sources. The first is the five-dollar fee per nominating voter that each candidate is required to raise. The second source is from the voluntary Clean Money Contribution check off box on each resident's state income tax return. The third source of funding is the $2 million provided annually from the $6.2 billion state budget. So, in order for the taxpayers of Maine to free their legislators from the clutches of wealthy special interests, it costs them .03 percent of the State Budget. Because Maine held its first Clean Money Elections in 2000, by 2003 the majority of Maine's sitting legislators had been elected by Clean Money.

Clean Money legislators are free to make decisions that they, and the public, feel will be in the public's interest or the general welfare of all. On the other hand, legislators who are financed by private special-interest money will usually feel obligated to first consider their donors' private interests and needs, not necessarily what's good for the general public.

Focusing on what's good for the general public, on June 18, 2003, Governor John Baldacci signed into law the Dirigo Health Reform Act. Over two thirds of the mostly Clean Money legislators had just passed the bill to make Maine the first state to seek universal health coverage for its residents. Dirigo, which in Latin means "to lead", was the first major health reform to be enacted in over a decade in any state. Since then other states have followed.

As required by the Maine Clean Elections law, once qualified and certified as Clean Money Candidates those state legislators were pledged to not accept any private money from organizations or individuals: no money from health care special interests such as insurance corporations, hospitals, HMOs, and any other big money interest that might have opposed the Dirigo health care law. Writing in the Hartford Courant in

October 2005, Republican representative Jim Annis, and Democratic representative John Brautigam stated, "Publicly funded legislators were free to support this legislation without any concern for the big-money special interests that might oppose such a law." In a *Yes! Magazine* August 21, 2006 post, Nancy Watzman, investigative director for Public Campaign, quotes Tammy Greaton, Executive Director of the Maine People's Alliance, one of the groups that pushed to pass the Dirigo health care law. Said Greaton, "Clean Elections make a huge difference. (Clean Money legislators) listen to people when they show up. They ignore lobbyists more than I've ever seen."

Let's face it, Clean Money Campaign funding made it possible for the majority of Maine legislators to pass and implement the Dirigo health care law. This law began phasing in near-universal healthcare in Maine, beginning in 2003. It began targeting and helping provide affordable health insurance to residents who had traditionally faced difficulty getting health coverage-- small employers, the self-employed, the unemployed, and other individuals who lacked access to employer-based insurance and also do not qualify for Maine's Medicaid program. DirigoChoice, as the plan is called, is administered through the private insurance market. But it also includes some features that are not always included in private health plans; features such as mental health parity, a prohibition on exclusion based on pre-existing conditions, and incentives for preventive care. As an example in 2007, an individual with a household income of $27,000 (135 percent of the federal poverty line) and a family of four buying a policy without an employer contribution would have a monthly cost of $1213 for family coverage but would receive a cash discount of $971, reducing their share of the health care premium to $243 per month. Employees of small businesses would have their personal contribution reduced further because of the additional contribution of their employer.

The Maine state government, driven by a majority of Clean Money legislators, provides subsidies for health insurance coverage through the Dirigo Health Agency (DHA) and its DirigoChoice plan. Tens of thousands of Mainers have been enrolled and provided with affordable health insurance in the last decade, by a Maine State Legislature that has been heavily dominated and led by Clean Money legislators. In fact, in

2014, 70% of the General Assembly and 86% of the State Senate in Maine won their seats with the use of Clean Money, rejecting the private money of wealthy special interests for their campaigns.

Maine State Representative **Tom Longstaff**, with whom I've had interesting conversations regarding Clean Money Elections and his own Clean Money election to the Maine House of Representatives, had this insightful observation:

> "Even as a clean election candidate I have felt a sense of obligation to those who have supported me. I am sure that the sense of obligation must be considerably stronger for those who are privately financed. It is less a sense of obligation due to pressure from those who have supported me than a self-imposed sense: if someone (individual or business) has supported me and the time comes when I must vote on a measure that could help (or harm) that individual or business I stop and think. Here is someone who has helped me. Now the time comes when I could help them. Do I pretend not to care whether what I do is helpful or not?"

Arizona Was the First State to Elect a Clean Money Election Governor, Janet Napolitano

As I've mentioned earlier Arizona became the second state in the union to pass a citizens' initiative in 1998 and implement Clean Money Elections in the year 2000. The Citizens Clean Elections Act is quite similar to the Maine Clean Election Act, with a few differences.

Unlike the State of Maine and most other states, Arizona's State Representatives and State Senators are elected from the same district. There are 30 legislative districts in Arizona, each with an average population of 216,000 residents. Approximately 71,000 registered voters on average in each district. Similar to prospective Clean Money

317

Candidates in Maine, those in Arizona are also allowed to begin by raising a maximum amount of seed money of $3813. The maximum individual contribution for seed money is $160. The candidate can provide a maximum of $700 of his own money as part of the seed money. As in Maine the prospective Clean Money Candidate needs to raise five dollars each of qualifying contributions from registered voters in his district. In Arizona these qualifying contributions must come from 250 registered voters in his district. Once she or he meets these requirements and is certified as a Clean Money Election candidate, the candidate is provided with $15,253 for his contested primary election campaign, and $22,880 for his contested general election campaign. As in Maine the Clean Money Candidate may spend this money to reach the registered voters he will need to win. As of 2014, 37% of Arizona legislators had run on Clean Money and the majority of them have been elected.

The State of Maine recently discontinued its Clean Money funding option for campaigns for governor. However, legislation is being introduced in Maine that would almost triple the clean money funds available to be spent by Clean Money Candidates for the Maine State Legislature. While Maine has never elected a Clean Money financed candidate for governor, Arizona has. Janet Napolitano, who later became the U.S. Secretary of Homeland Security and is currently University of California President, was a Democrat elected in 2002 and 2006 as Governor of Arizona, in a Republican majority state. In 2014 a prospective Clean Money Candidate for governor will have to collect five-dollar qualifying contributions each from 4500 registered voters statewide. This enables her or him to be certified as a Clean Money candidate and receive $753,616 in the contested primary election and $1,130,424 in the contested general election.

Prior to a June 27, 2011 U.S. Supreme Court ruling, both Maine's and Arizona's Clean Money Elections systems included matching fund provisions. According to these provisions, if a privately financed opponent kept on raising far more money than a Clean Money Candidate, "matching funds" would be triggered automatically. These were extra funds provided to the Clean Money Candidate, by the state Clean Elections fund, to help "level the playing field", so that the Clean Money Candidate's voice would not be drowned out.

However, in the 2011 Supreme Court case *Arizona Free Enterprise Club* v. *Bennett*, writing for the 5 to 4 majority, Chief Justice John Roberts broadly held that (1) the triggered matching fund provisions of Arizona's public financing system substantially burden free speech of privately financed candidates and independent expenditure groups without fulfilling a compelling government interest. (2) Public financing is an acceptable vehicle to combat corruption or the appearance of corruption so long as it is "pursued in a manner consistent with the First Amendment," but Arizona's program went "too far". (Brennan Center for Justice, New York University School of Law).

One has to wonder how Clean Money Elections burden the free-speech of privately funded candidates, when those very candidates had a choice to run as Clean Money Candidates and receive the same trigger funds, if necessary. However, the slim 5-4 Supreme Court majority invalidated trigger fund provisions in Arizona and other public campaign financing programs in states such as Maine, while validating the constitutionality of public financing programs without such provisions. In response to the Arizona ruling, legislation has been introduced in the Maine State Legislature that would increase funding beyond the initial Clean Money allocation based on additional signatures of registered voters gathered by certified Clean Money Candidates. Maine Citizens for Clean Elections qualified a bill to strengthen Clean Money Elections for the November 2015 ballot. It passed by a 54.96% to 45.04% solid margin.

Former Arizona Governor Janet Napolitano, elected in 2002 and reelected in 2006 as a Clean Money candidate, could focus on the voters and not big-money donors. Napolitano said, "I got to spend time with voters as opposed to dialing for dollars or trying to sell tickets to $250-a-plate fundraisers. This was much better". Because she refused money from special interests or powerful lobbyists, she could weigh the merits of policy without succumbing to pressure from big-money donors.

That's why on her first day in office in 2003 Governor Napolitano was able to sign a prescription drug discount plan. She stated that without Clean Elections, lobbyists would have held their campaign contributions over her head. She was quoted in a Public Campaign blog as saying, "none of that happened, because special interests had nothing to hold over me. I was lobbied heavily by all sides of this issue. But I was able to create this program based on one and only one variable: the best interests of Arizona's senior citizens." Napolitano said the following to PBS's NOW reporter David Brancaccio, "I think what Clean Elections allows you to do is be a better candidate and a better officeholder, because you're not all the time having to raise money." She went on to say that Clean Elections "empower people at the grassroots level to participate. Because anybody can give $5 dollars as opposed to $500 or $5000... I think once you've given $5, you're an investor."

Napolitano said poignantly "I think we all share an ideal vision in which elected officials come to their capitols free of the encumbrances of special interests. They take their seats and conduct the business of the people just as we and the Founding Fathers envisioned, and just as we have the right to expect."

(www.publicampaign.org/blog/2007/05/09/profile-arizona-gov-janet-napolitano).

Common Cause is a "nonpartisan, grassroots organization dedicated to restoring the core values of American democracy, reinventing an open, honest and accountable government that serves the public interest, and empowering ordinary people to make their voices heard in the political process."

(http://www.commoncause.org/site/pp.asp?c=dkLNK1MQIwG&b =4773855)

It points out that Clean Money (citizen funded) Elections are supported broadly across the political spectrum. Even former President Barack Obama supports Clean Money Elections and, when he was a U.S. Senator, cosponsored the Fair Elections Now Act, a federal clean money elections bill which has languished for several years in Congress. Obama's 2008 presidential opponent Senator John McCain supported Clean Money Elections in Arizona and even appeared in television commercials for the program.

Some Support Among Elected Officials for Clean Money Elections

There is some support among elected officials at the federal and state level for Clean Money Elections. The following elected officials, Republicans and Democrats, have made public statements in support of Clean Money Elections:

In his State of the Union address on December 3, 1907, President Theodore Roosevelt called for (Clean Money) public financing of elections. Others have followed: at the federal level, Senator Dick Durbin of Illinois, former Senator John Edwards of North Carolina, former Senator Russ Feingold of Wisconsin, former Senator Warren Rudman of New Hampshire, former Senator Alan Simpson of Wyoming, former Senator Jon Corzine of New Jersey, and Rep. Barbara Lee of California. At the state level, Governor M. Jodi Rell of Connecticut, Former Governor Janet Napolitano of Arizona, State Representative Jim Annis of Maine, State Senate President Beth Edmonds of Maine, State Representative Steve Gallardo of Arizona, State Representative Leah Landrum Taylor of Arizona, Corporation Commissioner William Mundell of Arizona, State Representative Chris Rector of Maine, State Representative Nancy Smith of Maine, and State Senator Ed Youngblood of Maine. Every day dozens more elected officials are becoming supporters of Clean Money Elections. And thousands more American voters and activists are working to raise awareness and support for Clean Money Elections, particularly at the state level. Many states are serving as laboratories, proving the viability of Clean Money Elections. Our federal elected officials must be made to take notice and support Clean Money Elections at the Congressional and Presidential levels. Only then can we transform our system of government from "Dollar Democracy" which serves the super wealthy few, to one of Real Democracy "by the people, of the people, and for the people" which serves all Americans.

As Common Cause has so simply but eloquently stated, "One of the things that has people so excited about Clean Elections is its ability to bring new people into the political process, restoring the promise of

321

democracy by allowing all citizens a fair opportunity to compete in the electoral arena." Common Cause illustrates this point by providing remarkable profiles of four elected officials who won their elections using clean money:

Deborah Simpson, Maine State Representative

When Deborah Simpson decided to run for the Maine legislature in 2000 to represent the old mill town of Auburn, she was a single mother waiting tables at TJ's, a local restaurant, while she also went to college. She made half the minimum wage per hour, plus tips.

Although Simpson had always been active in her community— her family, she says, was the sort that always volunteered for campaigns— she had never seriously thought of running for office. She certainly didn't have any connections to big campaign donors. But when she learned about Maine's new Clean Elections program, which went into operation that year, she thought she could do it.

During her tenure in the legislature, Simpson (D-ME) has used her seat on the Judiciary Committee to champion issues that affect regular people and affected her in earlier years, as a single mother and a victim of domestic violence. "Every year I try to do things I think make the laws work better for people – people who have difficulty."

Chris Rector, Maine State Representative

As a small publisher, ice cream purveyor, and former art gallery owner, Christopher Rector (R-ME) didn't consider himself much of a political insider. But after working with a citizens group in his town of Thomaston on how to deal with a newly empty state prison located on the highway nearby, he got the bug to run for office in 2002.

When Fall 2002 came, he pulled together a committee of friends in the community to help run his campaign and he set out on a door-knocking campaign to talk to his future constituents.

After two months of door knocking, he had reached out to some 95%

322

of households in his district. When election day came, Rector won the district by a vote of 56 to 44 percent.

"I never would have run if I had to do fundraising and make those kinds of connections," he said. "That held no interest for me at all. I wanted an issues-based campaign."

Mark Spitzer, former Arizona Corporation Commissioner

When the ballot initiative for Clean Elections first came up for a statewide vote in Arizona in 1998, Mark Spitzer voted no. He thought that the proponents were trying "to take politics out of politics and that just doesn't work."

Just two years later, Spitzer (R-AZ) changed his mind. He ran for the state's Corporation Commission and won using the Clean Elections system.

"I'm running for an office that is very powerful in the state, that regulates utilities. Does it make sense for me to go hat in hand to those utility companies to ask for campaign contributions and then if I win the election turnaround and – and vote on their rate cases?' he asked. that didn't make sense."

Spitzer became a quick convert. "Under Clean Elections you've got 5 million people that can participate. And I mean I raised in my little race for the Corporation Commission over 2,300 five-dollar campaign contributions from ordinary citizens, many of whom had never been involved in politics before," he said.

Kyrsten Sinema, Arizona State Representative

State Representative Kyrsten Sinema (D-AZ) likes to stay busy. Aside from being a member of the Arizona House of Representatives, she's a college professor and a lawyer. After graduating from college at the age of 18, she began a career in social work as a way to help those in need.

"The best thing about running Clean is that when you're in office, no one can pressure you to vote in a certain way. I had to vote on a bill to benefit Cox Communications and I was able to vote no on that bill. They try to stop and see me, but I told them I would vote no."

"I treat every single person who walks through my door the same because I'm not beholden to special interests." (www.common cause.org/site/pp.asp?c= dkLNK1MQIwG&B=4773855)

Clean Money Elections at the Federal Level: (HR 269) the Fair Elections Now Act

There is a fight going on to implement Clean Money Elections at the federal level. One of the groups involved in this struggle is Americans for Campaign Reform, a nonpartisan organization dedicated to public financing of elections. It is chaired by former Democratic Senators Bill Bradley of New Jersey and Bob Kerrey of Nebraska as well as former Republican Senators Alan Simpson of Wyoming and, until his death in 2012, Warren Rudman of New Hampshire. This organization has endorsed the Fair Elections Now Act (HR 269). The best summary of the key provisions of this act are provided by Public Campaign, a non-profit, nonpartisan organization dedicated to effective campaign finance reform:

> The Fair Elections Now Act was reintroduced in the House of Representatives by Congressman John Yarmuth (D- KY.), along with 52 original cosponsors on January 15, 2013. The bill would allow federal candidates to choose to run for office without relying on large contributions, big- money bundlers, or donations from lobbyists, and they would be freed from the constant fundraising in order to focus on what people in their communities want.

Participating candidates seek support from their communities, not Washington D.C.

- Candidates would raise a large number of small contributions from their communities in order to qualify for fair elections funding. Contributions are limited to $100.

- To qualify, a candidate for the U.S. House of Representatives would have to collect 1500 contributions from people in their state and raise a total of $50,000.

- Since states vary widely in population, a U.S. Senate candidate would have to raise a set amount of small contributions amounting to a total of 10% of the primary fair elections funding. The number of qualifying contributions is equal to 2000 plus 500 times the number of congressional districts in their state. For example:

  - A candidate running for U.S. Senate in Illinois, which has 19 congressional (House) districts, would raise 11,500 qualifying contributions-- the base of 2000 donations plus an additional 500 for each of the 19 House districts.

  - A candidate running for U.S. Senate in Maine, with two districts, would require 3000 qualifying contributions before receiving fair elections funding.

  - Qualified candidates would receive Fair Elections funding in the primary, and if they win, in their general election at a level to run a competitive campaign.

  - Qualified House candidates receive $1,125,000 in fair elections funding, split 40% for the primary and 60% for the general.

  - The formula to determine the amount of funding for qualified Senate candidates is as follows: Qualified candidates receive $1.25 million plus another $150,000 per congressional district in their state. The funding is split 40% for the primary and 60% for the general election.

  - Qualified candidates would be also eligible to receive additional matching fair elections funds if they continued to raise small donations from their home state.

- Donations of $100 or less from in-state contributors would be matched by five dollars from the fair elections fund for every dollar raised. $100 becomes $600.
- The total fair elections funds available are limited to three times the initial allocation for the primary, and again for the general, available only to candidates who raise a significant amount of small donations from their home state.
- If a participating candidate is facing a well-financed or self-financed opponent, or is the target of an independent expenditure, they will be able to respond by utilizing this matching fund provision.
- Joint fund-raising committees between candidates and parties would be prohibited.
- Fair Elections helps offset fund-raising for, and the excessive cost of, media.
- Participating Senate candidates receive a 20% reduction from the lowest broadcast rates.
- Participating Senate candidates who win their primaries are eligible to receive $100,000 in media vouchers per congressional district in their state. Participating candidates may also exchange their media vouchers for cash with their national political party committee.
- Participating candidates could set up leadership political action committees but would be limited to a $100 contribution limit per individual per year.
- The funding mechanism for House races will be determined at a future point but will be revenue neutral and not taxpayer-funded. The cost of fair elections for Senate races would be borne by a

small fee on large government contractors.

- Largest recipients of federal government contracts would pay a small percentage of the contract into the fair elections fund.
- If the system proves as popular as similar laws at the state level, the new system could cost between $700 and $850 million per year.

(www.publiccampaign.org/fair-elections-now-act)

The Fair Elections Now Act (HR 269) amends the Federal Election Campaign Act of 1971 (FECA). It was introduced in the U.S. House of Representatives by Representative John Yarmuth (D-KY.) and referred to the Committee on House Administration on January 15, 2013. This committee of six Republicans and three Democrats is chaired by Republican Representative Candace Miller of Michigan. Almost a year later, the Fair Elections Now Act has 68 co-sponsors, including 67 Democrats and one Republican. The Committee Chair determines whether a bill will make it past the committee stage. As of December 31, 2013, it has not. According to govtrack.us, HR 269 has an 11% chance of getting past committee and a 1% chance of being enacted into law. (https://www.govtrack.us/congress/bills/113/ hr269). Govtrack gets its data from THOMAS.gov (The Library of Congress).

It appears that "Dollar Democracy" may be blocking the Fair Elections Now Act, which is based on the Clean Money Elections Concept. I was determined to find out how and why. On December 30, 2013, I called the Washington, D.C. office of Congresswoman Candace Miller, chair of the Committee on House Administration, where HR 269 was sent a year ago. This is the House oversight committee in charge of federal elections and the ongoing administration of the House of Representatives.

The member of Representative Miller's staff who answered the phone was courteous and patient. I asked her where I could find information regarding the status of HR 269, and perhaps some information as to why this bill has not become law yet. She provided me with the email address of Congresswoman Miller's press relations staffer

327

and asked me to contact her by email. I asked her if I could please have the staffer's telephone number so that I could communicate more effectively on this matter. I was told courteously that the only number that she could give me was the number that I was calling and if I use this number I would be able to leave a message for the press relations staffer. I then asked the staff member who was on the phone with me for her name. She would only give me her first name and said to me that she preferred not to give me her last name. I was attempting to set up a consistent channel of communication with members of Congresswoman Miller's staff so that I could fully and clearly understand what has happened to the Fair Elections Now Act, which seems to me to be one of the best ways of limiting or eliminating the power of corporate special-interest money over members of Congress and their decisions regarding what's good for America.

On July 26, 2017, the Fair Elections Now Act, was introduced in the Senate and sponsored by Senator Richard Durbin (D-IL). It is co-sponsored by Senators Bernie Sanders, Elizabeth Warren, Kirsten Gillibrand, and 21 other senators.

Congressman John Yarmuth (D-KY) is moving ahead by introducing a constitutional amendment to get big money out of politics:

> On January 24, 2019, Yarmuth introduced the amendment in the House as H. J. Res. 33. It would amend the Constitution to clarify that financial expenditures and in-kind contributions would no longer qualify as forms of protected speech under the First Amendment. First introduced by Yarmuth in 2011, this amendment would also enable Congress to establish a public financing system for campaigns that would be the sole source of all campaign funding, diminishing the influence of wealthy donors on elections and expanding opportunities for more citizens to run for office.

(https://yarmuth.house.gov/news)

With HR-269 bottled up endlessly, a new bill has emerged. HR-1

Because of grassroots public pressure to get the pernicious influence of big corporate private money out of politics, the Democratic controlled U.S. House of Representatives overwhelmingly passed the "For the People Act of 2019" (HR-1) on Friday, March 8, 2019 by a party line vote of 234 to 193. The victorious majority House Democrats called it an anti-corruption and pro-democracy reform bill. HR-1 covers three main areas of reform: 1) Campaign Finance, 2) Strengthening the government's ethics laws and 3) Expanding voting rights. If the bill becomes law, it would accomplish several things:

Campaign Finance

- Establishing public financing of congressional and presidential campaigns funded by small donations. For every dollar raised in small donations by the candidate, the Federal government would provide $6 matching funds. The maximum small donation that could be matched would have a cap of $200. Funding for this would come from adding a 2.75 percent fee on criminal and civil fines, fees, penalties, or settlements with corporations and banks that commit corporate malfeasance.
- Supporting a constitutional amendment to end *Citizens United.*
- Passing the Disclose Act which would require Super PACs and "dark money" political organizations to make their donors public.
- Passing the Honest Ads Act which would require Twitter and Facebook to disclose the source of money for political ads on their platforms and reveal how much money was spent.
- Disclosing political spending by government contractors and slowing the flow of foreign money into elections by targeting shell companies.
- Reducing the number of Federal Election Commissioners from six to five.
- Prohibiting any coordination between Super PACs and

candidates

Ethics

- Requiring the President and Vice-President to each disclose ten years of tax returns. Candidates for those two offices must also do so.
- Preventing members of Congress from using taxpayer money to settle sexual discrimination or harassment cases.
- Providing more oversight and enforcement by the Office of Government Ethics. Implementing stricter registration requirements for lobbying, including more oversight of foreign agents by the Foreign Agent Registration Act.
- Creating a new ethical code for the U.S. Supreme Court, ensuring that all branches of government are impacted by the new law.

Voting Rights

- Creating new automatic voter registration. Promoting early voting, same day registration, and online voter registration.
- Making Election Day a holiday for federal employees and encouraging the private sector to do the same; requiring poll workers to provide a week's notice if poll sites are changed and making colleges and universities voter registration agencies.
- Ending gerrymandering in federal elections and ending voter roll purging. The bill would stop the use of non-forwardable mail being used in removing voters from the polls.
- Strengthening election security, including requiring the director of national intelligence to do regular checks on foreign threats.
- Recruiting and training more poll workers before the 2020 election in order to cut down on long lines at the polls.

(https://www.vox.com/2019/3/8/18253609/hr-1-pelosi-house-democrats-anti-corruption-mcconnell)

Well before HR-1 was passed in the House, Senate Republicans and the Trump Administration had voiced their opposition. Senate majority leader Mitch McConnell attacked the bill and President Trump issued an intent to veto the bill.

Why are Senate Republicans and President Trump intent on blocking this bill? Have they been so captured by Dollar Democracy that they lack the capacity to truly serve the public interest? Instead, it appears they are serving their own personal interests and that of their corporate sponsors.

Move To Amend Coalition's "We the People (28th) Amendment" to the U.S. Constitution

In addition to successful efforts at the state level, and not as yet successful efforts at the federal level involving Clean Money Elections, a nationwide grassroots people's movement has arisen to support a 28th amendment to the U.S. Constitution that will eliminate the ability of wealthy corporate special interest money to buy American elections and politics. It has been organized and lead by the Move To Amend (MTA) Coalition made up of hundreds of organizations and tens of thousands of individuals "committed to social and economic justice, ending corporate rule, and building a vibrant democracy that is genuinely accountable to the people, not corporate interests. (They) call for an amendment to the U.S. Constitution to unequivocally state that inalienable rights belong to human beings only, and that money is not a form of protected free speech under the First Amendment and can be regulated in political campaigns." (movetoamend.org)

MTA calls this amendment the "We the People Amendment", which was re-introduced in the 116th Congress (2019-2020) as House Joint Resolution 48 on February 22, 2019 by lead sponsor Congressperson Pramila Jayapal (D-WA), and co-sponsors

Congresspersons Betty McCollun (D-MN), Eleanor Holmes Norton (D-DC), Peter DeFazio (D-OR), Ro Khanna (D-CA), Tim Ryan (D-OH), Earl Blumenauer (D-OR), Mark Takano (D-CA), Janice Schakowsky (D-IL), Suzanne Bonamici (D-OR), Tulsi Gabbard (D-HI), Mark DeSaulnier (D-CA), Jared Huffman (D-CA), Barbara Lee (D-CA), Seth Moulton (D-MA), Ilhan Omar (D-MN), Mark Pocan (D-WI), Paul Tonko (D-NY), Jamie Raskin (D-MD), Chellie Pingree (D-ME), Debra A. Haaland (D-NM), Jesus Garcia (D-IL), Stephen Lynch (D-MA).

(https://www.congress.gov/bill/116th-congress/house-joint-resolution/48/cosponsors?q=%7B%22search%22%3A%5B%22hjr48%22%5D%7D&s=2&r=1&overview=closed#tabs:)

Exhibit 10-1 | We the People Amendment

WE THE PEOPLE AMENDMENT

The House Joint Resolution 48 introduced February 22, 2019

Section 1. [Artificial Entities Such as Corporations Do Not Have Constitutional Rights]

The rights protected by the Constitution of the United States are the rights of natural persons only.

Artificial entities established by the laws of any State, United States, or any foreign state shall have no rights under this Constitution and are subject to regulation by the people, through Federal, State, or local law.

The privileges of artificial entities shall be determined by the People, through Federal, State, or local law, and shall not be construed to be inherent or inalienable.

Section 2. [Money is not Free Speech]

Federal, State, and local government shall regulate, limit, or prohibit contributions and expenditures, including a candidate's own contributions and expenditures, to ensure that all citizens, regardless of their economic status, have access to the political process, and that no person gains, as a result of their money, substantially more access or ability to influence in anyway the election of any candidate for public office or any ballot measure.

Federal, State, and local government shall require that any permissible contributions and expenditures be publicly disclosed.

The judiciary shall not construe the spending of money to influence elections to be speech under the First Amendment."

Section 3.

Nothing contained in this amendment shall be construed to abridge freedom of the press.

Under the slogan, "End corporate rule. Legalize democracy", The Move to Amend (MTA) Coalition states,

"On January 21, 2010, with its ruling in *Citizens United* v. *Federal Election Commission*, the Supreme Court ruled that corporations are persons, entitled by the U.S. Constitution to buy elections and run our government. Human beings are people; corporations are legal fictions.

"We, the People of United States of America, reject the U.S. Supreme Court's ruling in Citizens United and other related cases, and move to amend our Constitution to firmly establish that money is not speech, and that human beings, not corporations, are persons entitled to constitutional rights.

"The Supreme Court is misguided in principle, and wrong on the law. In a democracy, the people rule.

"We Move to Amend."

Exhibit 10-2 | Press Release

Press Release Updating Move to Amend's Campaign For the 28th Amendment

Groundbreaking Constitutional Amendment Introduced in Congress

Monday, February 25, 2019

Ensures Constitutional Rights for People, Not Corporations

Rep. Pramila Jayapal and House Members Respond to Hundreds of Local Resolutions Calling for "We the People" Amendment

(Washington D.C.) - The movement for Constitutional reform that would end what organizers call "corporate rule" has arrived in the chambers of the 116th Congress. Today, members of the U.S. House of Representatives lead by Pramila Jayapal (WA-07), joined Move to Amend by announcing their sponsorship of the "We the People Amendment," which clearly and unequivocally states that:

1   *Rights recognized under the Constitution belong to human beings only, and not to government-created artificial legal entities such as corporations and limited liability companies; and*

2   *Political campaign spending is not a form of speech protected under the First Amendment making it possible once again for Congress and state governments to institute campaign finance reform.*

"Our Constitution says 'We the People,' not 'We the Corporations,' stated Representative Jayapal. "When I first ran for Congress I took Move to Amend's Pledge because I believe corporations exist to serve the public welfare, not for the public to serve them. That same year, Move to Amend won a ballot initiative in my home state of Washington — now they've passed resolutions in over 700 communities across the United States. It is time for Congress to catch up. We are supposed to be the People's House and we need to start acting like it. Big corporate money has been working against the interests of Americans for far too long. We have to restore the voice of the people in our democracy, and that starts with passing the We the People Amendment."

"When corporations are able to claim Constitutional rights it makes meaningful regulation of their behavior impossible," said Kaitlin Sopoci-Belknap, Move to Amend's National Director. "Our government is currently legally beholden to billionaires and their corporations because of this doctrine that was invented by a Supreme Court overreach. We must overrule the Court and make clear that human rights come first. Our ability to address life and death issues like climate change, or the opioid epidemic, or astronomical healthcare costs, depends on passing the We the People Amendment."

The Move to Amend coalition was formed in 2009 in preparation for the Supreme Court's 2010 *Citizens United v. Federal Election Commission* decision. Today, the coalition of over 462,000 people and hundreds of organizations has helped to pass over 700 resolutions in municipalities and local governments across the

335

country calling on the state and federal governments to adopt this amendment. Eighteen state legislatures have passed similar resolutions.

Addressing money as a form of free speech is a non-partisan issue with overwhelming support from Americans across the political spectrum. 88 percent of Americans want to reduce the influence large campaign donors wield over lawmakers. Three-fourths of survey respondents — including 66 percent of Republicans and 85 percent of Democrats — back a constitutional amendment to address the problem.

The Move to Amend coalition makes a point of differentiating themselves from the other proposals that have come forward in response to *Citizens United*. "The *Citizens United* decision is not the cause, it is a symptom of the systemic problem of the Courts extending constitutional rights under the 1st, 4th, 5th, 14th Amendments to corporations," stated Sopoci-Belknap "The public has voted for an amendment to outlaw corporate personhood over 300 times, in liberal and conservative communities alike. The message is clear: we must stop giving away our Constitutional rights to corporations and we must remove big money and special interests from the legal and political process entirely."

In addition to lead sponsor Pramila Jayapal (WA), initial Co-Sponsors are: Betty McCollum (MN), Peter DeFazio (OR), Ro Khanna (CA), Tim Ryan (OH), Eleanor Holmes Norton (DC), Earl Blumenauer (OR), Mark Takano (CA), Jan Schakowsky (IL), Suzanne Bonamici (OR), Tulsi Gabbard (HI).

Corporations Are Not People, and Money Is Not Speech Under the First Amendment

MTA Coalition proceeds to quote Supreme Court Justice John Paul Stevens, January, 2010, "... corporations have no consciences, no beliefs, no feelings, no thoughts, no desires. Corporations help structure and facilitate the activities of human beings, to be sure, and their 'personhood' often serves as a useful legal fiction. But they are not themselves members of "We the People" by whom and for whom our Constitution was established."

The Move to Amend Coalition has been working diligently for four years to raise awareness and build support for the adoption of this constitutional amendment. It then collected hundreds of thousands of signatures across the country in support of it. Its members have started a move to get state legislators to pledge their support for it. And they have been successful in getting some county and city governments, most recently the Los Angeles City Council, to vote to endorse the proposed amendment. As they themselves have stated, "Amending the Constitution will take nothing less than an organized, disciplined, mass movement of millions." (https://movetoamend.org). Those who are interested in laying the structural foundation for building a democracy of, by, and for the people should visit their most informative and comprehensive website: https:/movetoamend.org.

In January 2014, I spoke extensively with **Ann Porter**, a member of the leadership team of the Los Angeles area chapter of the Move to Amend Coalition. For over 10 years Ann has been educating herself and others on the rise of corporate power to the detriment of the American people's power. Ann and the Los Angeles area activists of Move To Amend were successful in getting six neighborhood councils as well as the Los Angeles City Council to pass resolutions reflecting the two major principles in the We the People Amendment: 1) corporations are not persons and do not have constitutional rights, and 2) Money is not free speech. Members of two other groups, Common Cause and Money Out Voters In, as well as the LA Area Move to Amend and other activists were heavily involved in the overwhelming passage of Proposition C with 76% of the vote in the May 2013 Los Angeles City Election. Prop C was a resolution that instructed local and state officials to promote the overturning of *Citizens United* v. *Federal Election Commission.* (Huffington Post, 5/22/2013).

In the 2010 *Citizens United* case, the U.S. Supreme Court held that spending by corporations on political campaigns is protected by the First Amendment. This momentous decision was based on earlier Supreme Court rulings stating that corporations are people (have personhood) in *Southern Pacific Railroad* v. *Santa Clara County* (1886), and stating money is free speech in *Buckley v. Valeo* (1976). With the passage of Prop C, the second-largest city in the U.S., Los Angeles, joined San

337

Francisco, Chicago, and 175 other American cities that have voted to urge the overturning of *Citizens United*. Of course, the success of resolutions such as Prop C across the country have inspired thousands of activists to support a 28th amendment to the U.S. Constitution that would abolish corporate personhood and establish that spending money to influence elections is not speech under the First Amendment. As Ann Porter emphatically said to me, "corporate personhood is the root of much evil."

David Cobb, the 2004 Green Party presidential candidate and national board member of the Move To Amend Coalition, which has led much of the national grassroots organizing, stated, "we are doing movement building in order to win a constitutional amendment within a decade. We have a meta-perspective about what is going on, but we also have a sense of movement history; in recognizing what it takes to actually get a lot of people in motion demanding systemic change. Our call is no more radical or will be no more difficult than the abolitionist movement, the women's suffrage movement, trade union movement or the Civil Rights movement."

(www.salon.com/2012/01/21/the_hard_truth_of_citizens_united/).

Recently I had the opportunity to talk with David Cobb about the Move To Amend Coalition's principles, goals, and methods that drive what is fast becoming an American Social Movement. It is rooted in the fundamental recognition that the concepts of "Corporate Personhood" and "Money is Speech" are not found in any of the founding documents of the U.S., including the Constitution. Yet the U.S. Supreme Court "found" them to exist. As of March 12, 2019, over 463,248 members of the Move To Amend Coalition, who have signed the "We The People Amendment" petition, are actively working to enlist the support of the American people, state legislators and members of Congress to abolish these two unconstitutional concepts through the 28th Constitutional Amendment.

As part of the National Leadership Team of the Move To Amend Coalition, Cobb and the other Team Members had organized the 2014 campaign around 1) barnstorming the country in the tradition of the Populist Movement that fought Corporate Rule 125 years ago, 2) getting written pledges from State Legislators to back the amendment, 3) recruiting affiliated groups, 4) providing recommended reading on the subject for members of the public, 5) providing "take action toolkits" and 6) providing outreach material to spread the word to more people. David Cobb told me, "I live my politics everyday", including in this fundamental fight to return power and Democracy to the American people and away from Corporate Rule.

Another member of the Move To Amend Executive Committee and Field Organizing Coordinator for the campaign, **Kaitlin Sopoci-Belknap** said, "We recognize that the Citizens United decision is a problem, but it is not the problem. Citizens United is not the cause, it is a symptom.

"The real problem is that a small group of wealthy individuals have hijacked our sacred right to self-government, and are using the political and legal systems to legitimize that theft. We must get money out of elections, to be sure. But we have to go deeper than that to address the reality that corporate lawyers use a legitimate doctrine of 'corporate constitutional rights' to overturn public health, environmental protection, and worker safety laws – and have for decades. Such laws relate to political questions that should be decided through public debate, discourse and the opportunity to vote and participate. When the decisions are made in the courts, 'We the people' are relegated to spectators.... The grassroots movement to press it (the We The People 28th Amendment) forward in the Congress grows steadily. Since 2010, over 300,000 have signed a petition and nearly 500 municipal resolutions and citizen initiatives have passed calling on state and federal governments to adopt an amendment ending corporate 'personhood' AND 'money as speech,' " Says Sopoci-Belknap.

Both David Cobb and Kaitlin Sopoci-Belknap are also members of the Program on Corporations, Law and Democracy (POCLAD), a collective of activist intellectuals who came together over a decade ago to educate and activate the public on the need to create a true and deep democracy, by putting corporations back in the place they had been in the first 80 years of the American Republic. The late Richard Grossman, a co-founder of POCLAD, along with Frank T. Adams, published a pamphlet in 1993 with clarity and focus on how corporations in America rose from state chartered strictly regulated entities with strict rules and limited duration, to large industrial giants with full personhood and constitutional rights granted to them by the U.S. Supreme Court. Because Grossman's and Adam's pamphlet, "Taking Care of Business", is written in the right combination of analytical and narrative style, it is informative and easy for the average reader to comprehend. So that the reader can directly read what they're saying, and not have to only rely on my interpretation of their pamphlet, visit: http://www.ratical.org/corporations/TCoB.html.

When the American revolutionaries overthrew King George, they overthrew his chartering of powerful private corporations, such as the East India Company and the Hudson's Bay Company, and the tremendous power that he gave them. American leaders, particularly in the states, decided to give the state governments the sole power to charter corporations, the power to dictate the terms of operation and rules to follow, and the right to revoke their charters, if they broke the rules. There was also overall recognition that corporations exist to some extent in order to serve the public good. Charters were granted for set periods of time and the state governments decided whether to renew them or not. For example, in Massachusetts, the Turnpike Corporations Act of 1805 gave the legislature the authority to dissolve the turnpike corporations when their receipts surpassed the cost of construction plus 12%. At this time the turnpike became public. Massachusetts was an example of how the various states, in multiple ways, controlled and held ultimate power over the corporations that they chartered.

Then came step-by-step rulings by the U.S. Supreme Court limiting the power of the state governments over corporations while expanding corporate power. The seminal ruling by the U.S. Supreme Court which solidified corporate power was the 1886 decision in *Southern Pacific Railroad* v. *Santa Clara County* "that a Corporation was a natural person under the U.S. Constitution, sheltered by the Bill of Rights and the 14th amendment." ("Taking Care of Business, Citizenship and the Charter of Incorporation", Grossman and Adams) (http://www.ratical.org/corporations/TCoB.html).

The American Corporation, originally a dead artificial entity created by the state for temporary limited purposes, was given life, and grew

340

rapidly into a domineering giant that has limited the individual American's freedom and power in politics, economics, and life. Dr. Frankenstein's monster has come to life and taken over our election and campaign finance system, as well as our government and public policies, through the corporate dominance of Dollar Democracy, with Liberty and Justice for Some.

It's time to tame the corporate Frankenstein monster and put it back in its rightful place. Corporations as living, breathing persons with fundamental unalienable rights, do not exist in America's founding documents: the Declaration of Independence and the United States Constitution. Before the 1860s, corporations were artificial, temporary entities, with only privileges, not rights, granted by the states, with strict conditions. Over the past 128 years, the U.S. Supreme Court "discovered" corporations in various parts of the U.S. Constitution. In so doing, the Supreme Court breathed life into the corporation, turning this artificial temporary entity, a "legal fiction", into an uncontrolled monster with personhood and constitutional rights. The very nature and actions of this post-1886 multinational corporation, whose allegiance is not to the American people but only to its major stockholders and CEOs, has undermined American democracy and is turning the American Dream into an American Nightmare for the bottom 99% of Americans. On the other hand, this transformation has been very lucrative for the top 1%, the American super rich.

To bring greater clarity to the picture that exists let's take a closer look at the top 1% of Americans. According to U.C. Berkeley economist Emmanuel Saez, in the so-called economic "recovery" of 2009-2012 the top 1% captured 93% of the total growth in income. However, it must be noted that the upper half of the top 1% (the top 0.5%) has far more wealth and income that the lower half of the 1%. The incomes of the lower half, which includes many hard-working professionals such as doctors, lawyers, and small business people, begin at $400,000 annually, and their net worth begins at just over $1.2 million. The upper half's (the top 0.5%) incomes are over $500,000 annually and their net worth begins at $1.8 million. The incomes of the top 0.1% begin at $2.5 million annually, and their net worth begins at $5.5 million. The incomes of the top 0.01%

begin at dozens of millions to hundreds of millions to over $1 billion annually, and their net worth begins at $25 million and goes into the billions of dollars.

The vast majority of the income of the top 0.5% of America comes from profits, dividends, rents, and interest derived from ownership of great corporate wealth in the form of stocks, bonds, real estate investments, and investments in technology, financial services and other industries on Wall Street. This is even truer of the top 0.1%. Sociologist G. William Domhoff notes that in 2008 only 19% of the income reported by the 13,480 individuals or families making over $10 million annually came from wages and salaries. (Who RulesAmerica.net). Over 80% of that income came from the corporate ownership and investments of the mega-rich.

The income of this mega-rich is income that is generated primarily from the labor of others: from the labor of Indonesian women in Nike factories paid 35 cents an hour; from the workers in Chinese factories who are paid just over $1 an hour to produce Apple iPhones; from workers in General Motors factories in Mexico paid $4 dollars per hour including benefits compared to $62 per hour including benefits in unionized U.S. auto factories; from the high-tech software engineers working in Microsoft's computer parks in India paid $25,000 a year (instead of the pay for an American of over $100,000); it is the hundreds of billions of dollars generated in the value of products created by these underpaid workers in low-wage countries that is bloating the income of the corporate CEOs and stockholders on Wall Street. It is the billions of dollars generated for corporate CEOs and stockholders, by this generation of Americans who have been forced by two-tier contracts to take half the factory wages of their mothers and fathers.

Take the example of **Karl Hoeltge**. He is working at a General Motors factory near St. Louis, Missouri for $15.78 an hour on the lower tier of a two-tiered contract that is capped at $19.28 in several years. His father Gary is working in the same factory in the upper tier of the contract for $28 per hour. The cumulative trillions of dollars in corporate profits made in this way, have been finding their way into the pockets of the corporate CEOs, stockholders, and Wall Street bankers over the last few decades and currently.

As my friend Dr. **Michael Parenti**, a Yale University Ph.D. and the author of *Democracy for the Few*, once said, "The secret to becoming rich in America is not to work hard, but to get others to work hard for you." This is exactly what the super-rich corporate owners of late 19th Century and early 21st Century America did, and their counterparts are doing today. They, and specifically those who owned the railroad corporations, in the late 1800s, used their wealth, corporate influence and connections, through campaign contributions and lobbying, to get legislation they wanted from Congress, and to get Supreme Court justices appointed that would free their big corporations from government regulation, supervision, and control. The biggest achievement of these corporate "Robber Barons" was getting the U.S. Supreme Court to declare in 1886 that corporations are persons with full personhood including constitutional rights. The *Southern Pacific Railroad* v. *Santa Clara County* decision granting U.S. corporations full personhood was the same as Dr. Frankenstein giving life to the artificial creature which became a dangerous out of control real monster. In subsequent Supreme Court decisions *Buckley v. Valeo* (1976), the Court ruled that money is free speech, and *Citizens   United* v. *Federal Election Commission* (2010), the Court ruled that the government may not ban political spending by corporations in candidate elections, based on the corporation's supposed First Amendment rights. In the 2014 McCutcheon ruling, the Supreme Court removed all limits on aggregate campaign donations given by a super wealthy individual to Congressional candidates and political parties. The super-rich can now buy all members of Congress and the political parties, blatantly.

We cannot let the Frankenstein corporate monster ravage the American countryside. POCLAD clearly states this by saying, "the corporate perversion of rights and the Constitution have resulted in the destruction of our communities, economy, politics and natural world in many ways for a very long time." POCLAD goes on to say that "all corporate constitutional rights should be abolished." These include at least the following:

- **1st Amendment Free-Speech rights.** Corporations use these rights, meant to protect human beings from the power of the state, to influence elections through political 'contributions' (more like 'investments'); to advertise for guns, tobacco and other dangerous products over the objections of communities; to avoid having to label genetically modified foods.

- **4th Amendment Search and Seizure rights**. Corporations have used these rights to avoid subpoenas for unlawful trade and price fixing, and to prevent citizens, communities and regulatory agencies from stopping corporate pollution and other assaults on people or the Commons.

- **5th Amendment Takings, Double Jeopardy and Due Process corporate rights.** Corporations must be compensated for property value lost (e.g. Future profits) when regulations are established to protect homeowners or communities. Corporations cannot be retried after a judgment of acquittal in court. The granting of property to a corporation by a public official cannot be unilaterally revoked by a subsequent public official or act of Congress.

- **14th Amendment Due Process and Equal Protection corporate rights.** These rights originally enacted to free slaves from oppression, were gradually extended to corporations by the courts. Corporations have used these rights to build chain stores and erect cell towers against the will of communities; oppose tax and other public policies favoring local businesses over multinational corporations; and resist democratic efforts to prevent corporate mergers and revoke corporate charters through citizen initiatives.

- **Commerce Clause related corporate rights.** Corporations have used this section of the Constitution (Article 1, Section 8), for example, to ship toxic waste from one state to another over the health, safety, and welfare objections of communities claiming the waste is actually not waste, but 'commerce'.

- **Contracts clause-related corporate rights.** The Supreme Court ruled in *Dartmouth* v. *Woodward* (1819) that a corporation is a party in a private contract based on the Contracts Clause (Article 1, Section 10) rather than being a creature of public law. Even though the state creates a corporation when it issues a charter, that state is not sovereign over the charter, merely a party to the contract. Thus, corporations became 'private contract' with the state and therefore, shielded from many forms of control by We the People. (poclad.org., November 2010).

As mentioned earlier, the Move To Amend coalition's 28th amendment to the U.S. Constitution would end corporate personhood and declare that money spent to influence election campaigns is not speech protected under the 1st Amendment. Of the three approaches to ending the pernicious influence of "Dollar Democracy" in our society, discussed in this chapter, the most challenging and comprehensive solution for building a deep and real democracy is the adoption of the We the People (28th) Amendment to our U.S. Constitution, which requires nothing less than a 21st Century social movement led by the people of the United States of America. "When the people lead, the leaders will follow." (Gandhi). The Move to Amend Coalition and its allies are doing just that.

WOLF-PAC: Grassroots Organizing for Article V Convention to Propose a 28th Amendment to Make Elections Free and Fair

Another group that has been working for a 28th Amendment to get big money out of politics is Wolf-PAC. I spoke with founder of Wolf-PAC Cenk Uygur and Wolf-PAC Executive Director Michael Monetta about their work for an Article V Constitutional Amendment to get big money out of politics.

Cenk Uygur is the founder of Wolf-PAC, The Young Turks (TYT) network social media news, and the Co-founder of Justice Democrats. When I interviewed him, Cenk said there is no point in "chipping away at the problem (of the pernicious influence of Big Money in Politics). We must attack the root of the problem right now." That is why Cenk Uygur and Wolf-PAC National Director Michael Monetta, along with 50,000 volunteers nationwide, have been working hard to convince state legislatures in 2/3 of the 50 states in the U.S. (34 states) to pass Free and Fair Elections resolutions. These resolutions call for a national convention to propose a constitutional amendment that will remove the pernicious effects of Big Money in American Politics.

In my interview with him, Mike Monetta said that the reason for such a 28th Amendment to the Constitution is "to ensure that our government is responsive to the needs of its citizens, rather than only to the wealthy elites and special interests that can afford to buy influence."

Cenk Uygur noted to me the big gap between average Americans in the 50 states and the political and party leaders in Washington, as well as their elite sponsors. He said that "97% of Americans support background checks for gun purchasers, and yet it doesn't get passed." He pointed out that 75% of Americans support raising taxes on the rich, yet Congress and Trump did the opposite. This of course is due to the tremendous amount of influence that special-interest wealthy donors and corporate lobbyists have over our politicians in Washington. This is why Wolf-PAC is focusing their efforts on getting state legislators to pass the Free and Fair Elections Resolution that will result in producing the convention and a 28th Amendment. As Cenk Uygur points out, "no one at the top has an interest in changing the system, because they benefit from the system." (Cenk Uygur interviewed by Peter Mathews on May 16, 2019).

Uygur and Monetta both told me that Wolf-PAC believes in working from the ground up, as all successful American social movements have done. In their view there is no point in attempting to persuade Congress directly to sponsor a Constitutional Amendment that would stop the influence of Big Money in politics. It is much more effective they said to get the states to call for a convention to accomplish this goal. They point to the 17th amendment in the U.S. Constitution (to require the direct election of U.S. Senators) as a historical example: When 32 states out of the requisite 33 passed resolutions calling for an Article V convention to draw up an amendment calling for direct election of U.S. Senators, Congress gave in and formally proposed the amendment.

Wolf-PAC says, "Since the Supreme Court has taken a wrecking ball to the wall of separation between wealth and state and Congress has been complicit, we are pursuing a Free and Fair Elections Amendment via the state-based convention route. The Article V convention route for proposing amendments was our founders' safeguard for representative democracy in case our federal government ever became unresponsive to the people."

Article V of the U.S. Constitution provides for procedures to amend the Constitution. At the proposal stage article V offers two options: 1) two thirds of each house of Congress votes to propose the amendment; 2) two thirds of the states' legislatures (currently 34 states) call for a convention to propose the amendment. For adoption of the amendment to the Constitution, three quarters of the 50 states (currently 38 states) must ratify the amendment. Fears of a possible "runaway convention" that could end up proposing unrelated or dangerous amendments to the Constitution, are basically unfounded, according to several constitutional, legal, and historical experts.

In "The Other Way to Amend the Constitution: The Article V Constitutional Convention Amendment Process," the Harvard Journal of Law & Public Policy says, "Much of the fear surrounding a convention is unfounded. The Convention Clause's text and history indicates that it grants power to the States to limit the scope of any such convention. In addition, the States have the ability to reject any amendments proposed by a convention through the ratification process." In other words, the safety check on the actions of a potential "runaway convention" is the 38 state requirement for ratification in order to adopt a new amendment to the Constitution.

Toward the end of our interview, Cenk Uygur boldly and clearly stated:

> We must have a solution to money and politics that matches the size of the problem. This one issue is blocking progress on every other issue - and everyone knows it. Yet from what is widely acknowledged as the number one problem in

politics no one has a comprehensive plan to fix it - other than Wolf-PAC. If you keep dinking and dunking to end the corruption it will take decades to fix it. So, it is perfectly obvious that we must have an amendment to fix this issue; it is equally obvious that 2/3 of this corrupt Congress is not going to voluntarily give away their base of power. So, that leaves any logical person with only one choice - we must pursue a convention to propose an amendment! It's stunning to me that this is not plainly obvious to everyone who works in politics or covers it.

Three quarters of Americans believe climate change is real you don't need more persuasion. 97% of Americans want federal background checks on guns. You don't need more persuasion. Three quarters of Americans also believe we should raise taxes on the rich, but yet we did the exact opposite. You don't need more persuasion. You need to end corruption.

Everyone knows that corporate donors are not giving millions of dollars to politicians for their health. No one in their right mind would believe that. In fact, 93% of Americans say that our politicians work for their donors rather than their voters. We all know this system is built on corruption yet no one on TV or in politics calls it by its name. In fact, all of the so-called journalists in America are scandalized by the idea that the politicians are not honest actors who have legitimate policy differences but are actually shills for their donors and do as they are paid to do. They find that idea outrageous, the American people find it obvious.

If you don't fight for a convention you are blocking all opportunity at fixing this obviously broken system. We must have a convention so we have a realistic chance of getting an amendment that brings back free and fair elections.

So far, thanks to Wolf-PAC's efforts, the five states of Vermont, California, Illinois, New Jersey, and Rhode Island have passed Free and Fair Elections resolutions calling for an Article V convention to propose a Free and Fair Elections 28th Amendment. That's 15% of the 34 states needed.

Emphasizing Wolf-PAC's bi-partisanship, Mike Monetta says, "there are people from all sides of the political spectrum who want to make our elections work better for the average American, but they may have different ideas of how we get there. We are forcing a much-needed national conversation on the issue of campaign finance reform, without dictating the amendment language. For example, some people say that we must declare that money isn't speech to solve this problem, but we're not convinced that is a requirement. For example, when our volunteers testify at committee hearings we are often limited to two minutes per person. This is clearly limiting speech to allow for more voices to be heard. So even if money does equal speech, it can still be limited in America with probable cause. Allowing more voices to be part of the solution has brought a lot of bi-partisan support to our legislation, and we believe that will help us find a solution that can be ratified by 38 states.

"I got involved in this movement because it's obvious to me that if we don't take real action soon our country, and the world, is going to be in serious trouble. I was immediately drawn to Wolf-PAC's plan of action because it allows citizens to work together with our state legislators at the local level to push for much-needed Constitutional change that Congress refuses to give us. I believe this issue is far too urgent not to use every tool of democracy available to us." (Michael Monetta interview with Peter Mathews on May 16, 2019).

This is the state of Idaho's proposed resolution asking for an Article V convention to discuss, write, and vote for a Free and Fair Elections 28th Amendment to the U.S. Constitution:

Exhibit 10-3 | Free and Fair Elections

Idaho Resolution to Restore *Free and Fair Elections* in the United States

Applies to Congress for a limited national convention for the exclusive purpose of proposing an amendment to the United States Constitution that will ensure balance and integrity in our elections.

WHEREAS, the framers of the Constitution of the United States of America intended that the Congress of the United States of America should be "dependent on the people alone" (James Madison, Federalist 52); and,

WHEREAS, that dependency has evolved from a dependency on the people alone to a dependency on powerful special interests, through spending by third-party groups, campaigns or out of state donors, that has created a fundamental imbalance in our representative democracy and eroded the people's trust in government; and

WHEREAS, Americans across the political spectrum agree that elections in the United States of America should be free from the disproportional influence of special interests and fair enough that any citizen can be elected into office; and

WHEREAS, the Constitution of the State of Idaho states that "all political power is inherent in the people," that "government is instituted for their equal protection and benefit," and the people have the right to alter or reform their government whenever they may deem it necessary (Article I, Section 2); and

WHEREAS, Article V of the United States Constitution requires Congress to call a convention for proposing amendments to the federal Constitution on the application of two-thirds of the legislatures of the several states; and

WHEREAS, the Idaho Legislature perceives the need for an amendments convention in order to ensure balance and integrity in our elections by proposing an amendment to the federal Constitution that will permanently protect fair elections in America by addressing, inter alia, issues raised by the decisions of the United States Supreme Court in Citizens United v. Federal Election Commission (2010) 130 S.Ct. 876 and related cases, and desires that said convention should be so limited; and

WHEREAS, a national convention would give us an opportunity to come together, as a nation, to discuss solutions on how to ensure the integrity of our elections, and renew the American people's trust in government; and

WHEREAS, Article V of the U.S. Constitution clearly states that any amendment, whether proposed by Congress or a convention, must be ratified by 75% of the states, presently 38 states, ensuring that only the most reasonable proposals with widespread support become part of our Constitution; and

WHEREAS, Notwithstanding any federal or Idaho law to the contrary, the State of Idaho desires the delegates to a national convention be composed equally of individuals currently elected to state and local office, or be selected by election, in each congressional district in Idaho, though all individuals elected or appointed to federal office now, or in the past, be prohibited from serving as Idaho delegates, and the State of Idaho intends to retain the ability to enforce the responsibility and conduct of its delegation within the limits herein expressed.

WHEREAS, the State of Idaho intends that this be a continuing application considered together with applications calling for a convention passed in the 2013-2014 Vermont

351

legislature as R454, the 2013-2014 California legislature as Resolution Chapter 77, the 98th Illinois General Assembly as SJR 42, the 2014-2015 New Jersey legislature as SCR 132, the 2015-2016 Rhode Island legislature as HR 7670 and SR 2589, and all other passed, pending, and future applications until such time as two-thirds of the several states have applied for a convention for a similar purpose and said convention is convened by Congress.

NOW, THEREFORE, BE IT RESOLVED, that the people of the State of Idaho speaking through its legislature, and pursuant to Article V of the United States Constitution, hereby apply to the United States Congress to call a convention for the exclusive purpose of proposing an amendment to the Constitution of the United States of America that will permanently protect fair elections as described herein, as soon as two-thirds of the several states have applied for a convention for a similar purpose; and

BE IT FURTHER RESOLVED, that the Chief Clerk of the Idaho [*House of Representatives or Senate*] transmit copies of this resolution to the President of the United States; the Vice President of the United States in his capacity as presiding officer of the United States Senate, the Speaker of the United States House of Representatives, the Minority Leader of the United States House of Representatives, the President Pro Tempore of the United States Senate, to each Senator and Representative from Idaho in the Congress of the United States with the respectful request that the full and complete text of this resolution be printed in the *Congressional Record*, to the presiding officers of each legislative body of each of the several states, requesting the cooperation of the states in issuing an application compelling Congress to call a convention for proposing amendments pursuant to Article V of the U.S. Constitution.

If the spirit of the Wellstone No Corporate Funding Campaign continues to be carried forward by people like Bernie Sanders, Alexandria Ocasio-Cortez, and Elizabeth Warren, and the Clean Money Elections Campaigns, the Yarmuth Constitutional Amendment to get big money out of politics, the Move To Amend Coalition's We The People Amendment, or Wolf-PAC's Free and Fair Elections Amendment are implemented nationwide, American society and government would have moved away from **Dollar Democracy on Steroids: With Liberty and Justice for Some, to a Real Democracy: With Liberty and Justice for All. The Middle-Class Dream could then become a reality for all!**

Because of massive campaign donations and lobbying money spent on members of Congress by wealthy corporate special interests, a type of "legalized bribery", hundreds of corporations enjoy corporate tax loopholes and government subsidies (handouts) given to them by Congress. This results in negative income taxes for the corporations and lack of federal funding for investment in America's schools, higher education, infrastructure, jobs, health care, and a clean sustainable environment. Read this to understand solutions to this crisis and take action:

"When the People Lead, the Leaders will follow."

--Mahatma Gandhi

"Power concedes nothing without a demand."

--Frederick Douglass

ACTION PLAN: WHAT IS TO BE DONE? A PEACEFUL POLITICAL-ECONOMIC REVOLUTION TO RESTORE THE MIDDLE-CLASS DREAM AND MAKE IT A REALITY!

https://www.house.gov/representatives
https://www.senate.gov/senators/index.htm

Use the above website to locate your member of Congress, obtain their phone number and email address. Or **use the list of all the members of Congress from your own state that we have provided you on the following pages** and ask for your own U.S. Representative and U.S. Senators and **email** or **call** them and **demand** that they:

-- Serve the American people, not big corporations. They must:

- give up campaign money from corporate lobbyists, and win without it, as Professor Paul Wellstone did in his grassroots campaign and became the U.S. Senator from Minnesota

- get big money out of politics by immediately passing HR-1, the For the People Act, expanding voting, reforming campaign finance and promoting ethics.

- run as Clean Money candidates

- rely on volunteers and small donations from individuals

- close unnecessary corporate tax loopholes to bring in money to invest in America and pay down the national debt

- create high paying green jobs and stop outsourcing jobs

- bring back quality tuition free education as in all other advanced countries and as in California from 1960 to 1980

- guarantee Medicare for All single-payer Universal Health Care

- stop big corporations from destroying our air, water and soil, and switch from fossil fuels to renewable energy

- immediately pass the Green New Deal to create high-paying green energy jobs and save the nation and planet from the worst effects of disastrous Climate Change/Climate Disruption.

- stop big corporations from endangering our lives with harmful chemicals, pesticides and genetically modified foods (GMOs), and require clear and honest labeling of GMOs

- break up the big banks and re-regulate them to prevent another Great Recession by restoring the Glass Steagall Act

- implement a Financial Transaction Tax on Wall Street to make it pay for destroying the American Economy, and to invest in rebuilding the Middle Class

- end waste, fraud and abuse in military spending by auditing the Pentagon, the only government department not audited

- create small business opportunity by providing low interest loans and lowering taxes on small business

- **Sponsor the "We the People" (28th) Amendment to the** U.S. Constitution that states that corporations are not persons with natural rights, and that money is not equal to speech, and can be strictly regulated. This will get big money out of politics, prevent corporations from buying our government, and return our government to the American people.

If your Senators and Congresspersons are not responsive, let them know that you are organizing thousands of neighbors/voters in your area to vote them out and support non-corporate bought candidates in the next election.

Above all, share the information in this book with your friends and neighbors. This is how peaceful revolutions begin.

www.EPeterMathews.com

Table 10-4 | Congress Contact List

Congresspersons' Contact Phone Numbers

U.S. SENATORS AND U.S. REPRESENTATIVES (2019-2020) Members of the 116th Congress Contact Phone Numbers in Washington DC. For more information go to www.house.gov/representatives and see www.votesmart.org.

Alabama

District	Name	Party	Phone
Senators			
	Jones, Doug	D	(202) 224-4124
	Shelby, Richard	D	(202) 224-5744
Representatives			
1	Byrne, Bradley	R	(202) 225-4931
2	Roby, Martha	R	(202) 225-2901
3	Rogers, Mike	R	(202) 225-3261
4	Aderholt, Robert	R	(202) 225-4876
5	Brooks, Mo	R	(202) 225-3261
6	Palmer, Gary	R	(202) 225-4921
7	Sewell, Terri A.	D	(202) 225-2665

Alaska

District	Name	Party	Phone
Senators			
	Murkowski, Lisa	R	(202) 224-6665
	Sullivan, Dan	R	(202) 224-3004
Representatives			
1	Young, Don	R	(202) 225-5765

Arizona

District	Name	Party	Phone
Senators			
	McSally, Martha	R	(202) 224-2235
	Sinema, Kyrsten	D	(202) 224-4521
Representatives			
1	O'Halleran, Tom	D	(202) 225-3361
2	Kirkpatrick, Ann	D	(202) 225-2542
3	Grijalva, Raul	D	(202) 225-2435
4	Gosar, Paul A.	R	(202) 225-2315
5	Biggs, Andy	R	(202) 225-2635
6	Schweikert, David	R	(202) 225-2190
7	Gallego, Ruben	D	(202) 225-4065
8	Lesko, Debbie	R	(202) 225-4576
9	Stanton, Greg	D	(202) 225-9888

Arkansas

District	Name	Party	Phone
Senators			
	Boozman, John	R	(202) 224-4843
	Cotton, Tom	R	(202) 224-2353
Representatives			
1	Crawford, Rick	R	(202) 225-4076
2	Hill, French	R	(202) 225-2506
3	Womack, Steve	R	(202) 225-4301
4	Westerman, Bruce	R	(202) 225-3772

California

District	Name	Party	Phone
Senators			
	Feinstein, Dianne	D	(202) 224-3841
	Harris, Kamala	D	(202) 224-3553

Representatives

1	LaMalfa, Doug	R	(202) 225-3076
2	Huffman, Jared	D	(202) 225-5161
3	Garamendi, John	D	(202) 225-1880
4	McClintock, Tom	D	(202) 225-2511
5	Thompson, Mike	D	(202) 225-3311
6	Matsui, Doris O.	D	(202) 225-7163
7	Bera, Ami	D	(202) 225-5716
8	Cook, Paul	R	(202) 225-5861
9	McNerney, Jerry	D	(202) 225-1947
10	Harder, Josh	D	(202) 225-4540
11	DeSaulnier, Mark	D	(202) 225-2095
12	Pelosi, Nancy	D	(202) 225-4965
13	Lee, Barbara	D	(202) 225-2661
14	Speier, Jackie	D	(202) 225-3531
15	Swalwell, Eric	D	(202) 225-5065
16	Costa, Jim	D	(202) 225-3341
17	Khanna, Ro	D	(202) 225-2631
18	Eshoo, Anna G.	D	(202) 225-8104
19	Lofgren, Zoe	D	(202) 225-3072
20	Panetta, Jimmy	D	(202) 225-2861
21	Cox, TJ	D	(202) 225-4695
22	Nunes, Devin	R	(202) 225-2523
23	McCarthy, Kevin	R	(202) 225-2915
24	Carbajal, Salud	D	(202) 225-3601
25	Hill, Katie	D	(202) 225-1956
26	Brownley, Julia	D	(202) 225-5811
27	Chu, Judy	D	(202) 225-5464
28	Schiff, Adam	D	(202) 225-4176
29	Cardenas, Tony	D	(202) 225-6131
30	Sherman, Brad	D	(202) 225-5911
31	Aguilar, Pete	D	(202) 225-3201
32	Napolitano, Grace	D	(202) 225-5256
33	Lieu, Ted	D	(202) 225-3976
34	Gomez, Jimmy	D	(202) 225-6235

35	Torres, Norma	D	(202) 225-6161
36	Ruiz, Raul	D	(202) 225-5330
37	Bass, Karen	D	(202) 225-7084
38	Sanchez, Linda	D	(202) 225-6676
39	Cisneros, Gilbert Ray Jr.	D	(202) 225-4111
40	Roybal-Allard, Lucille	D	(202) 225-1766
41	Takano, Mark	D	(202) 225-2305
42	Calvert, Ken	R	(202) 225-1986
43	Waters, Maxine	D	(202) 225-2201
44	Barragan, Nanette	D	(202) 225-8220
45	Porter, Katie	D	(202) 225-5611
46	Correa, J. Luis	D	(202) 225-2965
47	Lowenthal, Alan	D	(202) 225-7924
48	Rouda, Harley	D	(202) 225-2415
49	Levin, Mike	D	(202) 225-3906
50	Hunter, Duncan D.	R	(202) 225-5672
51	Vargas, Juan	D	(202) 225-8045
52	Peters, Scott	D	(202) 225-0508
53	Davis, Susan	D	(202) 225-2040

Colorado

District	Name	Party	Phone
Senators			
	Bennet, Michael F.	D	(202) 224-5852
	Gardner, Cory	D	(202) 224-5941
Representatives			
1	DeGette, Diana	D	(202) 225-4431
2	Neguse, Joe	D	(202) 225-2161
3	Tipton, Scott	R	(202) 225-4761
4	Buck, Ken	R	(202) 225-4676
5	Lamborn, Doug	R	(202) 225-7882
6	Crow, Jason	D	(202) 225-7882
7	Perlmutter, Ed	D	(202) 225-2645

Connecticut

District	Name	Party	Phone
Senators			
	Blumenthal, Richard	D	(202) 224-2823
	Murphey, Christopher	D	(202) 224-4041
Representatives			
1	Larson, John B.	D	(202) 225-2265
2	Courtney, Joe	D	(202) 225-2076
3	DeLauro, Rosa L.	D	(202) 225-3661
4	Himes, Jim	D	(202) 225-5531
5	Hayes, Jahana	D	(202) 225-4476

Delaware

District	Name	Party	Phone
Senators			
	Carper, Thomas R.	D	(202) 224-2441
	Coons, Christopher A.	D	(202) 224-5042
Representatives			
1	Blunt Rochester, Lisa	D	(202) 224-4165

Florida

District	Name	Party	Phone
Senators			
	Rubio, Mark	R	(202) 224-3041
	Scott, Rick	R	(202) 224-5274
Representatives			
1	Gaetz, Matt	R	(202) 225-4136
2	Dunn, Neal	R	(202) 225-5235
3	Yoho, Ted	R	(202) 225-5744
4	Rutherford, John	R	(202) 225-2501
5	Lawson, Al	D	(202) 225-0123
6	Waltz, Michael	R	(202) 225-2706
7	Murphy, Stephanie	D	(202) 225-4035

8	Posey, Bill	R	(202) 225-3671
9	Soto, Darren	D	(202) 225-9889
10	Demings, Val	D	(202) 225-2176
11	Webster, Daniel	R	(202) 225-1002
12	Bilirakis, Gus M.	R	(202) 225-5755
13	Crist, Charlie	D	(202) 225-5961
14	Castor, Kathy	D	(202) 225-3376
15	Spano, Ross	R	(202) 225-1252
16	Buchanan, Vern	R	(202) 225-5015
17	Steube, W. Gregory	R	(202) 225-5792
18	Mast, Brian	R	(202) 225-3026
19	Rooney, Francis	R	(202) 225-2536
20	Hastings, Alcee L.	D	(202) 225-1313
21	Frankel, Lois	D	(202) 225-9890
22	Deutch, Ted	D	(202) 225-3001
23	Wasserman Shultz, Debbie	D	(202) 225-7931
24	Wilson, Frederica	D	(202) 225-4506
25	Diaz-Balart, Mario	R	(202) 225-4211
26	Mucarsel-Powell, Debbie	D	(202) 225-2778
27	Shalala, Donna E.	D	(202) 225-3931

Georgia

District	Name	Party	Phone
Senators			
	Perdue, David	R	(202) 224-3521
	Isakson, Johnny	R	(202) 224-3643
Representatives			
1	Carter, Buddy	R	(202) 225-5831
2	Bishop Jr., Sanford D.	D	(202) 225-3631
3	Ferguson, A. Drew	R	(202) 225-5901
4	Johnson, Henry C. Jr.	D	(202) 225-1605
5	Lewis, John	D	(202) 225-3801
6	McBath, Lucy	D	(202) 225-4501
7	Woodall, Robert	R	(202) 225-4272
8	Scott, Austin	R	(202) 225-6531

9	Collins, Doug	R	(202) 225-9893
10	Hice, Jody	R	(202) 225-4101
11	Loudermilk, Barry	R	(202) 225-2931
12	Allen, Rick	R	(202) 225-2823
13	Scott, David	D	(202) 225-2939
14	Graves, Tom	R	(202) 225-5211

Hawaii

District	Name	Party	Phone
Senators			
	Schatz, Brian	D	(202) 224-3934
	Hirono, Mazie	D	(202) 224-6361
Representatives			
1	Case, Ed	D	(202) 225-2726
2	Gabbard, Tulsi	D	(202) 225-4906

Idaho

District	Name	Party	Phone
Senators			
	Crapo, Michael	R	(202) 224-6142
	Risch, James	R	(202) 224-2752
Representatives			
1	Fulcher, Russ	R	(202) 225-6611
2	Simpson, Mike	R	(202) 225-5531

Illinois

District	Name	Party	Phone
Senators			
	Durbin, Dick	D	(202) 224-2152
	Duckworth, Tammy	D	(202) 224-2854
Representatives			
1	Rush, Bobby L.	D	(202) 225-4372
2	Kelly, Robin	D	(202) 225-0773

3	Lipinski, Daniel	D	(202) 225-5701
4	Garcia, Jesus "Chuy"	D	(202) 225-8203
5	Quigley, Mike	D	(202) 225-4061
6	Casten, Sean	D	(202) 225-4561
7	Davis, Danny K.	D	(202) 225-5006
8	Krishnamoorthi, Raja	D	(202) 225-3711
9	Schakowsky, Jan	D	(202) 225-2111
10	Schneider, Bradley	D	(202) 225-4835
11	Foster, Bill	D	(202) 225-3515
12	Bost, Mike	R	(202) 225-5661
13	Davis, Rodney	R	(202) 225-2371
14	Underwood, Laurin	D	(202) 225-2976
15	Shimkus, John	R	(202) 225-5271
16	Kinzinger, Adam	R	(202) 225-3635
17	Bustos, Cheri	D	(202) 225-5905
18	LaHood, Darin	R	(202) 225-6201

Indiana

District	Name	Party	Phone
Senators			
	Braun, Mike	R	(202) 224-4814
	Young, Todd	D	(202) 224-5623
Representatives			
1	Visclosky, Peter	D	(202) 225-2461
2	Walorski, Jackie	R	(202) 225-3915
3	Banks, Jim	R	(202) 225-4436
4	Baird, James	R	(202) 225-5037
5	Brooks, Susan W.	R	(202) 225-2276
6	Pence, Greg	R	(202) 225-3021
7	Carson, Andre	D	(202) 225-4011
8	Bucshon, Larry	R	(202) 225-4636
9	Hollingsworth, Trey	R	(202) 225-5315

Iowa

District	Name	Party	Phone
Senators			
	Grassley, Charles	R	(202) 224-3744
	Ernst, Joni	R	(202) 224-3254
Representatives			
1	Finkenauer, Abby	D	(202) 225-2911
2	Loebsack, David	D	(202) 225-6576
3	Axne, Cynthia	D	(202) 225-5476
4	King, Steve	R	(202) 225-4426

Kansas

District	Name	Party	Phone
Senators			
	Roberts, Pat	R	(202) 224-4774
	Moran, Jerry	R	(202) 224-6521
Representatives			
1	Marshall, Roger	R	(202) 225-2715
2	Watskin, Steve	R	(202) 225-6601
3	Davids, Sharice	D	(202) 225-2865
4	Estes, Ron	R	(202) 225-6216

Kentucky

District	Name	Party	Phone
Senators			
	McConnell, Mitch	R	(202) 224-2541
	Paul, Rand	R	(202) 224-4343
Representatives			
1	Comer, James	R	(202) 225-3115
2	Guthrie, S. Brett	R	(202) 225-3501
3	Yarmuth, John A.	D	(202) 225-5401
4	Massie, Thomas R.	R	(202) 225-3465
5	Rogers, Harold	R	(202) 225-4601
6	Barr, Andy	R	(202) 225-4706

Louisiana

District	Name	Party	Phone
Senators			
	Cassidy, Bill	R	(202) 224-5824
	Kennedy, John	R	(202) 224-4623
Representatives			
1	Scalise, Steve	R	(202) 225-3015
2	Richmond, Cedric	D	(202) 225-6636
3	Higgins, Clay	R	(202) 225-2031
4	Johnson, Mike	R	(202) 225-2777
5	Abraham, Ralph	R	(202) 225-8490
6	Graves, Garret	R	(202) 225-3901

Maine

District	Name	Party	Phone
Senators			
	Collins, Susan	R	(202) 224-2523
	King (I), Angus	I	(202) 224-5344
Representatives			
1	Pingree, Chellie	D	(202) 225-6116
2	Golden, Jared	D	(202) 225-6306

Maryland

District	Name	Party	Phone
Senators			
	Van Hollen, Chris	D	(202) 224-4654
	Cardin, Ben	D	(202) 224-4524
Representatives			
1	Harris, Andy	R	(202) 225-5311
2	Ruppersberger, CA Dutch	D	(202) 225-3061
3	Sarbanes, John P.	D	(202) 225-4016
4	Brown, Anthony	D	(202) 225-8699

5	Hoyer, Steny H.	D	(202) 225-4131
6	Trone, David	D	(202) 225-2721
7	Cummings, Elijah	D	(202) 225-4741
8	Raskin, Jamie	D	(202) 225-5341

Massachusetts

District	Name	Party	Phone
Senators			
	Ed Markey	D	(202) 224-2742
	Warren, Elizabeth	D	(202) 224-4543
Representatives			
1	Neal, Richard E.	D	(202) 225-4735
2	McGovern, James	D	(202) 225-6101
3	Trahan, Lori	D	(202) 225-3411
4	Kennedy III, Joseph P.	D	(202) 225-5931
5	Clark, Katherine	D	(202) 225-2836
6	Moulton, Seth	D	(202) 225-8020
7	Pressley, Ayanna	D	(202) 225-5111
8	Lynch, Stephen F.	D	(202) 225-8273
9	Keating, William	D	(202) 225-3111

Michigan

District	Name	Party	Phone
Senators			
	Peters, Gary C	D	(202) 224-6221
	Stabenow, Debbie	D	(202) 224-4822
Representatives			
1	Bergman, Jack	R	(202) 225-4735
2	Huizenga, Bill	R	(202) 225-4401
3	Amash, Justin	R	(202) 225-3831
4	Moolenaar, John	R	(202) 225-3561
5	Kildee, Daniel	D	(202) 225-3611
6	Upton, Fred	R	(202) 225-3761
7	Walberg, Tim	R	(202) 225-6276

8	Slotkin, Elissa	D	(202) 225-4872
9	Levin, Andy	D	(202) 225-4961
10	Mitchell, Paul	R	(202) 225-2106
11	Stevens, Haley	D	(202) 225-8171
12	Dingell, Debbie	D	(202) 225-4071
13	Tlaib, Rashida	D	(202) 225-5126
14	Lawrence, Brenda	D	(202) 225-5802

Minnesota

District	Name	Party	Phone
Senators			
	Klobuchar, Amy	D	(202) 224-3244
	Smith, Tina	D	(202) 224-5641
Representatives			
1	Hagedorn, Jim	R	(202) 225-2472
2	Craig, Angie	D	(202) 225-2271
3	Phillips, Dean	D	(202) 225-2871
4	McCollum, Betty	D	(202) 225-6631
5	Omar, Ilhan	D	(202) 225-4755
6	Emmer, Tom	R	(202) 225-2331
7	Peterson, Collin C.	D	(202) 225-2165
8	Stauber, Pete	R	(202) 225-6211

Mississippi

District	Name	Party	Phone
Senators			
	Hyde-Smith, Cindy	R	(202) 224-5054
	Wicker, Roger F.	R	(202) 224-6253
Representatives			
1	Kelly, Trent	R	(202) 225-4306
2	Thompson, Bennie G.	D	(202) 225-5876
3	Guest, Michael	R	(202) 225-5031
4	Palazzo, Steven	R	(202) 225-5772

Missouri

District	Name	Party	Phone
Senators			
	Blunt, Roy	R	(202) 224-5721
	Hawley, Josh	R	(202) 224-6154
Representatives			
1	Clay Jr., William "Lucy"	D	(202) 225-2406
2	Wagner, Ann	R	(202) 225-1621
3	Luetkemeyer, Blaine	R	(202) 225-2956
4	Hartzler, Vicky	R	(202) 225-2876
5	Cleaver, Emanuel	D	(202) 225-4535
6	Graves, Sam	R	(202) 225-7041
7	Long, Billy	R	(202) 225-6536
8	Smith, Jason	R	(202) 225-4404

Montana

District	Name	Party	Phone
Senators			
	Daines, Steve	R	(202) 224-2651
	Tester, John	D	(202) 224-2644
Representatives			
1	Gianforte, Greg	R	(202) 225-3211

Nebraska

District	Name	Party	Phone
Senators			
	Sasse, Ben	R	(202) 224-4224
	Fischer, Deb	R	(202) 224-6551
Representatives			
1	Fortenberry, Jeff	R	(202) 225-4806
2	Bacon, Don	R	(202) 225-4155
3	Smith, Adrian	R	(202) 225-6435

Nevada

District	Name	Party	Phone
Senators			
	Cortez Masto, Catherine	D	(202) 224-3542
	Rosen, Jacky	D	(202) 224-6244
Representatives			
1	Titus, Dina	D	(202) 225-5965
2	Amodei, Mark	R	(202) 225-6155
3	Lee, Susie	D	(202) 225-3252
4	Horsford, Steven	D	(202) 225-9894

New Hampshire

District	Name	Party	Phone
Senators			
	Shaheen, Jeanne	D	(202) 224-2841
	Hassan, Margaret Wood	R	(202) 224-3324
Representatives			
1	Pappas, Chris	D	(202) 225-2841
2	Kuster, Ann	D	(202) 225-5206

New Jersey

District	Name	Party	Phone
Senators			
	Booker, Cory	D	(202) 224-3224
	Menendez, Robert	D	(202) 224-4744
Representatives			
1	Norcross, Donald	D	(202) 225-6501
2	Van Drew, Jefferson	D	(202) 225-6572
3	Kim, Andy	D	(202) 225-4765
4	Smith, Chris	R	(202) 225-3765
5	Gottheimer, Josh	D	(202) 225-4465

6	Pallone Jr., Frank	D	(202) 225-4671
7	Malinowski, Tom	D	(202) 225-5361
8	Sires, Albio	D	(202) 225-7919
9	Pascrell Jr., Bill	D	(202) 225-5751
10	Payne Jr., Donald	D	(202) 225-3436
11	Sherrill, Mikie	D	(202) 225-5034
12	Watson Coleman, Bonnie	D	(202) 225-5801

New Mexico

District	Name	Party	Phone
Senators			
	Udall, Thomas	D	(202) 224-6621
	Heinrich, Martin	D	(202) 224-5521
Representatives			
1	Haaland, Debra	D	(202) 225-6316
2	Torres Small, Xochitl	D	(202) 225-2365
3	Lujan, Ben R.	D	(202) 225-6190

New York

District	Name	Party	Phone
Senators			
	Schumer, Chuck	D	(202) 224-6542
	Gillibrand, Kirsten	D	(202) 224-4451
Representatives			
1	Zeldin, Lee	R	(202) 225-3826
2	King, Pete	R	(202) 225-7896
3	Suozzi, Thomas	D	(202) 225-3335
4	Rice, Kathleen	D	(202) 225-5516
5	Meeks, Gregory W.	D	(202) 225-3461
6	Meng, Grace	D	(202) 225-2601
7	Velazquez, Nydia M.	D	(202) 225-2361
8	Jeffries, Hakeem	D	(202) 225-5936
9	Clarke, Yvette D.	D	(202) 225-6231
10	Nadler, Jerrold	D	(202) 225-5635

11	Rose, Max	D	(202) 225-3371
12	Maloney, Carolyn	D	(202) 225-7944
13	Espaillat, Adriano	D	(202) 225-4365
14	Ocasio-Cortez, Alexandria	D	(202) 225-3965
15	Serrano, Jose	D	(202) 225-4361
16	Engel, Eliot	D	(202) 225-2464
17	Lowey, Nita	D	(202) 225-6506
18	Maloney, Sean Patrick	D	(202) 225-5441
19	Delgado, Antonio	D	(202) 225-5614
20	Tonko, Paul D.	D	(202) 225-5076
21	Stefanik, Elise	R	(202) 225-4611
22	Brindisi, Anthony	D	(202) 225-3665
23	Reed, Tom	R	(202) 225-3161
24	Katko, John	R	(202) 225-3701
25	Morelle, Joseph	D	(202) 225-3615
26	Higgins, Brian	D	(202) 225-3306
27	Collins, Chris	R	(202) 225-5265

North Carolina

District	Name	Party	Phone
Senators			
	Richard Burr	R	(202) 224-3154
	Tillis, Thom	R	(202) 224-6342
Representatives			
1	Butterfield, G.K.	D	(202) 225-3101
2	Holding, George	R	(202) 225-3032
3	Jones, Walter B.	R	(202) 225-3415
4	Price, David	D	(202) 225-1784
5	Foxx, Virginia	R	(202) 225-2071
6	Walker, Mark	R	(202) 225-3065
7	Rouzer, David	R	(202) 225-2731
8	Hudson, Richard	R	(202) 225-3715
9	**VACANT**		(202) 225-1976
10	McHenry, Patrick T	R	(202) 225-2576
11	Meadows, Mark	R	(202) 225-6401

| 12 | Adams, Alma | D | (202) 225-1510 |
| 13 | Budd, Ted | R | (202) 225-4531 |

North Dakota

District	Name	Party	Phone
Senators			
	Hoeven, John	R	(202) 224-2551
	Cramer, Kevin	R	(202) 224-2043
Representatives			
1	Armstrong, Kelly	R	(202) 225-2611

Ohio

District	Name	Party	Phone
Senators			
	Brown, Sherrod	D	(202) 224-2315
	Portman, Rob	R	(202) 224-3353
Representatives			
1	Chabot, Steve	R	(202) 225-2216
2	Wenstrup, Brad	R	(202) 225-3164
3	Beatty, Joyce	D	(202) 225-4324
4	Jordan, Jim	R	(202) 225-2676
5	Latta, Robert E.	R	(202) 225-6405
6	Johnson, Bill	R	(202) 225-5705
7	Gibbs, Bob	R	(202) 225-6265
8	Davidson, Warren	R	(202) 225-6205
9	Kaptur, Marcy	D	(202) 225-4146
10	Turner, Michael	R	(202) 225-6465
11	Fudge, Marcia L.	D	(202) 225-7032
12	Balderson, Troy	R	(202) 225-5355
13	Ryan, Tim	D	(202) 225-5261
14	Joyce, David	R	(202) 225-5731
15	Stivers, Steve	R	(202) 225-2015
16	Gonzalez, Anthony	R	(202) 225-3876

Oklahoma

District	Name	Party	Phone
Senators			
	Inhofe, James	R	(202) 224-4721
	Lankford, James	R	(202) 224-5754
Representatives			
1	Hern, Kevin	R	(202) 225-2211
2	Mullin, Markwayne	R	(202) 225-2701
3	Lucas, Frank	R	(202) 225-5565
4	Cole, Tom	R	(202) 225-6165
5	Horn, Kendra	D	(202) 225-2132

Oregon

District	Name	Party	Phone
Senators			
	Wyden, Ron	D	(202) 224-5244
	Merkley, Jeff	D	(202) 224-3753
Representatives			
1	Bonamici, Suzanne	D	(202) 225-0855
2	Walden, Greg	R	(202) 225-6730
3	Blumenaur, Earl	D	(202) 225-4811
4	DeFazio, Peter	D	(202) 225-6416
5	Schrader, Kurt	D	(202) 225-5711

Pennsylvania

District	Name	Party	Phone
Senators			
	Casey, Robert	D	(202) 224-6324
	Toomey, Patrick J.	R	(202) 224-4254
Representatives			
1	Fitzpatrick, Brian	R	(202) 225-4276
2	Boyle, Brendan	D	(202) 225-6111
3	Evans, Dwight	D	(202) 225-4001

4	Dean, Madeleine	D	(202) 225-4731
5	Scanlon, Mary Gay	D	(202) 225-2011
6	Houlahan, Chrissy	D	(202) 225-4315
7	Wild, Susan	D	(202) 225-6411
8	Cartwright, Matt	D	(202) 225-5546
9	Meuser, Daniel	R	(202) 225-6511

Rhode Island

District	Name	Party	Phone
Senators			
	Reed, Jack	D	(202) 224-4642
	Whitehouse, Sheldon	D	(202) 224-2921
Representatives			
1	Cicilline, David	D	(202) 225-4911
2	Langevin, Jim	D	(202) 225-2735

South Carolina

District	Name	Party	Phone
Senators			
	Graham, Lindsey	R	(202) 224-5972
	Scott, Tim	R	(202) 224-6121
Representatives			
1	Cunningham, Joe	D	(202) 225-3176
2	Wilson, Joe	R	(202) 225-2452
3	Duncan, Jeff	R	(202) 225-5301
4	Timmons, William	R	(202) 225-6030
5	Norman, Ralph	R	(202) 225-5501
6	Clyburn, James E.	D	(202) 225-3315
7	Rice, Tom	R	(202) 225-9895

South Dakota

District	Name	Party	Phone
Senators			
	Rounds, Mike	R	(202) 224-5842
	Thune, John	R	(202) 224-2321
Representatives			
1	Johnson, Dusty	R	(202) 225-2801

Tennessee

District	Name	Party	Phone
Senators			
	Alexander, Lamar	R	(202) 224-4944
	Blackburn, Marsha	R	(202) 224-3344
Representatives			
1	Roe, Phil	R	(202) 225-6356
2	Burchett, Tim	R	(202) 225-5435
3	Fleischmann, Chuck	R	(202) 225-3271
4	DesJarlais, Scot	R	(202) 225-6831
5	Cooper, Jim	D	(202) 225-4311
6	Rose, John W.	R	(202) 225-4231
7	Green, Mark	R	(202) 225-2811
8	Kustoff, David	R	(202) 225-4714
9	Cohen, Steve	D	(202) 225-3265

Texas

District	Name	Party	Phone
Senators			
	Cornyn, John	R	(202) 224-4944
	Cruz, Ted	R	(202) 224-3344
Representatives			
1	Gohmert, Louie	R	(202) 225-3035
2	Crenshaw, Dan	R	(202) 225-6565
3	Taylor, Van	R	(202) 225-4201

4	Ratcliffe, John	R	(202) 225-6673
5	Gooden, Lance	R	(202) 225-3484
6	Wright, Ron	R	(202) 225-2002
7	Fletcher, Lizzie	D	(202) 225-2571
8	Brady, Kevin	R	(202) 225-4901
9	Green, Al	D	(202) 225-7508
10	McCaul, Michael T.	R	(202) 225-2401
11	Conaway, K. Michael	R	(202) 225-3605
12	Granger, Kay	R	(202) 225-5071
13	Thornberry, Mac	R	(202) 225-3706
14	Weber, Randy	R	(202) 225-2831
15	Gonzalez, Vicente	D	(202) 225-2531
16	Escobar, Veronica	D	(202) 225-4831
17	Flores, Bill	R	(202) 225-6105
18	Jackson Lee, Sheila	D	(202) 225-3816
19	Arrington, Jodey	R	(202) 225-4005
20	Castro, Joaquin	D	(202) 225-3236
21	Roy, Chip	R	(202) 225-4236
22	Olson, Pete	R	(202) 225-5951
23	Hurd, Will	R	(202) 225-4511
24	Marchant, Kenny	R	(202) 225-6605
25	Williams, Roger	R	(202) 225-9896
26	Burgess, Michael	R	(202) 225-7772
27	Cloud, Michael	R	(202) 225-7742
28	Cuellar, Henry	D	(202) 225-1640
29	Garcia, Sylvia	D	(202) 225-1688
30	Johnson, Eddie Bernice	D	(202) 225-8885
31	Carter, John	R	(202) 225-3864
32	Alred, Colin	D	(202) 225-2231
33	Veasey, Marc	D	(202) 225-9897
34	Vela, Filemon	D	(202) 225-9901
35	Doggett, Lloyd	D	(202) 225-4865
36	Babin, Brian	R	(202) 225-1555

Utah

District	Name	Party	Phone
Senators			
	Romney, Mitt	R	(202) 224-5251
	Lee, Mike	R	(202) 224-5444
Representatives			
1	Bishop, Rob	R	(202) 225-0453
2	Stewart, Chris	R	(202) 225-9730
3	Curtis, John R.	R	(202) 225-7751
4	McAdams, Ben	D	(202) 225-3011

Vermont

District	Name	Party	Phone
Senators			
	Leahy, Patrick	D	(202) 224-4242
	Sanders, Bernard	D	(202) 224-5141
Representatives			
1	Welch, Peter	D	(202) 225-4115

Virginia

District	Name	Party	Phone
Senators			
	Warner, Mark	D	(202) 224-2023
	Kaine, Tim	D	(202) 224-4024
Representatives			
1	Wittman, Robert J.	R	(202) 225-4261
2	Luria, Elaine	D	(202) 225-4215
3	Scott, Robert C.	D	(202) 225-8351
4	McEachin A. Donald	D	(202) 225-6365
5	Riggleman, Denver	R	(202) 225-4711
6	Cline, Ben	R	(202) 225-5431
7	Spanberger, Abigail	D	(202) 225-2815
8	Beyer, Don	D	(202) 225-4376

9	Griffith, Morgan	R	(202) 225-3861
10	Wexton, Jennifer	D	(202) 225-5136
11	Connolly, Gerrald E.	D	(202) 225-1492

Washington

District	Name	Party	Phone
Senators			
	Murray, Patty	D	(202) 224-2621
	Cantwell, Maria	D	(202) 224-3441
Representatives			
1	DelBene, Suzan	D	(202) 225-6311
2	Larsen, Rick	D	(202) 225-2605
3	Herrera, Beutler, Jamie	R	(202) 225-3536
4	Newhouse, Dan	R	(202) 225-5816
5	Rodgers, Cathy McMorris	R	(202) 225-2006
6	Kilmer, Derek	D	(202) 225-5916
7	Jayapal, Pramila	D	(202) 225-3106
8	Schrier, Kim	D	(202) 225-7761
9	Smith, Adam	D	(202) 225-8901
10	Heck, Denny	D	(202) 225-9740

West Virgina

District	Name	Party	Phone
Senators			
	Capito, Shelley Moor	R	(202) 224-6472
	Manchin (III), Joe	D	(202) 224-3954
Representatives			
1	McKinley, David	R	(202) 225-4172
2	Mooney, Alex	R	(202) 225-2711
3	Miller, Carol	R	(202) 225-3452

Wisconsin

District	Name	Party	Phone
Senators			
	Johnson, Ron	R	(202) 224-5323
	Baldwin, Tammy	D	(202) 224-5653
Representatives			
1	Steil, Bryan	R	(202) 225-3031
2	Pocan, Mark	D	(202) 225-2906
3	Kind, Ron	D	(202) 225-5506
4	Moore, Gwen	D	(202) 225-4572
5	Sensenbrenner, F. James	R	(202) 225-5101
6	Grothman, Glenn	R	(202) 225-2476
7	Duffy, Sean P.	R	(202) 225-3365
8	Gallagher, Mike	R	(202) 225-5665

Wyoming

District	Name	Party	Phone
Senators			
	Enzi, Michael	R	(202) 224-3424
	Barrasso, John	R	(202) 224-6441
Representatives			
1	Cheney, Liz	R	(202) 225-2311

These are non-voting Congressional Delegates from U.S. "territories":

American Samoa

District Name	Party	Phone
Delegate		
Radewagen, Amata	R	(202) 225-8577

District of Columbia

District Name	Party	Phone
Delegate		
Norton, Eleanor Holmes	D	(202) 225-8050

Guam

District Name	Party	Phone
Delegate		
San Nicolas, Michael, F. Q.	D	(202) 225-1188

Puerto Rico

District Name	Party	Phone
Resident Commissioner		
Gonzalez Colon, Jennifer	R	(202) 225-2615

U.S. Virgin Islands

District Name	Party	Phone
Delegate		
Plaskett, Stacey	D	(202) 225-1790

INDEX

INDEX

Fair Elections Now Act (HR-269),
320, 324, 327, 328
See also Clean Money Elections
Fair Trade (*see also, Free Trade vs.
Fair Trade), 45, 70, 74, 95-101,
128, 215, 216, 310*
Fallon, William J., Retired four star
Navy admiral, 294
Family Farming, 25
Family Sustaining Wage, 28
FEC (*see Federal Election
Commission)*
Federal Bailout Money
See Wall Street (banks) bailout
Federal Election Campaign Act of 1971
(FECA), 327

Federal Election Commission (FEC),
<www.fec.gov>, 34, 64, 302, 329,
333, 335, 337, 343, 351
*See also Citizens United v. FEC
See also McCutcheon v. FEC*
Federal Funding, 124, 126, 354
Federal Water Pollution Control Act, 58
Ferdinand Marcos, *see Marcos,
Ferdinand*
Fifth Amendment to the U.S.
Constitution, (Double Jeopardy and
Due Process), 228, 344
Figueroa, Yadira, 4, 5
Financial Services Modernization Act,
218
See also Gramm-Leach-Bliley Act,
Finmeccanica, 262
FIRE industries (Finance, Insurance,
Real Estate), [Table 8-1] 211; 34,
210, 211
First Amendment, U.S. Constitution,
(Freedom of Speech), 78, 319, 328,
331, 333, 335-338, 343, 345
Flanagan, Kevin (case history: job lost,
forced to train his replacement who
was a foreign guest worker), 213-

214
Foglesong, Robert "Doc", retired Air
Force General, 289
Follow the Money,
<followthemoney.org>, 90, 143
Food Democracy Now!, 200
Food and Water Watch, 191, 192, 194,
195, 200
Foothill College, 83, 104-106, 137
Foothill-De Anza Community College
District, (attended by Steve Jobs
and Steve Wozniak, and Peter
Mathews' first teaching job in
California), 105
*See also De Anza College
ForeignPolicy.com, Fortune 500, 276*
Fountain, Colorado, 102, 104, 112
Fourth Amendment to the U.S.
Constitution, (Search and Seizure),
344
Fourteenth Amendment to the U.S.
Constitution, (Due Process and
Equal Protection), 303, 336, 344
Fourth National Climate Assessment,
12, 14, 15, 18
Fracking, [Table 6-1] 187; 8, 57, 167,
172, 173, 182-187
*See also Acidizing and Gravel
Packing*
*See also "Stop Fracking Long
Beach"*
France, 76, 88, 140, 145, 152, 158, 171
Frank Greenthaler, *see Greenthaler,
Frank*
Frank, Joshua (investigative reporter
with the *OC Weekly*), 184
Franklin Delano Roosevelt, *see
Roosevelt, Franklin Delano*
Freedom of Speech, *see U.S.
Constitution, 1st Amendment*
Freeman, Dr. Benjamin, 281
Fremont, California, 102
Fremont Elementary School, Long

Made in the USA
Coppell, TX
28 May 2020